THE RISE AND FALL
— OF THE —
FRENCH AIR FORCE

THE RISE AND FALL
— OF THE —
FRENCH AIR FORCE

FRENCH AIR OPERATIONS AND STRATEGY 1900–1940

GREG BAUGHEN

FONTHILL

Fonthill Media Language Policy

Fonthill Media publishes in the international English language market. One language edition is published worldwide. As there are minor differences in spelling and presentation, especially with regard to American English and British English, a policy is necessary to define which form of English to use. The Fonthill Policy is to use the form of English native to the author. Greg Baughen was born and educated in the United Kingdom; therefore, British English has been adopted in this publication.

Fonthill Media Limited
Fonthill Media LLC
www.fonthillmedia.com
office@fonthillmedia.com

First published in the United Kingdom and the United States of America 2018
Reprinted 2019

British Library Cataloguing in Publication Data:
A catalogue record for this book is available from the British Library

ISBN 978-1-78155-644-3

Typeset in 10pt on 13pt Sabon
Printed and bound in England

Acknowledgements

My thanks to the Staff of the Service Historique de la Defénse (SHD) and the former Service Historique de l'Armée de L'Air (SHAA). Also thanks to the staff of the National Archives, the Imperial War Museum, and RAF Hendon for their help over many decades. Once again, my thanks to Tony Buttler, Phil Butler, and Ian White for their help with finding photographs. Thanks also to my wife, Lynda, for helping out on my visits to Paris.

Contents

Introduction

In the spring of 1940, little more than twenty years after the 'war to end all wars', France, Great Britain, and Germany once again found themselves facing each other across the field of battle. This time, the neutral Netherlands, as well as Belgium, would be drawn into the conflict. Over 6 million men, 6,000 tanks, and 8,000 warplanes prepared to take part in a titanic struggle, which many believed would determine the fate of Europe for generations to come. The long-awaited German offensive finally came on 10 May 1940. With the opposing forces seemingly reasonably well-matched, not even the most optimistic German general anticipated what was about to happen. Within six weeks, the mighty French Army had been defeated, France had surrendered, and the military balance of power in Europe had been transformed. Britain stood alone, facing imminent defeat.

The Germans were astonished by how easy it had been. An enemy with more men, tanks, and artillery had been comprehensively defeated. Perhaps most surprising of all was the absence of any effective opposition in the skies. Reconnaissance planes were scarcely ever encountered and Allied bombers seemed mysteriously reluctant to strike the all too vulnerable German columns. The baffled Germans even began to suspect the Allies must be deliberately holding them back for some reason.[1]

The surprise was no less great among Allied ground forces. The skies appeared to be full of German and empty of Allied planes—what had gone wrong? The French and British air forces each possessed front line strengths close to 2,000 planes. The Dutch and Belgian air forces brought the total number available to around 4,000. The French Air Force should have been able to put around 800 fighters, 400 bombers, and 600 reconnaissance planes into the air. Yet nothing like this number appeared in the skies above the struggling French Army.

In the decades that followed, a debate raged about what really happened in the May–June 1940 campaign and where the preparations for war had gone wrong. Many theories abounded. There seems to be a reasonable case for arguing France started to rearm too late. France did start later than other countries, but still had time to build 5,500 planes before the country was attacked.[2] Indeed, French production was about to overtake German production. Some claimed that the French had thousands of aeroplanes that they just failed to use. Others thought that it was the quality, not the quantity, that was the problem. At the time, and later, the failure to match the speed, range, and bomb load of German bombers was seen as a major problem, yet in 1940, it was the plane that had the lowest speed, range, and bomb load, the Ju 87 Stuka, that caused the French the most problems. Anglo-centric accounts tend to focus on the lack of any radar controlled air defence system, although this had no effect on the crucial tactical air battle taking place over the front. Some have even suggested that the Allied air forces had not done so badly and might even have won the war in the air; it was only the armies that lost, as if the two battles were entirely separate issues. French conservatism is another popular explanation; French generals are often accused of trying to fight the Second World War with the weapons and ideas of the First World War. In the air, the very opposite is true; with the sort of tactical air force they had in 1918, the outcome in 1940 might have been very different.

Complacency was not a reason for the defeat. Not for one moment did Frenchmen believe that victory in the First World War had brought to an end the long-running Franco-German feud. Unlike her First World War allies, France continued to keep powerful military forces in existence. All military thought focused on how to stop the next German invasion. The lessons of the First World War were analysed, the significance of new weapons assessed, but when put to the test, all these efforts appeared to have been to no avail. The defeat of France was as crushing and rapid as it was unexpected.

Yet the one-sided nature of the defeat was perhaps misleading. The French military were far closer to understanding what was required to defeat Germany than her British ally. Excellent new combat planes were just beginning to reach the squadrons. If France had been granted just a few more months, the French Air Force would have been in a far better position to provide the French troops on the ground with the support they needed. As the brief campaign progressed, the French generals at the top and soldiers at the front were beginning to learn how to cope with the German *blitzkrieg*. If the French Army had hung on just a little longer, the course of the Second World War might have been very different.

1

The Seeds of Future Problems

At the dawn of the twentieth century, France could quite rightly claim to lead the world in aeronautics, yet it was during this golden era that many of the seeds of future problems were sown. Many of the principles that would prove so damaging in the decades to come would be well-established long before the first French aircraft was ever used in combat.

The French were pioneers in the military use of aircraft. As early as 1794, the French Army was using a hydrogen-filled balloon to observe the enemy during the Battle of Fleurus. By the end of the nineteenth century, observation balloons tethered to the ground were standard Army equipment. They were especially useful for directing artillery over the much greater ranges guns could now fire. While the Artillery learned to exploit the captive balloon, another branch of the French Army, the Engineers, was experimenting with airships. By the end of the nineteenth century, these were capable of navigating hundreds of miles, opening up the possibility of operations deep in the enemy rear. They could do more than just observe; they could also carry bombs and attack targets on the ground. Some envisaged these slow, clumsy craft engaging in a three-dimensional version of naval warfare, with fleets of airships patrolling enemy airspace for weeks at a time.

Meanwhile, the aeroplane had arrived. In 1890, Clément Ader came close to achieving the world's first officially recognized heavier-than-air flight when his *École*, powered by a steam engine, made an uncontrolled hop of around fifty metres. The War Ministry inspected the machine in 1891 and were sufficiently impressed to invest in a second version with two engines. For the required performance, the War Ministry only had the airship as a guide, which made some aspects of the requirement rather ambitious to say the least. The Army wanted a reconnaissance bomber with a maximum speed of just 50 km/hr (30 mph) but an endurance of six hours. Ader enthusiastically set about trying to achieve this, but was soon demanding more money to keep the project going. In several test runs, his *Avion 3* barely left the ground and when it crashed in October 1897, a disappointed War Ministry withdrew its support. The decision was perhaps a little hasty, but at the time, the airship looked far more promising. Despite its failure, Ader's '*avion*' left its mark. Ader had not just created the French word for the aeroplane; his project had also set the standard for future designs. A twin-engined machine with a 300-km range would remain the War Ministry requirement for many years to come.[1]

Ader gave up building aeroplanes and instead set about warning the authorities about the dangers this new invention posed. He suggested that unscrupulous enemies would not hesitate to use them to attack civilian as well as military targets. The French capital was not that far from the frontier and looked especially vulnerable. He warned that 5,000–10,000 enemy bombers, each carrying 200 kg of bombs, might raze Paris to the ground in hours.[2] In 1909, Ader published a book, *L'Aviation Militaire*, outlining his ideas, and, to make sure his views were known in official circles, he sent copies to various politicians and military figures, including General Pierre Roques and General Auguste Hirschauer, both leading figures in military aeronautics. He also sent copies to various up and coming young officers, including a certain Captain Joseph-Édouard Barès, who would go on to become one of the most powerful advocates of the long-range bomber.

At the time, it seemed rather fanciful to suggest that aeroplanes might be capable of wreaking such devastation. Early flights in Europe only lasted seconds. However, in the summer of 1908, the Wright brothers arrived in France with their latest 'flyer' and, on the very last day of 1908, enthralled crowds watched the Wright brothers fly the plane for over two hours, covering nearly eighty miles. This rekindled War Ministry interest and officers from the Army Engineers were sent along to see what the various machines taking part in the August 1909 Reims air show could do. They were impressed by what they saw. The planes on display were scarcely ideal, but they already had some military value. The Engineers' director at the Chalais-Meudon research centre, Col. Bertrand, went even further, warning that if foreign rivals established a lead in the development of the aeroplane, it would be disastrous for the 'honour and security' of France. Officers 'gifted in this sport' should be given the chance to become more familiar with some of the practical aspects of aviation.[3] In 1910, the Army acquired some single-engined Blériot, Farman, and Wright planes but the long-term aim remained the development of a much larger, longer-range, two-seater, twin-engined aircraft.[4]

Meanwhile, a group of forward-thinking artillery officers, led by Col. Estienne, were also taking an interest in the aeroplane. The captive balloons Artillery was using were not ideal. In gusty conditions, a balloon was a rather unstable platform to observe from, with the luckless observer often succumbing to severe airsickness. The balloons were also vulnerable to ground fire and were rather cumbersome to move around in the kind of mobile warfare French generals were envisaging. Estienne and his colleagues had also been impressed by the aeroplanes on show at Reims. Just as the Engineers saw the aeroplane as an alternative to the airship for long-range missions, so the Artillery viewed it as an alternative to the captive balloon in the short-range observation role. They only needed a light single-seater capable of flying short distances and operating from primitive airstrips near the front, and the planes at Reims already seemed capable of this. To make sure their needs were not overlooked, the Artillery set about challenging the right of the Engineers to be the sole Army department responsible for developing military aviation. It was the beginning of a long-running feud between those who saw the aeroplane primarily as a tactical tool and those who envisaged a broader, more independent, strategic role.

By the end of 1909, the Artillery had ordered their first aircraft and had set up their own research establishment at Vincennes to rival the Engineers' Chalais-Meudon centre. Some claimed that it was not ideal having two departments ordering and experimenting with planes. Since existing aeroplanes were only capable of short-range observation, there was a case for leaving their development in the hands of the Artillery. This would leave the Engineers free to focus on the possible strategic uses of the airship. Roques, the Director of the Engineers, strongly disagreed, arguing that it would be unwise to allow a single branch of the Army with a relatively narrow field of interest, like the Artillery, to have total control. With aeroplanes now capable of flying nearly 400 miles, much more than short-range observation was becoming possible. In 1910, Roques got his way and the Vincennes centre was placed under the control of the Engineers.[5]

Roques had no doubts about the importance of military aviation. In a report requested by the War Minister, he claimed that there were virtually no limits to the ways in which aviation might be used with some already talking of fleets of bombers destroying cities.[6] His fervour persuaded the War Ministry to grant the new air arm a degree of autonomy. A new inspectorate was created to oversee the development of military aviation and Roques became its first inspector.[7] In March 1912, a separate air service, the *Aéronautique Militaire*, was created. Soon after this, Roques handed over control of the Air Force to another Army Engineer, General Hirschauer.

The Engineers' claims about the destructive capabilities of the aeroplane were hardly borne out by trials carried out at Vincennes and Meudon. Far from laying waste to cities, it was difficult to see how they could possibly destroy anything. The planes available at that time were not capable of carrying anything like the bomb loads suggested by the likes of Ader and the only way of hitting anything was to fly very low, which made the plane very vulnerable to ground fire. Against tactical targets, losses might be reduced if surprise was achieved or if the troops being targeted were already in action, but the risks involved seemed to suggest that low-level attacks could only be justified as a last resort. Larger targets in the rear, such as army barracks, might be easier to bomb from a safer altitude.[8] However, for true long-range bombing, the airship, with its vastly superior lifting capability, was still far superior to the aeroplane. Reports coming in of the poor results achieved by Italian bombers in Tunisia seemed to confirm this.[9] Even with improved performance, there was a growing suspicion that the problems of hitting a target from a safe altitude would always limit the success bombing could achieve. There seemed to be no justification for developing a specialist bomber. If required, bombing would be carried out by the twin-engined plane the War Ministry was still expecting the French aircraft industry to develop.

In the reconnaissance role, progress was far swifter. During 1910, planes were used to direct artillery fire and wirelesses were soon being used to transmit information directly to the ground. Cameras were also being tried, to provide a permanent record of what observers could see. It would take time to turn these experiments into standard operational procedures, but the promise was clear.[10] In the meantime, the 1912 and 1913 Army manoeuvres demonstrated just how much information a pair of eyes could gather. For the visionaries, it was all rather disappointing. Army plans for using the Air Force contained no hint of the massive aerial assaults on civilian and military targets some were predicting. The most ambitious plan simply involved using all available airships and aeroplanes to monitor the build-up of a mobilising enemy army. Even in this role, it was felt that the airship would probably be more useful than the aeroplane.

Only the Artillery seemed to need aeroplanes. With interest elsewhere on the wane, the Artillery managed to persuade the War Minister that military aviation was not making much progress under Hirschauer. An Artillery officer, General Bernard, was ordered to investigate; on 31 December 1913, a new department, the 12th Directorate (*12ème Direction*), was created and the Inspectorate abolished. By this time, Hirschauer had already resigned in protest at the way his role was being scrutinised and General Bernard became the first director of the new department.[11]

Although their priorities were different, both the Artillery and the Engineers broadly agreed on the types of plane the Air Force would need. Both saw the need for a light single-engined, single-seater observation plane and the larger twin-engined, two-seater reconnaissance bomber. The ever-increasing threat posed by the airship, both as a vehicle for reconnaissance and as a bomber, led both to consider the use of the aeroplane as an interceptor; this role was taken on by the twin-engined reconnaissance bomber. A smaller, more specialised 120 km/hr (75 mph) single-engined, two-seater interceptor was also required. In 1913, specifications for all these were issued to French aircraft companies.[12] Very little changed when the Artillery took over in 1914. The long-range combat plane was now expected to be a multi-seater and the multi-purpose *multiplace de combat*, which would so dominate French thinking for the next two decades, was born. To fill the growing gap between this and the light observation plane, a medium-range, single-engined, two-seater reconnaissance plane was added. No planes specifically designed to meet any of these requirements reached the squadrons before the First World

War. There were no twin-engined aircraft flying in France, but there were plenty of excellent single-engined planes to choose from.

On 3 August 1914, Germany declared war on France and the following morning, German troops crossed the Belgian frontier. For two weeks, as the French nation mobilised, 150 planes and four airships reported German movements directly to the French High Command. Unfortunately, most of the sorties were flown along the Franco-German frontier where the main German offensive was expected and the strength of the German advance through central Belgium came as a surprise. Strategically, the air effort was therefore a failure, but many of the sorties flown provided local army commanders with useful tactical information.

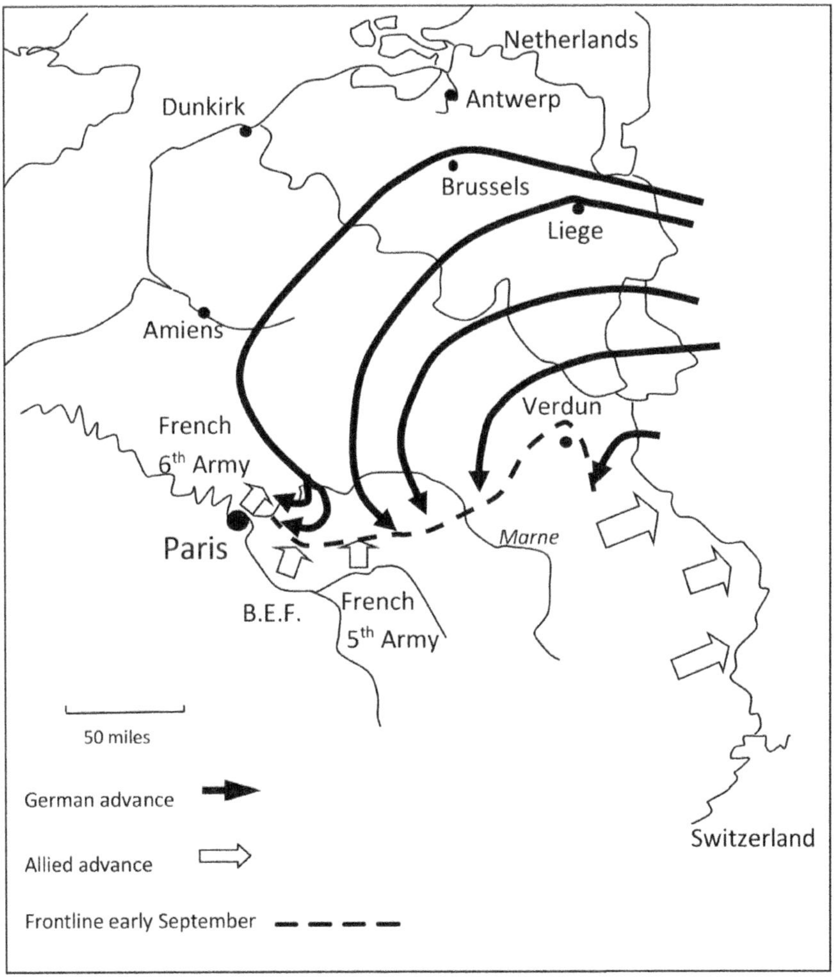

German advance, 1914.

As soon as fighting between the French and German forces began in earnest, all the aircraft were distributed among the various armies for tactical reconnaissance and artillery spotting duties. The aeroplanes soon proved their worth. The most spectacular success was achieved by planes dispatched by the commander of the Paris garrison. These were able to confirm that General von Kluck's First Army had turned in a south-westerly direction away from the capital, exposing its right flank to French forces in the Paris region. The French, with British support, attacked the exposed flank, forcing the Germans to halt their advance and ending German hopes of a quick victory. The Air Force was not the sole source of information on German intentions, but it was a dramatic demonstration of what aerial reconnaissance was capable of.

General Joffre, the commander of the French Army, was sufficiently impressed by these successes to order an expansion of the Air Force and Barès, the commander of the Fourth Army's air units, was given the task. No doubt inspired by the book that Ader had sent him, Barès saw the aeroplane as an excellent way of bombing targets beyond the range of the artillery. The chances of these ideas getting more attention were improved in October when Hirschauer replaced Bernard as the War Ministry Director of Aeronautics. The Artillery general had made the unfortunate error of assuming the war would only last a few weeks and so decided to close all air force training schools and dispatch the personnel to the front. Hirschauer and Barès both wanted a much broader role for the Air Force but they could not agree on much else. In theory, Barès was responsible for directing operations at the front, while Hirschauer controlled services in the rear. Hirschauer's duties included deciding the types of aircraft that should be ordered but Barès felt he should have the final say in the aircraft that he would be expected to use. Not for the last time in the history of the French Air Force, it was not clear who was in charge.

This conflict was resolved in September 1915 by abolishing Hirschauer's post. Instead, an under-secretary of state for war, with responsibility for the Air Force, was appointed to coordinate services at the front and in the rear. The transfer of control of military aviation from the War Ministry's 12th Directorate to this new civilian post was a worrying development for the Army. It seemed like a first step towards an entirely independent air ministry with its own ideas on how the Air Force should develop. The Army lobbied for the appointment of René Besnard, a politician who, they believed, would ensure the War Ministry kept full control of aviation. Besnard, however, would prove to be more open to the idea of an independent role for the Air Force than the Army bargained for.

Barès's first expansion plan was agreed on 8 October 1914. This required Air Force strength to increase from twenty-three squadrons to sixty-five. There would be sixteen long-range reconnaissance-combat squadrons attached to the armies; thirty observation squadrons would be assigned to the various army corps and three 'cavalry' squadrons would be equipped with high-speed single-seater reconnaissance planes.[13] There would also be sixteen bomber squadrons. Compared with pre-war plans, Barès had dropped the single-engined interceptor and brought in the bomber. It was a reasonable reflection of Barès's own ideas on how military aviation should develop. Nevertheless, it had been the success of aerial reconnaissance that had prompted the Army's decision to expand the Air Force; making sure that the generals continued to get the information they needed had to be Barès's priority.

With stalemate along the front, tactical reconnaissance became even more crucial. With trenches stretching from the Channel coast to Switzerland, there were no flanks for the armies to attack. The only option was to blast a path through the barbed wire and machine guns with artillery, so the success of any offensive hinged on whose artillery was the more effective. Army commanders needed to know where enemy batteries and trenches were and aircraft could provide this information and ensure the artillery hit them. As early as October 1914 Army commanders were demanding better photographic coverage of enemy lines. By 1916 and the Battle of Verdun, Army commanders could expect to have photographs of enemy positions in their hands within hours of them being taken. To correct artillery fire, initially aircraft simply dropped flares or waggled their wings, but by the end of 1914, wireless sets were already in use. With wireless equipment still too heavy for soldiers to carry into battle, wireless operators in planes were also used to report the position of advancing friendly forces.

For the French, aerial reconnaissance was especially vital. German forces were often willing to withdraw to more easily defendable lines with higher ground to make it easier to observe French positions. Fighting on her own soil, the French did not feel inclined to concede any more ground to the invader and often found themselves defending positions which offered the defence few advantages. French commanders had to rely more heavily on information provided by their airmen so it was not surprising that they soon came to regard tactical reconnaissance as by far the most useful contribution the French Air Force could make. Barès tried to broaden the role of the Air Force. When he arrived at the French Army headquarters, he insisted efforts to bomb the enemy should be stepped up and suggested that planes working for the artillery might as well aim a few bombs at the target themselves while they were observing. Crews on all reconnaissance missions were encouraged to carry bombs and to attack any target they came across.

However, as the front stabilised and the German troops dug in, the number of suitable targets dwindled and in any case, the bombs were often only hastily converted artillery shells. It seemed rather pointless to aim one or two of these in the general direction of the enemy when, by concentrating on their primary reconnaissance and artillery spotting tasks, they could ensure a stream of identical shells hit the same target. The information the planes brought back was far more important than any damage the odd bomb might cause. Squadrons were told to abandon these freelance bombing sorties and concentrate on their primary mission. However, bombing targets that artillery could not reach did seem worthwhile. The outcome of battles seemed to depend on artillery and the explosives they use needed chemicals. With her greater industrial capacity, Germany had a huge advantage, but if chemical and explosives factories could be bombed, German output of shells would drop. Barès was keen to encourage this sort of thinking.

Barès's first expansion plan had called for the creation of sixteen specialist bomber squadrons. In September, the first bomber squadrons were formed and in December, all bomber squadrons were put under the control of Joffre.[14] The only planes available were single-engined Breguet and Voisin pushers, neither of which could carry much more than 200 kg of bombs, but Barès pushed ahead with his plans to form a bomber fleet. In November, the first *groupe de bombardment*, GB 1, was created with three squadrons.[15] In a new expansion scheme approved in January 1915, the number of required bomber squadrons was increased to twenty-one with a strength of 126 machines. By March 1915, four bomber groups existed.[16]

Initially, these attacked tactical targets such as army barracks and railway stations near the front line, but in April, industrial targets were bombed for the first time. The most spectacular raid was carried out on 26 May 1915, when eighteen bombers flew 250 miles to drop at least four 155-mm and eighty-three 90-mm converted artillery shells on an explosives and gas factory in Ludwigshafen and the nearby Oppau research establishment. Anti-aircraft defences were by no means negligible, and the charismatic leader of the French bomber force, Commandant de Goÿs, was shot down, but the Germans were taken by surprise and the bombing was accurate. Reports from French agents in Germany suggested that the raid had caused considerable damage; after the war, the Germans agreed that of the many British and French attacks on Ludwigshafen, this was the most successful.[17] This success came at a time when there was no movement on the ground and bombing seemed to be a way of breaking the stalemate. Joffre approved a plan to increase the bomber force to fifty squadrons with 500 planes. Others wanted to go further. One senator, M. Flandin, proposed a 750-strong bomber force to destroy Essen and its armaments industry, which he believed would soon bring an end to the war.[18]

During June and July, all four French bomber groups were gathered together at Malzéville and large-scale attacks were launched against various industrial targets. The biggest operation took place on 25 August when sixty-two aircraft bombed the blast furnaces at Dillingen. Much damage was claimed at the time, although it would seem that these claims were somewhat exaggerated. Four planes were hit by anti-aircraft fire and two failed to return. The increasing losses were becoming a major concern. Stronger anti-aircraft defences forced French planes to fly higher, making accurate bombing more difficult. To add to their problems, armed German planes began intercepting the French bombers. Flying in formation, and thereby increasing the number of guns the bombers could bring to bear on the interceptors, provided a partial solution, but losses continued to rise. Either the French had to find a way of escorting the bombers or they would have to start operating by night; this would make it difficult to find the target, never mind hit it.[19]

The Ludwigshafen raid proved to be the exception. No subsequent operation achieved the same success and interest in the whole idea of strategic bombing soon began to fade. In September 1915, the bomber groups operating from Malzéville were dispersed and used mainly against tactical targets close to the front line. 'Communication centres' and 'enemy billets' were common targets. However, as a British report noted, in practice, this meant the random bombing of French and Belgian towns and villages, which was bound to provoke much bitterness among their inhabitants. In the words of one Belgian informant, these raids were 'worse than useless'.[20]

On 1 February 1916, the bomber groups were placed under the orders of army group commanders. If the Army was about to launch an offensive, the bombers would be used tactically, as long-range artillery. Enemy airfields and communications leading to the front were also listed as suitable targets and the government might require reprisals against civilian targets. When no ground operations were underway, the plan was still to use the bombers against industrial targets.[21] French intelligence had identified four main areas with chemical works, explosives plants, and iron foundries: Mannheim and Ludwigshafen, the Main Valley, Cologne, and the SaarLorLux regions.[22] However, long-range bombing by day was still too risky and, by night, it was extremely difficult. Even after Barès managed to persuade British naval squadrons to join the French offensive, little was achieved. Advocates of strategic bombing could claim, with justification, that results were poor because the bombers used were inadequate. Indeed, they were just converted Breguet, Voisin, and Farman reconnaissance planes. For strategic bombing to have a chance, better bombers were needed.

There was still a lot of political support for Barès's long-range bomber force. In Army circles, however, interest was on the wane and with it went the inclination to develop better bombers. As the air battle intensified over the front, more and better reconnaissance and fighter aircraft were the priority, not long-range bombers, and many of the bomber squadrons were converted to reconnaissance or fighter squadrons.[23] Political pressure forced the War Ministry to organise a series of trials to find a better bomber. The winning entry need only carry 300 kg (661 lb) around 300 km (186 miles), which was hardly demanding. French designers, however, showed almost as little interest as the Army. Nothing much better than the existing pushers emerged and when a design did manage to meet the requirements, the politicians decided it was too expensive. French squadrons would have to continue to make do with the relatively cheap Voisin pushers.[24] Without a better bomber, there was little prospect of improving on the results so far achieved. During the winter of 1916–17, bombing by day virtually ceased and bombing by night was achieving little.

While the bomber was in decline, the fighter was becoming the key factor in the air war. There were supposed to be two types of fighter—the small and fast single-engined two-seater (the *avion de chasse*) and the larger, twin-engined multi-seater (the *avion de combat*)—both preferably armed with cannon. At the outbreak of war, prototypes of planes like the single-engined Nieuport Destroyer and twin-engined Dorand biplane were being tested, but no successful designs had emerged and the planes in service were hardly capable of carrying any weapon into the air. Barès was not interested in single-engined fighters but as soon as suitable twin-engined multi-seaters became available, he planned to use them to equip his sixteen army squadrons. Barès expected all planes to play some part in the struggle for air superiority, but these large fighter-reconnaissance planes would lead the way.

Despite the lack of any specialist equipment, French pilots were soon making improvised attempts to shoot down enemy planes. Like most air forces, the French assumed a fighter had to carry a gunner to aim a weapon and pushers provided a good forward field of fire. On 5 October, the French Air Force achieved its first aerial victory when a machine gun-armed Voisin III pusher shot down a German Aviatik reconnaissance plane. Victories were few and far between. Carrying a machine gun as well as a gunner slowed the planes so much, airmen had to resort to rifles and even pistols. From 1915, more powerful engines made it easier to carry machine guns, but planes weighed down by a gunner and his gun still found it difficult to catch lighter, often unarmed planes.

Just as Barès had demanded, any machine capable of carrying a gun was having a go. Ironically, this led to a solution that Barès had not anticipated. Barès had wanted his Army long-range reconnaissance and combat planes to spearhead the fighter force but speed was the key asset and the fastest planes available to the army squadrons were some Morane-Saulnier L two-seater parasol monoplanes. Some pilots decided they would be even faster without the gunner and flew the plane as a single-seater. Flying the plane and aiming a gun was not easy but Roland Garros tried fixing a gun to fire forward through the propeller arc, with armoured wedges attached to the propellers to make sure he did not shoot off his own propeller. All he had to do was point his plane at the enemy and open fire. It worked and in the summer of 1915, the Morane-Saulnier Type 'N' monoplane, with the same deflector system, became the first plane to be ordered by the French as a specialist single-seater interceptor. At around the same time, the fighters that Barès wanted (two-seater pushers armed with cannon) began to arrive, but it was the much lighter single-seaters that were the more successful.

By the spring of 1915, armed French planes had established a degree of dominance over the Western Front, but this would not last long. In April 1915, Roland Garros was forced down in enemy territory and the Germans discovered that the French had been achieving their recent successes with a fixed forward-firing gun. The French deflectors could not cope with German machine guns but the importance of the synchronised systems German engineers had been working suddenly became clear. Work on these was hurriedly completed and Anthony Fokker fitted one to his Fokker Eindecker monoplane; this was soon causing French reconnaissance planes problems. The Army had come to rely on unimpeded access for their reconnaissance planes and by the summer of 1915, the French had a fleet of some 500 and planned to double this number. However, the majority were Farman, Breguet, and Voisin pushers. Their slow speed and excellent stability made them ideal for observing the enemy, but this also made them sitting ducks for the Fokkers. The standard mode of German attack was to dive on the rear of the French planes, using the sun to hide their approach whenever possible. With their pusher engines making it very difficult to fire backwards, the French reconnaissance planes became death-traps for their crews.

Barès, however, still saw his twin-engined multi-seater as the best solution. As a first step, he wanted three-seaters with nose and dorsal gunners initially with machine guns, but eventually cannon-armed, armoured planes would be required.[25] These powerful machines would be capable of battling their way through to their target without any escort and could be used for reconnaissance, observation, bombing, and air combat.

French designers and pilots were not so enthusiastic. Only one twin-engined plane had reached the squadrons: the Caudron G.4 two-seater; it was hardly the powerful combat plane Barès had in mind. Many pilots feared that these planes would be too difficult for the average pilot to fly and were taking French fighter development in the wrong direction. Pilots at the front were making it very clear what they wanted. Speed and agility were required, not two engines and cannon. Soon, the pilots of two-seater, single-engined Nieuport 10 reconnaissance planes began following the example of the Morane-Saulnier L parasol pilots. The Nieuport was already one of the fastest planes available to the French and with the rear seat covered over and the plane flown as a single-seater, it was even faster. Pilots did not need to fire through the propeller; they simply fixed a gun firing straight ahead to the upper wing and went searching for enemy reconnaissance planes. Without a second crew member, it did not need to have so much wing area, so Nieuport built a scaled-down, single-seater version, the Nieuport 11 *Bébé*, which was even faster and more manoeuvrable. It was the best fighter produced so far by any nation.

However, commanders in the rear were slow to appreciate the importance of what the pilots had stumbled across. Barès's November 1915 plan called for a front line strength of 1,310 planes by the spring of 1916. The vast majority of these would be twin-engined, three-seater, dual-purpose, bomber-reconnaissance planes. Only 250 were categorised as fighters and most of these were: twin-engined Caudrons, cannon-armed pushers, or two-seater Nieuport 10s or 12s. Only a very small proportion would be Nieuport 11 single-seaters. Besnard supported Barès's demand for larger combat planes, but the aircraft manufacturers claimed that no such plane existed and it would simply be impossible to develop one before the spring of 1916. Caudron was one of the few companies making a serious effort to develop twin-engined planes. Their latest attempt, the Caudron R.4, may not have been the all-powerful armoured combat plane Barès had in mind, but it was the closest to it so far and Barès was anxious to get it into service as quickly as possible. These plans received a major setback when the first prototype crashed in December 1915, not only delaying production but also focusing attention on the difficulty of designing and flying large twin-engined designs.[26]

The influential Parliamentary Army Commission also thought that it was unlikely that a suitable multi-purpose plane could be developed in time. In any case, it doubted that a single type could ever be capable of tasks as diverse as artillery observation, reconnaissance, bombing, and air combat. A commission was set up to look into Barès's re-equipment plan and this concluded that the number of 'combat' planes should be increased to 500, out of a total strength of 1,430. However, with the terms '*avion de chasse*' and '*avion de combat*' both being used interchangeably, there was nothing to stop Barès using multi-seaters in the combat role, nor did the report specify the sort of plane that the bomber and reconnaissance squadrons should be equipped with. Barès's multi-purpose combat plane was still very much alive.

The winter of 1915–16 proved to be a difficult one for French reconnaissance crews with German Fokkers prowling the skies. Yet despite their success, Barès was still reluctant to give fighters the same priority as bomber and reconnaissance planes. The strategic reconnaissance Army squadrons were still largely responsible for challenging the enemy in the air. However, as the front stagnated, there was less call for strategic reconnaissance and fighting became their main role. Gradually, Army squadrons metamorphosed into fighter squadrons. For a time, the terms '*escadrille d'Armée*' and '*escadrille de chasse*' were used interchangeably. However, they were not getting the single-seaters they needed. Barès only ordered small numbers of the specialist Nieuport 11 and still wanted all planes to play their part in the struggle for air supremacy.

Barès's faith in twin engined and two-seater fighters was not shared by those who had to fly them. The Caudron G.4 lacked the speed and manoeuvrability to intercept enemy planes or deal with the Fokker. As for the two-seater Nieuport 12, pilots at the front covered up the rear cockpit and flew the plane as a single-seater as they had done with its Nieuport 10 predecessor. The extra speed and manoeuvrability was more valuable than rearward defence. By early 1916, common sense had prevailed. The Caudron G.4, R.4, and the Nieuport two-seaters were now seen as reconnaissance planes, and the single-seater Nieuport 11 was finally recognised as the best fighter available. The multi-seater fighter concept seemed dead. The demand for yet more speed and agility would grow during the forthcoming Battle of Verdun.

On 1 February, three weeks before the German Verdun offensive was launched, the French had over 1,000 front line planes. Of these, only 135 were classed as fighters with ninety Nieuport 11s and thirty-six cannon-armed pushers the principal types.[27] On the eve of the offensive, Col. du Peuty, the commander of the French Air Force units in the Verdun area, had just sixty planes and just two of the fifteen Nieuport fighter squadrons. When the Germans launched their attack on 21 February 1916, Barès immediately rushed units and the best pilots from quieter sectors of the front to Verdun. Within a week, six Nieuport squadrons were operating in the area and to ensure their actions were coordinated, they were brought together as a *groupement de chasse* under Commandant de Rose. For the first time, fighter effort could be focused where it was required.[28]

Du Peuty and de Rose had very strong ideas on how these fighters should be used. Rather than using them as close escorts, both believed in using the fighters aggressively in groups, with pilots working together as a team. Enemy planes could be swept from the skies, allowing friendly reconnaissance planes to perform their tasks unhindered. De Rose ordered his squadrons to take the initiative with offensive patrols at squadron or half squadron strength 3 to 4 miles behind enemy lines. As du Peuty made clear, it was impossible to stop all German activity over French lines, especially with the limited fighter resources available. He also accepted that long-range missions should have a close escort and that on short-range missions, fighter patrols should coincide with the activities of the corps planes. It was a controlled offensive; the fighters would never be too far from the reconnaissance planes. The tactics used were essentially correct, although their effectiveness was watered down to some extent by individual pilots who did not accept the teamwork ethic and set off on their own looking for targets. French losses were still sometimes heavy, du Peuty conceded, but he insisted German losses were heavier.[29, 30]

Any losses among the reconnaissance squadrons tended to provoke demands for closer escorts, but this was not possible because there were far too many reconnaissance planes, and far too few fighters. Both du Peuty and Barès had to believe the general air superiority established by the roving French fighter patrol would, in the long run, create the conditions in which the short-range reconnaissance planes could operate. Clearly, it would help if the reconnaissance squadrons had something better than the vulnerable pushers many of them still had. Barès still hoped that when reconnaissance and observation squadrons began to get his well-armed multi-seaters, they would be more than capable of dealing with any German fighters that broke through the defensive ring and might even make the single-seaters unnecessary. Unfortunately for Barès, the large twin-engined planes he wanted were not materialising. Whoever was right about how fighters were used, one thing was becoming very clear: far more fighters were needed.

With so few fighters, du Peuty's strategic offensive could only succeed if the zone they were trying to dominate was limited. During the Battle of Verdun, the French tactics worked well because the fighting was taking place over a limited sector of the front and French fighters were never too far from the planes they were protecting. The French fighter force was also very well equipped. In March 1916, the Nieuport 11 was joined by the Nieuport 17. This was a much tougher, faster machine with a synchronised machine gun and far superior to any German fighter. The French were also fortunate that the Germans were still very much feeling their way in this new era of aerial combat and had not yet appreciated the value of specialist fighter units. Their fighters were still mostly attached to the reconnaissance squadrons and were still flying in small formations.

During the second half of 1916, the situation changed dramatically. In July, the length of the front was greatly increased by the opening of the Allied offensive along the Somme. A second fighter formation, Group Cachy, was created to support the French forces involved. Initially, only one French army was committed and Group Cachy was at the disposal of its commander. However, in August, a second army joined the offensive and Group Cachy was put under the Army Group commander, who deployed the fighter unit over the army he believed was in most need. The two armies engaged were only allowed to keep one or two fighter squadrons under their direct control.[31] Neither army commander was happy with this arrangement, but in the circumstances, there was nothing else that could be done—there were simply not enough fighters to go around. Over the much-extended front, French fighters were not able to achieve the same concentration they had in the skies around Verdun.

To add to the problems the French faced, the German Air Force was now reorganising their fighters into more aggressive, independent '*Jagdstaffel*' (Jasta) hunting packs. These units also began to receive the first examples of the deadly, twin-gun Albatros D-series fighter, with its streamlined, liquid-cooled Mercedes engine. The lighter French fighters, with their less powerful rotaries, could still climb faster and were much more manoeuvrable, but in terms of diving and horizontal speed, the Albatros had a clear advantage. By chance, the French were also developing fighters powered by liquid-cooled engines and the first of these, the sturdy Hispano-Suiza-powered SPAD S.VII, proved to be even faster than the Albatros and these began to reach front line squadrons in September 1916, at about the same time as the German fighter. The French were not being left behind in terms of the technology, but in future, it would be a much more even contest.

Barès now accepted that single-seater fighters had a crucial role to play, but it was not the agility of the single-seater that impressed him; for Barès, the three key qualities were climbing, diving and horizontal speed. He preferred the SPAD to the Nieuport because the former had all three, whereas the latter could only climb fast. His ideal fighter would be handy at 19,000 feet and have a top speed of 125 mph at 6,000 feet.[32] Dogfighting escorts were not part of Barès's plans—his heavily armed multi-seaters would not need any escort—so he did not need the Nieuport's agility. Unfortunately for French pilots, SPAD fighters were in short supply. Technical problems delayed deliveries and even by February 1917, there were still only seventy in front line squadrons, compared to the nearly 300 Albatros fighters they faced.[33]

The last months of 1916 were a very difficult time for the French reconnaissance squadrons. These were still almost entirely equipped with pushers, or the barely less vulnerable Caudron G.4. Losses began to rise alarmingly and insistent Army demands forced the fighter squadrons to revert to direct escort. Du Peuty remained convinced that this was not the way to use fighters. The aerial struggle could not be confined in space; only a strategic air offensive, as practised at Verdun, would bring success. If anything, even more offensive patrols, deeper inside enemy territory, was the path to take. Initially, losses might be heavy, but it was just a case of persevering and accepting this as the price that had to be paid for the domination of the air that would inevitably come. Discord in the rear would soon put du Peuty in a position to give his theories an extended trial.

Problems had been brewing since the winter of 1915–16. There were doubts about Barès's multi-purpose combat plane and the long-range bombing offensive Barès had advocated was not producing any worthwhile results. Worst of all from the Army's point of view, German fighters were preventing their fleet of tactical reconnaissance planes from bringing back the information they needed. Early in 1916, with controversy raging over Barès's proposed Air Force expansion plans, the Artillery felt the time was right to make another bid for control of the Air Force.

On 8 February 1916, Besnard's post was abolished and the Director of Aeronautics (12th Directorate) post was restored. The Artillery lobby in the War Ministry moved quickly to make sure that an artillery officer, Col.

Régnier, got the job. As compensation, Barès was elevated to the new position of *commandant de l'aéronautique aux armée*. The different outlooks and priorities of the two commanders inevitably led to friction. Régnier felt that Barès was not entitled to his new higher rank as no such position existed in any other branch of the Army. For his part, Barès argued that the Air Force was not like any other branch of the Army and strongly objected to the artillery style organisation Régnier was trying to impose.[34]

General Guillemin was called in to investigate the lack of liaison between the rear and the Air Force command at the front. In an attempt to resolve the problem, Guillemin was himself appointed *directeur générale de l'aéronautique*, with authority over both Barès and Régnier. Barès objected rather too strongly, and with growing criticism of the way he was running the Air Force, the Minister of War took the opportunity to sack him. For Barès, it was the beginning of a long spell in the wilderness and by no means the end of his days in command. Guillemin now appointed du Peuty in Barès's place, although with the reduced rank of *directeur d'aéronautique*. It was enough to ensure du Peuty would be able to impose his offensive fighter tactics during the forthcoming 1917 Allied spring offensive.[35]

General Nivelle's Chemin des Dames offensive was perhaps one of the most ill-conceived of the First World War. Frustrated by three years of static trench warfare, Nivelle believed the *élan* of the French infantry would carry them through the barbed wire and machine guns. The French made little effort to disguise their intentions. The Germans were expecting the offensive and had even withdrawn to a more easily defensible line in anticipation.

Both sides fielded considerably expanded air forces for the new campaigning season and both sides now appreciated that fighters were the key. By April 1917, the Germans had assembled a fighter force of over 500 planes and the French had almost as many. The French army corps reconnaissance fleet had grown from under 700 machines in June 1916 to over 1,000 in April 1917, but there was little corresponding improvement in quality. The Caudron R.4, the first of Barès's twin-engined combat planes, had begun arriving in 1916 and it would be joined by the first Letord 4 multi-seaters in April 1917. Neither proved as successful as Barès had hoped, nor was the more conventional replacement for the pusher types, the single-engined Dorand AR.2 two-seater reconnaissance plane, a great success. The French tried using SPAD and Nieuport fighters for aerial reconnaissance duties and their speed and manoeuvrability made them far less vulnerable. However, an observer was still considered necessary for most missions.

Nivelle's offensive involved an assault by three French armies along a 40-mile front with each army having just one fighter squadron under its direct control. The bulk of the fighters were concentrated in three *groupements de combat*, GC 12, 13, and 14. Later, 'GC' would come to stand for *groupe de chasse*. These three groups received their orders direct from the headquarters of the army group coordinating the entire offensive. Each army indicated where their corps planes would be operating and the army group headquarters decided where the fighter groups should operate. Unfortunately, du Peuty was becoming rather too zealous in his determination to be offensive. Fighter squadrons were ordered to hunt down the enemy on offensive patrols 'without restriction'. Patrol lines were to be ten miles inside enemy airspace—far deeper than at Verdun—and it would seem that in their enthusiasm to be offensive, pilots strayed even deeper. As well as being in a poor position to provide the local air superiority the army corps machines required, they were also poorly placed to prevent the German planes operating over the front. The distant patrol lines were far too easy to bypass. It did not help the French cause that the Nieuport 17, which still equipped most of the fighter force, was not suited to the offensive tactics du Peuty was using. It lacked the speed to catch the Albatros, and it was up to the German pilots whether they engaged or not. The offensive French patrols posed no great threat and unless the odds particularly favoured them, German fighter pilots simply chose to ignore the roving French formations. Instead, they operated over the front where their own and enemy reconnaissance planes were. French losses began rising and frustrated Army commanders demanded that the fighters work more closely with the reconnaissance planes. The best way to do this, they insisted, would be to put the fighters under their direct control so they could assign fighter escorts directly to their reconnaissance planes. Du Peuty remained adamant that close escort was not the way forward and he had no intention of handing any fighters over to Army commanders. He did, however, feel obliged to coordinate reconnaissance and fighter sorties more closely and pilots were instructed to stick to their patrol lines. However, it was not enough to stem the flow of losses.[36] Ironically, the Nieuport was better suited to the close escort role the Army commanders were demanding. Enemy pilots could not ignore its presence, so its lack of speed was not so critical, and its agility made it a tricky opponent. The way any fighter is used is as much to do with its particular qualities as abstract theories on how fighters ought to be used.

Du Peuty's offensive fighter policies were blamed for inflicting on air units a scale of losses comparable to the infantry losses on the ground. How heavy air losses actually were is not clear. Some accounts state that nearly 300 French aircraft were either destroyed or damaged in April, but actual outright losses in combat were probably only around sixty-five planes.[37, 38] However, the perception at the time was that the French Air Force had been overwhelmed, and the lack of control over the available fighter resources was to blame. Only after the offensive was called off did du Peuty finally agree to allow the fighter groups to be placed under the operational control of the armies at the front.

Du Peuty was right that providing every reconnaissance plane with an escort was not possible. However, it is no good patrolling aggressively miles away from where you are needed. The volume of airspace that any air force can control depends on the quantity and quality of the fighter force available. As a last resort, it might be that the fighters available are only capable of controlling the air space in the immediate vicinity of the reconnaissance plane. This would mean fewer reconnaissance sorties could be flown, but that is the price that has to be paid for losing control of the skies.

Du Peuty's tactics were too offensive for the quantity and quality of the fighters available and the distrust that this policy generated between Army and Air Force commanders would not be forgotten. The dispute over who should control the fighter force would become a long-running bone of contention. Parcelling fighters out to army commanders makes it more difficult to concentrate them where they are needed, but if centrally controlled fighters are going to be misused, army commanders are likely to prefer fewer fighters they can control rather than a larger force they cannot control. In the decades ahead, this is what French Army commanders would opt for.

2

Towards a Modern Air Force

On 15 May, Nivelle was sacked and his place was taken by the more pragmatic General Pétain, who had made his reputation commanding the French forces in the bitter defensive victory at Verdun. Do or die offensives were not in his nature. He could not have taken over at a more difficult time. Morale at the front was rock bottom; along certain sectors of the front, French troops had mutinied, agreeing to defend the lines they held but refusing to take part in any more senseless offensives.

The fortunes of the *Aéronautique Militaire* had also reached an all-time low. Squadrons were under strength and poorly equipped. Some squadrons were still using the Farman F.40 pusher and the tractor replacements that had been delivered had not proven particularly successful. French bombers were unable to venture out by day and by night, they were not achieving much. Within the fighter arm, there was uncertainty about how the force should be used. Better equipment and a complete reassessment of Air Force tactics were needed. Pétain had no doubts about the importance of tactical air support and he was anxious to modernise and expand the Air Force. He believed that the Air Force had tended to go its own way far too often, and was determined to bring air policy more into line with Army requirements.

In the aftermath of the Chemin des Dames offensive, du Peuty requested, and was granted, permission to return to his regiment. He was killed in action in the spring of 1918 while leading an infantry assault. In du Peuty's place, Pétain appointed Col. Duval. The new Air Force commander did not have an aeronautical background and was by no means an obvious candidate for the post. Pétain, however, had been impressed by the leadership that he had demonstrated while commanding an infantry brigade and his organisational skills as the 6th Army's chief of staff. His lack of any previous involvement in Air Force affairs at least meant that he did not belong to either the Artillery or Engineers and Barès clique and could approach the problems with an open mind.[1]

Duval was fortunate that his appointment coincided with the arrival of several excellent new French designs, benefiting from a new generation of more powerful motors, which were especially efficient at high altitudes. In the summer of 1917, the first examples of the single-engined Breguet 14 A2 began to reach the army corps squadrons. This tough reconnaissance plane was well-armed, was very nearly as fast as the best German fighters and, if required, could operate at altitudes that German pilots found difficult to reach. The Breguets were later joined by the equally fast and rugged but smaller, lighter and more manoeuvrable Salmson 2. Both these planes were awkward targets for German fighters. For the first time, the army corps squadrons had planes that had a reasonable chance of defending themselves.

Given the state of the bomber force, and the problems it had encountered in the previous two years of war, there were those who believed daylight bombing should be abandoned altogether, but Duval resisted the temptation.[2] It was a decision that would be justified by the appearance of a bomber version of the Breguet 14, although this was not immediately obvious when the bomber variant first appeared. The plane's robustness, speed and ability to operate from high altitude enabled French bomber squadrons to venture out once more by day, but not everyone was impressed. It had not been designed with the bomber role in mind, and its range and bomb load were limited, scarcely what the bomber advocates wanted. Nor could great accuracy be expected bombing from high altitude. Some doubted the Breguet was worth having as a bomber and suggested that the bomber squadrons equipped with the plane would be more usefully employed as two-seater fighters to protect the Army observation planes, at least until a bomber 'worthy of the name' became available.[3]

Pétain, however, was keen to retain a day bomber capability, whatever its limitations. He was determined that the long-suffering infantry should have as much fire support as possible and the bomber was another way of providing it. Pétain wanted bomber support both on and beyond the battlefield, but it was the latter the Air Force was more interested in. The advocates of strategic bombing were constantly having to downgrade their expectations. The SaarLorLux region was not the most important industrial region, but it was the closest and easiest to bomb and useful results might be achieved by focusing French effort here. It was a pragmatic approach, but it rather underlined how little chance bombing had of denting overall German industrial output.[4] Bombers would also be used to attack rail communications to the west of the Rhine and the airfields the Germans were using to bomb Paris. However, as soon as the front became 'active', the bombers would switch to tactical targets, although the Air Force preference was still that these should be well behind the front line.[5]

As well as receiving new equipment, the bomber fleet was also reorganised. In January 1918, the force was divided into eight groups, with each unit specialising in either day or night missions. Soon after, two of the day bomber groups were brought together to form a day bomber wing, *Escadre de Combat* 12. On 7 March 1918, two new tactical formations, *Groupements* Villeneuve and Cramaille, were formed, both of which were mixed formations with fighter and bomber squadrons. The former took in *Escadre* 12 while the letter had the remaining day bomber group, GB 3. Both formations had a wing of SPAD fighters.[6] The aim of this reorganisation was to revive the offensive policies that had failed so miserably in Nivelle's offensive, but were still favoured by many in the Air Force. The bombers were there to provoke German fighters into taking on the SPAD escort, giving the French fighters the opportunity to win air superiority.[7] A fortnight after they were formed, the new formations would find themselves being used for a very different purpose.

Meanwhile, the altitude fighters could now reach meant even more were needed. Combat was now regularly taking place at 5,000 metres or higher as each side sought to gain a height advantage. At best, pilots could only be expected to see planes 2,000 m above or below them, so fighters flying at much lower altitudes were needed to take on the enemy reconnaissance planes and bombers. These in turn needed fighters above them to provide protection, which meant fighter formations might have to fly at three or even four different altitudes.[8] The German Air Force had come to the same conclusions. The French correctly estimated the Germans planned to double their fighter force during the winter of 1917–18. By the spring, half of the German front line strength would be fighters. The French matched this by increasing the number of fighter groups from five when Duval took over to eleven by March 1918.[9]

The French were also becoming aware that different types of fighter would be needed at different altitudes. The faster more powerful SPAD S.XIII, which was taking over from the SPAD S.VII, was a superb medium and low-level interceptor, but, like its predecessor, it lacked the manoeuvrability to dogfight with the enemy, nor did it have the performance at altitude required to intercept high-flying aircraft or protect friendly fighters operating below. To fill this gap, the French had a Morane-Saulnier rotary-powered parasol, which was lighter and more manoeuvrable than the SPAD; it could also fly higher than the SPAD and retained its superb manoeuvrability at high altitude. The fighter came in two versions: the Morane-Saulnier MoS.29 with two guns, and the lighter MoS.27 with less fuel and only one gun, but even better performance.[10]

Large numbers of both the SPAD and Morane fighters were ordered, the first SPAD S.XIII reaching the squadrons in May 1917 and the first of the thousand Morane-Saulnier fighters on order arriving in January 1918. Unfortunately, the Morane design never won the confidence of its pilots. It was rumoured to have structural defects and its rotary engine proved unreliable. Very few squadrons were ever equipped with the type and all had been withdrawn from front line service by May 1918. The failure of the Morane-Saulnier fighter deprived the French Air Force of a valuable dogfighter, the need for which would soon become apparent.[11]

French aircraft production was now getting into its stride. Average monthly output rose from 650 in 1916 to over 1,200 in 1917. The appointment of Albert

Caquot in January 1918 helped push this up to around 2,000 a month.[12] It was now possible to bring squadrons up to full strength, establish a reasonable reserve and still have sufficient fighters to expand front line strength. Fighter, bomber and reconnaissance squadrons had never been as well equipped as they were in the spring of 1918. The SPAD S.XIII, Breguet 14, and Salmson 2 were all high-performance, sturdy, reliable warplanes. Their ruggedness would stand them in good stead as a new generation of German fighters rose to challenge the air superiority established by the French in the winter of 1917–18.

While the French were forced to abandon the manoeuvrable dogfighter, the enemy was beginning to rely on them. The agility of the French Nieuports and British Sopwith Triplanes had impressed the Germans and they were determined that their next generation of fighters would be just as agile. The result was planes like the Fokker Dr.1 triplane, Fokker D.VII biplane, and Fokker D.VIII parasol monoplane. Their engines were not as powerful as the latest British and French designs, but German engineers had become expert at maintaining engine output at high altitudes. By keeping the weight of the fighter as low as possible and making full use of high-lift wings, German companies were able to design fighters that were very fast and manoeuvrable at high altitudes. Structural problems limited the use made of the Fokker Dr.1 and the Jastas would have to wait for the Fokker D.VII before they could take full advantage of this new approach. Before it could reach the front, the German Army was making its last bid to win the war.

With the Russian decision to withdraw from the war, Germany was able to concentrate all her forces on the Western Front for one final all-out effort. The first of a series of offensives was an attempt to drive a wedge between the British and French armies. The Germans hoped the French would retreat towards Paris and the British to the Channel ports, opening up a gap for the German Army to drive through. To break through the British front, the German Army would use new tactics which relied on surprise rather than lengthy artillery barrages, with groups of infantry working their way forward, bypassing rather than trying to take strong points.

On 21 March 1918, the German army attacked on a 40-mile stretch of front, from Arras to La Fère, covered by the British Third and Fifth Armies. The main weight of the attack fell on the northern Third Army, but it was the Fifth Army in the south that was soon in trouble. By the evening of the 23rd, the Germans had advanced 15 miles against weakening resistance, and, more ominously, the British had lost contact with the French armies to the south. The long sought-after breakthrough had been achieved and German units were pouring through the breach in the Allied lines. General Haig, the British commander, asked the French for support and General Fayolle, the commander of the French Reserve Army Group, dispatched divisions from his First and Third Armies to cover the southern flank of the breakthrough, halt the drive on Amiens, and re-establish contact with the British armies to the north. The situation was desperate and the British were already throwing all available aircraft, bombers, fighters and reconnaissance planes, against the advancing German columns. Pétain ordered the French Air Force to follow suit and on the afternoon of the 23rd, Duval passed these instructions on to his units. It was not what *Groupements* Cramaille and Villeneuve had been created for, but the combination of Breguet bombers and SPAD fighters would prove very effective.

The French were well behind the British and Germans in the development and use of low-level close air support. Within the RFC and the German Air Force, these were already normal missions; the French still believed they were too risky and only justified in an emergency. When the order was given to

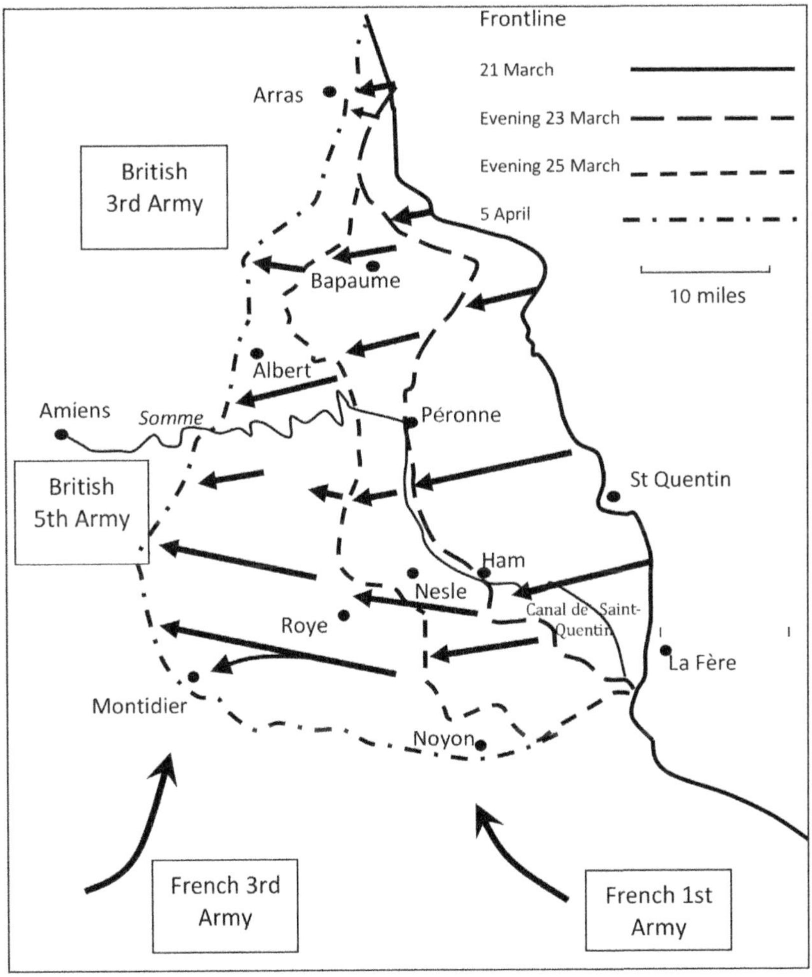

German offensive, March 1918.

throw all resources into slowing down the German drive, the French were not as well prepared either in terms of material or mindset as their British Allies. Initially, only the Breguet 14s of GB 3 and the night bombers of GB 8 were available, as the French were expecting a German offensive further south. On the night of 22nd–23rd, GB 8 bombed roads around La Fère and St Quentin railway station, but it was not until the 24th that GB 3 began bombing by day, hitting targets in the St Quentin, La Fère, and the recently occupied Ham regions. Throughout the 24th, 25th, and 26th, the eighty odd Breguets, flying in flights of six, set off to bomb and strafe German forces advancing along the southern sector of the breakthrough, from St Quentin to La Fère. In what were rather melodramatically referred to as 'missions of sacrifice', the SPAD escorts joined in these attacks as did reconnaissance and observation planes when the opportunity arose.[13, 14] The night bombers contributed by switching their attention to targets on or close to the battlefield, with planes often bombing and strafing from low level. On the 27th, the Germans occupied Montdidier, which was 40 miles from the original front line and had been a vital detraining point for French reinforcements. On this day, *Groupement* Villeneuve finally joined in the assault with its two Breguet and three SPAD groups. Targets included bridges over the Canal de Saint-Quentin and troop columns as far north as Péronne, but with the main effort in the Ham, Nesle, Roye, and Noyon regions.[15] With no artillery in place, aircraft provided the only way of supporting the arriving French forces trying to close the gap with their British allies further north. The SPAD escorts had already been joining in these attacks but on 28 March, Fayolle ordered all available fighters to suspend normal patrols and join the assault on the advancing German columns.[16]

This message was reinforced by General Foch who, on 1 April, assumed command of all Allied forces on the Western Front:

> At the present time, the first duty of fighting aeroplanes is to assist the troops on the ground, by incessant attacks, with bombs and machine-guns on columns, concentrations or bivouacs. Air fighting is not to be sought except so far as necessary for the fulfilment of this duty.[17]

The French and British planes found no shortage of targets on the roads leading to the front. Marching troop and horse-drawn artillery and supplies, all proved extremely vulnerable to the low-flying Allied planes. Although neither the SPAD nor the Breguet had been designed for low-level ground-attack, the ruggedness of both stood their crews in good stead during these hazardous missions. On 30 March and 4 April, two final attempts by the Germans to take Amiens made little progress against the rapidly stiffening Allied resistance. The crisis had passed.

It was a brilliant demonstration of how flexible air power could be. The French had not been as quick as the British to react, but French air support still arrived long before reinforcements on the ground. Aircraft had demonstrated how versatile they could be. Fighters had proven particularly effective in a ground-attack role. Fighters are designed to shoot down other planes, and this has to be their primary role, but there will always be circumstances where they can contribute more in the ground-attack role than air combat. The way any plane is used has to be dictated by circumstances at the time and not pre-determined, rigid, theoretical dogma.

Allied air power was far from being the only reason for the German failure to exploit their initial success, but the delays it imposed on the German advance were a major factor. Until French artillery arrived on the 30th, the French Air Force had been providing the only effective fire support for the French First Army. Air power had substituted for artillery and had proved very effective against troops denied the protection of trenches. At the time, French Army commanders appreciated the efforts made and success achieved by the Air Force. After the war, there would be a fierce debate over the value of such close air support. Ironically, the German Army entered the battle with specialist close air support units, but in the end, their ground-attack efforts were overshadowed by the more improvised Allied assault. Two decades later, a new German Army would make sure it had more comprehensive air support and protection for its advancing columns.

The full significance of what the French had stumbled upon was not immediately appreciated. Once the German offensive had been halted, French fighters and bombers returned to their normal duties. Even in the closing days of the German attack, there were concerns that using all available fighters for ground-attack had allowed the German Air Force to become more active. The battle for air superiority, the original purpose of the *groupements*, could not be abandoned. The SPADs and Breguets were switched to bombing communication targets in the rear, once again in the hope of provoking the German fighter force into action. However, the bombers were not capable of inflicting sufficient damage to warrant a response, and unless the odds were particularly favourable, the German fighter force declined to engage.[18]

On 14 May, command of the combat wings was centralised when the two wings were combined to form the Air Division, which would be under the direct control of Duval. Two weeks later, the new unit was required to intervene in a new German offensive, this time across the Aisne. This was the first time a French sector of the front had borne the full weight of the new style German offensives. To counter the German tactics on the ground, Pétain organised a more flexible defence in depth, which meant German forces had to advance further before they reached the main line of defence. This meant that even if the defensive line held, a degree of movement was returning to the battlefield, and with it, more opportunities for aircraft to intervene.

On the first day of the offensive, 27 May, the Germans advanced more than ten miles, and a further ten by the evening of the 29th, far further than the new flexible defence was supposed to allow. The French response in the air was slow. The Air Division was still based further north on the Picardy front, but there was also still a reluctance to accept the role it could play and there was no immediate attempt to move it south. No close support missions were flown on the first day of the offensive. During the night, around fifty sorties were flown against lines of communication leading into the battle zone, and the next day the Breguet bombers of *Escadre* 12 were still concentrating on the rail station at Péronne, well in the German rear, despite the critical situation developing at the front. The only close support during the course of the day was provided by the courageous efforts of the crews of a few obsolete Voisin night bombers.[19]

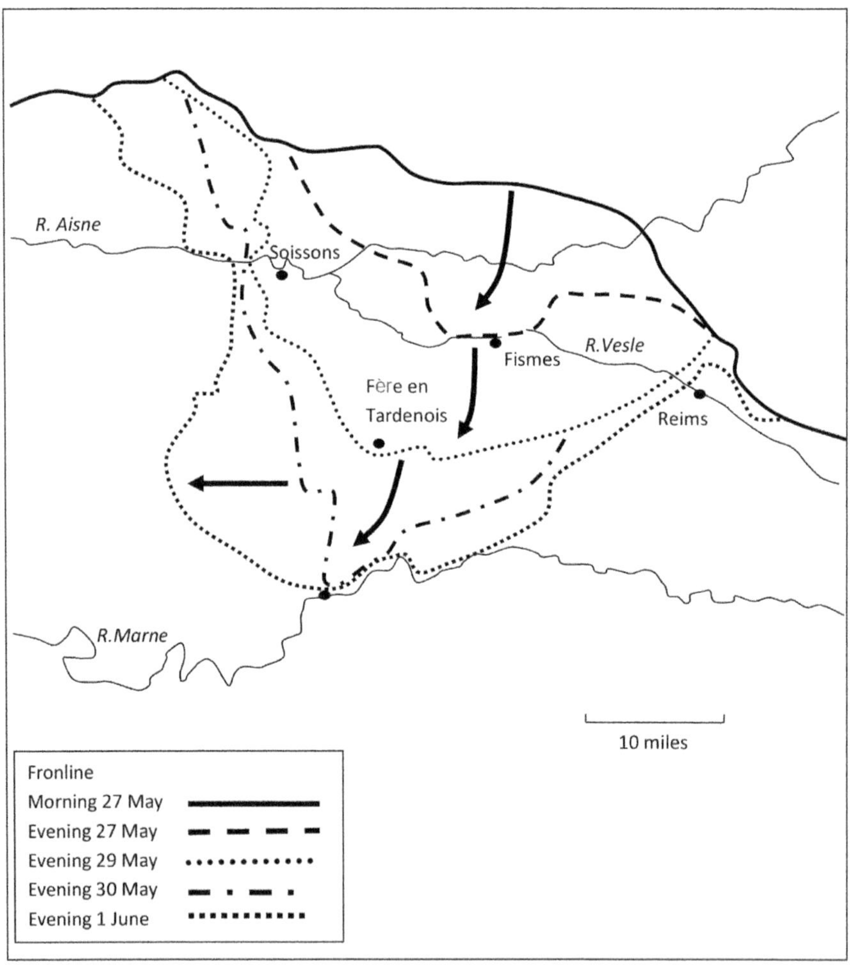

Marne, 27 May–1 June 1918.

By the 28th, the situation was so serious that the French squadrons behind the front were having to abandon bases threatened by the German advance. By the 29th, the day bomber wings were finally in a position to respond. *Groupement* Cramaille, now renamed *Groupement* Féquant, made its first intervention, attacking German forces around Fismes. The next day, *Groupement* Ménard (ex-*Groupement* Villeneuve), led by Commandant Victor Ménard, joined in with attacks on German forces pushing through Fère-en-Tardenois. From this point on, the French bomber squadrons were fully engaged. On the 31st, *Groupement* Ménard flew 223 sorties around Fère-en-Tardenois, causing heavy casualties and provoking frantic appeals from German commanders for better air cover.[20]

With their advance to the south blocked, the Germans turned westwards towards Paris and the Air Division promptly switched all its resources to halting this drive. On 1 June, *Escadre* 12 flew around 200 bombing missions, dropping 34 tons of bombs, followed by another 174 sorties the next day. This gave the French reserves the necessary breathing space to establish a new defensive line in the rear; by the time the Germans reached them, they were too weakened to break through. In one final demonstration of its power, on 4 June, *Groupement* Ménard was called upon to disperse German forces reportedly assembling in a ravine for an attack on French positions the following day. Despite losses and the wear and tear imposed by five days of continuous operations, the wing was still able to launch 100 sorties against the German forces. The next day, a grateful army commander was able to report the attack had been repulsed with ease.[21]

In both the 21 March and 27 May offensives, the Breguets had been called in as an emergency measure, but over the next few months, bombing operations in and around the battlefield would become a normal activity and the two French tactical *groupements* became a vital part of the Army's defensive strategy. The ability to switch these formations from one front to another provided the French High Command with an immediate way of reinforcing any threatened sector.

On 9 June, the Germans struck south of Noyon. This time the French were not caught by surprise and there was no hesitation about using the Air Division. After advancing nearly ten miles the offensive ground to a halt, but the French were not now merely content to contain the enemy. On the evening of the 10th, a counterattack on the flank of the German advance was hastily organised for the following day. Thanks to the work of General Estienne, this would be like no previous French counterattack. Having pioneered artillery-observing aircraft, Estienne had turned his attentions to developing the tank and with 300 Renault FT-17 light tanks taking part, this would be the first large-scale use of this weapon. Even more interesting was the decision to attack without the previously obligatory pre-offensive artillery assault. There was no time to organise this; instead, the French infantry would rely on the firepower of the French tanks and the Air Division.[22] Low-level close air support was no longer 'a mission of sacrifice' or a desperate measure in desperate circumstances—it had become a normal Air Force role.

Two fighter groups of the Third Army joined the Air Division for the attack. In total, there would be some 225 light bombers, 100 night bombers, and 550 fighters. The light bombers were assigned specific zones in the battle area, none of which were further than 5 miles from the front line. All fighters were responsible for establishing air superiority over the battle zone, but Air Division fighters would have the additional task of strafing enemy positions. The heavy bombers would provide indirect support by bombing stations up to 15 miles beyond the front line. The counterattack was launched on the morning of the 11th and during the course of the first day, around 500 fighter and bomber sorties were flown.[23] The attack on the ground did not win a decisive victory; the enemy were only pushed back 2 miles. Tanks were still mechanically unreliable and there was still much to learn about tank and infantry cooperation. Nevertheless, the Germans had been surprised by the power and speed of the French riposte.

In the early part of July, aerial reconnaissance spotted camouflaged ammunition dumps around Reims, confirming information gathered from captured German soldiers that a further major offensive was about to be launched. This advance information allowed the French to be a little more ambitious. The Germans would be attacking from a salient in the front line, so were already in an exposed position. Even before the Germans moved forward, the French were planning to launch a counterattack at the base of the salient. To halt the initial German advance, the French had the Air Division, fighter units attached to the threatened armies and an RAF wing. Altogether, there were over 800 fighters, 200 day bombers, and 100 night bombers. The fighter units attached to the armies were to escort the reconnaissance planes and protect the troops from enemy attack and observation. Air Division fighters were given the task of establishing air superiority, escorting the day bombers and strafing enemy positions.[24]

The attack was launched on 15 July. To the east of Reims, the German forces were comfortably contained, but to the west, the Germans surprised the French by audaciously ferrying troops across the Marne under cover of darkness and these were soon making rapid inroads into the French lines. To supply their advancing forces, German engineers hastily threw pontoon bridges across the river and these immediately became the targets for both French artillery and aircraft. By mid-morning, the French artillery had been forced to pull back, leaving the Air Force as the sole means of continuing the assault on the crossing points. It was not so different to the situation the French would face twenty-two years later at Sedan. During the course of the day, around 250 bomber sorties, covered by 900 fighters, were flown against the bridges and villages on the Marne. The bombers were operating no further than 3 miles beyond the front line and General von Hoeppner, the commander of the German Air Force, later testified to the effectiveness of these assaults. Although the bridges remained intact, German efforts were severely disrupted and considerable quantities of supplies were lost. Without adequate supplies, the Germans were not able to make further progress.[25]

On the 18th, Pétain launched his pre-prepared counterattack on the northern flank of the German salient. The French had plenty of time to move artillery into position to support the offensive but they preferred the surprise relying on tanks and aircraft would provide. Again, the French forces did not advance far—no more than a few miles. However, the Germans had been caught off balance and the French attack threatened to take Soissons, cutting off the German forces fighting along the Marne further south. Ludendorff had no choice but to withdraw from the salient. Once again, the French had shown that bombers could substitute for artillery, both defensively in an emergency, and, even more significantly, offensively by choice.

The last desperate offensives of the spring and early summer had significantly weakened the German Army. American troops were now pouring into France

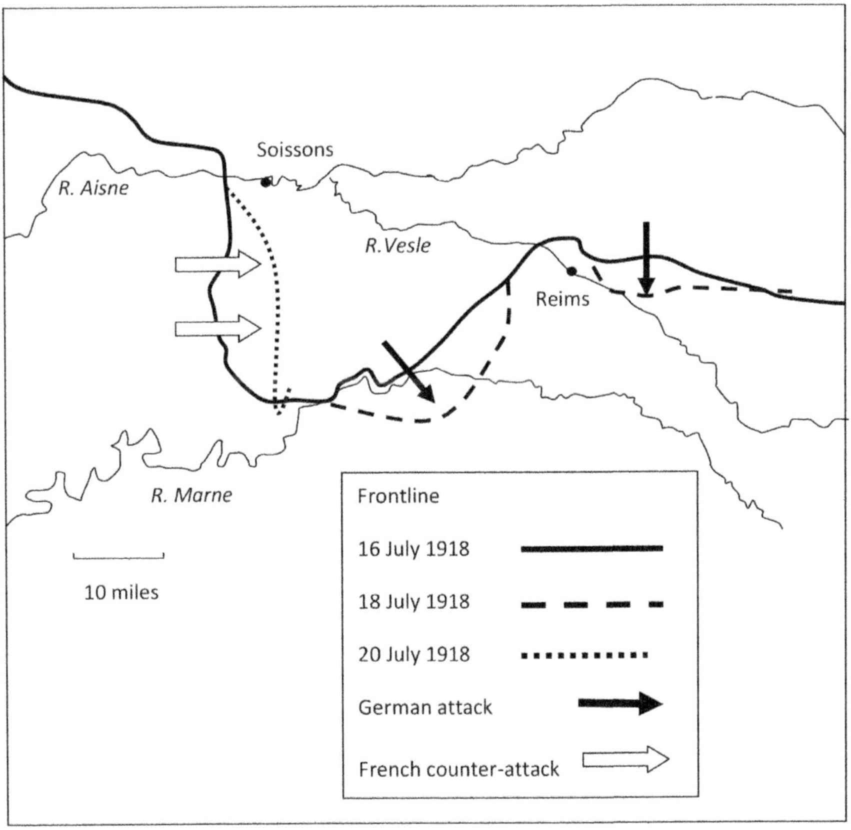

Marne, 16–20 July 1918.

and the tide of battle was inexorably turning in favour of the Allies. On 8 August, the Allies launched their first major offensive of the year from their positions east of Amiens. In addition to considerable quantities of tanks and artillery, the Allies had assembled a huge fleet of nearly 2,000 planes, of which around half were French. They included eighty fighters attached to the French First Army and a further 432 fighters and 195 day bombers with the Air Division.

The formidable array of firepower brought to bear on the German lines on the morning of 8 August had immediate effect. For the first time in the war, the morale of German troops began to crack, with units abandoning their weapons and fleeing the battlefield. For the German High Command, it was a major shock. The Allied attack might have achieved more if the RAF had not switched its effort from the battlefield to bridges over the Somme in the rear. The British bombers soon discovered destroying permanent bridges is difficult and, when they are close to German airfields, very dangerous. If the French attacks on the Marne pontoon bridges paralleled the 1940 attacks at Sedan, the RAF bombing of the Somme bridges was more akin to the 1940 attempts to destroy the bridges over the Albert Canal.

The Amiens offensive marked a turning point in the course of the First World War. From this point on, the Allies would advance steadily towards the German frontier. For the remaining three months of war, the French Air Division would be switched from one sector of the front to another to support each successive offensive. The final Franco-American Meuse-Argonne offensive, launched on 26 September, had the support of over 900 bomber and fighter sorties.[26] The pressure applied by Breguet pilots, often joined by strafing SPADs, was relentless and on occasion enabled the advance to continue when the lack of artillery support might have forced a delay.

When hostilities finally ceased in November the French were planning to form a second air division. By this time, the French day bomber squadrons had become a purely tactical force, rarely penetrating more than ten miles beyond the front line. The use of light bombers to intervene on and immediately behind the battlefield seemed well-established. Fighters too, it seemed, were now viewed as a tool for attacking ground targets as well as establishing air superiority. However, these ideas were less well embedded than it might seem. The Air Force still saw its main role as hitting targets much further behind the front line; the short range of most missions flown was largely because deeper penetrations were felt to be too risky. This close air and ground cooperation did not ease tensions between Army and Air Force. Army commanders still felt the Air Force was too independent and complained about a lack of liaison. Ménard retaliated by claiming the Army did not want liaison, it wanted control of the air units and accused its commanders of seeing the Air Division as no more than a way of protecting their observation squadrons.[27]

With the benefit of hindsight, the significance of the tank and tactical air support is clear enough. However, even with this support, the French had been unable to achieve the dramatic advance the German Army had managed in their spring offensive, without massive air support or indeed tanks. In November 1918, when Germany finally agreed to a ceasefire, their army was still holding a continuous front and had not even been pushed out of French territory. It was easy to be sceptical about the value of the tank and battlefield air support.

Nevertheless, there were those who saw the tank and air combination as the way forward. Using ideas developed by Estienne and his British counterpart, Colonel Fuller, Foch was planning to make bold use of the tank in offensives planned for 1919. He envisaged a force of 5,000 tanks, with heavy tanks bursting through enemy defences, faster medium tanks destroying enemy command centres in the rear and a pursuit force completing the rout. The Air Force would provide reconnaissance and act as airborne artillery.[28] The German surrender in November denied Foch the chance to see how these ideas would work out in practice.

By the end of the war, the *Aéronautique Militaire* had become a formidable weapon. Yet there were major gaps in its capability. The SPAD S.XIII was an excellent low and medium-altitude interceptor and ground-attack fighter, but its performance was not so good at altitude. Intercepting the high-flying German Halberstadt C.V and Rumpler C.VII reconnaissance planes had been a major problem. The SPAD also lacked the agility to deal with fighters like the Fokker D.VII; it was not a natural dogfighter or escort fighter.

Ménard had never been happy about using the single-seater fighter as escorts. He did not believe it was possible to use high-speed fighters and slower bombers together and the short range of the single-seater would also always limit the distance bombers could fly. In any case, the time would always come when a shortage of fuel would force the single-seater to retreat, and it would then be exposed to continuous assaults from the rear. Ménard tried to reduce the disadvantages by not tying the SPAD escorts so closely to the bombers so that they could use their high horizontal and diving speeds to better effect. However, a close escort would also be needed and the multi-seater combat plane flying in formation with the bombers, seemed the best option.

With the departure of Barès, the fate of the multi-seater combat plane had appeared sealed. The few Caudron R.4s and Letord 4s delivered had been used almost exclusively for long-range reconnaissance rather than air combat. However, the idea remained a strong feature of French thinking. Many fighter commanders agreed with Ménard that multi-seaters were better escorts than single-seaters.[29] The French had been impressed by the German Halberstadt CL.II and Hannover CL.II two-seaters that began to appear over the front in the summer of 1917. The British had also had some success with the Bristol Fighter. Not having something similar seemed to be a mistake and the French began developing their own. Two-seater fighters seemed to offer a compromise between the twin-engined multi-seater and the single-engined single-seater. The idea was to use them at low and medium-altitudes for interception and as an escort. By May 1918, Duval was proposing that eventually, two-thirds of the fighter force would be equipped with two or multi-seaters.[30] This was precisely what Barès had been proposing before Verdun.

Caudron had continued to develop the multi-seater combat plane with their R.11, a smaller, lighter more powerful version of the R.4. Its performance was almost identical to the Breguet 14, which, Ménard insisted, made it the perfect machine to accompany the light bombers. With its twin nose and dorsal machine guns and a fifth (and sometimes even a sixth) gun firing through a floor hatch, the plane was very well-armed.[31] Protection squadrons equipped with the Caudron R.11 began to be attached to the Breguet squadrons and the tactic appeared to work. German fighters seemed reluctant to press home their attacks when confronted with the combined firepower of the Caudrons and Breguets. The apparent success of the Caudron in the escort role secured the future of the still more powerful Caudron R.14, which, it was hoped, would be armed with cannon.[32] The trend away from using single-seaters for close escort was confirmed by the decision in September to divide the Air Division wings into independent homogeneous fighter and bomber brigades.

The defensive firepower of these French Caudron Breguet formations was indeed formidable and initially posed problems for German fighter pilots. However, as better fighters like the Fokker D.VII and Siemens-Schuckert D.IV reached the squadrons, German pilots learned to deal with the problem. For their part, the French probably underestimated the value of the indirect escorts the SPADs were providing. On 14 September, thirty-nine Breguet 14s and three escorting Caudron R.11s, with no single-seater SPAD escort, lost six Breguets and two Caudrons in a running battle with German fighters.[33]

The Hanriot HD.3 was chosen for the two-seater fighter role and large numbers ordered, although few reached the front before the Armistice. It was also suggested that single-seater fighters like the new SPAD S.XX should be capable of carrying a rear gunner if required, and fly as a so-called *monoplace protège*.[34] The wheel had turned full circle since the pilots of the Nieuport 10s and 12s had elected to cover the second crewman's position and fly the planes as single-seaters. Tactically, the reckless aggression of du Peuty's tactics had been replaced by an ultra-cautious defensive approach. At the heart of the problem was the lack of a highly manoeuvrable dogfighter. If the Morane-Saulnier MoS.27 and MoS.29 had not suffered from technical problems, the case for defensive two or multi-seater escort planes would not have been so strong.

The traditional single-seater fighter was still required and Duval recognised the need for specialist high and medium-altitude fighters. It was hoped that with the turbo-supercharger Rateau was developing, a high-altitude interceptor ought to achieve 240 km/hr (149 mph) and be able to climb to 7,000 metres (23,000 feet). The next generation of medium-altitude fighters were to be capable of no less than 270 km/hr (168 mph) at 4,000 metres. Given that the latest SPAD S.XIII could only manage 200 km/hr, this was a demanding requirement, and took speeds to the point where the low weight of the biplane no longer compensated for its high drag.[35] There was already talk of cantilever monoplanes with speeds of 265 km/hr at 4,000 m.[36]

These single-seaters, however, would only make up a third of the fighter force. The two and multi-seaters would predominate. This move towards much larger planes was also a feature of the next generation of tactical bombers. The Breguet 14 had proven vulnerable to ground fire and some armour had been fitted, but to carry more, greater engine power was required. To replace the Breguet 14, Duval wanted a heavily armoured, twin-engined, two-seater assault plane, for low-level bombing and strafing. Apart from the extra power, the second engine also provided more security and in years to come two engines would continue to be seen as a major advantage for any low-flying plane. Lioré et Olivier and Canton set about building prototypes to meet this requirement.[37]

However, the need to match the capabilities of ground-based artillery led to demands for an even larger plane. This would be an armoured three-seater armed with a 75-mm cannon. The cannon would not be fixed; the idea was that it could be elevated through 120 degrees and engage the enemy by indirect fire in the same way that land-based artillery could. It was effectively a flying tank. This produced one of the most remarkable ground-attack planes ever built. The Schneider 'Henri Paul' S.3 was huge, and required no less than four engines to haul its massive airframe into the air.[38] It seemed that size was no handicap for a French ground-attack plane.

While the French Army spent the First World War focusing on how to use air power to support ground forces, the politicians were more concerned about the way Germany was using bombers to undermine the morale of the French nation. The war had not begun with the massive aerial bombardments that some had predicted. However, as the stalemate at the front deepened, both sides began to consider using the bomber to achieve victory more directly by attacking the enemy's vulnerable civilian population.

Initially, German bombing was directed at communication targets. As early as November 1914, Le Havre was demanding planes to defend the town. During 1915, there were similar requests from towns as far in the rear as Bourges and Lyon. However, as the need for fighters at the front grew, so the Army became more reluctant to divert resources to the rear. It argued that fighters at the front were just as capable of intercepting bombers on the way to targets in the rear, a slightly dubious argument as bombers could always choose to cross the front where fighters were less likely to be encountered. As the war progressed, the German Air Force attacked more by night, and since it was almost impossible to intercept night bombers, the case for not deploying fighters in the rear became even stronger. The only sizeable interceptor force was created in the Paris region, although even here, the proximity of the capital to the fighting made these squadrons a frequent source of reinforcement for the front. As the war progressed and the aerial threat to Paris increased, the number of squadrons assigned to the capital actually decreased. To reduce the scale of attack, the French relied on raiding the airfields the Germans were using, although there was little evidence this achieved much.[39]

Barès had no doubts that the bomber should be used as a weapon of terror and in 1915, was proposing victory could be achieved by the systematic bombing of German towns.[40] It scarcely seemed a sensible strategy given that Paris was only sixty miles from the front line, while French bombers were not even capable of reaching Berlin. Indeed, very few German cities were within range of the bombers the French possessed. The French delivered the odd raid as retaliation, but their long-range bomber force lacked the striking power to deter. Germany on the other hand, had Zeppelin airships, which could carry over 3,000 lb of bombs. In 1917, Gotha aeroplanes that could carry over 1,000 lb appeared and towards the end of the war the Zeppelin-Staaken R.VI Giants that could lift over 4,000 lb. These were used to launch deliberate terror attacks on towns and cities in Britain and France. For most of the war, Paris was not bombed. The implications were not lost on the French; provided there was no retaliation against German cities, Paris would be spared.

It was a humiliating position to be in. The best French designed bombers were all single-engined and could only carry 600 lb of bombs. Caproni Ca.33 and Ca.45 multi-engined bombers were acquired from Italy but even they could not match the German 'Giants'. Given the lifting capability of French bombers and the proximity of Paris to German airfields, the French government was very cautious about retaliating. In March 1917, the French cabinet decided that raids on industrial targets should be avoided if there was any chance of German civilian casualties and French bombers began confining their attacks to German Lorraine, a largely French speaking region, and Luxembourg.

During the course of 1917, attacks on French towns increased in size and frequency with Nancy, Calais, and Dunkirk being particularly hard hit. The ineffectiveness of the defences was all too clear to the inhabitants and discontent grew.[41] At one point, the dockers at Dunkirk refused to work while the possibility of air attack remained. The country had no effective bomber force for retaliation and the Army did not seem to have done much about creating one.

In March 1917, French deputies were briefed on the inadequacies of the bomber fleet by one of its pilots, a certain Victor Laurent-Eynac, who would go on to become a major figure in the drive towards an independent air force.[42] The inadequacies he described provided more ammunition for critics of a government already reeling from the disastrous Nivelle Offensive. The government fell and the new administration recreated the post of under-secretary for air. The Army's 12th Directorate was not abolished, but it now shared responsibility for developing the air arm with the politicians. The latter were now able to ensure more effort went into developing a long-range bombing force. The departure of Nivelle and du Peuty, neither of whom had been great advocates of the long-range bomber, and the arrival of Pétain, who had expressed his concern about the lack of an effective French bombing deterrent, all helped the bomber cause. New specifications were released calling for a medium night bomber and also a heavy bomber capable of carrying a 1,000-kg (2,200-lb) bomb load to Berlin. The former led to the Farman F.50 and Breguet 16, the latter a stretched version of the Breguet 14. The Farman F.60, a scaled-up F.50, and the Caudron C.23 would meet the heavy bomber requirement. Apart from the Breguet 16, all these designs were twin-engined and appeared to offer the striking power the French needed.

In the meantime, the French government felt helpless. French bombers restricted themselves to lone precision attacks by particularly experienced crews, in the hope of avoiding German casualties. There was the occasional attempt at a reprisal, with accompanying leaflets to justify the action, but the French government were very aware of how feeble these efforts were.[43] To add to French problems, their British allies had decided that the time had come to act. A large bomber fleet would be built which would serve the dual purpose of retaliating for German raids on the UK and crippling German industry. The RFC did not have bombers with the range to do this from Britain so bases in France had to be used. Initially, the force would have just three squadrons. Pétain had no objections to the occasional powerful retaliatory raid, but he could not see the point of scattered raids on industrial targets with such a small force—they would only provoke heavier German reprisals, and these would almost certainly be against French cities, not British. He pleaded in vain for the British to use these bombers to reinforce French efforts against German airfields, but the British squadrons were soon attacking targets inside Germany and, just as the French had feared, the Germans attributed, or chose to attribute, them to the French.[44] On the night of 30–31 January 1918, German bombers struck Paris; sixty-one civilians were killed and another 198 were injured. It was the first of a series of raids that would last eight months.[45]

Right to the end of the war, the air defence of cities remained weak. In November 1918, only sixteen of the available ninety-eight fighter squadrons were based in the rear and nearly all of these were defending the capital or communication centres the Army wanted protected. The French government still had no way of retaliating effectively. The new Farman F.50 and Caudron C.23 night bombers were hastily rushed into production, but despite political pressure, the needs of the Army ensured that the planned long-range bomber force remained relatively modest. In 1918, French plans to increase Air Force front line strength to 4,000 planes involved a 1,000 strong bomber force, but most of these would be medium. Some Farman F.50s did reach the squadrons before the end of the war but before they could begin operations, the German raids on Allied cities suddenly ceased. The German High Command decided that bombing cities could not change the course of the war and the planes could be more usefully employed supporting the retreating German Army. French politicians saw things differently. Over 3,000 French civilians had lost their lives in bombing and long-range artillery fire.[46] Compared to the slaughter at the front, it was a relatively small number, but it was more than twice the British civilian death toll. The vulnerability of French cities and the frustration of not being able to retaliate effectively would not be forgotten.

France ended the First World War with 3,700 aircraft in front line squadrons and could claim to possess the most powerful air force in the world. Yet despite the experience gained in four years of operations, the way forward was far from clear. The Air Force had demonstrated that aircraft could play an important part in slowing down rapid enemy advances by intervening directly on and in the immediate vicinity of the battlefield. Offensively, the Air Division had been used in much the same way as the Luftwaffe would be used in 1940, but this would only become clear with hindsight. The more fluid battles of 1918 had been the exception rather than the rule and the struggle as a whole had been dominated by seemingly impregnable defences. Only on rare occasions had the continuous front being broken, and when it had, the defenders had always been able to restore the situation.

At precisely which level of command air units should be placed remained a thorny issue. The way in which it had been possible to switch the Air Division from one sector to another as the tactical situation required had demonstrated the value of centralised control. On the other hand, centrally controlled fighter forces had not always been used as army commanders wanted. For centralised control, there had to be trust between Army and Air Force commanders; this was often in short supply. What was apparently beyond dispute was the need for the largest possible fighter force. In 1916, the French Air Force had six times as many army corps planes as fighters. By the end of the war, fighter strength had almost caught up with reconnaissance strength and, if the September 1918 expansion plan had been completed, would have overtaken it. It seemed impossible to have too many fighters.

Long-range bombing had not played the decisive part some pre-war experts had predicted. Arguably, the French had made no sustained effort to develop an effective bomber and there was plenty of evidence to suggest bombing could have achieved more. The German capitulation had as much to do with the collapse of morale on the home front as it did with military defeat on the battlefield. Allied bombing could only claim to have played a minor part in achieving this, but it was tempting to suppose that the development of a more effective bomber force at an earlier stage in the war might have brought a collapse in German morale far sooner.

At the end of the war, the French were developing no fewer than fifteen types of combat plane (four fighters, six bombers, and five reconnaissance planes). The sheer variety of aircraft under development seemed to augur well for the future, but a growing number of these were large multi-seaters. Using these for ground-attack and escort was a dangerous path to follow. Combat at the front seemed to prove that Barès's multi-purpose combat planes were not the way to go, but by the end of the war, the concept was very much back in fashion.

3

The Air Force Loses Its Way

In the post-war years, the Army's air units continued to be run by the War Ministry's 12th Directorate. Naval and colonial aviation were controlled by their respective ministries. A civilian under-secretary of state for air within the Ministry of Public Works had the task of coordinating all aeronautical matters, civilian, and military. It was a rather complicated set-up. Spheres of responsibility overlapped and liaison between the various departments was not always easy. Flandin, the under-secretary of state for air, and Laurent-Eynac, now a prominent deputy, were openly campaigning for an independent air ministry, like Britain's. There also seemed a strong case for an independent air force, so that the potential of air power as a strategic weapon could be developed to the full.[1,2,3]

The Army did not object to an air ministry as long as it was a purely non-military body that concerned itself with the technical aspects of aviation. However, any civilian body that involved itself in how air power should be used, and certainly an Air Force command independent of the Army, was strongly opposed by Pétain and the Army General Staff.[4] Even within the framework of the War Ministry and Army command, the Air Force had demonstrated an inclination to go its own way. The Army was anxious to curb this tendency, not encourage it by granting the Air Force even more freedom.

If the First World War had continued, it is quite likely that Army objections would have been overcome and the French would have followed the example set by Britain with her independent Royal Air Force. In peacetime, however, it was not just the Army who objected; the French Treasury too had good reason to oppose a separate air organisation. The First World War had crippled the French economy, and while there was no intention of jeopardising the security of the nation by skimping on defence spending, an autonomous air force or air ministry seemed an unnecessary extra expense.

The end of hostilities resulted in a running down of front line strength. By 1920, the number of operational squadrons in France had been more than halved, falling from 251 to 105. This however was still a substantial force—

the RAF had been reduced to a mere handful of squadrons. French leaders, both military and political, were determined to maintain French strength. The post-war contraction had hardly got going before there were calls to reverse the process. By 1921, plans existed to create a 220 (194 in France) squadron strong Air Force, which was not far short of the number that had existed at the end of the war.[5, 6] A plan to increase Air Force strength to 186 squadrons was actually approved by the French Parliament, but France's dire financial position scuppered the plan.[7] Nevertheless, the French Air Force still maintained a front line strength of approximately 1,000 planes in France, with another 500 overseas, making it by far the most powerful air force in the world. These figures would remain virtually unchanged throughout the interwar years.

It was, however, a very different air force to the one the French had ended the war with. Each army corps and army still had its own observation and reconnaissance squadrons, but as divisions were disbanded, the number of these squadrons fell by nearly two thirds. Even so, the surviving units still constituted nearly half (45 per cent) of the front line peacetime strength. The growing importance attached to long-range bombing meant the number of bomber squadrons remained roughly the same, but this meant the proportion of bombers rose from around 15 per cent to 30 per cent of overall strength. What was left (around a quarter) made up the fighter force. Compared to the fighter force that existed at the end of the First World War, this was not only much smaller, it was also smaller as a proportion of total strength, reversing the wartime trend of a proportionally increasing fighter force. It was argued that fighters could be built relatively quickly and so the fighter force was the easiest to expand. This was perhaps reasonable, as long as the overriding importance of a powerful fighter arm was not forgotten.

Many of the orders placed for warplanes before the Armistice were either reduced in size or cancelled altogether. A massive contraction of the aircraft industry was inevitable, but the process was staggered to a certain extent to give the industry time to adjust. Nearly 4,000 machines were built in 1919, far more than the peacetime Air Force would need. Many of the surplus machines were either put into storage or exported to the fledgling air forces of France's new eastern allies, Poland and Czechoslovakia. By 1920, however, production had fallen from the 1918 figure of over 23,000 to under 1,000. It was not long, however, before production was rising once more. If war broke out suddenly, a healthy reserve of aircraft would be needed to cover initial losses while the aircraft industry was getting back to a war footing. Large orders were therefore placed for the latest Breguet bombers, Potez reconnaissance planes, and Nieuport fighters, all of which were far in excess of the needs of the remaining front line squadrons.[8]

This so-called '*politique de stocks*' was very much an army solution to the problem of preparing for war in peacetime. It was a policy that only made sense if the useful life of the stored items was reasonably long. This was true with most army equipment, but experience during the First World War did not suggest it was true for aircraft. Each year had seen the introduction of new, improved combat planes by both sides, which made previous equipment obsolete. On the other hand, it could be argued that this was only because the aeroplane was such a new invention. By the end of the First World War, it did not appear too rash to suppose that the aircraft had come of age, that the era of rapid evolution had come to an end and that in future the useful life of a combat plane would be considerably longer. Many decades later, they would have been right. Opponents of the policy argued that too much of the Air Force budget would go on production and not enough on research and development. However, the War Ministry argued that the need to compete in the rapidly expanding civil aviation market would force the aircraft industry to finance its own research. There was some truth in this, although not all areas of research are relevant to both civilian and military requirements.

There was no complacency among the French military. The euphoria of victory soon gave way to the realization that as long as the German state remained intact, it would continue to pose a threat to the security of France and how this threat could be best met was soon exercising minds. There were good reasons for relying on the mobile, flexible strategy Foch had been planning to use in 1919. Under the terms of the Treaty of Versailles, Germany was not allowed to station forces on the west bank of the Rhine and a 50-kilometre strip to the east of the river. The only way France could oppose German reoccupation of the Rhineland would be by a rapid advance into the area. This was also the only military way of supporting France's new allies in Eastern Europe. Even defensively, Foch believed the French would have to advance to the Rhine simply because the river represented the easiest line to defend.[9] This was the sort of strategy that would require fast-moving mechanised forces and the mobile firepower of the Air Division.

In the early twenties, some steps were taken to improve the mobility of the French Army by motorising some infantry and artillery units. In 1921, General Estienne was appointed director of tank studies and he was soon proposing a mobile force with 100,000 infantrymen, 4,000 trucks, and 8,000 tanks. Such a force, he claimed, would be capable of advancing up to 60 miles by day or night and could rapidly reoccupy the Rhineland if required.[10] General Buat, the French chief of staff, was another who favoured an initial advance to the Rhine in any future war with Germany and he too was interested in the possibilities of mechanised mobile warfare. His young adjutant, Jean-Henri Jauneaud, envisaged highly mobile armoured forces supported by bombers.[11] Maxime Weygand, Foch's old chief of staff, was another showing a keen interest in the concept of mechanised mobile warfare. These were still only ideas, but the elements of the future German *blitzkrieg* theory were certainly there.

Unfortunately, during the early twenties, many of the advocates of a more fluid type of warfare disappeared from the military scene. Early in 1920, the architect of the Air Division, General Duval, was replaced by General Dumesnil as Director of Military Aviation. Foch had made himself unpopular with French politicians by his insistence that the Rhineland should be annexed. When it came to appoint the Vice-President of the War Council, the highest post in the peacetime army, Pétain was preferred to Foch. Pétain had built his reputation during the war on sound defence and methodical advance, not dashing assaults. In 1923, Pétain's Chief of Staff, General Buat, died suddenly and the staunchly pro-Pétain General Debeney replaced him. In 1924, Jauneaud left for Brazil to work with the French Military Commission there. The loss of so many key figures did not help the mechanisation cause. The likes of Estienne and Weygand remained to fight for greater mobility, but the counter arguments were formidable.

Dashing advances in the First World War had invariably ended in bloody defeat. It was far from certain that the tanks could supply the mobile firepower that rapid advances required and relying on air support as a substitute seemed risky. Air superiority could not be relied on; the arrival of a new fighter could soon change the balance of power. Even if an air force possessed superiority, a spell of bad weather was enough to ground the force. Defensively, the ability to switch air units from one sector of the front to another was a major advantage, but exploiting this advantage required a huge expensive network of airfields. Aircraft were also expensive to build and required highly trained crews. Such a force might be eventually created in wartime, but it would cost too much to maintain on a peacetime budget. It was also argued that aircraft would always be vulnerable to ground fire. All in all, the aircraft appeared to be a rather unreliable weapon on which to base a defensive or offensive strategy. Pétain went back to the pre-First World War belief that low-level attacks on the battlefield could only be risked in an emergency. The normal role of the bomber should be enemy communications in the rear. The French Army were not doctrinally opposed to battlefield bomber support in the way the British Air Staff were (any support the Air Force could provide would be useful) but it could not be relied on.

Even Ménard, a commander in the First World War Air Division, had serious reservations about using aircraft on or around the battlefield. Although he admitted some useful results had been achieved against advancing German troop columns in March 1918, he did not believe these attacks had been in any way decisive. It had been the infantry, not the Air Force, that had restored the situation, which was true but did not take account of the extra time the intervention of the Air Force had bought the infantry. Ménard went further by claiming that the Air Division had been misused during the subsequent French advances. The bomber squadrons should have been used to supplement the army corps squadrons in the artillery observation role and the fighters should have concentrated on eliminating German spotter planes. The low-level bombing and ground strafing had undoubtedly inflicted casualties on the retreating German forces, but Ménard maintained that German casualties would have been even greater, and French casualties far fewer, if the Air Force had concentrated on supporting the artillery. Ménard was not much more enthusiastic about the indirect support Pétain favoured.[12, 13] Coming from an Air Division commander, these views carried some weight.

The Air Force Inspectorate came to similar conclusions. This body had been set up to advise the Army General Staff on how best to use aviation. Fayolle was put in charge, 'more on account of his temporary unemployment than because of his knowledge of aviation', the British air *attaché* in Paris unkindly noted.[14] Fayolle appointed a commission of experienced Air Force officers, headed by a Colonel Armengaud, to report on the lessons to be learned from the First World War. The commission conceded that in 1918 bombers had achieved some success against battlefield targets without suffering heavy losses. The report went on to suggest that in an emergency, reconnaissance and observation machines and even heavy night bombers could be usefully used in an all-out daylight offensive against tactical targets. However, the commission also argued that rather than being a means of reinforcing or substituting for artillery, the true value of the bomber lay in its ability to strike at targets beyond the range of artillery. As the accuracy and range of artillery increased, so the zone in which day bombers would normally operate would be pushed ever further into the rear. Fayolle did not see any need for a specialised ground-attack plane. In an emergency, those bombers being used against the enemy rear could always be switched to battlefield targets, as they had in 1918.[15, 16]

The consensus within the Army was that the bomber was not a battlefield weapon. The French had rejected an essential ingredient of the future German *blitzkrieg*. At this stage, however, the Germans were no more enlightened. The German Army, which had both used and experienced the effectiveness of close air support in the First World War, came to exactly the same conclusion for the same reasons. It was pointless to risk aircraft in attacks on battlefield targets that could be destroyed far more easily by artillery.

Discarding the aircraft as a way of providing close support left Estienne's mobile forces short of the firepower it needed to maintain an advance. Rather than rely on the power of manoeuvre, the French would use concrete and artillery to blunt any German attack. In 1929, work began on the Maginot Line and similar fortifications along the Albert Canal in Belgium would complete the defence of Western Europe. The static siege warfare envisaged would provide even fewer opportunities for aircraft to intervene tactically. As the element of mobility was squeezed out of French military thinking, the need for any sort of tactical close air support decreased.

This change in attitude was reflected in the post-war organisation of the Air Force. In 1924, the second Air Division planned at the end of the war was created, but it was no longer the specialised close air support unit it had become in the First World War. The new formations included captive balloon units and mixed fighter and reconnaissance regiments, reflecting Ménard's view that artillery spotting could be of more use to the Army than direct intervention on the battlefield. The night bomber units were incorporated into the two air divisions rather than the specialised heavy bomber brigade proposed in the original 1921 scheme. It was argued that these were more balanced formations, but this was just another way of saying they were no longer specialist army air support units. The 1st Air Division was supposed to be capable of instantly reinforcing French Air Force units based in Germany. The 2nd Air Division was viewed as a nucleus for the air units that would be required by the mobilising French armies. This 2nd Air Division did not possess any day bombers.[17]

The French Air Force was still largely a tactical air force, but reconnaissance and artillery observation would be the primary roles and the job of the fighters was to protect them. There was no redeployment of fighters to rear defence as had happened in Britain. Strategic air defence was no more important in the post-war French Army than it had been during the war. The rear defence squadrons that had existed in the First World War had been the first to be disbanded and during the twenties, just one experimental night fighter squadron was formed. As General Niessel, who took over from Fayolle in 1924, rather candidly admitted, any rear defence flights that might be formed would be to reassure the French public, not impress a potential enemy.[18] A nominal rear defence force would reduce potentially embarrassing public pressure in wartime to withdraw fighter squadrons from the front to defend French cities.

Indeed, the Army intended to keep the tightest possible control over the fighter force. At the end of the war, only one or two fighter squadrons had been rigidly attached to any particular army; most were with the General Reserve. Fayolle wanted more fighters permanently attached to each army. In an 'ideal air force' scheme drawn up in the early twenties, each of six armies was to have a fighter group with five squadrons. This would leave forty squadrons in a General Reserve, which could be deployed where they were needed most. This was still a substantial mobile reserve, but the proportion of the fighters that could be focused over any particular sector of the front was lower than it had been at the end of the First World War. The 'ideal air force' scheme also required far fewer fighters than the September 1918 expansion plan. The importance of having the most powerful fighter force possible was already being forgotten.[19] The 'ideal' organisation was applied to existing units with five of the ten fighter groups forming part of mixed fighter and reconnaissance regiments, one of which would be attached to each army, with the remaining groups in two regiments in the General Reserve.

The changes introduced after the war fundamentally altered the nature of the French Air Force. The 'air division' remained but it had effectively become an administrative label. The important tactical distinction now was between the tactical Observation Forces and General Reserve units. The former contained all observation and reconnaissance units, together with the fighter units in the mixed regiments. The two independent fighter regiments and all the bombers belonged to the latter. The Air Divisions were a mixture of General Reserve and 'Observation Forces'.

Initially, there was no radical reassessment of the types of aircraft that should equip these units. The end of hostilities saw some cutbacks in the aircraft development programme with the number of aircraft types required by the Army reduced from fifteen to eleven. However, there was little to suggest that the French were about to abandon their faith in the relatively small, specialised combat planes that had served them so well during the First World War. Indeed, in this first cull, three of the types to disappear were multi-seaters: a bomber, the heavy assault aircraft, and the escort fighter. The other type to go was the specialised long-range reconnaissance plane, which, it was argued, could easily be carried out by the two-seater fighter. The only plane required with more than two crewmembers was a four-seater heavy bomber. The new programme included two-seater medium bombers, armoured assault planes, and the two-seater day fighter, all essentially tactical aircraft.[20] With substantially higher performances at higher altitudes expected from all these aircraft, the future looked promising.

It looked particularly promising for fighter design. In 1940, the major weakness of all French fighters was their low top speeds, but in 1919, there was no suggestion this would become a problem. Balancing manoeuvrability and speed is always a dilemma for fighter designers but by the end of the war, the consensus was that the latter was more important than the former. High speed made interception easier and gave the pilot the initiative in fighter-versus-fighter combat. However, it was not just horizontal speed that was important: high climbing speed could be just as useful. At the end of the war, the French were planning two types of fighter; the high-altitude interceptor, with a ceiling of 9,000 metres (30,000 feet) and a high-speed medium-altitude interceptor, capable of reaching just 6,500 metres.[21] Given that the latest SPAD S.XX and Nieuport-Delage NiD.29 fighter prototypes could not manage 220 km/hr, the 270 km/hr target for the medium-altitude fighter was a challenge. A new generation of designers (De Marcay, Wibault, and Gourdou-Leseurre) were all working on fighters with speeds of between 230 km/hr and 250 km/hr, but still more would be required. With drag rising exponentially with speed, designers were already beginning to experiment with undercarriages and radiators that retracted and cantilever monoplanes that did not require supporting struts.

It was an approach which Laurent-Eynac was determined to promote when he became under-secretary of state for air in January 1921. Government cash incentives encouraged the development of more powerful engines like the 500-hp Hispano-Suiza HS 12G and 12H. These powered a whole series of record-breaking racers, culminating in the exquisitely streamlined, all-metal, cantilever monoplane Bernard V.2, powered by the 500-hp Hispano-Suiza 12G. The plane was in many ways years ahead of its time. The only advanced feature missing was a retractable undercarriage; even this had been considered, but only at a late stage and it was not possible to build wheel wells into the complicated fuselage structure. In December 1924, the Bernard monoplane shattered the existing world record with an extraordinary 448 km/hr (278 mph). With talk of 750-hp engines appearing soon, the 500 km/hr barrier seemed well within reach and work began on an improved Bernard V.3, this time with a retractable undercarriage.[22] Producing combat planes with the speeds of specialist racers was not possible, but Bernard was expecting 315 km/hr from a fighter version of his V.2 racer and Lioré et Olivier were aiming for 300 km/hr with their LeO 9, an all-metal cantilever monoplane fighter.[23] No one could accuse French designers of lacking ambition.

While these prototypes were being built, a major rethink was underway on future Air Force requirements. Many thought that the combat planes of the First World War were only small because they had to be hasty improvisations of a still very primitive technology. Now that the war was over, there was time to think about what was really required. There was talk in War Ministry circles of large multi-seater 'destroyers' that would hunt down enemy planes, and even larger 'dreadnought' type cruisers for reconnaissance, observation, and bombing. These would be equally capable of operating deep in the rear and over the battlefield.[24] It was argued that large planes capable of carrying cannon would always prevail over smaller single-engined aircraft, just as in naval warfare, where battleships would always outgun smaller vessels. Fayolle's staff concluded that an all-round defensive armament of heavy calibre machine guns or small calibre cannon would be needed. In order to man the guns, combat planes would need a crew of at least three. Planes like the four-engined, four-seater Latécoère (Laté) 6 were attracting a lot of interest in Air Force circles.[25]

Fayolle's staff saw these multi-seaters as no more than an extension of the policies being pursued at the end of the war. The two-seater fighter was back in vogue, but it seemed ideally, the rear gunner should also have a gun firing through the floor of the plane. A second gunner would be even better. It seemed that the two-seater was no more than a poor compromise between the light single-seater and the powerful multi-seater with all-round defensive armament. Fayolle still believed that fast single-seater fighters (250 km/hr) were needed but they would be complemented by a new generation of multi-seater combat planes. These tactical multi-seater fighters would be almost as fast as single-seater fighters (220 km/hr) and, despite their greater size and weight, true '*avions de chasse*'. They would provide both close escort and be able to hunt down enemy planes on offensive sweeps behind enemy lines. The plane could also carry more guns and bombs for the ground-attack role. The size of Fayolle's tactical fighter-bomber was not seen as a problem; it was not the first time large planes had been put forward for low-level ground-attack. Fayolle was quick to point out the similarities between his tactical fighter and the multi-seater bomber. Development costs could be kept to a minimum by adapting a single design to perform all fighting, bombing and reconnaissance roles.[26] The large multi-role combat plane was very much back.

In February 1920, General Dumesnil took over from Duval at the 12th Directorate; under the new regime, development programmes reflected a growing faith in larger combat planes. By 1922, the number of types required had been reduced from eleven to seven. This was partly to save money—building up aircraft reserves was an expensive policy and there was little left over for the development of prototypes—but the decision also reflected the growing confidence in a single type performing a variety of roles. The 1922 programme required a multi-seater that would be capable of carrying out some of the duties previously assigned to the low-level assault plane, the escort fighter and the two-seater fighter and reconnaissance plane, all of which were dropped.[27]

There was one other key type missing from the 1922 programme: there was no place for the medium-altitude high-speed interceptor. Once again, the motivation was partly economic as two single-seater fighter types were a luxury the peacetime Air Force could not afford; either the fast climbing, high-altitude interceptor or the high-speed, medium-altitude interceptor had to go. During the closing stages of the First World War, it had been the high-altitude performance of German planes that had caused problems and there were growing doubts that single-seaters could be used for medium or low-altitude escort duties. The new multi-seater tactical fighter was expected to take over some of the duties of the medium-altitude interceptor, but this relatively heavy plane would have a problem operating at high altitude. It therefore seemed logical to keep the high-altitude and drop the medium-altitude fighter, so designers were told to concentrate on achieving the best possible performance at altitude. Initially, the target remained 240 km/hr (150 mph) at 7,000 metres, but when it became clear that the turbo-supercharger Rateau were developing was still some way off, designers were told to aim for the same speed at a less ambitious 5,000 metres.

The Army was far from impressed with the planes their own 12th Directorate were suggesting. The idea that large armoured multi-seaters could carry out short and medium-range reconnaissance and observation duties was rejected out of hand. Instead, the single-engined, two-seater Potez 25 and Breguet 19, the sort of plane that had been successful in the First World War, continued to be ordered as short-range observation and longer-range reconnaissance planes. These were rugged and well-armed, came with a limited ground attack capability, and were capable of speeds reasonably close to those being achieved by contemporary fighters. In the literature of the day, they were often referred to as 'fighter/reconnaissance' planes. The Army would only agree to using the larger multi-seaters for longer-range reconnaissance.

Deciding that twin-engined multi-seaters could be used for ground-attack, bombing, reconnaissance, and air combat was one thing; designing and building such a plane was quite another. As during the First World War, most companies were reluctant even to try and the designs that did emerge were very disappointing. Much was expected of the four-engined Laté 6. This huge plane, larger than the Caudron C.23 heavy bomber and over 50 per cent heavier, was first exhibited at the 1921 Paris Air Show. It was credited with a top speed of 230 km/hr, which matched any existing French fighter, but came nowhere near this when it actually flew. It was the subject of endless modifications but even with the very latest Jupiter engines, the target speed was never achieved. Even if it had, it should have been clear that this massive plane was far too unwieldy for many of the duties it was supposed to perform. The four-seater, twin-engined Blériot 117 was only slightly smaller. Optimistically described at the time as a high-altitude fighter and escort plane, it was not even capable of the relatively undemanding task of accompanying bomber formations. The message should have been clear, but despite these disappointments, the multi-purpose, multi-seater continued to be a regular feature of aircraft development programmes, with air combat one of its roles.[28]

In the meantime, the ageing Breguet 14 equipping the bomber squadrons were in urgent need of replacement. As no successful multi-seater had emerged, a bomber version of the Breguet 19 was ordered as a stopgap. The same plane was also used to equip the close escort squadrons that were supposed to supplement the defensive firepower of bomber formations. The failure of the aircraft industry to produce a successful multi-role multi-seater should have been a warning, but instead of heeding this warning, advocates of the concept insisted that the idea could not be given a fair trial until a suitable plane emerged.

Meanwhile, designers were focusing on the high-altitude single-seater that the 12th Directorate still wanted. Such a fighter could not make much use of the advances made by low-level racers. Cantilever monoplane wings, stressed skin metal construction, and retraction mechanisms all added weight to a design, which was bound to reduce climb and altitude performance. With no superchargers, designers had to rely on high-compression engines, which limited the drop in power at altitude but only by reducing efficiency at lower altitudes. Thick, high-lift wings also helped improve climb and handling at altitude, but the extra drag was another barrier to high horizontal speed.

The emphasis on high-altitude performance ended the hopes of many promising fighter prototypes, with the cantilever monoplane designs particularly seriously affected. The Lioré et Olivier 9 could not fly higher than 6,000 metres. Bernard turned their racer into a fighter (the Bernard 1) but even after the wing area had been nearly doubled, it also could still not get higher than 6,000 metres, and by this time its speed had been reduced to a still respectable, but unremarkable, 248 km/hr. Perhaps the unluckiest contender in the 1921 program was another parasol design, the Buscaylet-de Monge 52. This was another racer turned fighter with a new much larger high-lift wing. The plane demonstrated how far French design had come in just a few years. Although powered by the same 300-hp Hispano-Suiza motor as the Nieuport-Delage NiD.29, the Buscaylet-de Monge fighter was some 50 km/hr faster, coming very close to meeting the requirements of the defunct 1919 high-speed fighter program. However, its service ceiling of 7,500 metres was not considered to be good enough for the high-altitude interceptor. The two planes eventually ordered were the Dewoitine D.1 and the Blériot-SPAD 81. Both were capable of climbing to around 8,000 metres but were only marginally faster than the NiD.29.[29] In 1923, designers were asked to try again. More powerful engines had become available but there was still no supercharging and the designs ordered into production (Nieuport-Delage NiD 42, 62, 622, Gourdou-Leseurre GL.32, and Wibault 7) offered little improvement. The French quest for performance at altitude was causing progress in all other aspects of performance to grind to a halt.

To make matters worse, in peacetime France, there was little urgency about getting these fighters into service. The Nieuport-Delage NiD 29 was not ordered until 1920 and did not enter service until 1922. Four years from trials to service introduction, nearly as long as the First World War, was a dangerous precedent to set. Structural problems delayed the entry into service of the Dewoitine D.1 until 1928. The Blériot-SPAD 81 reached the squadrons fairly quickly, but only eighty were ordered, enough to equip just five squadrons. Official trials for fighters designed to meet the 1923 programme were not held until 1926. The economic crisis facing France then delayed orders and the first examples did not reach the squadrons until 1928, five years after the specification had been released. Another two years passed before all the now ageing Blériot-SPAD 81s and even older NiD.29s could be replaced. The squadrons were no doubt grateful to have brand new planes, but they were not much faster than the fighters they were replacing. The French fighter force was being re-equipped with planes that would have been considered obsolete in most other air forces.

Meanwhile, government cutbacks were hitting high-speed research. In 1924, the French were forced to pull out of the Schneider Trophy race and there would be no more funding for several years to come. In 1926, Laurent-Eynac's post was abolished and with it went financial inducements for designers. There was also not much prospect of the Army funding research. Although the proportion of the military budget devoted to aviation gradually increased during the twenties, the Army policy of stockpiling continued, and the money spent on research and prototypes dropped. In the space of a decade, the French had lost their lead in high-speed flight and their position as a world leader in fighter design.

While France was slipping behind technically, colonial conflicts were a reminder of how important air power could be. The largest conflict was the Rif War. On 12 April 1925, forces of the recently established Rif state attempted to capture parts of French Morocco they believed was rightfully theirs. The mountainous terrain of that part of the world had little in common with the plains of northern France and the lightly armed Rif forces bore even less relation to the future Wehrmacht. Nevertheless, the fighting did bear some similarity to the type of warfare in which the French Army would find itself involved in 1940. Like the German Army, the Rif forces would rely on speed and surprise rather than artillery, and the terrain forced both sides to fight on narrow fronts with exposed flanks. The French Air Force units in the area were commanded by Fayolle's old chief of staff, Armengaud. He would now have the opportunity to see at first hand if the conclusions he had reached while working under Fayolle were correct.

The initial attack achieved complete tactical surprise. French outposts guarding the frontier were soon either overrun or bypassed and the French were in full retreat. It seemed that Fez and Taza might fall to the advancing Rifians. Just as had happened during the German Spring 1918 offensive, low-level ground-attack was the only immediately available way of relieving the pressure on the hard-pressed ground troops. Once again, the now ageing Breguet 14 was called upon to perform these missions. Initially, only six Breguet squadrons were available in North Morocco and these were quickly moved to the threatened zone. As the situation deteriorated, more squadrons were transferred from southern Morocco, Algeria, Tunisia, and even France. By the end of May, eighteen squadrons with around 100 planes were involved in the fighting.[30]

During the retreat, squadrons were held in the rear until the focus of the day's operations was decided. Squadrons then moved forward to temporary airstrips close to the front from which continuous sorties could be flown. Some pilots flew up to eight sorties per day. Supplies were moved forward partly by road but mostly by air. On 21 May, for example, seven squadrons moved forward to the advance landing strip at Drader, from which 170 bombing and reconnaissance sorties were flown before the approach of enemy forces forced the French units to pull back late in the afternoon. The Air Force was playing the same role as it had in the spring of 1918 and the Army was grateful. Marshal Lyautey, the commander of the French forces in Morocco, believed that only the intervention of the Air Force had saved Fez from falling.[31]

This reminder of how effective close air support could be in a defensive situation did not have the impact it perhaps should have done. French Army generals conceded that under some 'special' circumstances, some 'unusual' missions, including low-level ground-attack, had been forced on the Air

Force.[32] However, they were quick to point out that losses to enemy ground fire had been rather high and this reinforced the Army view that ground-attack could never be a normal Air Force mission. Once the initial crisis had passed, Armengaud was told to concentrate his efforts on bombing enemy targets to the rear of the battlefield, which was more in line with Army thinking.

In September 1925, French ground forces, now under the command of Pétain, went on the offensive. Armengaud soon found his units providing much more than just indirect support. French troops had to advance through narrow valleys and often found themselves threatened by enemy forces operating on their flanks. Aircraft were not only used to locate these enemy forces, they also intervened directly to break them up. The poor roads made it difficult for the artillery to keep up with the advancing French troops and ammunition was always in short supply. If Army commanders lacked the firepower to continue the advance, the Air Force was called in as a substitute. Some sophisticated procedures soon became standard practice. Reconnaissance planes radioed information on the position of enemy forces directly to bombers on standby, engines running, ready to take off. On occasion, new targets were transmitted to bombers after they had taken off.

The success of these air operations made a deep impression on Armengaud. In any war, he argued, the enemy was always likely to have an initial advantage in men and firepower. It took time to mobilise armies and move them to where they were required but aircraft could be moved far more quickly to any threatened sector of the front. Indeed, Armengaud believed the French Air Force should and could have reacted much faster. The quickest Breguet 14 squadron transfer had taken four days. Armengaud noted that a naval heavy bomber squadron sent in August 1925 had completed its move from France in thirty-six hours, thanks to the ability of its Farman F.63s to carry the ground crews and materials needed to get operations going. With their own transport planes, squadrons could be deployed to any sector of the front almost immediately. Once in place, low-level ground-attack missions could provide the supporting firepower the defending forces required until reinforcements arrived. All available aircraft, including reconnaissance planes and even heavy night bombers, could make a contribution. To ensure that, at the beginning of a conflict, effort was focused where it was needed, Armengaud stressed that all Air Force units had to be under a single commander. Only later, when the Air Force had expanded, would it be possible to attach squadrons to particular Army units.

Armengaud's squadrons also bombed enemy towns in the rear, partly to disrupt the movement of troops and supplies, but also to intimidate the local population. It was perhaps difficult to draw any definitive conclusions from these raids when there were so few crucial nerve centres to attack, but on balance, Armengaud thought they were a misuse of resources. Attacks on towns were only of any military value if the targets were close to the front and the attacks were coordinated with a ground offensive. Armengaud also argued that it was better to use a plane to fly six sorties against a target close to the front than one sortie that involved flying a great distance. Crucially, Armengaud also observed that even if substantial artillery was available and friendly forces were advancing, there would always be targets like fast-moving motorised columns, which were far easier for aircraft to attack. The bomber was more than just a way of extending the striking power of an army; it could both reinforce and complement artillery. Air support on the battlefield had to be a normal mission for all Air Force planes, not something that was only resorted to in an emergency. To make this possible, Armengaud wanted a large proportion of the Air Force equipped with a tactical 'front line plane' that would be equally capable of reconnaissance, ground-attack, or longer-range bombing missions. It also had to be capable of operating from primitive airstrips close to the front line, just as the Breguets had done in Morocco.[33]

Armengaud did not say what form his 'front line plane' should take. During the course of the campaign, three quite different aircraft were used in the ground-attack role. The vast majority of sorties were flown by the trusty Breguet 14. However, the four-seater Farman F.63 heavy bomber and the single-seater Nieuport-Delage NiD 42 fighter had also been used.[34] The former had been sent to North Africa to bomb towns but the large multi-seaters were also used for reconnaissance and tactical bombing, both by day and night, at medium and low altitudes. Armengaud's observation that the Farmans had not proved as vulnerable to ground fire as some had feared was reassuring for those who claimed that large planes could be used quite safely over the battlefield.

At the other end of the scale, the single-seater Nieuport-Delage 42 had been used as a fighter-bomber. The French had never shown much interest in arming fighters with bombs and the decision to employ three Nieuport-Delage fighters in the fighter-bomber role did not reflect any change of heart within the War Ministry. Fitting the fighter with six light bombs was the idea of the Nieuport test pilot Joseph Sadi-Lecointe, who had volunteered to serve in Morocco. Between 20 November and 21 December 1925, these planes flew some seventy sorties and the fighters proved well-suited to their new role.[35]

Armengaud was aware that any future war in Europe would be very different to a local conflict in North Africa. The lack of any aerial opposition in Morocco was one obvious difference. However, Armengaud was convinced that many of the lessons learned could be applied to a full-scale war and the German Wehrmacht would prove him right. In 1940, it would be the Luftwaffe being used as mobile artillery that supported the advance on the ground and broke up French counterattacks. French domination of the skies in Morocco was just a reminder of how valuable air supremacy was. In 1940, it would be the French struggling to cope with an enemy that dominated the skies.

Armengaud passed on the conclusions to the War Ministry where they were greeted with little enthusiasm. Centralised control of all Air Force units may have seemed logical enough, but it would take more than a colonial war for the Army to forget the way Air Force units not under their direct command had been misused during the First World War. Armengaud's proposal to equip Army squadrons with bomber and reconnaissance planes also attracted little interest. Knowing what the enemy was doing was too important to allow squadrons to be distracted by ground-attack and bombing duties. If there had been adequate warning of the enemy attack in Morocco, an emergency would never have arisen and ground-attack planes would not have been required. Better reconnaissance, not more ground-attack, was needed.

In any case, there were doubts that French bombing had been as influential as Armengaud claimed. Although aircraft had undoubtedly made an impression on the enemy, there was criticism that many attacks had not found their intended targets. Bombs had been wasted on what turned out to be empty villages and in the field, the enemy had soon learnt to disperse rapidly as soon as approaching aircraft were heard.[36] Losses to ground fire had been heavy and even Armengaud had been forced to concede that in a European conflict, anti-aircraft fire would be even more effective. Armengaud also had to admit that in the event of a First World War-style deadlock, his tactical 'front line' planes would be of little value. With plans for the Maginot Line taking shape, this was precisely the type of war the French were preparing for. As far as the French Army was concerned, the fighting in Morocco did not mean any rethinking was required.

In 1928, Armengaud gave his ideas a more public airing in the *Revue militaire francaise*. He concluded his article by recalling a statement made by Pétain in 1919. The French Marshal had pointed out that any advance by the infantry would always grind to a halt once it passed beyond the effective range of artillery. 'Only when the artillery could follow the infantry could one once more expect decisive victories to be achieved,' Pétain asserted.[37] Armengaud claimed that the fighting in Morocco had shown that his 'flying artillery' could provide the mobile firepower that Pétain wanted. Armengaud was soon incorporating the tank into his thinking. In 1932, he was describing how the speed and manoeuvrability of the tank and aircraft working together might once again make rapid victories possible. He also suggested that the best way of defeating an armoured assault on France would be to build up a fleet of specialised armoured, anti-tank versions of his 'front line' plane, which would be able to respond to any threat far quicker than land-based anti-tank artillery.

Changes at the top provided some encouragement for Armengaud. In the early thirties, first Debeney and then Pétain retired and the top two Army posts passed to the more flexibly minded Generals Maurice Gamelin and Maxime Weygand. Plans were soon being laid for light mechanised divisions with tanks, truck-borne infantry and towed artillery.[38] By this time, however, these ideas were being overshadowed by the debate raging over a quite different application of airpower. The bomber threat was rearing its head.

4

The Bomber Rules

Once the euphoria of victory in the First World War had passed, it did not take long for the French to begin fearing their powerful neighbour once more. Militarily, the Treaty of Versailles left France in a seemingly impregnable position. The German Army had been reduced to just 100,000 men, the German Navy had been scuttled, and military aviation was prohibited. France still had strong ground, naval, and air forces and her military advantage seemed overwhelming. However, there was one loophole in the Treaty of Versailles that was soon causing concern in both military and political circles. Although Germany was not allowed to have an air force, it was allowed to build civil airliners. German designers were soon focusing on this new challenge and building some very impressive planes. As far as the French were concerned, a civil airliner was just a bomber in disguise.[1]

As early as 1923, Fayolle was gloomily predicting that Germany was already capable of mobilising fifty bomber squadrons within twenty-five days of war breaking out. French superiority at sea and on land might count for nothing if German bombers could strike directly at French cities. French politicians, press, and people were obsessed by the German aerial threat.[2] The French were exaggerating the danger, just as they had done before the outbreak of the First World War, but it seemed real enough at the time. Long before Adolf Hitler came to power, France felt obliged to respond to the German bomber threat.

There were, in fact, very few in France who would deny this threat was real. Buat, Jauneaud, Foch, Pétain, Fayolle, and Ménard may have had their differences, but all agreed that this new weapon could not be ignored. They did not necessarily believe it could be decisive, but the terror German bombers had provoked during the First World War had not been forgotten. Enemy bombing causing civil unrest at a critical stage of a future war was a worrying prospect for both the military and the politicians. Insurrection was a constant fear. There was much talk in parliamentary debates of bomber fleets devastating countries with 'knock-out blows'.[3] Fayolle believed the need for a deterrent was so great that a French bomber force could never be too numerous or too powerful.[4] As under-secretaries of state for air, Flandin and then Laurent-Eynac both believed the country had to have a powerful long-range bomber force. Initially, they hoped that this could be done by matching German progress in civil aviation. As long as the French aircraft industry was producing large civil transports, France would always have available a bomber fleet in waiting.

At the end of the First World War, the French bomber force was still predominantly tactical, and this remained the case in the early interwar years. However, there was a growing belief that tactical night rather than day bombing was the way forward. Night bombers did not have to be high performance or carry heavy defensive armament so they could carry more bombs. They could also take risks by flying lower and with flares to illuminate the target, they could bomb more accurately. There seemed to be more scope for improving night bombing than there was for day bombing. The 1921 scheme had called for forty-eight day bomber squadrons and just sixteen night bomber squadrons but Fayolle's commission recommended a more balanced force with three day and four night bomber regiments.[5]

The need for a long-range bombing force saw this trend towards night bombing continue. The 1924 (186 Squadron) scheme required eighteen day and forty-four night bomber squadrons, and all of the latter would be heavy, long-range planes.[6] This was soon abandoned for economic reasons, but the more limited expansion that was agreed aimed for three day and five heavy night bomber regiments. In 1925, it was agreed that a start be made towards achieving the required five heavy bomber regiments by re-equipping one of the two existing Breguet day bomber regiments with the Farman F.60, but production of the Farman bomber was so slow, it would be 1931 before there would be enough to equip a third regiment.[7] Nevertheless, the trend was clear. The aim was to expand the long-range night bomber force at the expense of shorter-range day bombers.

Fayolle supervised the drawing up of two new bomber specifications in 1923. The first required a plane with a range of 1,000 km and 750-kg bomb load. A second, more ambitious, long-term project called for an ultra-heavy bomber, capable of flying to Berlin with 1,500 kg of bombs.[8] In 1926, the Lioré et Olivier LeO 20 was chosen as the best of the contenders, meeting the first requirement; in August, a first batch of fifty was ordered. It could lift 1,000 kg of bombs and was popular with the crews who flew it. The French had finally succeeded in producing a satisfactory long-range heavy bomber that was as good as any other design in the world. Over the next few years, orders would rise to over 300. It was hoped that a four-engined version, the LeO 206, would serve as the ultra-heavy bomber.

There was less interest in smaller single-engined bombers. The excellent Breguet 19 day bombers had replaced the Breguet 14, but only as an interim measure. The plane was an outstanding export success but in France, it was criticised for its lack of range and low bomb load.[9] When a satisfactory twin-engined multi-seater failed to materialise, another single-engined bomber, the Amiot 122, had to be ordered as a stopgap. This was a huge affair, powered by a mighty 650-hp Lorraine 18Kd engine. It was nearly twice as heavy as the Breguet it was to replace and was almost as large as the LeO 20 heavy bomber. The bomber's lifting capacity was phenomenal for a single-engined plane, but it was a slow, clumsy compromise. The final version was barely faster than the Breguet 19 and scarcely the sort of agile bomber that could carry out low-level tactical strikes, nor did it have the range of a plane like the LeO 20. Enough were ordered to equip just one bomber regiment, and it would be the last single-engined bomber ordered for some time. There seemed to be no place for single-engined designs in a long-range bomber force. The move towards a more strategically orientated bomber force drew no criticism from the War Ministry, partly because the Army recognised the need for a deterrent, but also because they saw no great need for tactical bombing.

The way French aeronautics seemed to be slipping behind the rest of the world technically and the slow progress towards an effective long-range bomber force were both attracting a lot of criticism. Many blamed the way aeronautics was organised. Four different ministries were running it and only an under-secretary of state of air attached to the Ministry of Public Works was providing any coordination. Many were coming around to the idea that aeronautics in France needed the clearer focus an air ministry would provide. Many also doubted that an Air Force controlled by the Army and War Ministry would ever develop the long-range bomber force France needed. Criticism grew when, to save money, the under-secretary of state for air was abolished in July 1926. Maurice Bokanowski's Ministry of Industry and Commerce took over the coordinating role, but he was criticised for ignoring aviation. The French press used a series of fatal accidents involving French planes to focus public attention on the problem. When, on 2 September 1928, Bokanowski was himself killed in yet another air crash, the public outcry enabled the Prime Minister, Raymond Poincaré, to act. Ignoring Army objections, he issued a decree on 14 September 1928, creating an independent Air Ministry, which would handle all aviation matters. The appointment of Laurent-Eynac left no one in any doubt about the direction the government expected the new ministry to take. The ex-under-secretary of state for air was both a long-time supporter of long-range bombing and a severe critic of the way the Army had been developing air power.

Laurent-Eynac called in Albert Caquot to head a new department, the *Direction Générale Technique*. Caquot had made his name during the closing stages of the First World War organising increased aircraft production. Now, he was set the task of improving quality rather than quantity by encouraging innovative design. The *politique de stocks* would be replaced by a *politique de prototypes*. To encourage companies to experiment, the Air Ministry agreed to pay, in advance, up to 90 per cent of the cost of any prototype that looked interesting.

The Army soon discovered their worst fears were fully justified. Laurent-Eynac announced that he intended to work towards an independent *armée de l'air* with its own strategy and a command structure paralleling the Army's. The Air Force would be commanded by its own peacetime inspector, who would assume command of air units in time of war. He would also head a decision-making Air Council, similar to the Army and Navy councils. As a first step towards an independent Air Force, all four existing bomber regiments and the two fighter regiments of the General Reserve would form a *Corps Aéronautique Autonome*.[10]

In February 1929, the post of *Inspecteur Général de l'Armée de l'Air* was created; to fill the new post, the Air Minister brought back none other than Joseph Barès, one of the staunchest protagonists of long-range bombing. For the former Air Force chief, it was a remarkable comeback. After being sacked in 1917, he had returned to the front as a regimental commander. After the war, he returned to aeronautics, heading the Inter-Allied Aviation Control commission in Austria. In October 1921, he took over at the *Centre d'Etudes Aéronautique* at Versailles, where he was no doubt able to impress upon young officers the value of long-range bombers and the potential of his cherished multi-purpose combat planes. In March 1924, he was appointed commander of the 2nd Air Division.[11] His promotion to Air Force Inspector meant that in the event of war, he would once more command the French Air Force—in theory, at least.

The War Ministry fiercely objected to the new order Laurent-Eynac was trying to impose. They disputed his criticism that the Army had held back development of a long-range bomber force. The 1923 specifications for heavy and ultra-heavy bombers were testimony to the War Ministry's commitment. No ultra-heavy bomber had emerged because it was not yet possible to build one, not because of any lack of War Ministry interest. This failure, the Army insisted, just proved that the bomber was not yet the destructive weapon some were claiming. Even when it was, the bomber force would still have to stay under Army control so that bomber operations could form part of the overall military strategy. Pétain was particularly scathing of any claim that bombers could achieve decisive results by attacking industrial targets. He believed that enemy air defences, both passive and active, would be far more effective than many imagined; even if the bombers managed to hit their targets, it was doubtful that this would have any significant effect at the front. The bomber would be more useful attacking tactical targets beyond the range of the artillery. Even here, the value was marginal. Discovering what the enemy was doing was the most important contribution the Air Force could make and a bomber force of any description could only be justified if the Army's minimum requirements for reconnaissance and fighter planes had been met.[12]

As for the *Corps Aéronautique Autonome*, the War Ministry did not accept the new Air Ministry had any right to create such a force. The decree setting up the Air Ministry had only intended a purely civilian body, not one with the authority to pronounce on military matters. Pétain had no objections to the new ministry specifying the technical aspects of aircraft specifications, but the Army had to decide on the types of plane that the Air Force needed. Pétain was quite happy to have a General Reserve with all the bombers and two fighter regiments, but it had to stay under Army control and it should only be created after the Army's air reconnaissance requirements had been met. The bombers in the General Reserve could be used by the government if it required retaliation, but the fighters had to be available to the Army for operations at the front.[13] The Army did not accept Barès as the wartime Air Force commander. Their own Air Force Inspector, General Hergault, would fill this position. Attempts to come up with a rewording that would satisfy both parties got nowhere. Even after contentious references to an independent *armée de l'air* with a chief of staff had been removed, there was no agreement.[14] As far as the proposed Air Council was concerned, the War Ministry simply ignored Air Ministry requests to discuss the matter. In October 1930, the Air Ministry created a chief of staff of aerial forces, but without an independent air force to command, the position was largely symbolic.

Laurent-Eynac had been out-manoeuvred and found himself under attack from all sides. The War Ministry was blocking the reforms he wanted to introduce but he was criticised by an impatient Parliament and press for not making quicker progress. The Army, sensing the tide was turning in their favour, were quick to add to the criticism. They claimed that the creation of an Air Ministry had not resulted in any improvement in the long-range bombing force and the War Ministry had dealt with the problem just as well if not better. The argument was persuasive and some politicians were already beginning to doubt the wisdom of creating an independent Air Ministry. In December 1930, Laurent-Eynac was forced to resign and the continued existence of an Air Ministry seemed very much in doubt when Paul Painlevé, a close friend of Pétain, replaced him. Painlevé immediately 'promoted' Barès to Chief of Staff, a position that still held no real power, and Hergault was appointed inspector for both the War and Air Ministries. The Army seemed to be well on the way to regaining full control over military aviation. The Barès faction, however, was about to gain valuable support from an unexpected quarter.

The Army had managed to frustrate the independent Air Force lobby but it could do nothing to stop the increasing public fear of the havoc bombers might wreak in a future war. The *Comité Permanent de la Défense Nationale* (CPDN: the military-political council that coordinated defence planning) tried to show the problem was being dealt with by appointing a single person to coordinate all air defence issues. On 9 February 1931, none other than the recently retired Pétain was given the task. The appointment of such an illustrious figure was a measure of how grave the problem was viewed. The new post carried very little real power, but Pétain's reputation ensured that his views would carry considerable weight. The creation of the new inspectorate, not to mention the appointment of Pétain, appeared to be yet another setback for those who wanted an independent Air Force. However, contrary to all expectations, Pétain would prove to be a useful ally.

Despite his age, Pétain energetically organised and supervised civil defence exercises throughout France, although this just served to fuel public concern by demonstrating how seriously the government was taking the threat. Pétain too seems to have been affected by his new responsibilities. The general clamour for a more effective deterrent and, no doubt, the memories of German bombing in the First World War, contributed to a dramatic change of heart. No longer was such a force of secondary importance to a tactical air force; it was now essential to the security of France and the maintenance of peace.[15] Pétain's views were officially endorsed by the CPDN on 30 July 1931. It was decided, with the grudging support of the Army, to give the highest priority to the creation of an effective long-range bomber force.

Weygand, who had taken over from Pétain as head of the Army, must have been as surprised as anyone by his former commander's sudden conversion. The Army now found itself increasingly on the defensive. The idea of an independent air council was revived and Weygand finally found himself obliged to consider the matter, rather lamely claiming that the two-and-a-half-year delay in replying to the original Air Ministry proposal had been due to the need to study the proposals carefully. In the climate prevailing at the time, the creation of the air council seemed inevitable. Weygand tried to ensure the Army, Navy, and Air Force all had equal representation, leaving the Air Force in a powerless minority.[16] However, the tide was now running against the Army and even this compromise was rejected. When the new Air Council was finally created in August 1931, it was a predominately Air Force body, headed by the Air Force Chief of Staff. However, by ensuring Hergault replaced Barès as the Air Force Chief of Staff, the Army still held the upper hand.

With both Army and Air Force factions feuding, any agreed policy seemed as far away as ever. Pétain suggested that a more coherent defence policy would emerge if existing War and Air Ministries and the commanders of the two arms were replaced by a Ministry of National Defence and a Chief of General Staff. The idea was right; the problem was finding someone with the authority and impartiality to impose a policy that all would accept. Pétain hinted that he might be the right person, and the concerns he was expressing about the bomber threat suggested that he might be more acceptable than most. However, rather than winning him new friends, his recent shift of opinion meant he was now viewed rather suspiciously by all. There would be no Ministry of Defence; the best that could be managed were bodies like the CPDN and other committees that were established, where the issues could be aired, but these were no more than forums for discussion.

The debate in France was fuelled by the publication in April 1932 of the French edition of Giulio Douhet's *Command of the Air*. The striking feature of the book was the similarity between Douhet's thinking and the ideas and fears that had, quite independently, developed in France. Douhet ridiculed the way aircraft in the First World War had been frittered away in attempts to support fruitless land and naval operations. In modern war, offensive action was only possible in the air. There would be no distinction between combatants and civilians and it was the vulnerable latter that an enemy would choose to target. The first objective in any war would be to win air superiority by destroying the enemy air force on the ground and wrecking his aircraft factories. To do this, Douhet proposed large multi-seaters. The defensive guns, bombs, and armour these carried could all be adjusted according to the mission and the strength of the likely opposition.[17]

The small, traditional warplanes currently attached to armies and navies would be 'worthless, superfluous and harmful' and could play no part in this new form of warfare.[18] Traditional single-engined interceptors would be blown out of the sky by his flying dreadnoughts. Any attempt at defence would be a futile waste of resources and would just hasten defeat. Attack was the best—indeed the only—means of defence. Once the bombers had achieved air superiority, they would be able to discard their defensive armament and armour for bombs. Cities would be defenceless. The combination of high explosives, gas, and bacteriological weapons would overwhelm civil air defence organisations, lay waste to entire cities, and break the morale of the civilian population.[19]

Just before he died in 1930, Douhet described a fictitious war between Germany and a Franco-Belgian alliance. The former had developed an independent air force along the lines described in his books. The latter had an independent air force, but planned to use it to support the advance of their armies to the Rhine. Within twenty-four hours, the Franco-Belgian interceptor force had been shot out of the skies by the firepower of the German bombers and their bombers lay wrecked on their airfields. With air supremacy established, the German bombers set about the systematic reduction of French and Belgian towns and cities to rubble. Before the allied armies had even completed their mobilisation, the French and Belgian governments were forced to surrender. It was a frightening scenario. It was what many in France had been predicting for some time; now an internationally recognised expert on the subject was confirming it. The Army found itself under even greater pressure to allow the creation of a fully independent Air Force.[20]

Not that everyone within the Air Force went along with the Douhet's vision or even wanted independence. General Pujo, the commander of the 2nd Air Division, emphasised the importance of the reconnaissance arm and believed that the Army should always retain full operational control over certain units. The first task of the Air Force in any future war would be to find out what the enemy was doing. However, he also saw an important tactical role for bombers both on and in the immediate rear of the battlefield. These might be needed on the very first day of war to stem an enemy advance and, rather prophetically in view of what was to occur in 1940, he warned that a sudden 50-kilometre advance by the enemy would be just as disastrous as any imagined assault on French cities.[21] At this time, Armengaud was also talking about the need for a mobile anti-tank aerial strike force.

However, even Pujo and Armengaud were influenced by the Douhet doctrine. Although Pujo insisted that reconnaissance squadrons remain under Army command in all circumstances, he was willing to concede that the Army could probably get by without the services of the bombers if they were required for long-range operations. Armengaud too felt obliged to admit the long-range bomber was a frightening weapon and that France must prepare for the possibility of Douhet style conflict.[22] However desirable his specialised ground-attack units might be, conventional land-based weapons would always be there to hit targets on the battlefield, whereas only the bomber could retaliate against enemy cities. If a choice had to be made between a purely tactical and a purely strategic bomber force, then even Armengaud believed the latter had to have priority. Everyone agreed a bomber deterrent was needed. Hitler had not yet come to power in Germany, but French intelligence estimated that the fleet of civil aircraft the country possessed was already close to matching the French bomber fleet.[23] No one was yet sure which side Mussolini would take, but if Italy was an enemy as well, the French would be in an extremely vulnerable situation.

Pétain was alarmed and insisted that the highest priority should be given to the development of a heavy bomber capable of carrying between one and two tons to Berlin. Only a force of 200 such machines could guarantee the security of the nation. He did not want this force to be under the control of the Army or Air Force. In peacetime, the Air Ministry would be responsible for training and equipment, but in wartime control should pass directly to the government.[24] Pétain did not believe that the long-range bomber could win the war for France, either by striking at enemy industry or by intimidating civilians, but he did fear that France might lose a war if it did not have an adequate bomber force. He did not want an independent Air Force, but the importance he attached to long-range bombing was encouraging for those who did.

Weygand now decided to take the initiative and demonstrate that the Army was quite capable of organising the sort of bomber fleet the politicians wanted and Pétain was proposing without a Douhet style independent air force. Weygand asked Hergault to prepare a discussion document for the *Haute Comité* on ways in which the long-range bomber force might be expanded. His proposals were presented on 3 June 1932.

Hergault decided that six heavy bomber regiments with 300 machines would be required to achieve the bomb tonnage target set down by Pétain. At that time, four bomber regiments existed, two with the LeO 20, one converting to the LeO 20, and one with the single-engined Amiot 122. The Amiot regiment was supposed to provide tactical air support, but these bombers were obsolete and needed replacing. The LeO 20 could carry 10-kg anti-personnel bombs and extra defensive armament for daylight operations, so it was equally capable of supporting the army. Hergault therefore suggested the Amiot regiment convert to the LeO 20. The Navy had some large Farman F.168 long-range torpedo bombers, so there was no reason why they could not transfer these to the General Reserve to form a fifth heavy bomber regiment. A sixth could be created by reducing the number of air units in French colonies. By 1939, all six regiments would re-equip with the LeO 206, the four-engined version of the LeO 20. Hergault was proposing the abolition of all the light and medium day bombers—the bombers most capable of supporting the Army.[25]

The Army might have been willing to part with its tactical day bombers, but the Navy was not. Vice Admiral François Darlan was horrified by the idea of handing over his bombers to the General Reserve. Hitting fast manoeuvring warships with torpedoes or bombs required specialist training. An Air Ministry only concerned with bombing fixed targets deep inside enemy territory would not provide it. The Navy was also far from convinced that planes like the large Farman F.168 were what they wanted. One Farman squadron was already re-equipping with the new, much smaller, single-engined Laté 290 torpedo-bomber. The Navy were also interested in the dive-bomber. The development of these shorter-range tactical aircraft might be jeopardised if naval squadrons had to be capable of making a contribution to the French long-range bomber fleet.[26] The Army had no such misgivings about the units they were handing over to the Air Ministry.

Darlan questioned the need for any major expansion of the bomber fleet. France did not have to match Germany in every respect. Naval bombers would contribute far more to the French cause by being used as they were intended: against naval targets. Hergault reasoned the Navy would benefit far more from the occasional intervention of the entire General Reserve than more regular attacks by a small number of bombers. Darlan countered that he preferred a few bombers when it mattered, rather than 200 arriving too late. Initially it was agreed that the naval bomber squadrons would form a rather ill-defined 'reserve of the reserve', cooperating with the main body of the General Reserve when the latter attacked targets of interest to the Navy.[27]

Hergault's scheme would have tripled the striking power of the French bomber fleet by 1939. The politicians would get their deterrent and the rest of the Air Force could be developed along the lines the army wanted. However, Painlevé decided that this scheme did not go far enough; Germany and Italy might already be very close to achieving the French 1939 target. The weak French economy ruled out a vast increase in defence spending. If the next war was to be decided by long-range bombing, then France could only survive by using its limited resources flexibly. France could no longer afford to distinguish between air units attached to the General Reserve and those belonging to the Army and Navy. If attacked, all aircraft, including those equipping reconnaissance and observation units, would have to play some part in striking back at the enemy heartlands. Army squadrons would have to be considerably more versatile than hitherto required and the belief that large combat planes were perfectly capable of flying low-level tactical missions over the front made such versatility seem possible.

General Armengaud, now an influential member of the Air Council, proposed making eight of the existing sixteen reconnaissance and four of the thirty-two observation squadrons available to the General Reserve for long-range bombing missions, if required. This was precisely the kind of reallocation of resources the Army feared most. Armengaud claimed that twenty short-range observation squadrons created from reservists during the first weeks of war would compensate for the lost reconnaissance and observation squadrons.[28] Poorly trained reservists, however, were a poor substitute for highly trained regular air force crews but the tide was moving against the Army. Barès, the champion of the multi-seater, multi-role combat plane, replaced Hergault. In January 1933, ill health forced Painlevé to resign and it would be left to his successor, Pierre Cot, to take these ideas to their logical conclusion.

The youthful, ambitious Cot was considered by many to be a little too dynamic for his own good. His brashness earned him many enemies and his views on the role of air power would do nothing to improve relations between Army and Air Force. Cot feared that an unscrupulous enemy might choose to deliver a knock-out blow when no immediate cause for conflict seemed to exist. At all times, all available fighter aircraft, including those belonging to the Army, had to be ready to intercept an incoming attack. All aircraft capable of carrying bombs had to be equally ready for an immediate counter-attack. This would only be possible if all aerial units were under a single commander. Cot wanted all Army reconnaissance and observation squadrons to be equipped with aircraft capable of bombing. Only the twenty reservist squadrons would be equipped with traditional single-engined, two-seater reconnaissance planes.[29]

On 20 and 27 March 1933, the *Haute Comité* was convened to consider Cot's proposal. In the discussions that followed, the Air Minister made much of the fact that the Army was not even contemplating any military operations during the first two weeks of war as both sides mobilised. This was precisely when France would be most vulnerable to air attack. Apart from a few strategic reconnaissance missions, most units would have nothing to do. Cot also pointed out that the Army's plans to stay on the defensive would not help France's eastern European allies. An aerial offensive was the only military support France could provide. Cot claimed an offensive air strategy perfectly complemented the Army's defensive strategy.[30] It seemed like a balanced military strategy, but it assumed that the French government would risk triggering an all-out aerial war and invite retaliation against French cities just to support a distant ally.

It was precisely what the War Ministry did not want but they were under pressure from Pétain to reach some sort of compromise and were forced to concede that there might be circumstances in which all Air Force units might be required for a Douhetian-style aerial struggle. It therefore agreed that all aircraft would have to be capable of playing their part, either defensively or offensively. An independent *armée de l'air* would be formed to embrace all squadrons attached to the General Reserve, Army, and Navy. Barès became the first inspector general of the newly independent Air Force and General Victor Denain was appointed his chief of staff. It was not a clear-cut victory for the Air Force. The Army and Navy had only agreed to an independent Air Force on the condition that they would have to approve which units were attached to the General Reserve. The struggle for control over Air Force squadrons was only just beginning.

The Air Ministry had not won full control over the Air Force, but it could control the type of planes that equipped its squadrons. The two key types Cot needed were the heavy bomber and a reconnaissance plane capable of bombing. There were supposed to be planes in the pipeline for both. For the heavy bomber role, the LeO 206 had an impressive lifting capability, but it was a biplane and scarcely looked like a plane of the future. The limitations of the original design meant that the four-engined version could not use engines more powerful than 320 hp. For the medium multi-seater, designers had been adopting a more modern monoplane approach for some time, but were finding it difficult to come up with anything even reasonably efficient. The latest attempt, the Blériot 127, entered service in 1929 but successive modifications so increased the weight that the wings developed the unfortunate habit of buckling dangerously in flight. After the briefest of operational careers, the plane was withdrawn from service. The next generation built to meet the 1928 requirements did not look like they were going to be any more successful. Designers struggled to produce anything that was reasonable and at the end of 1931, they still had nothing they thought worth putting forward for official trials. Planes like the Amiot 140 and Blériot 137 were not even managing the 240 km/hr (150 mph) expected of the observation and reconnaissance aircraft. The Breguet 27 for the observation role and the ANF Les Mureaux 110 reconnaissance plane were not outstanding performers, but at least they were ready to go into production.

Relatively few Breguet and Mureaux reconnaissance planes were ordered. These were not the powerful long-range aircraft the Air Ministry wanted and the War Ministry, for different reasons, was also beginning to have its doubts. Since the early twenties, Fayolle and others had been arguing that even short-range observation planes should be at least three-seaters. With a two-seater, the second crew member had to do his observing and watch out for enemy fighters at the same time. A specialist gunner was needed so that the observer could focus his attention on the task in hand. Also, a second engine would increase the chances of a damaged plane limping home. The result was the three-seater *avion de travail*, powered by two relatively low-powered engines, a requirement which would eventually lead to the Potez 566 T3. It was still supposed to be a relatively small, light plane capable of operating from primitive forward airstrips. Nevertheless, the plane the Army was asking for was drifting in the direction of the much larger twin-engined multi-seater the Air Ministry wanted to use for reconnaissance and bombing.

Meanwhile, the Air Ministry were developing their own ideas about giving multi-purpose planes a much more prominent role. The distinction between the heavy night bomber and medium day bomber was dropped. Henceforth all bombers would have to operate by day or night. Painlevé and his successor Cot now wanted this plane to fill the reconnaissance and short-range observation role as well. Armengaud enthusiastically hailed the new multi-purpose 'battle plane' as none other than the 'front line plane' he had advocated in the twenties.[31] A plane capable of bombing Berlin scarcely seemed likely to be anything like the plane Armengaud had been expecting to fly short-range tactical missions from airstrips near the front line, but Armengaud had not been dissatisfied with the large Farman F.63s used in Morocco. Unfortunately for the War Office, the Air Ministry multi-seater did not seem so different to the three-seater, twin-engined *avion de travail* the War Ministry wanted.

Cot also wanted this plane to have the speed and manoeuvrability to intercept enemy aircraft over the battlefield and, more importantly, bombers heading for French cities. He claimed that the single-seater fighter was an outdated concept; even in the First World War, they had been outclassed by larger enemy two-seater fighters.[32, 33] This scarcely justified the jump to the even larger multi-seater fighters, but there was nothing radical about using large planes as interceptors. Multi-seaters with an air combat role had been a regular feature of Air Force programmes. The 'destroyer' concept of the early twenties, Barès's First World War combat planes, and even the proposed pre-war twin-engined planes were all supposed to be capable of hunting down the enemy. Arguably, with the speed of modern planes reducing warning time, high-endurance interceptors that could fly lengthy standing patrols might have been quite an effective way of defending cities. However, the primary purpose of the multi-seater interceptor was to increase the number of planes that could carry bombs. Not even Cot dared eliminate the single-seater fighter but a quarter of his fighter force would be equipped with multi-seaters.

For those who sought a solution to the apparently conflicting requirements of the bomber radicals and the Army traditionalists, the flexible multi-purpose combat plane seemed to be the ideal solution. Given the problems French designers had had in the past developing a multi-seater capable of performing any useful role, the Air Ministry was remarkably confident that such a plane was possible.

The Army greeted the Air Ministry proposals with dismay. Weygand was willing to accept the multi-seater as a long-range reconnaissance plane, but the prospect of observation squadrons being equipped with such large planes horrified him. Weygand argued in vain that the multi-role combat plane was an anachronism in an age when specialisation in all fields was considered so vital. The Army chief questioned Cot's entire premise that the next war would open with massive aerial assaults on French cities with the Army playing very little part. In Weygand's view, a simultaneous attack in the air and on land was more likely, and if this was the case, the Army would need its specialist reconnaissance planes.[34]

To add insult to injury, the Air Ministry explained that they would have to reduce the number of reconnaissance and observation squadrons because the new multi-seaters were so much more expensive than the traditional smaller army plane. The Air Ministry claim that this reduced strength would be compensated for by the greater operational efficiency of the multi-seater cut little ice in Army circles. As far as the generals were concerned, they were being asked to accept reduced strength to accommodate a plane that was not ideal for reconnaissance and useless for short-range observation duties.[35] Development of the more specialised *avion de travail* would continue but only for the twenty reservist squadrons. The Army's sense of frustration was only increased by the shrewd way in which Cot presented his programme. Cot's new independent *Armée de l'Air* was, he claimed, quite clearly a balanced force because it had an equal number of bombers, fighters and reconnaissance planes. In fact, all the reconnaissance squadrons and eight of the fighter squadrons would be equipped with multi-seaters, and three-quarters of the force would be designed primarily for long-range bombing.

To accommodate the more expensive multi-seaters, overall strength would have to drop from around 1,400 to 1,010 in the three years it would take to complete the programme. In France itself, front line strength would drop from 1,074 in January 1933 to 826 by 1938. Overall, there would be a small increase in the bomber force, the fighter force would be cut by nearly a third, and the strength of reconnaissance squadrons reduced by more than a half. Twenty regional training centres would be set up for the reservists that would man the twenty observation squadrons. In line with the policy established by Laurent-Eynac, there would be no attempt to stockpile large quantities of equipment. Air Force reserves would be restricted to just one-third of front line strength. This first Air Ministry inspired reorganisation of the French Air Force, Plan I, was approved by the Air Council in June 1933 and the French cabinet in December.[36]

Cot's plans were not good news for Lioré et Olivier. The company had been led to believe that they had a winning design with their four-engined LeO 206 heavy bomber. Production of the first batch had begun in the summer of 1933 and more orders were expected. The company were already working on the next version: the LeO 208, a streamlined biplane with a retractable undercarriage. However, this was not the sort of flexible combat plane Cot had in mind and it was not the sort of modern design Caquot was trying to encourage. Much more to Caquot's liking was a design from an entirely new company established by Marcel Bloch. Lioré et Olivier were about to discover there was no market for their biplanes.

Bloch's first combat plane was the Bloch MB.200 four-seater heavy bomber. The cantilever monoplane was a major advance on Lioré et Olivier's biplane. Although intended to meet a 1928 specification, the work on the design began late enough to take advantage of the new supercharged 900-hp Gnome-Rhône 14K Mistral Major radials. It also incorporated the all-round defensive armament heavy bombers would require now that they were expected to operate by day and night. Bloch's bomber had nose ventral and dorsal gun positions, with gunners in manually operated turrets. The shape of the nose was determined by the profile of the turret and its standing gunner. The result was a blunt nose, which was far from ideal aerodynamically. The cockpit had to be set quite high so that the pilot could see over the turret and the turret slung below the fuselage for the ventral gunner and an ungainly fixed undercarriage added more drag. The plane looked frightening enough but was not going to win any prizes for aerodynamic finesse.

The first Bloch MB.200 took to the air in June 1933, just as the LeO 206 was entering production. Despite its unattractive appearance, it was an all-metal monoplane and with its two powerful Mistral Major engines providing more power than the four Titan engines of the LeO 206, the Bloch was faster and could carry a greater bomb load further. The Bloch bomber was ordered and no more contracts were placed for the LeO 206. Success had been plucked from Lioré et Olivier by a company willing to embrace the latest ideas on aircraft design and take a chance on new engines. It was a lesson Lioré et Olivier would not forget.

Not even the Bloch MB.200 satisfied the lifting requirements of the original 1923 ultra-heavy bomber. However, the improvement achieved by the twin-engined Bloch suggested that a bomber powered by four of the new Mistral Major engines might provide the French with the true heavy bomber they had been seeking so long. Farman were soon proving that this was indeed the case. Their latest heavy bomber was, by the standards of the day, huge. With its strut-supported high wing, low-slung engines, and its bulbous gun turrets, the plane was even less aerodynamically advanced than the Bloch MB.200. The prototype Farman F.220 flew in May 1932, but it was not until the Gnome-Rhône 14K became available in 1933 that its full potential was realised. As the Farman F.221, the bomber handsomely exceeded the requirements of the 1923 specification. With a top speed and defensive armament similar to the Bloch MB.200, it could carry twice the bomb load twice as far. France at last had a genuine ultra-heavy bomber which was at least the equal of any other in the world. The Bloch MB.200 was in danger of sharing the same fate as the LeO 206.

The Farman F.221's lifting capability gave France the option of meeting the political requirement for a bomber deterrent with a specialist force, without equipping army reconnaissance and fighter units with bombers. It was, however, expensive. It was far cheaper to rely on twin-engined bombers. Plan I required just one ultra-heavy bomber group. There would also be six heavy groups equipped with the Bloch MB.200, but the bulk of the offensive capability would be provided by the forty-four bomber, reconnaissance, and fighter groups equipped with the medium multi-purpose, multi-seater combat plane.

With over half the Air Force destined to receive the multi-purpose plane, the Air Ministry was anxious to get a suitable design into production as quickly as possible. The initial response to the 1928 specification was another string of failures. With their open cockpits and gun positions, the Amiot 140, Blériot 137, SPCA 30, and Breguet 410 were an ungainly collection of designs. The biplane Breguet 410 and the more modern Amiot 140 monoplane seemed the most promising. These were redesigned, with enclosed cockpits and turrets, and re-engined with the Gnome-Rhône 14K Mistral Major to become the Breguet 413 and Amiot 143 respectively. The compact Breguet looked like the sort of compromise design that might have short-range tactical and long-range strategic potential and fifty were ordered, but problems with excessive vibrations were never overcome and the order was eventually cancelled. The larger Amiot was also ordered, and was a more successful design, but was more a bomber than anything else. Something much more versatile was required.

Designers needed to start afresh. In June 1933, the Air Ministry issued a new specification for a bomber combat reconnaissance (BCR) plane. The aim was a new generation of ultra-modern, fast, manoeuvrable, powerfully armed twin-engined planes, which would be equally capable of artillery observation, army reconnaissance, tactical bombing, strategic reconnaissance, long-range bombing, escorting, and interception. With an anticipated top speed of 350 km/hr (217 mph), these planes were supposed to be as fast as any contemporary fighter. It had to have the manoeuvrability to intercept enemy bomber and reconnaissance planes and the all-round defensive armament to ward off an attack from any angle. For long-range missions, the plane would sacrifice speed and manoeuvrability for lifting capability.[37] It was expecting a lot, but the lucrative contracts the winning company could expect ensured that there was no shortage of companies willing to try. Four planes were the subject of prototype orders: the Amiot 144 (a slightly smaller more streamlined version of the Amiot 143), the Breguet 460, the Farman F.420, and the Bloch MB.130. All these planes were stressed skin, monoplane designs with retractable undercarriages, enclosed cockpits and turreted gun positions and they were all powered by the Gnome-Rhône Mistral Major radials.

There was one unofficial contender. In a casual conversation with Henri Potez, Victor Denain (the new Air Force Chief of Staff) explained how worried he was by the increasing cost of the BCR planes being developed. Spotting an opportunity, Potez suggested that if Denain was willing to consider an unofficial entry, he would guarantee it would be cheaper. Denain agreed and Potez designed and built his Potez 540 in four months; in December 1933, Potez was rewarded for his endeavour with a production order. The guaranteed lower price meant that initially Potez was building the plane at a loss, but with subsequent orders, the plane more than broke even. The lightweight, mixed wooden and metal, and rather fragile Potez design had its critics. With its braced wing and low-slung engines, it was not as advanced as the official entries, but it was cheap and its combination of speed, manoeuvrability, range, and bomb load meant that it came as close as any of the official contenders to meeting the almost impossible BCR requirement.

Cot's BCR plane was the culmination of a thirty-year quest for a twin-engined multi-seater, multi-role plane. The appearance of vastly more powerful engines like the air-cooled 900-hp Gnome-Rhône 14K Mistral Major and the 860-hp liquid-cooled Hispano-Suiza HS 12Y-31 seemed to provide the power to make the dream a reality. The 1933 specification took the idea to the very limit, expecting a single type to perform virtually every military role an aircraft can perform. The history of aviation is full of examples of planes designed specifically for one role but proving capable of performing a variety of roles. However, it is also full of planes designed to perform a variety of roles that are not capable of performing any of them satisfactorily; so it would prove with the BCR plane. The whole idea was leading French aviation down a dangerous path. Just as aircraft speeds were reaching the point where reducing drag had become critical, French designers were embarking on another generation of clumsy, turret-laden bombers. While French designers were using the much higher power now available to haul their cumbersome planes into the air, other nations were exploiting it to achieve speeds undreamed of in France.

In the summer of 1933, any change of heart over the multi-purpose combat plane seemed most unlikely. With Army objections decisively overruled, many leading aircraft manufacturers working on proposals and plans to equip more than half the Air Force with these aircraft, the concept had never been more firmly established. The decline and disappearance of the *multiplace de combat*, however, would be as rapid as it was unexpected. In little more than a year, the entire idea would be totally discredited.

The first problem for the BCR concept was the emergence of the cannon as a practicable air-to-air weapon. Its low rate of fire and the high recoil had previously been serious disadvantages but in the early thirties, Hispano-Suiza acquired the rights to the excellent 20-mm Swedish Oerlikon S cannon, and soon increased its rate of fire from an already impressive 300 rounds per minute to 400. The engine is always the most solid part of any plane, so to absorb the recoil, Hispano-Suiza built their HS 12X and 12Y engines around the cannon. The new weapon possessed four times the weight of fire of the standard Air Force machine gun and its explosive shells also had greater range. The 1932 fighter specification required designers to use the Hispano-Suiza *moteur-canon* and with the 1934 specifications, designers who did not want to use the Hispano-Suiza engine were told that their fighters would have to carry a cannon in each wing. Plans were also drawn up for a new twin-engined interceptor armed with two cannon mounted in the nose, which would lead to the Potez 630.[38]

The multi-seaters relied for defence on the ability to fire a machine gun in any direction, but cannon-armed interceptors would always be able to attack from outside the range of their defensive armament. The only solution was to arm bombers with cannon, but while an interceptor need only increase its firepower along a single direction, a bomber claiming an all-round defensive capability had to match this increase along every line of attack a fighter might take. Designing turrets that could absorb the recoil of cannon was difficult, and they were bound to be extremely heavy. All-round defensive armament with cannon looked impossible.

A first indication that the French were moving away from reliance on defensive firepower came in 1933 with the release of a specification for a high-speed reprisal bomber. The plane was to have approximately the same lifting capacity as the Bloch MB.200 (500 kg of bombs to 1,500 km), but it would only need carry a very basic defensive armament and top speed was to be in excess of 400 km/hr (250 mph). Prototypes were ordered from Amiot (the E7) and Bernard, with trials expected to be underway before the end of 1935.[39, 40] The specification was purely speculative and there were no plans at this stage to re-equip any part of the Air Force with such a plane. Nevertheless, it was a significant departure from previous thinking.

In February 1934, rioting in Paris brought the government down and the new right-wing government replaced Cot with General Denain. In September, Barès retired. The departure of these two leading advocates of the flexible multi-seater combat plane helped pave the way for some more rethinking. This time it was triggered by developments on the other side of the Atlantic. In October 1934, a report for the Air Council and Air Ministry painted a less than rosy picture of the existing and future capabilities of the French bomber fleet. The LeO 20 was completely out of date. More alarmingly, its replacement, the Bloch MB.200, was already considered inferior to the Junkers Ju 52, which was already in production in Germany. The Amiot 140 was an improvement, but even the performance of this plane was not expected to be anywhere near that of the remarkable Martin B-10 and B-12 bombers already entering service in the United States. Reports reaching the French suggested that these were capable of an astonishing 370 km/hr (230 mph), considerably faster than the Bloch MB.200 or Amiot 140, and faster even than the speed required by the 1933 BCR specification.[41]

The report blamed French inferiority on the need for all-round defensive armament and the bulky turrets this required, with the nose turret a particularly severe handicap. The report suggested that either bombers should be lightly armed, as had been proposed by the 1933 fast bomber specification, or they should be equipped with retractable dorsal and ventral turrets. In either case, there should be no nose turret. The emphasis should be on achieving the most streamlined plane with the highest possible speed. With the engines available at that time, the report concluded that there was no reason why a bomber with a powerful defensive armament based on retractable cannon-armed dorsal and ventral turrets should not be capable of achieving 400 km/hr (250 mph) and have sufficient range to bomb Berlin, Budapest, or Naples.[42]

A speed of 400 km/hr was indeed very possible. Unbeknown to the French, just two months after the report was written, the Russian Tupolev SB-2 prototype bomber, ironically powered by two French Hispano-Suiza HS 12Y-31 engines, achieved 404 km/hr. More ominously for the French, the following year the fifth Dornier Do 17 prototype, also powered by Hispano-Suiza engines, achieved over 390 km/hr. This was 100 km/hr faster than the Amiot 143. France had some catching up to do.

Given how entrenched the *multiplace de combat* concept was, the speed with which these recommendations were acted on was remarkable. The proposed high-speed bomber was hastily added to the agenda of the 17 November meeting of the Air Council, which immediately approved the project.[43] A full official specification for a four-seater 400 km/hr bomber was equally hastily drawn up and released. Unlike the 1933 high-speed bomber specification, this was not a speculative venture. Trials with the prototype were expected to begin in April 1937, with production to start in 1937; by 1940, virtually the entire bomber fleet would be equipped with the new plane.[44] Development of the BCR plane would continue, but it was now just a stopgap. Indeed, if it was not too late, designers were asked to consider the advantages of removing the nose turret from their BCR projects.

The new bomber was to be powered by air-cooled radials. Using bulkier radials seemed counter-intuitive when the emphasis was on streamlining, but the French had good reasons for believing these were the engines of the future. They were lighter than liquid-cooled engines, getting ever more powerful and the latest cowlings meant they were not generating as much drag as they had done.[45] Even record-breaking racers were using them; in September 1933, the radial-powered Wedell-Williams Model 44 managed 491 km/hr. Radials were also less prone to combat damage than inline engines with their vulnerable cooling systems. France was not alone in believing the air-cooled radial was the engine of the future. The Martin B-10 that had impressed the French used air-cooled radials and the United States, Japan, and Italy were all tending towards radial powered combat planes.

This trend had not gone unnoticed by Hispano-Suiza, the leading French manufacturer of liquid-cooled engines. In 1928, the company acquired the rights to manufacture American Wright radials and began developing two entirely new radials; the Hispano-Suiza HS 14AA, expected to produce more than 1,000 hp, and a scaled-down version, the HS 14AB with a predicted output of around 700 hp. For a company with no previous experience of radial engine design, these were ambitious projects. At the time, it seemed to be a perfectly sound commercial decision, but it would prove to have very unfortunate consequences for the French Air Force.

The new November 1934 bomber specification did not mean any change in Air Ministry strategy. The priority was still to create a long-range bomber fleet which could bomb Berlin, but there was no question of the new bomber equipping any observation or fighter squadrons. The Air Force was beginning to move back to more specialised, combat planes—the sort of planes that France would need in 1940 to deal with the German *blitzkrieg*.

Coincidently, at around this time, the idea of a more mobile defence, based on mechanised forces, was also gaining ground. Plans were being drawn up to mechanise elements of the cavalry, motorise some infantry units, and create a first light armoured division (DLM: *Division Légère Mécanique*). In 1934, de Gaulle published his *Vers l'Armée de Métier*, in which the young French officer described how a professional army, rather than a conscript force, built around powerful armoured divisions, provided the best way of defeating a surprise assault on France. There was also much talk in France of an *aviation d'arrêt*, a ground-attack force capable of intervening rapidly to halt a surprise armoured assault, along the lines of the anti-tank strike force Armengaud was proposing. The success of ground-attack missions in 1918 was recalled and the Japanese were known to be using ground-attack planes in the fighting in China. Italy, Russia, and the United States were all believed to be developing aircraft to provide their armies with direct support on the battlefield. The Junkers K 47 two-seater assault dive-bomber, developed by the Swedish branch of the German aircraft company, was attracting particular attention.[46, 47]

However, the *aviation d'arrêt* was seen very much as an alternative to de Gaulle's mobile armoured divisions, rather than as a means of complementing them.[48] Similarly, de Gaulle failed to factor in the support aircraft might provide. The two key elements of the future German *blitzkrieg* existed in France but there was still little interest in merging them into a single strategy. The Germans, however, were no nearer to achieving this. The Wehrmacht still mistrusted the tank, and bombers were still seen as a means of providing purely indirect support. France was not yet slipping behind; it was just missing the opportunity to take the lead.

Hitting small battlefield targets was not a problem that concerned the Air Force, but bomber commanders were worried that their bombers, operating from medium altitudes, would not be able to hit small targets in the rear like bridges. A smaller, two-seater, single-engined, more manoeuvrable plane, along the lines of the Junkers K 47, would be more suitable for precision low-level or dive-bombing attacks. In the first half of 1935, a series of trials were organised to see which aircraft were best for low-level attack. Planes taking part included the LeO 206 heavy bomber, the Bloch MB.200 and Potez 540 multi-seaters, and, interestingly, a Morane-Saulnier M.S.225 single-seater fighter. The bomber commanders were right to be worried. The trials revealed that the four- and twin-engined bombers were far too slow and unwieldy for low-level attacks. The Morane-Saulnier fighter, however, was considered suitable and effective. Overall, the trials suggested that aircraft operating at low level would be virtually immune to interception and should be able to evade ground fire. However, despite the success of the Morane-Saulnier single-seater, using fighters for ground attack was still not considered a good idea. A small plane was required, but two engines would always offer more security. Even the Potez 540, the lightest of the available twin-engined planes, was considered too large and heavy. It was suggested that an experimental unit should be set up at Reims and equipped with the Potez multi-seater until something better could be developed.[49]

Dive-bombing was another way of hitting small targets. The Air Force had been interested in the dive-bomber for some time, but were happy to let the Navy develop the idea. The Air Ministry was following with interest trials with the Gourdou-Leseurre GL-430 dive-bomber version of the single-seater fighter. The 200 km/hr GL-430 was considered far too slow for Air Force use, and it was not clear dive-bombing would be any more accurate than low-level attack, but the idea seemed worth pursuing. By the end of 1935, there were plans to form one dive-bomber and one ground-attack group for trials.[50, 51]

During the summer of 1935, the outlines of an entirely new, compact, three-seat reconnaissance bomber aircraft, capable of ground-attack and, possibly, dive-bombing began to emerge. A full specification was due to be released early in 1936. There was talk of this plane being a new lighter, higher performance version of the BCR multi-seaters. This was perhaps not what the Army wanted to hear, but there was much more chance of this turretless plane being a useful tactical weapon.[52] The single-engined Mureaux 113 R2 reconnaissance plane was upgraded to the Mureaux 115 R2B2 reconnaissance bomber with a 440-lb bomb load as an interim measure and the experimental ground-attack unit being set up at Reims was to use this instead of the twin-engined Potez 540.[53]

With the BCR concept abandoned, the Army expected more specialist reconnaissance planes to be developed. They still wanted a twin-engined design and suggested the new heavy cannon fighter might be the basis for such a plane. The Air Ministry agreed and began drawing up a specification for a plane, which, like all French reconnaissance and observation planes, would have a secondary ground-attack capability. By the end of 1935, the Potez 63 reconnaissance variant had the highest priority. Significantly, the Army insisted that the bombing capability of these new planes must not in any way impair their ability to perform their primary reconnaissance mission. A nervous War Ministry did not want a return to the BCR concept by the back door.[54]

Interestingly, now that the *multiplace de combat* had been abandoned, the two-seater, single-engined tactical fighter was back in fashion for escort and intruder missions. It was a contentious concept. It might seem obvious that a plane weighed down by a second crew member could never hope to compete on equal terms with a single-seater. However, it could also be argued that as combat planes got heavier, the weight of the second crew member was becoming proportionally less significant. If the two-seater tactical fighter had earned its place in combat operations in 1918, then surely it would have a role to play in the thirties.[55] Whatever the merits of the single-engined two-seater, it was another specialised aircraft. The Air Ministry was also considering a smaller, simpler alternative to the plane required by the November 1934 high-speed B4 bomber specification. The new machine would only have a crew of three and the complex retractable dorsal and ventral turrets would be replaced by cannon or machine guns on simple mountings. With the reduced weight and better streamlining, it ought to be even faster than the 1934 project. A specification was drawn up for a 480 km/hr (300 mph) three-seater medium bomber.[56, 57]

Suddenly, the future was looking very bright, with a whole new generation of smaller, high-performance, more specialist combat planes in the pipeline. The original 1933 'reprisal bomber' was expected to begin trials before the end of 1935. The 1934 high-speed bomber specification was supposed to produce concrete results by the summer of 1936. The first high-speed reconnaissance planes would emerge the following summer followed by the first reconnaissance bombers and, eventually, the dive-bomber.[58] All these types were due to enter service during the late thirties. Until they arrived, the Air Force would have to rely on the multi-seaters already in service and the BCR planes being developed. The Amiot 143 was ordered as a medium bomber. The Bloch MB.200 would be used solely as a night bomber and a more advanced version of the plane with retractable turrets and undercarriage; the Bloch MB.210 was ordered as a precaution against delays with the new high-speed bombers. Planes designed to meet the 1933 'BCR' specification would now be used by reconnaissance squadrons. Initially, only the Potez 540 was ordered, while designers did their best to incorporate some of the new thinking into their BCR proposals. The Bloch MB.131 (an updated Bloch MB.130 with no nose turret) would eventually emerge. More Mureaux 117 two-seaters were ordered as interim tactical reconnaissance bombers. By 1940, most of these interim designs were supposed to be replaced by a new generation of specialist planes. The only remnant of the *multiplace de combat* era would be the updated Bloch MB.131.[59]

The new Air Force proposals received a mixed reception from the Army. They were delighted the large multi-seater would no longer be used for observation. In the long-range strategic reconnaissance role, the Army were happy with the Bloch MB.131 and the reconnaissance version of the twin-engined fighter (the future Potez 637) for tactical reconnaissance. For short-range observation, the Army still wanted the smaller *avion de travail* three-seaters they had specified in 1932.[60]

The proposed ground-attack planes and dive-bombers produced more controversy. The Air Ministry were keen to introduce these but did not want to reduce the deterrent value of the long-range bomber fleet by equipping some of these squadrons with short-range bombers. The Air Ministry hoped to get around this problem by equipping eight reconnaissance and seven observation groups with the reconnaissance bomber.[61] To the Army, it was just another multi-purpose combat plane, as ill-conceived as its BCR predecessors. They did not see any urgent need for a ground-attack capability and did not want their reconnaissance and observation squadrons infiltrated by aircraft designed for dive-bombing and ground-attack.[62] Significantly, they did not try to persuade the Air Ministry to equip some of the strategic bomber force with tactical bombers. Ground-attack was not on the Army agenda. The War Ministry seemed so opposed to the idea that the Air Ministry felt it best not to even mention the one or two specialist dive-bomber and ground-attack units the Air Ministry were thinking of slipping into the long-range reconnaissance force by 1940. However, at this stage, the German Army commanders thought the same. Arguably, the French were one step ahead of their enemy across the Rhine; at least the French Air Force was considering direct bomber intervention on the battlefield.

In January 1936, the Laval government fell and Denain was forced out of office. During his brief time at the Air Ministry, he had presided over a remarkable change in Air Force thinking. When he had taken over from Cot, he had been the staunchest supporter of the multi-purpose combat plane. Two years later, a whole range of specialist aircraft were being lined up to replace the stillborn BCR concept. However, it was easier for the Air Ministry to change direction, than the aircraft industry. Most of the major manufacturers were heavily committed to BCR projects and were loath to abandon the work done and start afresh. There was very little on the drawing boards that even remotely resembled the sort of combat planes the Air Force now wanted. By the end of 1935, the only specification released for the post-BCR era was the November 1934 B4 long-range medium bomber. Denain's successor would need to act quickly to get French aircraft design back on track.

5

Fighter Design: Squandered Opportunities

The much smaller, more specialised bomber and reconnaissance planes the Air Ministry wanted to develop might yet be the salvation of France, but they would need effective fighters to protect them. The twenties had been a disastrous decade for French fighter design. The quest for better performance at high altitude had resulted in two generations of fighters with totally inadequate horizontal speeds. In 1928, even at ground level, the latest French designs were scarcely capable of exceeding 270 km/hr (168 mph), which was little more than 20 mph faster than the decade-old Nieuport-Delage NiD.29.

There was no reason why French designers could not do much better. The newly created Air Ministry was encouraging French companies to test their talents in the competitive world of high-speed racing. Engine manufacturers were told to aim for 2,000-hp engines to power them and some advanced racers emerged. Valuable experience in monoplane design was gained and powerful engines like the Hispano-Suiza HS 12X and HS 12Y inline motors and the air-cooled Gnome-Rhône 14K Mistral Major emerged.

Crucially, the French had identified where they were going wrong with their fighter designs. A report written in the late twenties blamed the insistence on high-altitude performance as the reason for the backwardness of French fighters. It described how at medium altitudes, where enemy planes were most likely to be encountered, the latest French fighters would be hard pushed to intercept anything. In future, French designers should be told to concentrate on achieving the highest possible speed at altitudes between 3,500 and 4,000 metres, rather than 5,000 metres. Both manoeuvrability and rate of climb could be sacrificed to achieve this. Speed, however, was not the only issue. The report also highlighted the poor pilot view in all previous fighter designs and suggested designers should adopt the low-wing monoplane configuration to solve this problem.[1] The latest racers were demonstrating that this was necessary anyway for purely aerodynamic reasons, so it was apparently a fortuitous suggestion.

For the 1928 programme, designers would have the latest 500-hp Hispano-Suiza engines. The highest possible horizontal velocity at medium altitude was now the first priority, the low-wing monoplane had been selected as the best configuration, and more power was available. Even in Britain, where speed was also the top priority, there was still a reluctance to abandon the biplane and the superior climbing performance it offered. In Germany, thinking had changed little since the First World War; rate of climb was the first priority, manoeuvrability was second, and high horizontal speed a poor third.[2] The French appeared to be poised to establish a clear lead in fighter speeds over their main European rivals.

Unfortunately, the speed required by the 1928 fighter programme was not very ambitious. The French multi-seater combat planes, with their emphasis on defensive firepower rather than speed, were partly to blame. The French estimated that any fighter should have at least a 50–60 km/hr advantage over its intended target. This was a reasonable expectation, but the French did not expect their reconnaissance planes to fly faster than 240 km/hr, and their multi-seaters were not capable of doing any better. It was therefore felt that 300 km/hr (186 mph) would be enough. This was only 30 km/hr higher than the speed required ten years before. News that the RAF was a about to get the 286 km/hr Bristol Bulldog should have drawn attention to how low the target was.[3] Indeed, French designs were soon demonstrating this. An experimental 1926 specification had asked designers to investigate what could be achieved with a lightweight fighter carrying minimum fuel and equipment. The main purpose was to produce cheaper rather than faster fighters, but in 1929, the neat Bernard 20, using the experience gained with the Bernard V.2 racer, flew, achieving 305 km/hr at ground level and 280 km/hr at 5,000 metres, with a 400-hp engine.[4] Its 110 km/hr (68 mph) landing speed was rather high, but 300 km/hr scarcely seemed a demanding target for a new generation of fighters that would be using far more powerful engines.[5]

Reports were soon reaching France that fighters being developed in Britain had already exceeded 300 km/hr; the 320 km/hr American Boeing F4B was already in service. This information, together with the appearance in France of the first supercharged engines, prompted the French Air Ministry to edge the speed requirement up to 325 km/hr (202 mph). During the course of 1930, there were reports that the British Hawker Fury and Fairey Firefly II had already managed 350 km/hr (217 mph).[6] The French appeared to respond to this by increasing their own requirement to 350 km/hr early in 1931. The French were following trends rather than setting targets.[7]

The response from French companies was not quick, perhaps because of the repeated updates. Three years after the specification was released, there were still few prototypes to test and trials to decide on the winner would not take place until late in 1932. As a stopgap, the French ordered another fighter that had emerged from the 1926 lightweight fighter programme. Morane-Saulnier had turned the 250 km/hr M.S.221 into the 328 km/hr M.S.225 and the fighter's low weight and supercharged engine ensured that, far from sacrificing climbing performance, the plane actually climbed far faster than any previous service fighter. Despite its high wing loading, with its excellently harmonised controls, it was easy to fly and superbly manoeuvrable. The Morane-Saulnier reached the squadrons in October 1933 and was beyond doubt the best fighter so far produced by the French. It was still only broadly comparable to the British Fury, which had entered service over two years before but it was far superior to the Heinkel He 51, which would not reach German squadrons until the following year. The M.S.225's entry into service came none too soon for French fighter pilots. In an embarrassing incident three months earlier, a squadron of Nieuport-Delage NiD 622s had been instructed to escort a formation of Italian flying boats, led by the renowned General Bilbao, in a flypast over Strasbourg. Much to the amusement of the Italians, and the embarrassment of their hosts, the French pilots found they could not keep up.

Émile Dewoitine did not seem to think the 350 km/hr target speed was too challenging. With the 500-hp Hispano-Suiza 12M (the Ministry's preferred engine), he estimated he could achieve 376 km/hr. If he was allowed to use the heavier 700-hp Lorraine Pétrel, 400 km/hr (250 mph) was within reach.[8] Then, in the summer of 1931, the vastly superior 650-hp Hispano-Suiza HS 12X appeared. This was actually lighter than the HS 12M, but 30 per cent more powerful and superior to anything available to German or British designers. French designers seemed very well-placed to take the lead in fighter design.

Unfortunately, during the course of 1931, concern in France regarding fighter speeds seemed to recede. It seemed the performance of certain foreign fighter designs had been exaggerated. The American Boeing F4B was now only credited with a shade over 300 km/hr and Hawker were only claiming 328 km/hr for their Fury. Multi-seaters like the Amiot 140 were struggling to achieve 240 km/hr, so the existing 350 km/hr target speed seemed to provide a more than adequate speed advantage. When the fighter requirements were adjusted at the beginning of 1932, it was not felt necessary to increase the required speed, even though the far more powerful HS 12X was now available. The 350 km/hr requirement was not particularly low by international standards; German designers had the same target, but they did not have the engine power available to the French. The Air Ministry was not stretching French designers.

It was particularly unfortunate because below 400 km/hr, the lower drag of heavier cantilever wings and retractable undercarriages did not compensate for the reduced climb rate and manoeuvrability. The larger radiators required to cool the more powerful engines were also not such a huge problem. The ease with which the Air Ministry speed requirement could be achieved with engines like the Hispano-Suiza HS 12X did not encourage designers to make much effort to reduce drag. Even the low-wing monoplane configuration, adopted by four of the ten contenders, was inspired more by the Air Ministry insistence on an excellent upward view for the pilot rather than the higher speeds it might lead to.

Instead of attempting to maximise speed, French designers turned their ingenuity to improving the pilot's view, something that the Air Ministry were also very concerned about. Designers went to extraordinary lengths to provide the least obstructed view. None contemplated a fully enclosed cockpit as this would restrict the pilots' ability to look down over the side of the fuselage. Nieuport persisted with the traditional parasol wing for their NiD 122, even though this configuration was considered to be ten per cent slower than an equivalent low-wing cantilever design and then added to the drag by cutting a huge hole in the wing for the pilot to see up. Three of the prototypes ordered—the Loire 43, Mureaux 170, and Gourdou-Leseurre GL-482—hoped to avoid the poor upward view of the parasol winged plane by adopting the 'gull wing' configuration. Morane-Saulnier opted for the more efficient low-wing format, but to improve the downward view, cut a section out of the wing root. This increased drag and the wing junction was so weakened it had to be supported by bracing struts, adding even more drag. Since most of the fighters managed the 350 km/hr target, these draconian measures seemed entirely justified.[9]

The Dewoitine D.500 was eventually selected for production. With its cantilever low wing and rakish monocoque fuselage, the design had many of the hallmarks of a truly modern fighter. However, the excellent lines of the plane were broken by the fixed undercarriage, which increased total frontal area by no less than a quarter. To improve the pilot's view, sections were cut out of the wing roots and while they were not as extensive as those on the Morane-Saulnier M.S.325, they cut speed by 30 km/hr. The bulky radiator, with its water coolant, was another major source of drag. Using ethylene-glycol for coolant meant smaller radiators and less weight, but the Air Ministry thought it was too corrosive and French engines would not be able to cope with the higher temperatures. Even so, the fighter still managed 359 km/hr, exceeding the Air Ministry target. It was robust, manoeuvrable, and easy to fly. The D.501 version, with its engine-mounted 20 mm cannon, was one of the most heavily armed fighters in the world.

The final performance of the Dewoitine D.500 may not have taken advantage of the French lead in engine design but it was still far superior to the contemporary He 51. However, fighter performance in Germany and Britain was about to surge forward at an unprecedented rate. Whereas the French had used their ungainly multi-seaters to establish the criteria for fighter speeds, the British were being driven by the speeds of their high-speed light bombers and the Germans by their high-speed airliners. In Germany, this led to the 465 km/hr (290 mph) Jumo-powered Messerschmitt Bf 109. The German fighter did not fly until three years after the D.500, but the comparison is interesting. Both were powered by liquid-cooled engines of similar output. The French fighter was better-armed, lighter, could climb faster, fly higher, accelerate faster, and was more manoeuvrable. It was easier to fly and provided the pilot with a far better view. However, the Bf 109 was 100 km/hr faster.

Dewoitine knew more was possible. Since early 1933 the Dewoitine design team had been toying with the idea of fitting their D.500 fighter with a retractable undercarriage, but they were worried by the weight of the mechanism and the problems of fitting the wheels in the slim wings. A more aerodynamic fixed undercarriage seemed almost as good. They believed that this version, with the 650-hp HS 12X ought to be capable of topping 400 km/hr.[10] By this time, the Air Ministry had decided that the heavier 36-litre 860-hp HS 12Y-31, originally intended for bomber designs, would also be suitable for fighters. A version of the D.500 was ordered with this engine, but this immense power was going to be wasted if nothing was done about reducing drag.

During the course of 1933, evidence was mounting that the existing 350 km/hr requirement was far too low. The French had issued their own 400 km/hr reprisal bomber specification. In April 1933, the Heinkel He 70 had established a new world record by carrying 1,000 kg over a distance of 500 km at an average speed of 355 km/hr. The Heinkel was precisely the sort of plane the French had always feared could be easily converted into a bomber. With the 50–60 km/hr speed advantage the Air Ministry considered necessary, more than 400 km/hr was needed to deal with planes that were already flying never mind potential successors.

It was against this background that the next fighter specification was formulated. The motor to be employed was to be either the 860-hp HS 12Y-31 inline, the 900-hp Gnome-Rhône Mistral Major radial, or the even more promising and much anticipated 1,000-hp Hispano-Suiza 14AA radial. However, despite the abundance of power, when the specification was finally released in July 1934, the maximum expected speed was set at just 400 km/hr. This might have seemed reasonable when compared to the 350 km/hr expected of the BCR plane but would not be enough to catch the experimental high-speed reprisal bombers the Air Ministry had ordered from Amiot (the E7) and Bernard.

Émile Dewoitine achieved the required speed by simply fitting the HS 12Y-31 to a standard D.500 airframe. Two prototypes were ordered as the D.510. He went further, suggesting that if the cantilever undercarriage he had previously proposed for the D.500 was used and wing span was reduced, a top speed of 450 km/hr (280 mph) should be possible. A prototype of this version, the D.511, was ordered as well.[11] There was no need for designers to weigh their planes down with a retractable undercarriage or attempt any other aerodynamic refinements if the target speed could be achieved so easily.

Late in 1934, everything changed, with the Air Ministry abandoning the BCR plane and ordering the development of a 400 km/hr high-speed bomber. However, while the new bomber requirement was pushed through with real urgency, it took longer for the implications to filter through to the fighter programme. In January 1935, there were reports in France of how British designers were already aiming for 400–450 km/hr, but the French were slow to follow suit.[12] Required speed was increased to 450 km/hr, but this was soon looking just as modest. An early study by Amiot claimed their A.340 design could manage 470 km/hr with two HS 12Y-31 engines. If the new HS-14AA generated the promised 1,200 hp, even higher speeds would be possible.[13] To retain the necessary 50–60 km/hr speed advantage, target fighter speeds needed to be in excess of 500 km/hr, well over 300 mph. French fighter requirements were out of step with the anticipated performance of their own future bombers.

The 400 km/hr of the original July 1934 specification did not provide any great incentive to experiment. Blériot-SPAD saw no reason to abandon the biplane format while Dewoitine tinkered with his D.500 design. The only new fighter to emerge was the Morane-Saulnier M.S.405. Given the low speed required, it is surprising that the plane incorporated as many innovations as it did. It was a low-wing cantilever monoplane with fully enclosed cockpit and fully retractable undercarriage. Other modern features included flaps to reduce take off and landing speeds. The engine would be cooled by ethylene-glycol, despite Air Ministry reservations, and the radiator retracted at high speed in an effort to keep drag down. It did not adopt some of the more extreme measures to improve pilot view, but with its tubular plywood-covered structure, it was technically less advanced than the monocoque, all-metal Dewoitine D.500 it was supposed to replace.

As the speed required was edged up, other designers felt obliged to turn to more advanced monoplane fighter projects. Nieuport abandoned the parasol wing and produced the neat Nieuport 160 cantilever monoplane, powered by the HS 12Y-31. Even the tail wheel was fully retractable. Nieuport hoped to get rid of the external radiator completely by implanting it in the wing, with the cooling air passing through the wing. When the Air Ministry cancelled Dewoitine's 450 km/hr D.511, he too was forced back to the drawing board. The D.513 incorporated an elliptical wing, copied off the He 70, and a fully retractable undercarriage, improvements which Dewoitine hoped would help give his new fighter a speed in excess of 500 km/hr. As with the Dewoitine D.500, a neat design was marred by the bulky radiator. Air-cooled engines avoided this problem. Loire built a neat fighter around the HS 14AA radial (the Loire 250) and at the beginning of 1935, Bloch joined the race with their first fighter, the Bloch MB.150, designed around the Gnome-Rhône Mistral Major. All these fighters were expected to be capable of achieving between

460 km/hr and 500 km/hr, a speed which was in excess of even the updated Air Ministry requirement. The designers, rather than the Air Ministry, were setting the pace.

Manufacturers were also invited to take another look at the lightweight fighter approach. Earlier programmes had produced interesting designs, like the Bernard 20, and one outstanding success in the shape of the M.S.225. Designers would be helped by the fact that a new generation of small (14–19 litre) 400–500 hp inline engines being developed by Potez, Salmson, and Renault, which did not need radiators. In 1934, a Caudron racer powered by a 350-hp engine had demonstrated what was possible by exceeding 500 km/hr. Caudron set about building a cannon-armed fighter along similar lines.

Apart from the Blériot-SPAD 710, all the fighters designed to meet the 1934 fighter program were low-wing cantilever monoplanes. The success of the Dewoitine D.500 seemed to have assured the future of this configuration. During the first half of 1935, however, doubts about the low-wing monoplane resurfaced. Once again, it was the pilot's view that was causing concern. The low wing improved the pilot's upward view but blocked the view downwards. The high-wing parasol offered an unrestricted view down and the gull wing attempted to combine a good upward and downward view. Some even preferred the biplane, claiming that two wings with reduced span was less of a handicap than the much greater span of a monoplane. Uncertainty on the best fighter configuration was reflected in the orders placed in 1935. A small batch of D.510s were ordered, but so were the gull-winged Loire 46, the parasol Dewoitine D.371, and the biplane Blériot-SPAD 510, all of which were slower than the Dewoitine D.510.

In August 1935, the first of the next generation of fighters, the Morane-Saulnier M.S.405, took to the air. With a top speed of 475 km/hr (295 mph), it comfortably exceeded even the revised 450 km/hr target.[14] It was easy to fly and extremely agile. At official trials early in 1936, test pilots were so impressed by the machine that there was never much doubt that it would be ordered for the Air Force. The Morane-Saulnier decision to push through the development phase as quickly as possible had not resulted in a particularly sophisticated fighter, but the company had virtually won the contract before its more advanced rivals were ready for trials. Aerodynamically and structurally, it may not have been the most advanced fighter in the word, but thanks to its HS 12Y-31 engine, it was far superior to the early Jumo-powered Bf 109. The praise heaped upon the plane by those who flew it did at least silence once and for all the critics of the low-wing monoplane.

However, even at this stage it should have been clear that the M.S.405 was not fast enough. Towards the end of 1935, details of the new 500 km/hr Hawker Hurricane began to emerge. By the spring of 1936, the British were publicly proclaiming that the new Supermarine Spitfire was even faster. This information was greeted with some scepticism in France. It was suggested that such high speeds were only being achieved by prototypes as yet unburdened by full military equipment.[15] It was also argued that these designs were intended purely as bomber interceptors and did not possess the qualities required to engage opposing fighters. There was some truth in this, but it was a dangerous attitude to adopt.

By June 1936, it was clear to the Air Ministry that with engines like the promising HS 14AA radial, the next generation of bombers should be capable of achieving far more than the 450-km/hr 1934 program. The latest three-seater medium bomber specification required 480 km/hr. However, fighter requirements were only increased to 500 km/hr. A 20 km/hr speed advantage over a bomber was not enough by the Air Force's own criteria. In September 1936, the required speed was cautiously advanced to 520 km/hr (323 mph), but even this was still far too un-ambitious. The French had no idea just how far behind they were slipping. The Spitfire had already comfortably exceeded the 520 km/hr target and while the French had not yet fallen behind the Germans in terms of performance achieved, they were well behind in terms of expectations. Towards the end of 1936, the German Air Ministry released a 600-km/hr (375 mph) fighter specification, a speed that was far in excess of anything the French were considering.[16]

While French designers were working on the next generation of fighters, the Air Ministry was reassessing how they should be used. Until Pétain took an interest in air defence, very little had been done to organise an effective defence of targets in the rear. The 1928 programme had required the creation of four night fighter squadrons but the Air Ministry was in no hurry to create them.[17] In the early thirties, only one existed and this was equipped with an improvised night fighter version of the Breguet 19 bomber. The plan was to replace this with an equally improvised night fighter version of the Mureaux 117 reconnaissance plane. This was the only squadron assigned to rear defence. The two day fighter regiments with the General Reserve were still seen as a tactical force to reinforce the front.

When Pétain became Inspector of Aerial Defences in May 1932, he demanded the immediate creation of the three additional night fighter squadrons that were already supposed to exist and wanted a 200-strong interceptor force to protect French cities against day and night attack.[18] Barès saw no reason why the two fighter regiments attached to the General Reserve should not be given this task, and plans were drawn up for a defensive belt of fighters along a line running through Lyon, Dijon and Reims.[19, 20] What Barès had casually agreed to was a fundamental redeployment of fighter resources. Rear defence had suddenly become an important task for the fighter force. However, instead of creating the resources it needed, the Army's reserve fighter force was diverted to the task. The number of fighters available to the Army had effectively been halved.

Air defence now became a top priority. Pétain made sure an adequate early warning and tracking system was set up. During 1935 and 1936, trials were carried out with a network of observation posts using optical and sound location equipment, similar to those employed by anti-aircraft batteries. A central command post in the rear collated the information gathered, and transmitted the path of the bomber formation to fighters patrolling behind the belt of observation posts.[21] Like many nations, the French were looking into the possibility of using radio waves to detect and track enemy formations. During 1935, trials with a primitive radar system succeeded in detecting aircraft flying at altitudes up to 8,000 metres. Speed, direction, and size of formations were assessed with reasonable accuracy but there were problems estimating the altitude. Range was limited to just 5 km, which would clearly need to be improved, but it was seen primarily as a tracking rather than an early warning system, so huge range was not required. The idea was that it would replace the extensive and expensive ground observer network.[22] The results were encouraging enough for research to continue.

Another idea was flying command planes to shadow the enemy formation. Heavier armament would also be needed to shoot down large long-range bombers. To fill both these roles, a new type of fighter emerged. Extra endurance would be needed to maintain standing patrols and shadow bomber formations. This would also give the fighter a bomber escort capability. In the fighter direction role, a specialist wireless operator would be required and a rear gunner would be useful. Two or three crew members would therefore be needed. Two Hispano-Suiza HS.9 cannon would provide the firepower required and the fighter would use two of the new lightweight, low-powered engines Gnome-Rhône and Hispano-Suiza were developing; the latter, the HS 14AB, was a scaled-down HS 14AA. It was hoped that the plane would be no more than 20 per cent heavier than a single-seater and the Air Ministry were assured it could be just as manoeuvrable. It was an ambitious requirement. The new specification was released in October 1934.[23]

The advances in air defence technology led some to argue that perhaps France should rely more on fighters rather than bomber retaliation to protect French cities. Plenty of good reasons were put forward. A retaliatory strike on a prepared enemy would be unlikely to achieve as much success as the initial surprise attack. Operations in the First World War had demonstrated bombing enemy airfields achieved little. Airfields were difficult to locate and it was far too easy to disperse planes. With Paris, the third largest city in the world, twice as near the Franco-German frontier as the less densely populated German capital, France had far more to lose by escalating a bombing war. With the arrival of the cannon-armed fighter, it seemed the tide might finally have turned against the bomber. The fighter provided a much more direct means of defending cities and each victory gained meant not just the destruction of a bomber, but also the loss of its crew. Fighters were also much cheaper. Three Dewoitine D.500 fighters could be bought for the price of a single Bloch MB.200. Even a modest reduction in the proposed bomber force would enable the fighter arm to be doubled.[24]

The growing interest in air defence was a mixed blessing for the Army. There was a danger that in a war, limited fighter resources would be split between Army needs and defending cities. On the other hand, if the advocates of a more defensive air policy got their way, the Air Force would have far more fighters. Even if many of them were defending cities, provided these bomber interceptors were not too different to a tactical fighter, they would be available for use over the front. Short-range interceptors were of far more use to the Army than long-range bombers.

At this stage, however, the official line remained that the interests of France were best served by the existence of a powerful long-range bomber fleet. Precisely the same views prevailed in Britain and Germany at this time for broadly the same reasons. Politicians preferred large intimidating bomber fleets to bolster their confidence at the conference table. A strong fighter defence would not deter anyone. For the time being, there would be no expansion of the fighter force, but the issue was now on the agenda.

Early in 1936, the long-term prospects of the Air Force appeared brighter than they had for a long time. The conceptually flawed multi-seater, multi-purpose combat plane had been abandoned and the way cleared for a whole new generation of smaller, more specialised combat planes. If Denain's plans were implemented, by 1940 (the significance of the date would only became clear with hindsight), the French would have a far more flexible Air Force. The new, smaller, high-speed bombers would give France the capacity to strike at tactical or strategic targets. At the front, they would be supplemented by specialised ground-attack planes and possibly dive-bombers. High-speed reconnaissance aircraft would provide the Army with the tactical and strategic information they required. All tactical operations would be protected by an as yet undecided mix of single and two-seater fighter planes. On long-range missions, French bombers would be escorted by new twin-engined fighters. Cities in the rear would be protected by single and twin-engined interceptors. These would be guided to their targets by information provided by a network of ground stations, possibly making use of radar, and flying command posts. It was a bold vision, but to achieve it by 1940 as Denain had proposed, did not appear to be overly ambitious.[25]

6

Back to the Bomber

In January 1933, Adolf Hitler came to power and immediately left no one in any doubt about his intentions. Although the existence of the new German Luftwaffe would not be officially announced until March 1935, long before this, it was an open secret that the German aero-industry was expanding rapidly and military air units were being created. During the twenties, the potential German threat had caused enough alarm in France; now, the threat was very real and France had to start worrying about the quantity as well as the quality of its aircraft. During the twenties, the French had been building around 600 planes a month, but the Air Ministry's policy of investing in research had seen this drop to just 200 by 1934. This was scarcely likely to please French aircraft manufacturers, and Caquot soon became the target for some intense criticism. Some of it was justified. Caquot's desire to encourage innovation had resulted in some self-proclaimed inventors making a living out of some not very practicable ideas. When Denain took over at the Air Ministry at the beginning of 1934, Caquot was dismissed and his department was abolished. However, it was not just Caquot's emphasis on research that was limiting orders.

Plan I had been agreed in principle in the spring of 1933, but the shaky French economy meant any slight easing in international tension was used to justify delaying its introduction. It was July 1934 before any funds were released. Cot and Denain were also reluctant to waste the limited funds available on too many 1928 generation planes (the Breguet 413 and 414, the Amiot 140, and the Bloch MB.200) when the supposedly vastly superior 1933 BCR generation would soon be available. Germany's withdrawal from the Geneva disarmament talks and the League of Nations in the autumn of 1934 helped trigger limited orders, but by this time it was becoming clear that the much-vaunted BCR plane was a mistake and Denain was reluctant to waste too much money on them. Orders placed in 1934 did not even use up the limited funds that had been made available.[1, 2, 3]

Hitler's announcement in March 1935 that the Luftwaffe already existed was accompanied by commitments to create a large army and navy, but it was only the German Air Force that worried the French. It is easy now to underestimate the dread with which the bomber was viewed at that time. The possible use of chemical and bacteriological weapons against civilian targets on a vast scale led many to believe that any second world war would leave the planet much as future generations would imagine the consequences of a nuclear holocaust. In judging military strength, the number of bombs an air force could lift was all that mattered, and French intelligence estimated that the Germans were already capable of delivering more than twice the bomb load of the French. Even with the full implementation of Plan I, the gap could only widen. The relative proximity of Paris to the frontier made the French feel even more nervous. It was estimated that by April 1936, the Luftwaffe would be capable of dropping 1,450 tons of bombs on Paris in a single raid, while the French fleet would be able to carry just 245 tons to the German capital.[4] French politicians desperately needed their own Air Force to match the German threat. As it turned out, the threat to the French nation was not the long-range bomber. French survival in a future war would depend on whether her leaders could see beyond the apparently unimaginable horrors bombing would bring.

Denain was in no doubt that war with Germany was inevitable and might even break out before the end of 1935. Early in 1935, Denain proposed bringing forward the completion date of Plan I by one year to December 1935 and initiating a crash program to double the bomber fleet and bring Air Force strength up to 1,500 by October 1936. In fact, the Air Force was still at its pre-Plan I level of approximately around 1,500 planes with 1,200 based in France.[5] In effect, Denain was merely proposing that the personnel that were going to be freed by the reduction in strength of the reconnaissance and observation force should be used to form new bomber squadrons.

There was no formal approval for this plan, but the French government released some of the funds set aside for the second stage of Plan I. Denain immediately used these, together with those he had held back from the first stage, to order 300 more planes, with 200 of these (all Bloch MB.200 and Potez 54 bombers) to be delivered before the end of 1935. Still dissatisfied, he got approval to order another 520 aircraft, even though this involved funding Parliament had not yet agreed to. Most of these were also supposed to be delivered before the end of 1935.[6] The new contracts meant that French factories would be expected to produce over 1,000 machines during the course of 1935. Such a rapid increase in production was not realistic, although it was perhaps the encouragement the industry needed to expand and it was precisely the sort of stimulus the German aircraft industry was getting.

It was a gamble. Parliamentary approval was far from assured and there were soon objections. The Parliamentary Air Commission, headed by Cot, did not believe the increase in production was sustainable. If war broke out soon, it might well be the right decision, but if there was no war, France would not be able to maintain this level of production, and the industry would be forced to contract once more. In May 1935, France signed a pact with the Soviet Union, and this seemed to suggest rearmament was not so urgent. The Prime Minister, Pierre Laval, decided to suspend the proposed increase and Laval took it upon himself to decide when and how much extra resources should be released for the Air Force. The funds eventually made available did not even cover the initial batch of supplementary orders. Many contracts could not be confirmed, delivery schedules were put back and some orders had to be cancelled altogether. The critics had been proved right, but it was very much a self-fulfilling prophecy. The lack of long-term planning and consistency in government policy was destroying what little confidence remained within the industry.[7]

In January 1936, Laval was forced to resign and a caretaker government was formed under Albert Sarraut while the country prepared for a summer general election. Marcel Déat was given temporary control of the Air Ministry. It was this caretaker administration that would guide France through her first major confrontation with Hitler's Germany. As Denain had feared, this would occur far sooner than most had anticipated. For some time, it had been clear that Hitler planned to move military forces into the demilitarised Rhineland; under the terms of the Treaties of Versailles and Locarno, France would be perfectly entitled to oppose any reoccupation with military force. However, France would be on her own. Britain saw no reason why, eighteen years after her defeat in the First World War, Germany should not have the right to move her own military forces where she wished within her own frontiers.

The French government knew that on land and at sea, France was far stronger. In fact, the politicians grossly underestimated how much stronger. In the air, the Air Ministry correctly believed French designs were far superior, thanks largely to their excellent supercharged engines. They were also correct to believe that the Bloch MB.200 was superior to the Junkers Ju 52 and Dornier Do 23. The new Amiot 143, which had started to arrive in the summer of 1935, increased the French advantage and the Bloch MB.210 and Farman F.221, which were both about to enter service, were, in terms of lifting capacity at least, vastly superior to anything the Germans possessed.[8] The *multi-place de combat* may have lacked development potential and may have been leading French aircraft design down a dangerous technical and tactical cul-de-sac, but in 1936, the bombers that emerged from the concept were, by the standards of the day, fast and well-armed.

Tactically, the French did not believe they had too much to fear. The French believed their Mureaux reconnaissance planes were broadly equivalent to the German Heinkel He 45 and 46, the Dewoitine D.500 and D.501 to be the equal of the Heinkel He 51. On both counts, they were being unduly pessimistic; the French planes were far superior, especially at altitude.[9] Numerically, however, the French were convinced that the Luftwaffe had an overwhelming advantage in long-range bombers. Again, the French were overestimating the threat but the fear that the Germans could drop more bombs on France than the French could drop on Germany would dominate the debate about whether to oppose the reoccupation of the Rhineland.

Sarraut ordered Gamelin to prepare for possible military intervention but the plan the Army commander came up with was not impressive. Gamelin explained that the French Army was trained and equipped for a purely defensive war and he could only contemplate a very limited advance. Gamelin was certain that the Germans would resist fiercely and the peacetime French Army simply lacked the strength to defeat the German forces. Full mobilisation would have to be ordered and war declared. French cities would then be exposed to German bombing attacks. The front line would probably stabilise and stalemate would follow, as in the First World War. Gamelin insisted only the Air Force would be capable of taking any decisive action.[10] This was of course what Cot had always claimed. Gamelin must have known that the Air Force was not going to be used like this. For all Cot's talk, it was unthinkable that France would respond to German bands marching into their own Rhineland by bombing German cities.

Gamelin had also focused Sarraut's mind on what was the crux of the matter. French cities were vulnerable to air attack and France did not have as many bombers as Germany. Gamelin was confident that his Army, and even his tactical air force units, were capable of dealing with the Germans on the ground. However, neither Gamelin, Déat, nor Pujo (the new Air Force commander) had any confidence in the ability of the French bomber fleet to deter or retaliate for attacks on French cities. They all warned Sarraut that if the intervention of the French Army resulted in war and the Luftwaffe launched terror raids on French cities, the civilian casualties would be extremely high. With the political and social unrest in France at that time, such attacks might even lead to the disintegration of the Third Republic. Sarraut was not going to risk such a catastrophe over the Rhineland.

For the politicians, it was a reminder of how important it was to have an effective long-range bomber force. The French had spent nearly twenty years trying to ensure that never again would they suffer the sense of inferiority and helplessness they had experienced in the First World War. If there was one matter the politicians, Army, and Air Force had been able to agree on, it was the need for an effective bomber deterrent. The Rhineland crisis underlined the need for a bomber fleet that could reassure and bolster the political leadership of a nation in a moment of crisis. After twenty years preparing for this moment, the French bomber fleet had failed to provide the required reassurance.

The irony was that Hitler had no intention of using his bombers aggressively. Like the French, he only wanted bombers to deter attack. He too feared a knockout blow might topple his regime. Hitler could no more afford to initiate a Douhet style aerial war than the French. In the event of war, the initial targets for German bombers would have been French airfields. Targets in civilian areas would only have been bombed as reprisals.[11] The priority Hitler attached to the expansion of his deterrent bomber fleet left the fighter and reconnaissance forces extremely weak. The 100 odd D.500 and D.501 fighters available to the French would have had little difficulty in establishing a degree of superiority over the battlefield. If Hitler had not won the war of bluff with his bombers, he would have lost the real war that would have followed.

The Rhineland crisis was, in fact, the last opportunity for the French to oppose Hitler with a clear advantage in air power. Soon, German pilots would be acquiring combat skills in the skies over Spain and French intelligence would be collecting information on a new generation of combat planes: the Bf 109 fighter, Ju 87 dive-bomber, and the He 111 and Do 17 medium bombers. The new bombers carried far fewer bombs than the Ju 52, but they were far faster; however, the significance of this was not appreciated. The new bombers were far more suitable for supporting an advancing army than terrifying a nation.

The Rhineland crisis came as a great shock to the French nation. With little warning, France had been pushed to the brink of war. French superiority on land and at sea had counted for nothing because of her apparent inferiority in long-range bombers. Douhet had almost been proved right, but it was not independent bombing that had rendered armies and navies superfluous; just the threat of the bomber was enough to ensure the French Army did not intervene.

In the wake of the Rhineland crisis, immediate steps were taken to raise the state of readiness of the existing bomber fleet. All bomber groups were issued with the targets they should attack in the first twenty-four hours of war. Daylight attacks at 6,000 metres would strike targets 50 miles inside German territory; dusk attacks at 1,200 metres would hit targets up to 100 miles inside enemy air space and night attacks would strike further afield. Bombing operations against tactical targets were not ruled out, but the Air Force was now far too pre-occupied with a Douhetian style *bataille aérienne* to worry too much about what these might comprise.[12]

In May 1936, the Popular Front came to power and Pierre Cot returned to the Air Ministry. Denain's 1,500 plan was revived and approved as Plan II. However, Cot planned a far more radical reorganisation. The aim of the new plan was to increase the bomb tonnage the bomber fleet could carry to Berlin to 850 tons by 1939. To maximise available resources, the majority of squadrons would be centralised in two corps. The Light Defence Corps would be used to deal with enemy raids on French cities or to protect the French Army, as required. There would also be ten regional fighter squadrons permanently defending targets in the rear. All reconnaissance and observation units would join the bomber squadrons in the Heavy Defence Corps, which would be responsible for delivering the retaliatory strike. There was no question of these being multi-purpose squadrons. They would be re-equipped with bombers like the Bloch MB.200, the Bloch MB.210 and the Amiot 143. Lest there be any doubt about their new role, all reconnaissance and observation units in France would be renamed *groupes de bombardment*. At a stroke, this would increase the planned bomber fleet from twelve to thirty-six groups. Another ten observation groups in North Africa and Syria would also be converted into bomber formations. More groups would then be created to bring the French striking force up to sixty groups with 720 machines by 1939.[13]

To replace the Army's reconnaissance and observation groups, the twenty reservist *Centres Aériens Régionaux*, established under Plan I, would be mobilised to form twenty-six short-range observation squadrons, with a further seventeen created by the end of 1937. However, each group would have just six reconnaissance planes and three autogyros.[14] Even when all the new units had been created, the force would still be far smaller than the reconnaissance and observation squadrons they were replacing. If war were to break out before the new units were formed, the Army would be left without any tactical reconnaissance units whatsoever under its command. The Army was being asked to sacrifice its entire air reconnaissance capability in order to create an instant bomber force. As a concession to the Army, Cot initially proposed to use specialist reconnaissance planes (at this stage still an ill-defined Potez 63 A3) in ten of his 'heavy' squadrons, but the first of these would not be created until the summer of 1939 and later versions of the plan had some of these equipped with four-seater Bloch MB.131 reconnaissance bombers. In essence, Plan II was essentially Plan I with the reservist observation squadrons mobilised in peacetime and no pretence that the regular reconnaissance and observation squadrons would be used for anything other than long-range bombing.

In theory, Cot's proposals made it possible to concentrate virtually the entire Air Force for either a Douhetian style strategic struggle, or direct support of the army in a conventional land battle. In practice, Cot was clearly thinking primarily in terms of the former. He emphasised once again how only the bomber could provide the offensive aggressive element in an otherwise defensive French strategy. He enthusiastically described grandiose schemes whereby French bombers operating from bases not just in France but also Belgium, the Netherlands, Czechoslovakia, Poland, Yugoslavia, Romania, and even Switzerland would ensure the destruction of the German Air Force on the ground and elimination of key industrial targets, while the French Army defended the frontier.[15] Cot's ideas on how the Air Force should be employed had changed little during his enforced absence from the Air Ministry.

Cot's return had an immediate effect on Air Force development programmes. It was the end of many of the smaller, more specialised planes, Denain had been suggesting. Cot replaced the 480 km/hr three-seater bomber by a slightly slower four-seater with greater range and bomb load. The two-seater fighter also went. This had almost become a barometer of Air Force thinking. Its presence in French development programmes meant the focus was on developing tactical air power. Its absence suggested an independent strategy prevailed. Cot's September 1936 program made no mention of the type. Denain's three-seater tactical reconnaissance bomber was another plane to disappear. The proposed experimental ground-attack unit at Reims was never set up, the development of a specialised ground-attack plane was abandoned completely and the proposed dive-bomber was shelved. The only survivors of Denain's 1935 proposal were the high-speed three-seat reconnaissance plane (Potez 63 A3) and the twin-engined, three-seater observation plane (*avion de travail*).[16]

Gamelin was horrified by the re-emergence of ideas he thought he had seen the last of. The Army had lost control of all their remaining fighter, reconnaissance, and observation forces, and would be relying on the whim of an air force commander to provide the Army with any air support.[17] In the short term, Cot got his way. Cot did not have the authority to impose his new organisation on air units under Army or Navy control, but the apparent weakness of the Air Force in the Rhineland crisis had left such a deep impression on French politicians that the government simply ignored Army objections and approved Cot's proposals. A decree dated 3 September 1936 created Cot's two aerial corps. A few days later, the French cabinet agreed to Plan II and the following month, it was formally approved by the French parliament. The Army had been hoist with its own petard. It had been Gamelin that had used the frightening spectre of uncontrolled aerial warfare to restrain the politicians from involving the Army in attempts to oppose the Rhineland re-occupation. Now, the Army was powerless to prevent the Air Force from being almost exclusively prepared for such a Douhetian-style *lutte aérienne*.

The Army was furious by the way the reorganisation of the Air Force had been hustled through without their approval. The CPDN meeting on 17 December 1936 provided Gamelin and his deputy, General Georges, with an opportunity to vent their dismay. There was no Army objection to the shelving of Air Force plans to form more tactically orientated bomber units. If the Army had any concerns about the loss of bomber support, they were insignificant compared to the implications of losing their reconnaissance fleet and fighter cover. Georges pointed out that it might make sense to centralise fighter resources if the task was the same but intercepting mass bomber formations and establishing air superiority over the front required different tactics and equipment. Similarly, crews of the long-range reconnaissance squadrons would also find themselves unprepared for the kind of mission the Army would require of them. They insisted that the Army had to retain control of at least one fighter and one reconnaissance group per army, with two strategic reconnaissance groups available to the High Command. It was also time to make a stand on fighter strength. The continuing contraction of the fighter force had gone far enough. It was time to reverse the trend. Using some of the arguments put forward the year before by some within the Air Ministry, Georges pointed out that the arrival of cannon-armed fighters had transformed the prospects for the defence. Shooting down bombers attacking French cities made more sense than building expensive bomber fleets to retaliate. Crucially, he pointed out that if fighters were now required for rear defence and winning air superiority over the front, this alone meant far more fighters would be needed.[18] The fighter lobby was gaining momentum.

Convinced the government was still firmly on his side, Cot refused to even consider relinquishing the control the September decree had given him. On the question of an expanded fighter force, he was quite willing to spend any increase in the percentage of the military budget assigned the Air Force on fighter units.[19] In effect, Cot was suggesting the Army pay for the fighters they wanted out of their own pocket. On the issue of control, Georges and Gamelin would only accept Cot's reorganisation as a peacetime arrangement. Once war had broken out, fighter and reconnaissance squadrons would have to return to Army control. Unfortunately for Cot, memories of the Rhineland crisis were already fading fast, and with it the political will to support him. Cot was forced to accept this compromise.

Meanwhile, Cot had set about ordering the aircraft he felt the Air Force needed for its strategic role. Most of the ex-reconnaissance and observation groups were equipped with Potez 25, Breguet 19, and Breguet 27 single-engined planes. They were bomber groups in name only. As a first step, these two-seaters would be replaced with Potez 540s and Bloch MB.200s, with the Amiot 143 and Bloch MB.210 to follow. With its impressive ability to carry more than 4,000 lb of bombs, the Bloch MB.210 seemed the best and most immediate way of increasing the bomb load the Air Force could lift, but the basic design was being stretched too far. With its bulky nose turret and slab-sided fuselage, it retained the unattractive lines of its predecessor, and its retractable turrets and undercarriage only gave it a slight performance advantage over the Amiot 143. It was very much a product of the *multiplace de combat* era. While there was little to choose, in terms of performance, between the Bloch MB.210 and early versions of the Heinkel 111 bomber, the German machine had the potential to take advantage of more powerful engines as they became available. The Bloch MB.210 was the end of an era in French bomber design. Its Mistral Major engines were barely capable of dragging its bulky frame into the air. Accidents were common and the plane only became reasonably safe to fly when more robust Gnome-Rhône GR 14N-10 motors became available in 1937.

By the beginning of 1937, the conversion of the ex-reconnaissance and observation groups was well underway. Cot had installed the loyal General Philippe Féquant as Air Force commander. Even previously passionate advocates of tactical air support such as Armengaud and Jauneaud, now Cot's top adviser, remained firmly under the spell of the seemingly all conquering long-range bomber. The all-consuming desire to match German bomb loads was sending the French Air Force down the wrong path. There was no place for the tactical bomber in the French Air Force of the future. Then, in the first few months of 1937, the arrival of the first intelligence reports on the fighting in the Spanish Civil War sparked a rethink. Suddenly, the tactical uses of air power were back on the agenda.

The initial impetus for change would come from Féquant's chief of staff, General Aubé. A summary of the main features of the initial fighting in Spain, circulated within the Air Ministry in mid-January 1937, described how Republican assault planes had been very effective attacking Nationalist artillery positions and airfields. Planes used included low-performance Polikarpov R-5 two-seater reconnaissance biplanes. The report noted how remarkably similar to the French Potez 25 these were.[20] Aubé was impressed and he took it upon himself to reactivate the ground-attack programme Denain had ordered in 1935. The plan to set up an experimental unit at Reims had never been formally abandoned; it had simply been forgotten. On 27 January, Aubé wrote to the commander of the Reims unit, explaining, rather unconvincingly, that the Mureaux planes that were supposed to have arrived the previous April had been held up by a shortage of airscrews, and promised their immediate delivery. That same day Aubé ordered two Mureaux 117s to be dispatched to the unit. He also sent Cot a note, drawing the Air Minister's attention to the reports coming in from Spain.[21]

At the beginning of February, Aubé took the process a step further by ordering the immediate development of a manoeuvrable, armoured, high-speed assault plane. The plane was to be a twin-engined design capable of flying at low level on just one engine. Aircraft meeting the October 1936 twin-engined, lightweight fighter programme, an update of the 1934 programme, seemed to offer a likely basis for such a plane. However, larger three-seater and smaller single-seater attack planes might also be required and trials took place with Dewoitine D.500 and D.501 single-seater fighters as well as two-seater

Potez 25. Even 190 mph Caudron Simoun liaison planes were considered. Trials were also ordered to decide on the armour the future specialist assault plane would need.[22] Cannon would be an important part of the assault plane's offensive capability. With the Hispano-Suiza HS.9, the French possessed the most penetrative 20 mm cannon in the world and its successor, the HS 404, with twice the rate of fire, was about to enter production. Trials conducted in April 1937 demonstrated that these could be useful weapons against ground targets, including lightly armoured tanks.[23]

Quite by chance, at around this time the commanders of the bomber units were once again airing their views on the inadequacies of the aircraft available to them. In a report dispatched in February 1937, they again made it quite clear that many of the targets outlined in the various bomber plans would be impossible to hit from the sort of altitude medium bombers would be operating at. A more specialist low-level attack plane was needed.[24] By this time, reports were coming in of the fighting taking place around Guadalajara in March 1937, where ground-attack planes proved particularly effective against troops on the move and had seriously affected enemy morale. The report also noted many European countries were now developing specialist ground-attack planes.[25]

A detailed specification was hastily drawn up outlining the form such a plane should take. A two-seater with a top speed of 520 km/hr (323 mph) was called for. The aircraft was to have 150 kg of armour and be capable of attacking targets with cannon and 400 kg of bombs. Again, the French opted for the greater security two engines could provide, which meant it would be relatively large, but it was an approach that was popular in many countries at the time. The new programme was officially approved by Cot on 30 April and released to French manufacturers.[26]

It was not long before Armengaud and Jauneaud were once more advocating the direct intervention of aircraft on the battlefield. The new Air Ministry attitude was spelt out in an 'Instruction' issued in Cot's name in May 1937. In the introduction Féquant spoke of the growing importance of ground-attack aircraft and the need to adapt aerial operations to the needs of mechanised and armoured forces. The main text was largely the work of Jauneaud. Once more, Cot's top adviser was enthusiastically describing how ground-attack aircraft could be used to halt advancing armoured formations.[27]

Even Cot enthused over this new role for aviation. In September 1937, in a remarkable letter to Edouard Daladier, the War Minister, Cot explained that a very marked evolution had taken place in the way air power could be used. Cot was now extremely critical of Air Force policy in recent years, describing how the ill-fated theories of Douhet had taken root in 1934 and 1935, which happened to be the years he was out of office. The Douhetian doctrine had been accepted, he went on, because of superficial assessments of imported ideas and the vivid imagination of Douhet's supporters. He now admitted that the preparation of the vast majority of Air Force units for independent aerial warfare outlined in his July 1936 Instruction was a risky policy. Cot was not suggesting that France abandon the long-range bomber as a deterrent, but he did concede that in future, more account would have to be taken of how bombers could be used tactically.[28]

It was the latest twist in the long and chequered history of French battlefield close air support. Direct air support had been used successfully towards the end of the First World War and later in colonial conflicts without ever becoming accepted as a normal Air Force role. The development of specialist assault planes had been ordered in 1918, only to be abandoned four years later. In 1935, Denain had revived the idea only for it to be blown away by the Rhineland crisis. Now, Cot had been forced to relearn the lessons of his predecessor. Once again, bombing in direct support of ground forces was firmly back in favour, but this time, it was back to stay. There were still many problems to overcome, not the least of which was persuading the Army that it needed direct air support and finding room for these units within the existing framework of the Air Force. However, as far as the Air Ministry was concerned, bomber support on the battlefield now had a permanent place in their plans.

Another valuable year had been lost, but even in 1937, the French had not yet slipped behind their enemy across the Rhine. The German Army had been as surprised as anyone else by the success of close air support in Spain. In April, the same month that Cot approved the French armoured assault plane programme, the Germans issued a remarkably similar specification which would eventually lead to the twin-engined, armoured Henschel HS 129 assault plane. However, rather than wait for the development of a new plane, the Germans looked to what they already had. Planes like the Henschel Hs 123 biplane fighter, Ju 87 dive-bomber, and Do 17 light bomber were drafted in as stopgaps. Units equipped with these, with fighters to protect them, would go to form Richthofen's specialist army support VIII Corps, a formation remarkably similar to the French Air Division of the First World War. The French needed to move just as quickly.

There were options open to the French. The French were aware that the Polikarpov R-5 the Republicans were using in Spain was very similar to the obsolescent Potez 25. The success of the Russian plane was partly responsible for Germany adapting the obsolete Hs 123 fighter for the ground-attack role. The Luftwaffe would still be using this plane for ground-attack in the 1940 French campaign. Aubé thought about using the Potez 25 but did not believe that such drastic solutions were called for. The Potez biplane was single-engined, slow and old. France was not at war yet and had time to come up with something better. Two planes—the Bloch MB.170 and the Potez 63—seemed to offer more promise.

The origins of the Bloch 170 are a little obscure. The original design may have been an early response to the short-lived June 1936 high-speed, three-seater bomber programme. The plane was, in effect, the smallest airframe that could be built around two of the most powerful engines available to the French, an approach that always has a good chance of producing a successful plane. Nine pre-production Bloch 170s were ordered in 1937, but the first prototype was not expected to get into the air until the following year. The Potez 63 twin-engined fighter, on the other hand, was flying and a light bomber variant had flown as early as January 1937. With its low-powered engines and light airframe, it was a very different plane to the Bloch 170. Its lightweight origins did not perhaps provide the ideal starting point for a rugged assault bomber but by November 1937, Potez had a mock-up of the Potez 639 armoured version ready for inspection.[29] The plane seemed to provide a quick way of establishing a ground-attack force and in October 1937, Potez were told to begin preparing for the production of sixty-five of the assault version.[30]

None of this would be any use if the Army did not want close support and the more static French strategy was, the weaker the case for air intervention on the battlefield. However, Army strategy was changing. The Rhineland crisis had required rapid movement and the *post-mortem* that followed the occupation highlighted the French Army's lack of mobility. With German forces now up against the Maginot Line, the need for manoeuvre seemed to have disappeared, but then, in September 1936, Belgium declared its neutrality in any Franco-German conflict. If Germany attacked France through Belgium, the French Army would have to advance rapidly if it was to come to her neighbour's aid and, perhaps more importantly, fight the war on Belgian rather than French soil. Movement was back on the Army agenda, and with it, more opportunities for air forces to intervene.

A war of manoeuvre meant tanks would be even more important and the way the German Army was developing panzer divisions did not go unnoticed in France. In October 1936, Gamelin pointed out that the French Army needed similar units to lead French assaults and to counterattack enemy armoured units.[31] The first tentative steps were taken towards the creation of heavy armoured divisions (DCR: *Division cuirassée de réserve*) to supplement the light mechanised divisions (DLM) that were already forming.[32] The 1936 Army tactical manual discussed the use of tanks in mobile operations and even mentioned the possibility of using ground-attack planes to support them. These, it suggested, might be more effective than artillery against targets on the move. However, the vulnerability of low-flying planes was again seen as a problem and the assault plane could never entirely substitute for artillery. Nevertheless, when, in April 1937, the Air Ministry told Gamelin about their plans to develop specialised assault planes, the Army chief was interested.

They might be very useful attacking troops and armoured vehicles. He thought that something more powerful than 20-mm cannon might be needed against heavily armoured tanks, but he was keen for the idea to be investigated.[33]

The evidence from Spain continued to mount. The French military *attaché* in Spain in a report to Daladier explained how the common factor in every major breakthrough achieved by either side had been the large-scale intervention of ground-attack planes on the battlefield. Significantly, he noted that it was not so much the physical damage air attack caused but the demoralising effect these attacks were having on the infantry that was proving so decisive. The report emphasised how even combat hardened troops had been seriously shaken by air attack.[34] Three years later, at Sedan, the French would discover the effectiveness of air attack on less experienced soldiers.

The report went on to say that if sufficient aircraft were employed, the defences could be swamped and if the air attacks were followed by an immediate ground assault, then the defending forces often found themselves in serious difficulty. The report also described how aviation was being used to apply immediate pressure to new defensive lines the retreating forces were attempting to establish. Attacking forces were able to continue to advance without having to wait for supporting artillery to be moved up. The French *attaché* might have been describing the German drive to the Meuse and beyond in 1940.[35]

Yet there was still enough in the report to suggest no major rethink was required. The report also stressed that if the attacking air force encountered strong opposition in the air, then the effect of the bombing was seriously reduced.[36] Others noted the relative weakness of the reconnaissance forces available to both sides in Spain. Any successes achieved on the ground were, it was argued, more the result of achieving surprise than the influence of ground-attack aircraft. With an adequate fleet of reconnaissance planes to provide warning and a powerful fighter arm to protect them, the French would have nothing to fear from the tactics used in Spain. It was the reconnaissance and fighter arms of the Air Force, the Army insisted, that needed strengthening.

Also, in the final analysis, air support on the battlefield had not resulted in decisive victories. Even when the action of assault planes had helped to rupture the enemy's defences, tanks had not been able to exploit these breakthroughs.[37] As the fighting in Spain entered its second year, there was little evidence that tanks or aircraft, or a combination of both, could result in the rapid advances some had predicted. Rather than pour resources into a ground-attack force that might retrieve the situation once a breakthrough had been achieved, it seemed better to have a powerful fighter and reconnaissance arm to ensure a breakthrough was not achieved in the first place. Instead of being viewed as another useful option, the Army tended to see ground-attack forces as a distraction from the key task of creating adequate fighter and reconnaissance forces.

The Army's lukewarm response to ground-attack planes did not delay their development; for some time, the Army had very little say in the type of equipment developed for the Air Force. The problem for the Air Ministry was where to put squadrons equipped with these planes. They would not have the range or the bomb load to contribute anything to the strategic bomber force. Equipping bomber squadrons with these planes would make it impossible for the Air Force to achieve the 850-target bomb tonnage laid down by the CPDN. The Army was battling to retain its reconnaissance force and was certainly not going to allow the ground-attack planes to water down the quality of what might be available. Again, the only solution seemed to be a readjustment of the military budgets of the two services. Since these assault units would only benefit the Army, it seemed reasonable that they should provide the funds required to form the new units.[38] It was a somewhat optimistic solution. Given that the Army had refused to pay for the fighter forces it wanted, it was hardly likely to pay for a ground-attack force it did not feel it needed. For the time being, no detailed plans could be drawn up for how many and which units would eventually receive the new assault planes.

The Army was quite correct in believing that knowing what the enemy is doing is crucial, but by allowing this need to dominate their air policy, they were ignoring other important ways of using air power. The failure to see the potential of battlefield air support meant that all planning was based on the speed artillery could move. The French Army was denying itself a valuable asset and limiting its ability to advance rapidly. Even more seriously, French commanders believed that an enemy would be similarly restricted.

7

Chaos Reigns

While the Army and Air Force pondered the lessons of the fighting in Spain, Cot was trying to replace the planes that were the products of the now discredited multi-purpose, multi-seater concept. The 1933 and 1934 specifications had both required the development of bombers capable of achieving 400 km/hr, which the Air Ministry believed ought to be possible with existing engines. The Air Ministry had expected the first prototypes to be undergoing trials by the summer of 1936 and the planes to enter production in 1937.

The 1933 programme had been entirely speculative and even a successful design might not be ordered, so it was hardly surprising that only two companies (Amiot and Bernard) put forward proposals. The 1934 four-seater bomber specification was supposed to be a very different matter. The Air Force planned to re-equip virtually the entire bomber fleet with the successful entry. However, it seems the Air Ministry failed to convey to manufacturers how lucrative the final contracts could be. Only four companies put forward proposals: Dewoitine, Latécoère, Romano (CAER), and Lioré et Olivier. Of these, only Lioré et Olivier had ever produced a successful long-range bomber. The other traditional producers of bombers—Farman, Amiot, Breguet, and Bloch—were reluctant to abandon the BCR planes they had put so much effort into, and for which they could still expect lucrative stopgap orders.

In the summer of 1936, when the B4 bomber official trials were supposed to be taking place, the only contender on which any serious progress had been made was the Lioré et Olivier LeO 45, and even this had not got very far. When the Air Ministry had released the 1934 specification, the Lioré et Olivier company was still recovering from the shock of discovering that the previously officially favoured LeO 206 and the more advanced LeO 208 had been overtaken by the monoplane Bloch MB.200, and their biplanes were no longer needed. The company was not involved in the BCR programme and suddenly had no major projects capable of winning government contracts. The 1934 bomber programme was the perfect opportunity for the company to re-establish its credentials as a leading manufacturer of bombers. The company now planned to turn the tables on their rivals by designing a machine that would make planes like the Bloch MB.200 look as outdated as the LeO 206. A new design team was assembled under the dynamic M. Mercier and the drawings for an ultra-modern bomber were rapidly completed; the prototype was soon taking shape in the company workshops.

There could be no doubting the graceful lines of the new bomber. It was in every respect the antithesis of all previous French bomber design. The Air Ministry preference for radial engines ruled out the excellent Hispano-Suiza HS 12Y-31. The company could have used the existing 900-hp 14K Mistral Major, but they, and indeed the Air Ministry, preferred the more advanced 1,000-hp HS 14AA radial Hispano-Suiza were developing. By adopting an untried motor, Lioré et Olivier were taking a chance, but no more of a chance than Bloch had taken with the Gnome-Rhône Mistral Major. Everyone seemed confident there would be no major problems with the engine. A distinguished company such as Hispano-Suiza could surely be expected to sort out any teething problems that might occur. The 400 km/hr target speed could have been achieved with the tried and tested Gnome-Rhône 14K but the prospect of even higher speeds with the HS 14AA was too tempting. The design was moving away from the original idea of the speedy development of a 400 km/hr bomber using existing technology.

At one point, it looked like the June 1936 specification for a smaller three-seater 480 km/hr (300 mph) bomber would replace the Lioré et Oliver bomber. When this was released, the company was told their LeO 45 would now only be needed for the 1937 element of the re-equipment plan, with the three-seater bomber taking over from 1938.[1] However, this was dropped when Cot returned with a new specification for a larger plane, requiring space for four crew members, a greater lifting capacity, and a slightly reduced top speed of 470 km/hr (292 mph).[2] This was broadly what Lioré et Olivier were already building to meet the 1934 requirement. At this point, Breguet and Bloch joined the race, but Lioré et Olivier were well ahead. Their decision to go for a design well in advance of the original 1934 programme had apparently paid off.

The LeO 45 was aerodynamically advanced but structurally very complicated. It took nearly two years to construct the first prototype, which did not bode well for plans to mass produce the plane. The retractable dorsal and ventral cannon turrets proved too ambitious. The ventral turret was kept, but would just have a machine gun. The dorsal turret was dropped and a cannon on a mount with limited traverse would cover the rear instead. It was argued that the bomber would be so fast, anything other than attack from the rear would be impossible. On 16 January 1937, the prototype was finally wheeled out for its first flight. Within minutes of take-off, the engines started overheating and the plane was demonstrating an unhealthy lack of stability.

The pilot immediately landed.[3] It was not an auspicious start. Larger vertical tail surfaces would help improve stability but the problems with the engines would prove to be far more difficult to solve.

With a top speed of 465 km/hr (290 mph), the bomber was some 80 mph faster than the Bloch MB.210 when the engines were working properly. This, unfortunately, was not very often. Trials continued, but the troublesome engines needed to be constantly replaced. For Lioré et Olivier, there was no turning back now. The plane was too heavy for the Gnome-Rhône 14K to haul through the air. On 29 November, Cot ordered twenty LeO 45s, which would at least give the company the opportunity to prepare for production. Seven days later, both engines failed simultaneously and only the skill of the pilot enabled him to land the prototype undamaged in a field.[4] Until the problems with the motors could be resolved, there was no chance of the plane going into production.

There was always the 1933 'reprisal bomber' programme to fall back on. The first prototypes were supposed to begin trials before the end of 1935. The speculative nature of the specification was apparent in the rather strange single-engined Bernard proposal, but the rival Amiot E7 was a much more practicable proposition. It was essentially a more refined version of the Amiot 144 BCR plane. The ventral step of the Amiot 144 had gone and a more efficient high aspect ratio wing was grafted on. The plane still had a nose turret, but rear defence was provided by simple gun mountings. With two Gnome-Rhône 14K Mistral Majors, the plane was expected to achieve 410 km/hr (256 mph). Ironically, the speculative 1933 programme had delivered what the 1934 programme had been supposed to achieve. There was perhaps already a good case for at least ordering a prototype, but with the LeO 45 promising far higher speeds, there seemed no need.

Amiot continued to refine the design. A more aerodynamic circular fuselage was introduced and, in line with the thinking behind the 1934 specification, the nose turret was dropped. During the course of 1935, a new design, the Amiot 340 BR3, gradually took shape. The plane was aerodynamically even more advanced than the LeO 45, with the graceful lines of the fuselage broken only by the raised cockpit. It was a much simpler design than the LeO 45. There were no turrets and defensive armament was limited to single machine guns on simple mountings in the nose, ventral and dorsal positions. However, this helped keep weight down, which meant existing proven power plants were good enough. Amiot believed 470 km/hr was possible with either the HS 12Y-31 or GR 14K. The plane was still a three-seater, as required by the original 1933 specification, but when the Air Ministry set out their requirements for a three-seater 480 km/hr (300 mph) bomber early in 1936, it seemed Amiot already had a solution. A full-scale mock-up was inspected in March 1936 and a prototype ordered. Even when Cot dropped the three-seater requirement, the Amiot still seemed well-placed to meet the new four-seater bomber requirement.[5]

Unfortunately, relations between Felix Amiot and the Ministry were not good. Amiot's company had been nationalised and he was in dispute over the compensation. Amiot put forward four-seater versions, but the Air Ministry showed no interest and the three-seater went ahead at a leisurely pace. The prototype was apparently completed in February 1937 but there was then a wrangle over the engines, with Amiot wanting to use the more reliable Gnome-Rhône radials rather than the untrustworthy Hispano-Suiza radials that the Air Ministry wanted all bombers to use. It was June before he was allowed to fit Gnome-Rhône engines, and it was another six months before the prototype took to the air.

Some of the delay might have been caused by the Air Ministry asking Amiot to concentrate on the Amiot 370 racer version for the 1937 Istres–Damascus–Paris air race. For this, Amiot was able to use the HS 12Y-31 and provided an idea of what would have been possible had the Air Ministry not insisted on air-cooled radials. The racer had the same wing as the A.340 but possessed an even more refined fuselage. The raised cockpit was eliminated and the two crew members located within the fuselage itself, rather like later versions of the Heinkel He 111. The rear crew position was deleted and a fuel tank replaced the bomb bay and crew communication passage. With a top speed of 475 km/hr, the French press were soon hailing it as a new 'wonder bomber' and Amiot did propose some militarised versions of the racer, but once again the Air Ministry were not interested.[6] The Air Ministry seemed convinced the problems with their preferred LeO 45 would eventually be resolved. The Amiot 340 prototype, powered by Gnome-Rhône radials, finally flew on 6 December, coincidentally, the very day the LeO 45 force-landed after both of its Hispano-Suiza radials failed.

The only other bombers Cot could order in 1937 were planes generated by the BCR requirement. Designers had been asked to consider how these might be made more streamlined, but it was difficult to do much with designs built around bulky turrets. The Breguet 460 M4 became the Breguet 462 B4, but it was obviously just a design that used to have a nose turret. The plane demonstrated that the 1934 report had been correct in believing that with some redesign 400 km/hr was possible and the Breguet 462 became the first French bomber to achieve this speed. A 250-mph bomber entering production early in 1937 might have been useful, but it was not ordered. The Air Ministry decided another revamped BCR plane was more promising. The Amiot 143 with a retractable undercarriage and more refined wing became the 350 km/hr Amiot 144. A small number were ordered, with deliveries due to begin in May 1937, but then it was decided the 50 km/hr speed advantage over its predecessor was not worth it and more Amiot 143 were ordered instead.

Marcel Bloch had undertaken a complete redesign of his Bloch MB.130 M4 to produce the Bloch MB.131 RB4. The result certainly looked more modern.

Following the success of the Bloch MB.200, the Air Ministry felt confident enough to convert the order for forty Bloch MB.130 into one for the Bloch MB.131 before the prototype had even flown. The new bomber took to the air in August 1936 and eventually managed a respectable 390 km/hr (242 mph). In 1937, Cot increased orders to over 100. Some of these were to be powered by the Hispano-Suiza 14AA radial (Bloch MB.132), which pushed speed up to 435 km/hr (270 mph), but with the problems this engine was encountering, this was scarcely an option to be relied on. Indeed, with Bloch prototypes suffering from excessive vibration at high speeds, there had to be doubts about any version of the plane being a success. Despite the problems, production of the plane went ahead, with first deliveries expected in 1938.[7]

There was one other option: the light bomber version of the Potez 63 fighter. This was a reasonable equivalent to the high-speed bombers, like the Blenheim, Dornier 17, and Tupolev SB-2, that other countries had produced in the mid-thirties while French designers had been sidetracked by the BCR plane. With a speed of 273 mph, the Potez 633 was as fast as any bomber in the world and had already won an order from the Romanian government. There were already plans to build the assault version. The problem was that with its limited range and bomb load, it could not contribute much to the deterrent bomber force and was therefore not the sort of bomber Cot or the government wanted. As 1937 drew to a close, the only medium bombers being delivered to the Air Force were the Bloch MB.210, the Potez 54, and the Amiot 143; the only modern looking bomber likely to roll off the production lines in the near future was the far from satisfactory Bloch MB.131.

Meanwhile, the next generation of fighters were also in trouble. The September 1936 requirement expected 520 km/hr (323 mph) but the Air Ministry soon became aware of how inadequate even this was, with the German Air Ministry happy to let the French know in the summer of 1937 that a DB 601-powered Bf 109 was capable of 545 km/hr (340 mph) and was already in production.[8] This was not actually true—this version was not yet in production—and the claim was clearly intended to impress the French. Such misleading information ran the risk of being counterproductive if it merely spurred on French efforts. French designers, however, felt there was little they could do about matching such speeds until they had more powerful engines to work with.

Both major French engine manufacturers were going through difficult times. The Gnome-Rhône Mistral Major had been a tremendous commercial success, both in France and abroad, but it had gained a reputation for not being entirely reliable. Gnome et Rhône's first priority was to put this right rather than increase power. The result was the more sophisticated GR 14N series engine, which became available in 1937, but initial versions only offered a marginal increase in power. Meanwhile, Hispano-Suiza, lured away from their traditional liquid-cooled motors by the Air Ministry's preference for air-cooled engines, was having a torrid time with their HS 14AA and 14AB radials. All the company's resources were being sucked into resolving the problems of these engines and development of liquid-cooled motors had virtually ground to a halt. When it first appeared, the 860-hp HS 12Y-31 was the best inline motor in the world, but by the late thirties it had been overtaken first by the British Merlin and then the German Daimler-Benz DB 600. The best the French could do were the HS 12Y-21 and 12Y-29, tweaked versions of the HS 12Y-31 which offered slightly more power (910–920 hp) using higher octane fuel.

However, the lack of engine power was not the biggest problem facing French designers; they were still not getting the best out of what was available. The 475 km/hr the M.S.405 had managed with 860 hp was not fast when compared to the 470 km/hr the Bf 109B achieved with 670 hp. The biggest problem was the ever-larger radiators liquid-cooled engines needed. The Nieuport 161 tried to hide the radiator in the wing, but the air entering and exiting the wing surface caused more drag than an external radiator. The prototype only managed 460 km/hr, 15 km/hr less than the M.S.405.[9] With the D.513, Dewoitine tried an annular nose radiator and an elongated ventral radiator, but failed to get above 450 km/hr.[10]

By this time, it should have been obvious that the British and Germans had solved the radiator problem. By using a flap at the rear to increase the flow of air at low speeds, radiators did not have to be so large. The flaps were clearly visible on published photographs and aeronautical journalists were commenting on them and even describing how, by careful design, the new ducted radiators were using the heated air to generate some forward thrust.[11, 12] French designers, however, seemed to be completely unaware of these breakthroughs.

At least Bloch, with their air-cooled Mistral Major, did not have to worry about radiators with their Bloch MB.150 fighter. The engine was powerful enough to get close to the 520 km/hr target; designers abroad were exceeding 500 km/hr with similar power. However, the first attempted flight of the Bloch MB.150 ended in fiasco when the plane failed to get off the ground. When a second attempt at a maiden flight was also abandoned, the project was shelved. The Loire 250 at least left the ground, but only managed 480 km/hr and this was only achieved with the unreliable Hispano-Suiza HS 14AA. There were no other contenders. Bernard had gone bankrupt and Blériot-SPAD were still persisting with the biplane.

It really did seem that the M.S.405 was as fast as fighters could go with the available power. It was assumed that the 545 km/hr claimed for the Bf 109 had only been achieved with a specially boosted engine. Some French estimates put the top speed of the 570 km/hr Spitfire as low as 480 km/hr (300 mph). A December 1937 intelligence report credited the Hurricane with 480 km/hr and grudgingly conceded the Spitfire might be capable of around 510 km/hr (317 mph).[13] Despite the strenuous efforts of the top French designers, none had managed to design a fighter significantly faster than the M.S.405. There was no reason to suppose designers abroad were having any more success. In the M.S.405, the French believed they had a fighter that would serve them well for many years to come. To an extent, they were right; the plane's excellently harmonised controls and superb agility were the equal of any fighter in the world. Its most serious drawback would prove to be its relatively low speed. If the French could get it to go a little faster, they would be in possession of an outstanding fighter.

The early development of the Morane-Saulnier M.S.405 was as rapid as any contemporary fighter abroad. Following the release of the specification in 1934, detailed design had been completed by January 1935 and the first flight took place eight months later. However, progress then slowed. The first prototype did not begin official trials until February 1936, and these dragged on for six months. The report on these trials, issued in July 1936, confirmed the excellence of the design. There were no serious rivals and under normal circumstances, the Morane-Saulnier company might have felt sufficiently confident to begin preparing for production even before receiving an official contract.

However, these were not normal times. It looked like the left-wing Popular Front might win the 1936 election and one of their policies was to nationalise part of the aircraft industry. Under these plans, any designs from companies that remained private would only be built by the nationalised industry. There was no point in Morane-Saulnier making any preparations to build the M.S.405 if there was a chance they would not be asked to build any.

The National Front won the election and put their nationalisation plans into effect. Major companies were organised into six regional groups, but Morane-Saulnier were not included in the scheme. The changeover in government caused more delays. Following the Rhineland crisis, the priority was expansion of the bomber fleet, not the fighter force so the order for the M.S.405 would not be large. Indeed, to save money, more of the cheaper Dewoitine D.510s were ordered, even though the first of these would arrive at about the same time as the first M.S.405. It was the end of November 1936 before the first contracts for the M.S.405 were placed. Morane-Saulnier were to build sixteen pre-production planes for testing and experiments, while SNCAO (using the ex-Breguet plant at Nantes) were chosen to build the first batch of fifty. Deliveries of the former were expected to begin in June 1937 and the latter a month later. The need to organise the construction of the fighter in a completely different factory introduced more delays and the contracts were only provisional, again to free available funds for bomber production. Confirmation of the Morane-Saulnier contracts would have to await the release of further funds in 1937.[14]

In the circumstances, the Air Ministry were rather optimistic in believing deliveries of the M.S.405 could begin the following June. By the beginning of 1937, the Air Ministry was, unjustifiably, becoming irritated by the lack of serious preparations for the production of the Morane fighter. Morane-Saulnier was accused of unnecessarily delaying the completion of the detailed design drawings SNCAO would need and not even bothering to order the raw materials required for the production of the sixteen pre-production planes. In February, the Air Ministry threatened to take over the company if immediate steps were not taken to rectify the situation.[15] However, the Air Ministry could hardly expect any urgency when the contracts remained provisional, especially as the Air Ministry had a habit of cancelling such orders.

The only new M.S.405 under construction at the beginning of 1937 was the second prototype, which flew in January 1937. Having designed and built the first prototype in thirteen months, it had taken another eighteen months to complete a second. Some small improvements pushed top speed up to 485 km/hr (301 mph) and this became the production version as the M.S.406. In the spring of 1937, funds were released to confirm the Morane-Saulnier and SNACO contracts. Then, in July, another eighty were ordered. The Air Ministry was still expecting the first fighter to be delivered in June, with deliveries rising to ten per month by the end of the year, when four groups were supposed to be equipped with the fighter.[16]

Even with the funding released and full-scale preparations for production finally underway, progress was slow. The complicated structure of the M.S.406 meant it was not ideal for mass production. Far from having four groups equipped with the fighter by the end of 1937, not a single production model had been completed. On 29 July, the second prototype crashed. A similar fate befell the first prototype the following December. Remarkably, at the end of 1937, two and a half years after the plane's first flight, not a single M.S.405 or M.S.406 existed.

One other modern fighter design could have been coming off the production lines in 1937. The prototype twin-engined Potez 630 had first flown in April 1936 and was delivered to the Air Force testing centre at Villacoublay the following December. Its excellent flying qualities soon won the praise of those who flew it and, like the M.S.406, there were no serious contenders. Although a twin-engined design, the plane was as manoeuvrable as many contemporary single-engined fighters and was only marginally slower than early versions of the Bf 109. With its twin nose-mounted cannon, the plane was a formidable opponent. It was even much easier to build than the M.S.406.

At a relatively early stage, Potez were told that they could expect substantial orders for their design; in February 1937, it was hoped to have at least a couple of squadrons operational on the plane by the end of the year.[17] However, it was May 1937 before the first contracts were placed. A pre-production batch of sixteen machines, including light bomber and reconnaissance variants as well as fighter prototypes, was ordered, with the first production batch of eighty Potez 630 and thirty Potez 631 fighters. The former was to be powered by the Hispano-Suiza HS 14AB radial, the scaled-down version of the troublesome HS 14AA. The Potez 631 was to get the promising Gnome-Rhône 14M *Mars*, another small (19-litre) engine which was even lighter than the HS 14AB and produced slightly more power. As with the Morane-Saulnier M.S.406 contracts, none of these were confirmed, so expecting deliveries to begin as early as August 1937 was unrealistic. The Air Ministry could not expect companies, even nationalised companies, to forge ahead on the strength of a provisional contract. By the end of the year, no Potez fighters had been completed. It was all in stark contrast to what was happening elsewhere in Europe. By February 1937, as the second M.S.405 prototype took to the air, the Germans were already testing six Bf 109 prototypes. They had rushed three off to Spain for operational trials and the first production Bf 109B was about to roll off the assembly line. By the end of April, *Jagdgruppe* 88 in Spain was fully operational on the fighter.[18]

The prospects for the reconnaissance and observation squadrons were no better than the bomber and fighter elements of the Air Force. Little had been done to turn the twin-engined Potez 63 into the reconnaissance plane that Denain had promised in 1935. The initial batch of sixteen pre-production Potez 63 ordered in June 1937 included a three-seater observation prototype. A provisional order for forty-five Potez 63 A3 had even been placed in October 1937, but no detailed specification for this plane had yet emerged and there were no plans to equip any squadrons with the type until 1939. Only the low-performance Potez 566 T3 *avion de travail* had been ordered, and the prototype of this did not fly until December 1937. By the end of 1937, the French Air Force was in a dire state. Only three aircraft intended to meet specifications issued since 1933 (the Morane-Saulnier M.S.406, Potez 63, and Bloch MB.131) had been ordered and none reached the squadrons before the end of 1937.

Part of the problem was that many still feared rearming too soon would be a mistake. When new expansion plans were proposed early in 1937, Cot did not believe France could afford them. He feared that the weak French economy and limited industrial capacity made the Plan II 1,500 target the most the country could hope to achieve. He tried to compensate for the lack of orders by ordering more machine tools and modernising existing plants so that they would be better prepared when the time came for full-scale rearmament, but it was no substitute for large orders. Plan II required 950 planes a year, but this was soon reduced to 700 and then to just 500; even this proved to be too ambitious. Indeed, while both Germany and Great Britain were striving to increase output, the number of war planes built in France was actually falling.

Opponents of the nationalisation programme were quick to blame this for the drop in output. In the short term, this had caused some disruption, but the change was not as radical as it appeared. Ex-owners were running the six nationalised groups in much the same way as they had their private companies. Some disruption was caused by the unions exercising their newly won right to strike, but inconsistent government procurement policy was far more disruptive. Much is often made of the artisanal methods of production, but they were good enough to turn out over 2,000 planes a month in the First World War and the French aircraft industry had not been slow to switch to modern all-metal designs. If companies are given large orders, they will find ways to build them. In the mid-thirties, this was not happening in France. Instead of ordering a substantial number of the best fighter available (the Dewoitine D.510), Denain had ordered small batches of no fewer than four different types: the Dewoitine D.510, the Loire 46, the Blériot-SPAD 510, and the Dewoitine D.371. Even when relatively substantial orders were placed, production was divided between several plants. The initial contract for eighty Bloch MB.210s was spread between three companies. The number on order eventually rose to 250 but no fewer than six companies were involved. The largest single contract placed was for just thirty-five planes. Companies tooled up for production runs that would only keep the plant busy for a few months. Production would then cease while preparations were made for the delivery of an entirely different plane. One factory spent most of 1937 completing a batch of just sixteen Bloch MB.210. Often, a factory found itself putting the same plane back into production. Following the decision to abandon the Amiot 144 and revert to the Amiot 143, there was a twelve-month gap in deliveries while the old production line was reactivated. Production runs were not continuous. A contract placed by Cot for the Mureaux 117 in 1937 meant the plane was going back into production for the third time.[19, 20] The small contracts ruled out more efficient mass production techniques and pushed the price up, which meant fewer planes could be ordered. It could be argued that there was no point in wasting money on obsolete bombers when the LeO 45 would soon be available, but it was an argument that only applied to bombers. The M.S.406, Potez 63, and even the Mureaux 117 were as good as any planes serving in other air forces and could have been ordered in larger numbers, but they were not the bombers Cot wanted.

Cot the politician did not hesitate to paint the rosiest picture possible of the state of the French Air Force. In a speech in June 1937, he claimed that since he had taken over, the potential production capacity of the aircraft industry had increased by 30 per cent, production of modern planes was up by 110 per cent, and the striking power of the Air Force had been improved by 400 per cent. In Europe, he claimed the French Air Force was second only to the Soviet Air Force. Such optimism in public statements was perhaps needed to reassure the public and impress enemies, but he was scarcely less optimistic in private. He assured Daladier, the War Minister, that although Britain was spending more money on its air force than France, his nationalised industry was producing just as many planes. Cot also gave every impression that the lessons of the Spanish Civil War were being incorporated into French thinking and that the much-expanded bomber fleet was now capable of taking a more active part in the land battle.[21] Daladier and Prime Minister Camille Chautemps were pleased that all was well within the Air Force. Such illusions would not last long.

One critic described Cot as 'an illusionist' whose claims went 'beyond the limits of decency' and there was indeed an element of sleight of hand in many of his claims.[22] The arrival of the first Bloch MB.210 and Farman F.221/222s had resulted in an increase in the bomb tonnage the Air Force could lift, but much of the claimed increase in striking power had been achieved by just renaming reconnaissance squadrons as bomber squadrons. The new machine tools ordered by Cot had increased the potential production capacity of the industry, but his claim to have doubled the production of modern planes depended very much on Cot's definition of 'modern'. Some steps had been taken to develop aircraft capable of intervening on the battlefield, but the bomber squadrons remained equipped with aircraft that front line commanders themselves had described as totally unsuited for this type of mission. The British air *attaché* at military manoeuvres conducted in September 1937 expressed his horror at the sight of large heavy bombers flying at just a few hundred feet in mock ground-strafing attacks on artillery positions.[23]

Britain was now beginning to take a very close interest in her ally's rearmament plans and what they were hearing from their air *attaché* in Paris was not encouraging. He considered Cot 'quite untruthful' and 'a disaster' for the French Air Force.[24] When Cot turned down invitations to come to London to discuss ways in which the French might accelerate aircraft production, it was decided to raise the matter directly with the French Prime Minister. On 30 November, Chautemps visited London and Chamberlain and his Air Minister, Swinton, left the French Prime Minster in no doubt about how seriously they viewed the current state of the French Air Force. They claimed that no modern aircraft existed in France and nor did the means exist to mass produce any. The British were far from satisfied with their own efforts, but French production was running well behind British output. For the French Prime Minister, it was an enormous shock to discover just how alarmed his hosts were.[25]

On his return to Paris, Chautemps immediately summoned Cot to explain the startling British accusations. The French Air Minister was forced to concede that French production might be lower than the British, but, he insisted this was only because the Air Force was not getting enough funding to keep production lines going. He also admitted that if nothing changed France was extremely unlikely to attain the very modest target of 500 combat planes in 1938. With a fair share of the defence budget, he promised to increase annual production to 1,800 planes by 1940.[26, 27]

It was a much-subdued Cot that attended the 8 December CPDN meeting. He now admitted that Britain was producing between 175 and 200 planes a month, Germany was building 300, while France could only manage fifty; even this was not accurate. In no single month in 1937 had the French managed to produce fifty warplanes; the monthly average was nearer thirty. On the question of quality, Cot was even more vulnerable to criticism. None of the planes coming off the production lines could be classed as modern. The French were aware that other countries were getting aircraft into production much quicker. In Germany, it seemed just three-and-a-half months separated service trials and large-scale production. Reports from Britain suggested some planes had been ordered after trials lasting just a few days or even straight off the drawing board. In France, an interminable period of time seemed to pass before prototypes were considered sufficiently tested to be put into production.[28, 29]

Much of this criticism was true, but it was also missing the point. The inability to get modern aircraft into service had not been the result of bungling French incompetence, as the British had tended to assume. Funding was an issue, but so was Cot's, and indeed his government's, single-minded determination to expand the bomber fleet at the expense of all else. Cot was very anxious to get the LeO 45 into production. The British Air Staff would have undoubtedly approved of this determination. At the time, they were being forced by their own government to switch efforts to fighter defence, against their better judgement. They believed that talk of an interceptor force beating off a bomber assault was dangerous wishful thinking. Only bombers could provide security in peacetime and victory in wartime. As for using ground-attack aircraft to support the Army, this was not even on the British Air Staff agenda. Their view on how air power should develop was very close to Cot's. Ironically, their criticisms of the French Air Force would give Cot's critics the opportunity to overturn these policies.

Chautemps's discovery of how weak his Air Force was came when the threat to France was growing rapidly. On 1 November 1937, Mussolini had announced the Rome-Berlin Axis. With Italy now definitely siding with Hitler's Germany, France would have to guard her south-eastern border. In Spain, Franco seemed to be winning, exposing the south-western frontier. The time had come to rearm. The Luftwaffe was credited with a front line strength of 2,800 planes and the French needed parity. Plan II was aiming for a front line strength of 1,500, so another 1,200 would have to be found. In January 1938, the French Parliament approved the necessary funding. For the first time, France was actually planning to increase front line strength beyond the 1,500 figure it had remained at since the end of the First World War.

This decision was significant enough, but it was overshadowed by an even more dramatic change of policy. The Army wanted fighters to protect them from the sort of air attacks both sides in Spain had experienced. A faction in the Air Ministry felt it was time to rely less on retaliation and more on the new cannon-armed interceptors. Since the M.S.406 and Potez 63 fighters were the only modern planes ready to go into mass production, the case for switching to fighters was overwhelming. The call for an expansion of the fighter force was led by Aubé. The time had come to take to the defensive in the air as well as on land, he suggested. The Army agreed. Féquant opposed the move but the disgraced Cot was in no position to support his Air Force chief. For once, those who favoured reliance on the bomber fleet to defend French airspace found themselves in a minority.[30]

Aubé also demanded that assault planes and dive-bombers should be introduced into the French Air Force as rapidly as possible. For twelve months, the fighting in Spain had been demonstrating the value of these new weapons. The Air Ministry was developing assault planes, but had nowhere to put them. In the new expanded Air Force, it would be easier to accommodate them. If Cot had any objections, he did not voice them. Aubé's proposals were accepted.

The 8 December CPDN meeting marked a watershed in the development of the French Air Force. The 1934 high-speed bomber programme had seen the demise of the multi-role *multi-place de combat*, but Douhetian-style thinking still dominated. Now, the Air Force was beginning to move in a different direction. The bomber threat had not disappeared; the government and Air Staff still needed long-range bombers that could retaliate against Berlin and the increase in fighter strength was primarily to defend French cities. France was still preparing for the wrong war, but they were beginning to prepare for it with more of the right weapons. More fighters were going to be ordered and not all the bombers would be long-range. A tactical air force was beginning to re-emerge. Indeed, circumstances might force it to be far more tactical than the politicians wanted. The only modern planes ready to go into production were the M.S.406 fighter and the Potez 63 fighter, reconnaissance and light bombers. With the Mureaux 117 providing an adequate observation plane, the French had all the ingredients of an excellent tactical air force. With no long-range medium bombers to order, the French might find themselves reluctantly building precisely the air force they would need in 1940.

Immediately following the December CPDN meeting, Cot confirmed the orders for 110 Potez 63 fighters and fifty Potez 633 light bombers. Cot also began to show more interest in the three-seater Amiot 340. Having lost his production facilities to the nationalised industry, Felix Amiot was anxious to set up a new plant. He proposed building a small number of his three-seater bomber as an interim measure while he worked on the four-seater Amiot 350 the Air Ministry wanted. With no alternative bomber to order, Cot was interested and it seems he led Amiot to believe that an order for fifty would be placed in the near future.[31]

Before he could do this, Cot had gone. In January, Chautemps formed a new government, and there was no place for Cot in his cabinet. Cot had claimed France could not rearm any faster and was therefore not the right person to put the new government policy into practice.

8

Time to Rearm

In Cot's place, Chautemps appointed Guy La Chambre. If the new air minister had any illusions about the size of the task facing him, they were soon dispelled by a report from General Vuillemin, the commander of the French bomber fleet, which he found awaiting him. In it, Vuillemin did not mince his words. He told La Chambre that he did not have a single bomber capable of operating by day, and his best bomber, the Bloch MB.210, was not even a satisfactory night bomber. They might be able to operate by day with cloud cover, but Vuillemin did not think his crews had the navigational equipment to find their target flying in clouds, nor would they be able to find them under cover of darkness. If war should break out in 1938, Vuillemin concluded that the French Air Force would be wiped out in a week.[1] Doubtless, this report had some influence on the decision taken a few days later to appoint Vuillemin as the Air Force Chief of Staff in place of Féquant. Cot's old ally had always opposed the sort of policies the CPDN now wanted to pursue. Fresh faces were needed to launch the new expansion programme, and Vuillemin's frankness must have seemed refreshing after the distortions of the Cot regime.

Vuillemin was a popular and highly respected figure within the Air Force. During the First World War, he had commanded one of the Breguet 14 tactical light bomber wings, which had played such an important part in supporting French forces in the closing stages of the war. Highly intelligent but extremely sensitive, there was a fatalistic streak in his character, which would not always be to France's advantage during the forthcoming confrontations with Nazi Germany. Although a bomber commander, Vuillemin agreed with the CPDN decision to give priority to the expansion of the fighter arm. He also wanted the assault planes and dive-bombers his bomber crews had been demanding for some time for hitting small targets in the rear. These also happened to be the sort of planes needed for Army support on the battlefield. He was still a bomber man at heart. His pessimistic predications about heavy losses applied to bombers trying to reach Berlin, not short-range tactical air support. It was the Douhetian-style bomber war that dominated his thinking and the threat to French cities that most worried him.

The first task facing La Chambre and Vuillemin was to turn the vague proposals of the 8 December CPDN meeting into a concrete plan. The resulting Plan V was approved by the Air Council and the French cabinet in March 1938. Front line strength would increase to 2,617 by March 1941. It would not be a flimsy paper force with no reserves; it would be on a war footing with a 100 per cent fighter reserve and 70 per cent reserves for other types. This was later increased to 120 per cent and 200 per cent reserves respectively.[2] Within days of the plan being approved, Hitler annexed Austria; this latest German act of aggression persuaded the French government to bring forward the completion date to March 1940.

Vuillemin still believed something along the lines of Cot's fighter Light Corps and bomber Heavy Corps were needed. As Cot (and Armengaud before him) had pointed out, at the beginning of any future war, resources would be stretched and it would be necessary to focus all effort where it was required, either responding to an air only assault or a land invasion. However, the Army remained deeply suspicious and feared that the Air Force was still overestimating the threat to the rear and focusing too much attention on independent air warfare. On 2 September, Cot's bomber and fighter corps were officially abolished. All the reconnaissance and observation squadrons were put under Army command and each army would get one fighter group.

There would be far more fighters available; the fighter force was to be tripled to 1,081. However, with 649 assigned to defending bomber bases and other targets in the rear and 240 under the direct control of the armies, it was clear where the emphasis was. The balance of 192 formed a general reserve that could be used where it was needed. Dramatic though the increase was, planned fighter strength was still lower than it had been at the end of the First World War, when rear defence did not get much attention. Even assuming the Plan V general reserve would be used tactically, in 1918, the Army had three times as many fighters as the Plan V target.[3] Nevertheless, at least a powerful fighter force would exist and fighter squadrons in the rear would always be available for use over the front.

The bomber fleet would be expanded but more than half the force would be light, assault, or dive-bombers. The formation of these units was to begin immediately, with fifteen of the existing heavy bomber squadrons converting to nine light and six assault bomber groups by the end of 1939. The inclusion of these units meant that the expanded bomber force would be able to lift fewer bombs than the Plan II target. The rather half-hearted justification for this was that these units would be able to bomb more accurately.[4] In reality, it was a dramatic reversal of policy. A bomber deterrent was still required, but there would no longer be any effort to match the long-range striking power of the

Luftwaffe bomber for bomber, ton for ton. Given how terrifying the bomber threat was viewed, it was a brave decision. By concentrating on the expansion of the fighter arm, and creating room within the bomber fleet for tactical bombers, the Air Ministry was now aiming for something much closer to what would be required in the spring of 1940. As it turned out, Plan V was due to be completed just one month before the Germans would launch their attack. If the aircraft required by the plan could be built, if they were good enough, and the aircrews could be trained to fly them, then France could yet be in possession of an air force capable of playing an important part in defeating a German invasion.

It was an enormous task. Plan V required the production of 4,607 combat planes in just two years. Of these, 1,878, including 940 fighters, were supposed to be delivered in the following twelve months. At the time, the French aircraft industry was only building about thirty-five machines a month, of which only around half a dozen were fighters, and none of these were considered sufficiently modern to count towards the requirements of Plan V. Manning these planes was an even bigger challenge. Plan V required over 40,000 personnel to be trained, of which over 5,000 were to be aircrew. At the beginning of 1938, only six schools existed in France, with a total of just 2,532 students. New schools would have to be opened and equipped, large numbers of training aircraft would have to be built by an industry already stretched by the combat planes required by Plan V, and instructors would have to be trained to cope with the influx of new students. Once the new training facilities had been created, it would be the best part of a year before they could produce their first pilots.[5]

With a completion date of March 1941, this could have been possible. The plan was to increase pilot strength by 1,400 by training 240 men in 1939, rising to around 1,000 in 1940 and the remainder in the first months of 1941. When the deadline for the completion of Plan V was brought forward to March 1940, even the most optimistic forecast predicted a shortfall of 300 pilots. When a third stage was added to Plan V in March 1939, calling for the delivery of an additional 3,000 aircraft between April and December 1940, it was accepted that even in the most favourable circumstances, the shortage of personnel would limit the increase in front line strength to a mere 300 planes.

For the planes these pilots would fly, there was at least the option of calling on help from abroad. In Europe, nations were too preoccupied with their own rearmament programmes, but across the Atlantic lay the United States, France's ally from the First World War and the country that had introduced to the world the concept of mass production. President Roosevelt was sympathetic to the plight of the European democracies. He hoped to avoid direct involvement, but the United States was a potential 'arsenal of democracy' and might provide an instant solution. La Chambre estimated that it would take just two weeks to ship the planes across and another two weeks to assemble them.[6]

Even before Plan V had been officially approved, La Chambre dispatched senator Baron La Grange to the United States with instructions to purchase 1,000 combat planes for immediate delivery, hopefully by the summer of 1938. La Grange explained to Roosevelt how desperately inferior the French were in the air. Again, it was not the inability to gain air superiority over the battlefield that was the concern. The French were not looking for aircraft to protect and support their Army. It was still French civilians and industry that needed protecting. Roosevelt was sympathetic and assured La Grange of his personal support, although he warned the French senator to be discreet and not alert the American press. The Neutrality Act of 1935 did not forbid the sale of arms to nations not actually at war, but it was in the interests of both governments not to antagonise those who opposed any American involvement in foreign conflicts. Roosevelt also gave his personal assurance that if France went to war, a way around the Neutrality Act would be found.[7]

A reassured La Grange set off on his tour of American aircraft factories. What he saw came as a great shock. American companies were almost as poorly prepared for mass production as those back home. Even more discouraging was the dearth of suitable aircraft. There appeared to be only one combat plane that was even worth considering: the Curtiss H75 fighter. The plane was not armed with cannon, but in other respects appeared to be as good as the M.S.406. Even this would not be available immediately. The fighter was already in production for the United States Army Air Corps but the French would have to wait until these were delivered. It was also very expensive. With the weak French franc, the H75 was twice as expensive as home-produced fighters. However, France was desperate and 100 were ordered; the French also agreed to invest nearly one million dollars in a new production line so that deliveries could begin sooner.[8]

The limited assistance the American aircraft industry was capable of providing came as a bitter setback for La Chambre. Worse was to follow when it appeared he might lose even this. The decision to buy foreign aircraft was greeted with howls of protest in France. The American Neutrality Act meant that all arms had to be paid for in cash, and there were those who did not believe that France could afford to deplete her gold reserves. Aircraft manufacturers and unions were understandably aghast that after years of pitifully small orders placed with their own aircraft industry, the French government was now ordering foreign planes and pouring money into the expansion of the American industry. Opponents of the Curtiss fighter order called into question the quality of the American fighter. Thorough trials were demanded before any order was placed. These were duly held and the Air Force expressed their complete satisfaction. It was just as agile and just as fast as the M.S.406. Indeed, it was reassuring evidence that French fighter design was not slipping behind world standards. It was May before La Chambre was able to place the order. Rather optimistically, deliveries were expected to be completed by the following April.[9]

The order for the Curtiss H75 meant the French aircraft industry would still have to find another 840 fighters by April 1939. In April 1938, a further 895 M.S.406s were ordered from the nationalised industries—a massive contract by previous standards—with the nationalised plants at Billancourt (SNCAC) and Toulouse (SNCAM) joining the Nantes-Bouguenais (SNCAO) factory in the production programme. The policy of excluding private companies from government contracts was quietly forgotten and ninety were ordered from the Morane-Saulnier plant at Puteaux. Three years after the prototype had first flown, the company had finally received an order for the fighter it had designed. The new contracts brought the total on order to just over 1,000; not since the *politique de stocks* had a single design been ordered in such vast numbers. Even so, there was little chance of enough being built before April 1939 to meet the Plan V target. The M.S.406 was much criticised at the time for its complex design. The Air Ministry put the required man-hours to build one at 20,000.[10] Dewoitine, not pleased at having to build a rival's fighter, insisted he would need 30,000 hours. SNCAO claimed only 16,000 were needed and Morane-Saulnier insisted 13,700 hours was enough.[11] In truth, it was no more difficult to build than the Hurricane. The more serious problem was the supply of Hispano-Suiza HS 12Y-31 engines. The Air Ministry preference for air-cooled engines meant only the Dewoitine D.510 fighter and the Mureaux reconnaissance planes used the engine and production reflected this. In 1935, planned monthly output of the HS 12Y-31 was a mere twenty, compared to 130 of the smaller HS 12X and 200 Gnome-Rhône Mistral Major radials.[12] In 1937, total Hispano-Suiza production was down to fewer than fifty engines a month.

Suddenly, with the massive orders for the M.S.406, the HS 12Y-31 was in demand. It would take time to build up production of the engine and to make matters worse, the large orders placed for the radial HS 14AA and HS 14AB to power the LeO 45 and Potez 63 meant that much of the available capacity had been set aside for these. Even in the most favourable circumstances, it was estimated that there would only be enough HS 12Y-31 for 250 M.S.406s to be built by April 1939. This left a shortfall of some 600 fighters. The Air Ministry would have to find an alternative that did not use the Hispano-Suiza engine.

One option was a radial-powered fighter. Only two designs had emerged from the 1934 program. The Loire 250 had only achieved 480 km/hr (298 mph) and even this relied on the unreliable HS 14AA. This left the Bloch MB.150, powered by the Gnome-Rhône 14K Mistral Major. This project had been shelved in 1936 after two unsuccessful attempts to get the prototype into the air. During 1937, work resumed on a modified version, albeit with little sense of urgency. The prototype was re-engined with the first of the new Gnome-Rhône GR 14N-10 engines; with this, it finally managed to make its maiden flight in September 1937, but top speed was a miserable 434 km/hr (270 mph). Gnome-Rhône were promising that more powerful versions of the GR 14N engines were on the way, but even if the final speed could match the M.S.406, Vuillemin was in no doubt that it lacked the Morane-Saulnier's fighting capabilites. The alternatives, however, were limited. The Air Ministry toyed with the idea of reducing output of the HS 14AB radial to make way for more HS 12Y-31 production, which would mean the Bloch MB.150 would not be needed. However, there was a real belief that these light, relatively low-powered engines were the way forward, and they were needed for all the Potez 63 variants. Instead, it was decided to persevere with the Bloch fighter.[13] It was at least easier to build than the M.S.406; Bloch engineers reckoned it needed just 8,000 man-hours per plane.[14]

In April, a contract was placed for twenty-five pre-production Bloch fighters, with the promise of an order for further 450 if the manufacturers could improve performance. Little more than a year before the Air Ministry had found it impossible to finance the production of the M.S.406. Now a massive order for a clearly inferior fighter was on the cards. In June 1938, long before the revised prototype was ready to fly, the Air Ministry were already counting on the delivery of 300 of these fighters by April 1939.

Even this left the Air Ministry short of its target. The only remaining option was the 1934 lightweight fighter programme. The only serious contender, the Caudron C.713, had flown in December. In many ways, it was a remarkable fighter. Although it had a fully retractable undercarriage, cantilever wing, and stressed skin construction, it was still 30 per cent lighter than the M.S.406. Its remarkably low frontal area helped it achieve a top speed of 470 km/hr with just a 450-hp engine, making it as fast as the Jumo-powered Bf 109 and nearly as fast as the M.S.406. However, wing loading was extremely high and climbing performance was appalling. The crash of the prototype two months after its first flight seemed to be the end the project. However, times were desperate. Caudron were told if they could improve climbing performance, they could expect an order for 200. Caudron set to work on the improved C.714, but this could not possibly be in production before April 1939.[15, 16]

Even with their most optimistic forecast, the Air Ministry still saw no way of meeting the fighter requirements of the first stage of Plan V by the spring of 1939. Plans to re-equip six of the existing sixteen fighter groups by April 1939 and another eight by September looked impossible. The situation was even more desperate as so many of the fighter squadrons were still equipped with fighters as old as the Nieuport 62. Of the 426 fighters in service in June 1938, only sixty-seven were the reasonably modern Dewoitine D.510.[17] The situation was so serious and production of the M.S.406 so slow getting underway that the French even briefly considered putting the Dewoitine D.510 back into production yet again.[18]

In the desperate situation France found herself in, deliveries of the Potez 63 took on a new significance. Despite its twin-engined layout, the plane was still far superior to any single-seater in service in France. It was also easier to build than the M.S.406. The twin-engined Potez 63 was the only way of giving the single-engined fighter squadrons something reasonably modern fairly quickly. The first stage of Plan V only required 155 twin-engined fighters, a target SNCAN felt they could easily achieve. The order was therefore increased to 287, with 200 to be delivered by April 1939. The extra planes would go to single-seater squadrons, who would fly the twin-engined fighter as a single-seater. Given all the unnecessary delays, it was surprising how quickly the M.S.406 and Potez 630 began arriving. The first M.S.406 was eventually delivered in April 1938, but this was only four months after the first Hurricane. The following month, the Air Force took charge of its first Potez 630 fighter. However, by August, only twenty examples of these two fighters had found their way into the hands of the Air Force.

Deliveries of modern bomber and reconnaissance aircraft were even further behind. The bomber development programme was in such disarray that only 182 medium bombers of any description were expected before April 1939. Even this modest target seemed optimistic. There was still nothing that could go into production. The troublesome Hispano-Suiza engines ruled out the LeO 45. Other doubts about the bomber were, belatedly, also beginning to emerge. With the ventral turret retracted and the dorsal visor closed, the LeO 45 was a superbly streamlined and fast bomber. However, once the dorsal and ventral guns were deployed, speed dropped by 100 km/hr (60 mph). The defensive arrangements for the bomber might have to be rethought, but there was no time now to modify the bomber. The order was increased to 140 and the plane would go into production as it was, just as soon as the problems with the engines had been sorted out.[19]

The only reasonably modern plane in production was the Bloch MB.131. In the spring of 1938, the first examples started rolling off the production lines, but it was only now that the full implications of the plane's problems became apparent. To reduce the excessive vibrations that plagued the prototype, the structure of the plane had been reinforced and the wing tanks moved to the fuselage, taking up space required by the bomb load. These modifications meant the plane could only carry 500 kg of bombs, and top speed fully loaded was just 350 km/hr (217 mph). It was useless as a long-range bomber and hardly suitable for reconnaissance. The plane was close to being abandoned completely, but such was the desperation for any reasonably modern bomber or reconnaissance equipment, it kept its place in the production schedule.[20]

The Amiot 340 appeared to be the obvious alternative. In February 1938, Felix Amiot inquired what had come of Cot's promise to purchase fifty. So anxious was Amiot to set up a new production line to replace what he had lost in the nationalisation process, he was willing to start production with no more than the dubious security of a provisional contract.[21] Official trials revealed there was plenty wrong with the plane. The fuel tanks were unprotected and could only be replaced by taking the wings off. It was a three-seater, rather than the four-seater now required. The gun positions were no more than open hatches and the bomb load was only 1,000 kg. The prototype also had a single tail plane rather than the twin tail plane arrangement favoured by the Air Ministry to give the rear gunner a clear line of fire.

It was perhaps not the time to be too choosy. Its performance was good, with top speed a very respectable 454 km/hr (282 mph) and the plane was pleasant enough to fly. The official trials suggested that it might be capable of more than 500 km/hr with more efficient engine cowlings.[22] Amiot had plenty of variants on offer. One the Air Ministry found itself considering was a HS 12Y-31 powered version.[23] This was what had been possible ever since they released the reprisal bomber specification in 1933. The fact that the 423 km/hr Tupolev SB-2, powered by two Russian built HS 12Y-31 engines had been flying operations in Spain since October 1936, underlined the opportunity the French had missed. Indeed, had the French developed a HS 12Y-31 powered bomber, France would not only have a high-class plane with reliable engines already in production, but as a bonus, output of the Hispano-Suiza engine that the M.S.406 needed would be running at a much higher level. Air Ministry insistence on powering bombers by air-cooled engines had cost the country dear. In 1938, it was too late for a HS 12Y-31 powered bomber; the need for fighters was too great.

An Amiot 340 powered by air-cooled engines was still worth having. Given the disadvantage of the LeO 45's retractable turret, simple gun positions might not be such a disadvantage. Unlike the LeO 45, the Amiot 340 was flying with reliable engines. It was also much easier to build, requiring just 24,000 man-hours.[24] The initial LeO 45 production batch was expected to require 70,000 man-hours for each machine, and even when production was in full swing the most optimistic forecast did not see this figure dropping below 45,000.[25] Two Amiot 340s could be built for every LeO 45.

The idea of reducing the unsatisfactory Bloch MB.131 order in favour of the Amiot 340 was considered, but turned down. The Ministry seemed very reluctant to accept the Amiot bomber as the best available solution. At the end of March, twenty were ordered, but the Air Ministry wanted the plane brought fully in line with the 1936 B4 specification before going any further. Amiot was confident the required changes could be made within a matter of weeks and that a production rate of twenty a month by the following spring was still possible. A full-scale mock-up of the new four-seater Amiot 350 was speedily assembled and this was inspected and approved in April 1938. Orders followed in May and June for 120 Amiot 351/354s, with deliveries beginning in April 1939, but the struggling LeO 45 was still seen as the main medium bomber.[26]

The re-equipment of the reconnaissance and the new tactical bomber squadrons was complicated by the fact that both were relying on versions of the Potez 63. These included the three-seater reconnaissance plane (Potez 637), a two-seater light bomber (Potez 633), an armoured assault bomber (Potez 639) and a dive-bomber (Potez 63.13). There was no reason why they could not all be built using the production capacity idly standing by waiting for the problems with the LeO 45 to be sorted out. Ten Potez 63 bombers could be built for one LeO 45, but the long-range LeO 45 had become an immovable element of French planning. The LeO 45 was one plane the French never even considered dropping. With available production capacity limited, decisions had to be made about which versions of the Potez 63 should get priority. The Potez 633 light bomber was already in production, so it seemed sensible to continue with this version and the order was increased to 125. With Greek and Romanian contracts, some 200 were on order. For the time being, the provisional orders placed in 1937 for sixty-five Potez 639 assault and forty-five Potez 637 reconnaissance planes remained unconfirmed.

This, however, left the reconnaissance and observation squadrons in a worrying state. The Mureaux 117 was perfectly adequate for the short-range observation role, but this and its various variants had been in and out of production since 1932 and there were not nearly enough to equip all the observation units. More than half of these squadrons were still using the Breguet 27 and Potez 39 biplanes. Another 150 Mureaux 117s were ordered to ease the problem, but the plane was using the HS 12Y-31 needed by the M.S.406. The Mureaux plant was also involved in the Potez 631 fighter production programme. To speed up production of the Potez 631 and free more HS 12Y-31 motors for the M.S.406, the contract for the extra Mureaux was cancelled.

At about the same time, the Air Ministry realised that the ventral cupola they were insisting on for all reconnaissance and observation planes was too much of a handicap. The Potez 566 T3 *avion de travail* could not even manage 200 mph and was actually slower than the Mureaux 117 it was supposed to replace. The Potez 566 was cancelled and all companies developing reconnaissance planes were told to replace the ventral cupola with more streamlined glazed noses. The Potez 637 with its cupola was replaced by the Potez 63.11. This seemed to offer a satisfactory compromise between the requirements of the observer and the need for high performance. It was only slightly slower than the fighter version, retained much of its agility, and was not much inferior to the Jumo-powered Bf 109. The cancellation of the Potez 566 and Mureaux 117s made it even more important to order something to replace the aging Breguet and Potez biplanes, so it was decided the Potez 63.11 would be used by observation squadrons as well.

Re-equipping the reconnaissance and observation squadrons was the top priority so it was decided to switch to the Potez 63.11 reconnaissance version as soon as existing Potez contracts for fighters and light bombers were completed. To speed up deliveries, the Air Force agreed that the first sixty-five could be the original Potez 637 with the ventral cupola. In the end, the Air Force did not get any of the Potez 633 on order. Vuillemin had doubts about the two-seater Potez 633 light bomber, and preferred to wait for the three-seater Bloch MB.170, despite the less than encouraging early reports about the plane. The fighter version was urgently needed, so in May 1938, just as the first Potez 633 were coming off the production lines, Vuillemin cancelled the contract for the light bomber in favour of an equal number of the fighter version. The Greek and Romanian contracts for the Potez light bomber, however, would be honoured.[27]

La Chambre had not, so far, concerned himself with which planes were ordered but the decision to halt deliveries of the only modern bomber coming off the production lines alarmed the Air Minister. He failed to get Vuillemin to reverse the decision but he did get a bomber version of the Breguet 690 fighter ordered to replace it. This plane had been designed to the same 1934 two-seater, lightweight fighter specification as the Potez 63, but had ignored the weight restrictions and was therefore never a serious contender. The prototype did not even fly until March 1938. The plane was not as manoeuvrable as the Potez 63, but it was sturdier and had more potential. It was also as fast as the M.S.406 fighter, which led the Air Ministry briefly to consider ordering the plane to equip single-seater fighter units.[28]

Breguet were soon adapting the design as a two-seater bomber. Vuillemin was no more impressed with this than he was with the two-seater Potez 633, but La Chambre was adamant that France could not afford to wait until the ideal machine became available.[29] Indeed, the Bloch MB.170 was soon proving it was far from ideal. The second prototype proved to be no more successful than the first. One pilot reputedly gave up test flying for a desk job following a hair-raising flight in the machine.[30] The plane was abandoned and work started on the completely revised Bloch MB.174, but it would be some time before a prototype flew. The problems with the Bloch MB.170 strengthened La Chambre's case; he got his way and the Breguet 691 low-level assault bomber version was ordered instead. It was ironic that a politician should secure the production of a tactical bomber the Army believed it could do without.

The Breguet 691 was smaller and faster than the Potez 633, but it was not going to be available as soon as the Potez 633 would have been. Setting up a new production line would take time. It did not help that production was left in the hands of Louis Breguet's surviving independent firm rather than the nationalised Breguet plant, and, as Amiot was also discovering, it was more difficult for private companies to get the funding they needed. La Chambre did his best to hurry things along. Company trials had revealed no problems and La Chambre ordered the plane to be put into production without waiting for official trials of the Breguet 691 bomber version or even the Breguet 690 fighter prototype. The first contract for 100 was placed in June, but while the production line was being set up, the only tactical bomber being built, the Potez 633, was for export only.

9

To the Brink of War

Before Plan V could have any effect on French air strength, France again found herself on the brink of war. Germany was demanding the return of the German-speaking Sudetenland border regions of Czechoslovakia. France was pledged to come to Czechoslovakia's aid if attacked, and both Britain and Russia had promised to support France if she was forced to go to war. Everything, therefore, hinged on the action France took, and that depended on how confident France was about the country's military capabilities. In August 1938, at the height of the crisis, Vuillemin had the opportunity to judge at first hand Germany's military strength on an official visit planned some time before the crisis. Vuillemin set off in the knowledge that the only modern combat planes coming off French production lines were the Morane-Saulnier M.S.406 and Potez 63, and none of these had actually reached front line squadrons yet. In an attempt to impress the Germans, the Amiot 340 prototype was borrowed from its manufacturers to carry the Air Force Chief of Staff to Berlin. The aircraft cruised to its destination at an impressive average speed of 270 mph, and its graceful lines no doubt made an impression. This attempt to impress their German hosts, however, was nothing compared to what the Germans had in store for their French guests.

Hitler hoped that an impressive display of military might would dissuade the French from intervening in the German-Czechoslovakian dispute. Their German hosts made sure the French party were given every opportunity to appreciate the high performance of planes like the Heinkel He 111 bomber, Messerschmitt Bf 110 twin-engined fighter, and single-seater Bf 109. They were also shown the factories where these designs were being mass-produced. To emphasise the strength of the Luftwaffe, combat squadrons were gathered at airfields being visited by the French. At one point, the French were given the opportunity to fly in a Fieseler Fi 156 *Storch*, a liaison plane capable flying remarkably slowly. Erhard Milch, in charge of Luftwaffe expansion, had cunningly arranged for the 400 mph Heinkel He 100 prototype to make a high-speed pass over the slow-flying *Storch*. The French party were visibly shaken. On the ground, Vuillemin was allowed to overhear Milch being told the second Heinkel He 100 production line had just commenced deliveries and the third would follow in a couple of weeks. In fact, only prototypes of the fighter existed, the design was a failure, and there were no plans to put it into production. The Germans had made a very thorough job of misleading the French.[1]

The He 100 production lines may have been fictitious, but there was nothing imaginary about the devastating fire-power of the Bf 110 or the superb manoeuvrability of the twin-engined He 111 as it flew past on one engine or the ultra-modern production lines producing the planes at Rostock. Nor was there anything imaginary about the shortcomings of the French Air Force. The visit served to deepen the French Air Force chief's pessimism. On his return to France, he rather melodramatically informed Daladier, now Prime Minister, that if war should break out with Germany, he would ask to be relieved of his command and go and die in a bomber over some German city.[2] The choice of target said much about the sort of war Vuillemin was envisaging. He was not offering to sacrifice his life attacking German columns marching into France.

A month later, the Sudetenland crisis reached its climax. The Czechs, determined to resist any German effort to occupy the disputed territories by force, began mobilizing and the French were soon following suit. Daladier was initially determined to honour the French commitment to support the Czechs; however, his resolve gradually weakened. The British were anxious to avoid war at any cost and were soon reminding the French about the fate that would await French cities if it came to war. Gamelin assured his Prime Minister that, on land, the French Army still held the advantage. In the air, the French Air Force was undoubtedly weaker, but Gamelin believed the Air Force could provide the short-range air support the Army would need.[3]

Finally, with the memories of his recent visit to Germany still fresh in his mind, Vuillemin made his views clear. In a letter to La Chambre, which was passed on to Daladier, Vuillemin claimed that the French only possessed 700 machines in front line squadrons. Since he had taken over command of the Air Force, there had been no improvement in the capability of the French bomber fleet. He did not agree with Gamelin that the Air Force would be capable of supporting the Army. French fighters would not be capable of protecting Army reconnaissance machines, and French generals would have to fight their battles blind. Also, Army lines of communication would not be secure from attack, and industrial and civilian targets deep inside French territory would be vulnerable. Civilian loss of life would be huge. He estimated that French losses in the air would be 40 per cent at the end of the first month and 60 per cent of the remainder would be lost in the second.[4] French intelligence reports supported Vuillemin's pessimistic view. It was believed the German Air Force was 3,000 strong and nothing Vuillemin had seen in Germany contradicted these figures. Vuillemin's report perhaps more than any other single factor persuaded Daladier to bow to British pressure and German intimidation. Czechoslovakia was told that if she chose to resist any German occupation of the Sudetenland, there would be no military support from France. Germany duly moved into the disputed territories unopposed.

The French Air Force was indeed weaker than the Luftwaffe, although Vuillemin had tended to overstate the case. French Air Force strength in France was nearer 1,000 machines, as it had been since the First World War. Vuillemin had arrived at his more pessimistic figure by simply deducting short-range army observation squadrons, using the Douhetian logic that they could play no part in the all-important strategic air operations. The Douhetian-style *bataille aérienne* still dominated Vuillemin's thinking. The French intelligence estimate of German strength was precisely right; on 19 September, the Luftwaffe possessed 2,998 machines. In terms of quality, the Germans now had the edge. At the beginning of 1938, most German fighter squadrons were still equipped with the Arado Ar 68, which was markedly inferior even to the Dewoitine D.500, Loire 46, and Blériot-SPAD 510. However, by the autumn, the German fighter force had re-equipped with the Jumo-powered Bf 109, which was superior even to the Dewoitine D.510, although French engines still gave French fighters the edge at high altitude.

The tragedy for France was that the M.S.406 was superior in every respect to the Jumo-powered Bf 109. The plane had flown fewer than three months after the prototype Bf 109 but in the autumn, the Luftwaffe had nearly 600 Bf 109s while the French Air Force did not have a single M.S.406. The best French fighter in service, the Dewoitine D.510, would have had difficulty catching lone reconnaissance planes, but it was still capable of dealing with slower flying bomber formations. However, there were only about fifty Dewoitine D.510s in service and the fighter was not even in production. Some rear defence squadrons still had the hopelessly slow Nieuport 62. All the bombers available were products of the *multiplace de combat* era. The only reasonably modern equipment in service was the Mureaux reconnaissance plane.

France's ally, Czechoslovakia, was, in some ways, better prepared for conflict. The Czechs possessed nearly 400 of various versions of the Avia B-534 fighter, broadly similar to the Dewoitine D.500–510 series. Ironically, while the French were re-equipping bomber units with the Bloch MB.210, the Czech Air Force had started replacing the Bloch MB.200s it had bought from France with Russian Tupolev SB-2 light bombers, powered by the French HS 12Y-31 engine. In a tactical air battle, the Luftwaffe would have encountered stiffer opposition in the skies over Czechoslovakia than over the Western Front.

The orders Cot had placed had gone some way to achieving his goal of giving the French a reasonable deterrent. Planes like the Bloch MB.210 might have been totally unsuitable for tactical operations or indeed daylight operations of any sort, but it helped give the French bomber fleet the ability to deliver 530 tons of bombs. It might only have been capable of dropping these indiscriminately over German cities by night, but if the French government wanted retaliation, that was all that was needed. However, Vuillemin's pessimism convinced the government that it dare not act.

It is interesting to speculate what might have happened if a more assertive character, such as Cot, had exaggerated the potential rather than the shortcomings of the Air Force. Goering may only have told Hitler what he wanted to hear, but his brash confidence must have been reassuring in the political brinkmanship leading up to the Munich agreement. If France had gone to war, her cities would not have been ruthlessly bombed, as Vuillemin and the French government feared. Hitler could not risk the retaliation. The air battle would have been tactical. Even without Soviet support, the combined air forces of France, Britain, and Czechoslovakia were almost as strong as the Luftwaffe. On land, the alliance had a clear advantage. The German Army was not as well prepared for war as it would be a year or two later. The outcome was far from a foregone conclusion. But it was not the balance of power on land that was worrying the politicians. It was the inability of the French Air Force to counter or match Luftwaffe attacks on French cities that overrode all other factors, just as it had during the Rhineland crisis. The French Army could not protect French civilians from the German bomber. In the end, it was another victory for the bomber prophets of doom. Without dropping a bomb, the bomber had decided the issue.

The French betrayal of the Czech nation had bought more time to rearm, but only a rapid revival of French air power could justify the sacrifice of the Czech nation, not to mention the loss of her thirty-five divisions and 550-strong air force. The show laid on for Vuillemin during his visit to Germany had the desired short-term effect of helping to dissuade the French from intervening in 1938. However, in the long term, the German strategy could prove counter-productive if the extravagant attempts to impress her neighbour galvanised the French and accelerated their rearmament programme. Following the humiliating climb down at Munich, the French would be willing to go to virtually any lengths to strengthen her Air Force.

French leaders still did not see the real danger. They still did not see developing Army air support and ensuring air superiority over the battlefield as the priority. However, unlike what happened following the Rhineland crisis, there would be no knee-jerk reaction to expand the long-range bomber fleet at the expense of all else. The aim was to defend French cities and industry, but at least France was trying to build or find fighters. These were what the Army would require in 1940.

Desperate for quick solutions, France turned to any country that might be able to supply fighters or engines. Many nations had bought the rights to manufacture the Hispano-Suiza HS 12Y-31 under licence and some of them were now building more Hispano-Suiza engines than the French themselves. Ironically, the Czechoslovakian Avia company, short of orders now that the Czechoslovakian government had abandoned any attempt to defend what was left of their nation, was quick to offer the French the immediate delivery of 200 Avia B-534 fighters. The French, however, were more interested in the HS 12Y-31 engine that powered the plane. Skoda agreed to deliver twenty-five a month, but only a few arrived before Germany occupied the remainder of the country in March 1939. Attempts to buy 200 from the Soviets came to nothing. After being left out of the Munich talks, Stalin was trying to distance himself from his former ally. The only major success was 100 HS 12Y-31 engines acquired from the Swiss Saurer company.[5]

Foreign designers were queuing up to take advantage of the French plight. The Belgian Alfred Renard promised first deliveries of his Renard R.36 fighter within five months of a firm order being placed, but when the French discovered the excellent performance of the prototype had been achieved with the HS 12Y-21, which was not even in production, they soon lost interest. In the Netherlands, Frederick Koolhoven built his prototype F.K.58 in just eight weeks and immediately offered it to the French. Its armament was limited to four machine guns but its performance was broadly similar to the M.S.406. Koolhoven was so confident that he would find customers for the fighter somewhere in a war threatened Europe that production had begun before any orders had been placed, so he was able to promise rapid delivery. The French took advantage by ordering fifty. In December 1938, a second batch of 100 of the slightly improved Curtiss H75 A-2 were ordered from the United States, but these could not arrive until after April 1939.[6, 7]

With few options abroad, the French aircraft industry would have to come up with most of the fighters Plan V required. The latest version of the lightweight Caudron C.714 flew in the summer of 1938 and completed official trials in October. In an attempt to improve climbing performance, the two cannon had been replaced with four machine guns, but it did not help much; the C.714 climbed even slower than the Caudron C.713 prototype. Nevertheless, times were desperate and 140 were ordered.

There was still the Bloch MB.150 to fall back on. In August 1938, the modified Bloch MB.151 flew, but its performance remained well below the 480 km/hr (300 mph) target. However, more powerful versions of the Gnome-Rhône 14N engines were on the way and these enabled the Air Ministry to adopt a carrot and stick approach. An order for 432 was divided into three batches of 144. The first batch, powered by the 920-hp Gnome-Rhône 14N-35, need only be capable of 460 km/hr. This would at least enable production to get going and the planes could be used as trainers. The second batch, powered by the 1,000-hp GR 14N-25, would be expected to achieve 500 km/hr (311 mph). If the third batch, with the 1,060-hp GR 14N-49, did not manage 530 km/hr (329 mph), this contract would be cancelled. If, however, an additional 20 km/hr could be coaxed out of the design, then a further 100 would be ordered.[8, 9]

In the summer of 1938, the prospects for the bomber squadrons looked even bleaker. Only three modern bombers—the LeO 45, Amiot 351/354, and Breguet 691—had been ordered and none of them had even successfully completed official trials. The LeO 45 was still handicapped by its unreliable HS 14AA engines, Amiot had been asked to introduce extensive modifications to their bomber design and the Breguet interim assault plane had been ordered solely on the strength of company trials with the Breguet 690 fighter prototype. The more specialised fully armoured designs were a long way from becoming available. The Bloch team had been forced to return to the drawing board with their MB.170 and the Air Ministry wanted the revised version for reconnaissance and light bombing rather than low-level assault. The SNCASE SE.100, originally intended as a heavy fighter, and the armoured Dewoitine D.770 would not fly until 1939. As far as dive-bombers were concerned, the Air Ministry was still quite happy to leave the development in the hands of the Navy. The Navy, however, only wanted a plane that could operate against naval targets at sea, where, they believed, enemy fighter opposition was unlikely. The only plane they were seriously considering, the Loire-Nieuport LN.40, was a single-seater with no rear defence.

In the summer of 1938, there were, therefore, serious problems with all the major categories of bomber aircraft required, but things were about to improve. Confidence in the Breguet 690 increased when official trials confirmed the excellent performance claimed by the company. The assault bomber version of the fighter had still not flown but there was no reason to suppose the conversion would pose insuperable problems and the decision to put the plane straight into production seemed to have been justified. Construction of the first Breguet 691 prototype proceeded in parallel with the first production batch. The plane also looked good enough to cover some of the other gaps that had appeared. With the delays to the Bloch MB.170, a light bomber version with telescopic bombsight and larger bomb bay, was ordered as a substitute. The nationalised SNCAC was brought into the Breguet production program to produce this version (the Breguet 696). The Breguet design was also to be adapted as a dive-bomber (the Breguet 698), although production of this variant would only begin in the middle of 1940 when the initial batch of Breguet 691 assault planes had been completed. A small number of the single-seater Liore-Nieuport LN.411 dive-bomber were also ordered for the Air Force as a stopgap, with first deliveries expected before the end of 1939.[10]

Gnome et Rhône came to the rescue of the floundering LeO 45 project. The appearance in the summer of 1938 of the Gnome-Rhône 14N radials with virtually the same output as the HS-14AA finally enabled Lioré et Olivier to abandon the troublesome Hispano-Suiza engine. Renamed LeO 451, the Gnome-Rhône-powered version first flew in October 1938 and performance was virtually the same. Nearly two years after the bomber's first flight, production could finally begin. The new, more powerful Gnome-Rhône radials were also put to good use by the Bloch design team. A general redesign and the increased engine power transformed the disastrous Bloch MB.170 into the superlative Bloch MB.174. The prototype flew in January 1939; with a top speed of 530 km/hr (329 mph), it was faster than any French fighter. The initial version was a three-seater reconnaissance plane, with a secondary light bomber capacity, but as soon as the first batch of fifty was completed, production would switch to the Bloch MB.175 light bomber version. With an eventual planned monthly output of sixty Bloch MB.175 light bombers, compared to just forty LeO 451 medium bombers, the French seemed to be getting their priorities right.[11]

The Amiot bomber was also entering production. This too made use of the new Gnome-Rhône 14N radials. Turning the three-seater Amiot 340 into the four-seater Amiot 350 took far longer than expected; dressing up the Amiot prototype so that Vuillemin could impress the Germans had not helped. It was the following February before the Amiot 350 arrived at Villacoublay for official trials. Even then, there was still no provision for a rear gunner, and the new twin tail unit Amiot had designed was declared inadequate. It was agreed that the first fifty could be delivered with the original single tail unit while a new twin-tail plane was designed. As with the Bloch MB.150, these early production models would just be used for training and would not even be equipped for operations. The aim was just to get production going.

The French were now able to count on more American assistance. On his return from Munich, Daladier ordered La Grange back to the United States with instructions to get 1,000 planes delivered by the following summer. There seemed little reason to believe much would have changed since their last visit, but the French team discovered that two entirely new and very promising attack bombers were being developed: the Douglas DB-7 and the Martin 167; the former flew in October 1938, the latter in March 1939. The French delegation were, extremely generously, allowed to inspect these brand-new prototypes. Once again, they were warned this had to be done as discreetly as possible so as not to attract the wrath of the isolationists. Things were soon going very wrong. In January, the DB-7 prototype crashed during a test flight and worse was to follow when it transpired that an eagle-eyed reporter had noticed that one of the shaken survivors was not American. The revelation that a foreign power had been allowed to inspect a top-secret plane, which had not even entered service in the United States, sparked a wave of protests that for a time threatened to halt all further American aid to France.[12]

Roosevelt, however, refused to bow to public pressure and even insisted the French should have priority over any orders the US Army Air Corps might place. In February 1939, 115 Martin 167s and 100 Douglas DB-7s were ordered, even though the former had not flown and the latter had just crashed. Both were considered too large by the French for the low-level assault role, so it was planned to use the Douglas as a light bomber and the longer-range Martin as a reconnaissance plane. French faith in these untested designs was matched only by their optimism over delivery dates. The first Douglas DB-7s were expected to be handed over in June 1939 and the first Martins were supposed to follow a month later.[13] Given the speed with which the French were putting their own designs into production, they really had no right to expect such prompt deliveries from anyone else.

In October 1938, the LeO 451 had finally been cleared for mass production but although SNCASE had been preparing for this since 1937, the first production LeO 451 did not fly until March 1939; by the end of August, only twenty-two had been built. The simpler Amiot 350 was far easier to build, but there was little sign the company was doing any better. Nor was there any sign of relations between Amiot and the Ministry improving. Amiot was accused of focusing on expanding his factory space rather than building bombers and that subcontracting out some of the work would produce quicker results.[14] In January 1939, Amiot was still promising first deliveries the following April, but in reality, production was well behind schedule and his company was in serious financial difficulty, somewhat ironic given the money being pumped into American companies.[15] By the summer of 1939, no Amiot 351/354 bombers had been built. Breguet had more success in getting production going but even so, by August 1939, only a handful of Breguet 691s had been completed. As might have been expected, no Martin 167 or Douglas bombers had arrived from the United States. On the eve of the Second World War, fewer than fifty modern bombers of all types had been built, and only seventeen were actually in the hands of the Air Force. The French also had fifteen Potez 633 light bombers, planes that were supposed to be delivered to Romania and Greece, but which the French government had appropriated. The most numerous modern bomber available was one the French had decided not to order for their Air Force. In fact, the Potez 63 was the only twin-engined plane that had been built in any numbers for any role. The prototype of the Potez 637, with ventral cupola, had flown in the August 1938, followed by the more extensively modified Potez 63.11, with the fully-glazed nose, the following December. By August 1939, the first batch of sixty-seven Potez 637 and the first examples of the definitive Potez 63.11 had been handed over to the Air Force. In all, nearly 400 fighter, reconnaissance, and bomber versions of the Potez 63 had been built.

As far as fighters were concerned, in the autumn of 1938, any upturn in production seemed as far off as ever. Even worse, the twin-engined Potez 630 coming off the production lines were not proving satisfactory. The scaled-down HS-14AB engines the Potez 630 used were not thought to suffer from the problems of its HS-14AA big brother, but it soon became clear the engine could not cope with the rough handling it could expect in normal service use. Fortunately, the Gnome-Rhône 14M *Mars* engine was now available as a substitute. The Hispano-Suiza-powered Potez 630 was abandoned and production switched to the Gnome-Rhône *Mars*-powered Potez 631. The eighty Potez 630 would be used for training. However, this setback had one major consolation. The decision to phase out the Hispano-Suiza HS-14AB would leave more production space for the HS 12Y-31. Indeed, with the LeO 451 now using Gnome-Rhône radials, the HS-14AA was no longer required either and Hispano-Suiza could focus all their efforts on building liquid-cooled engines. Hispano-Suiza's foray into the radial engine market was finally over, but France had paid a heavy price.

With increased HS 12Y-31 output, M.S.406 production could be stepped up. Indeed, there were now fears the production of M.S.406 airframes might not be able to keep pace with HS 12Y-31 output. In a bid to speed up all aircraft production, France turned to Albert Caquot, the architect of the *politique de prototypes* in the early days of the Air Ministry but, more significantly, the man who had helped boost aircraft production in the closing stages of the First World War. Caquot immediately set about rationalising the production of all French aircraft, including the M.S.406. Instead of the three nationalised factories involved in the production programme each producing complete fighters, the Billancourt (SNCAC) plant would build the wing; Émile Dewoitine's Toulouse plant (SNCAM) the tail unit; and Nantes-Bouguenais (SNCAO) would build the fuselage, assemble the final product, and test it. Initially, this reorganisation slowed down deliveries, but by the spring of 1939, it was beginning to pay dividends. Before 1 April 1939, only 106 M.S.406s had reached the Air Force, but in the next five months, a further 466 arrived. By August 1939, seven fighters were being completed every day. Despite the years of delay, M.S.406 production was well ahead of the Spitfire and had even overtaken the Hurricane. The M.S.406 may not have been the easiest fighter in the world to mass produce, but it was clearly not impossible.

The overall situation was further improved by the prompt delivery of the American Curtiss H75s. The American company set up the French-sponsored production line with remarkable speed, and the first H75 arrived in France in December 1938, just seven months after the contract had been signed. By the end of August 1939, 176 had reached the Air Force. During the same month, the last of the 200 Potez 631s were delivered. By this time, the first Bloch MB.151 were arriving and the Caudron C.714 was on the way. In the

Netherlands, Koolhoven was scrambling to deliver his F.K.58s before war forced his country to impose an arms embargo. However, with over 1,000 Potez 631, Curtiss H75, and M.S.406s already delivered, it was beginning to look as if these back-up fighters might not be required after all.

In May 1939, the first step in the expansion of the fighter force took place when a third fighter group was added to four of the existing eight fighter wings. By the end of August, all except three fighter groups and the Regional Defence squadrons in the rear had modern fighters. With Polish forces preparing for a possible German attack and war looking unavoidable, these new planes had arrived none too soon. It seemed that the French aircraft industry had won this particular race against time. There was a sense of euphoria that a catastrophic situation had been averted in the nick of time.

It seemed France would have enough fighters, but the question was whether they would be good enough. Early in 1938, it was generally assumed that the M.S.406 and Curtiss H75 would, at the very least, hold their own against the German Messerschmitts. In the spring, the French had the opportunity to test a Jumo-powered Bf 109 captured by the Republicans in Spain. The French pilots were impressed by the simplicity of the design, the lightness of its construction, and its aerodynamic qualities. Ominously, it was considered to be remarkably fast, given the low output of its Jumo engine. Nevertheless, with an estimated top speed of around 460 km/hr, it was slower than the M.S.406, and climbing performance was vastly inferior. The French were still confidently claiming the Bf 109 with the more powerful DB 600 was only capable of 490 km/hr (304 mph), and it was believed that this speed had only been achieved by further reducing climbing performance.[16, 17]

There was, however, plenty of evidence to contradict this complacency. In June 1938, in a much-publicised record-breaking flight, a Heinkel He 100 flew 100 km at an average speed of 635 km/hr (nearly 400 mph). This was obviously a specially boosted racer, but no French designers were contemplating anything like this, even with a racer. Vuillemin's close encounter with this plane during his visit to Germany made sure its capabilities would not be forgotten. By the autumn of 1938, the Spitfire's speed had been upgraded to 581 km/hr (360 mph) and the Curtiss H81 (P-40) prototype, powered by the new Allison inline engine, was, the French believed, capable of 631 km/hr.[18]

The French Air Ministry had little choice but to believe the latest reports emanating from Germany, claiming that the production version of the Daimler-Benz DB 601-powered Bf 109E was capable of 570 km/hr. It seemed both Germany and Britain had fighters in service that were considerably faster than anything the French possessed, even in prototype form. There was still the hope that these speeds had only been achieved by sacrificing other essential qualities of a fighter. In Spain, many had observed that the high-speed Bf 109 had sometimes struggled against the more manoeuvrable Polikarpov I-15 biplane and similarly, the monoplane Polikarpov I-16 had problems with the Fiat CR.32 biplanes. It also seemed the high-speed monoplanes had suffered higher accident rates. It was all very well designing sophisticated combat planes for professional peace-time pilots, but in wartime training, standards inevitably dropped. Fighters had to be easy to fly.

The French had also had an opportunity to find out what the much-vaunted Spitfire was capable of. In June 1938, the French asked if they could test the plane. The British government had decided no nation would even be allowed to try out the plane until at least 100 had been delivered to the RAF, but an exception was made for the French and two top French test pilots, Michel Détroyat and Constantin Rozanoff, were allowed to fly it in September 1938. The Frenchmen were not over impressed. The fighter was extremely fast, but they considered it more difficult to fly and less manoeuvrable than French designs.[19] The British would almost certainly have turned down a request for deliveries of the fighter to France. As it was, the French did not even attempt to place an order. The Merlin engine was a different matter, and the French immediately set about acquiring the rights to manufacture the engine that powered the Spitfire.

The Spitfire was indeed more difficult to fly and less manoeuvrable at high speed than the M.S.406. The French were also right that the Spitfire had been designed as a bomber interceptor, not for fighter-versus-fighter combat. Nevertheless, speed is important. Deciding what aspects of performance should be sacrificed in the quest for higher speed is always a tricky balancing act. The history of fighter development is littered with designs that were either extremely fast but too difficult to fly, or superbly manoeuvrable aircraft that lacked the speed to be effective. The French were beginning to suspect that they were getting the balance wrong.

A first step towards redressing the balance in favour of speed was taken in the summer of 1938 with the release of a new fighter specification. Clearly influenced by the speeds being achieved elsewhere, the Air Ministry asked designers to aim for 570 km/hr (354 mph). Caquot did not believe even this was enough. He was convinced the Germans would be introducing 600 km/hr combat planes into service within a year.[20] Caquot was right that more speed was required, but given that the 1936 520 km/hr target had not yet been achieved by any French designer, the new target was ambitious enough. Indeed, it was not at all clear how even 570 km/hr could be achieved with existing engines.

It was not like the twenties, when faster fighters existed but were rejected for various reasons. In 1938, there was nothing flying that was faster than the M.S.406 and there was nothing in the pipeline. Neither Loire-Nieuport nor Dewoitine were even aiming for 570 km/hr with their latest projects, the LN.60 and D.520. The favourite to replace the M.S.406 was the M.S.450.

The plane kept the same wing, although four belt-fed machine guns replaced the two drum-fed guns, increasing firepower and eliminating the drag of the protruding drums. The fuselage was a more modern stressed skin structure but the company saw little reason to tamper too much with what had proven to be a very successful design. Many of the machine tools used for the M.S.406 could be used for the M.S.450, making it easier to introduce on the production lines. For more speed, Morane-Saulnier was happy to await the arrival the 1,000-hp HS 12Y-51 engine. The first prototype of this engine became available in the spring of 1939, and with it, the M.S.450 managed 560 km/hr.[21]

In the meantime, the Bloch MB.150 was also coming to be viewed as a successor to the M.S.406 rather than just a poor substitute. Given the disastrous performance of the first prototypes, this seemed rather optimistic, but the new low-drag Mercier engine cowlings and the more powerful radials Gnome et Rhône were now developing, led the Air Ministry to believe the 550 km/hr target they had set was obtainable. These hopes seemed even more optimistic when the first improved Bloch MB.152 prototype took to the air in October 1938. Powered by a 1,030-hp GN 14N-21, far from achieving the 520 km/hr expected by the company, it was barely capable of matching the speed of the Bloch MB.151. When re-engined with the GN 14N-25 specified by the Air Ministry, it managed just 470 km/hr; this was still slower than the M.S.406. The manufacturers experimented with every conceivable combination of engine cowling and propeller to increase speed, but with little success. With M.S.406 production increasing rapidly, the Air Ministry was not convinced it needed the Bloch fighter anymore and its future was hanging in the balance. Then, in May 1939, news came, stating that the latest version of the fighter had managed 530 km/hr.[22] It appeared that the company's persistence with the design had been rewarded. The third production batch was given the go-ahead and the order for the additional 100 Bloch MB.155 was also confirmed, but still with the proviso that it had to be capable of 550 km/hr.

This was still short of the 570 km/hr target and the only way of achieving this seemed to be more power. The Air Ministry were already taking steps to acquire the British Merlin, but it seemed unlikely that Britain would be able to supply large numbers, if any, and it would take time to set up production in France.[23] Gnome-Rhône were working on their 1,200-hp GR 14R, prototypes of which were due in 1939. With the HS 14AA and 14AB motors abandoned, Hispano-Suiza was now focusing on their liquid-cooled engines again but even the most optimistic did not foresee the 1,000-hp HS 12Y-51 entering production before the end of 1939. As the M.S.450 demonstrated, not even this seemed capable of taking French fighters beyond 570 km/hr. At a much earlier stage of development was the completely revised 1,200-hp HS 12Z, but the first prototype would not even begin bench trials until September 1939. Without substantially more powerful engines, the 570 km/hr target seemed beyond the reach of French designers.

The unconventional approaches the Air Ministry were willing to consider underlined how desperate they were. In 1936, the government had set up the *Arsenal de l'aéronautique* research centre to investigate the more speculative lines of research that might not appeal to commercial companies. They were soon coming up with ideas about how much higher speeds might be achieved with existing engines. The Arsenal-Delanne 10 made use of the special aerodynamic properties of the so-called tandem monoplane or Nenadovich biplane configuration, which allowed much higher speeds without impossibly long take-off runs. With the same take-off speed of a conventional fighter, and using the HS 12Y-31, a top speed of 600 km/hr (375 mph) was theoretically possible. Arsenal set to work building a prototype to test the theory. Arsenal also suggested a radical twin-engined fighter with two HS 12Y-31 engines in tandem driving coaxial propellers, which would offer twice the power without increasing drag. The Air Ministry hoped to have the Arsenal VG.20 prototype flying by 1939.[24]

The Air Ministry were pushing the development of both these project, but nothing this innovative was needed, and it was the Arsenal team that demonstrated this. The French lightweight fighter programmes had already produced some interesting results. The Arsenal's contribution to this line of research was the wooden VG-30, powered by an air-cooled 450-hp Potez 12D inline engine. By trying to achieve high speeds with low power, the French were artificially creating the situation German designers found themselves in when they only had the 650 hp of the Jumo engine at their disposal. Designs had to be as aerodynamically clean as possible. A mock-up of the sleek Arsenal VG-30 displayed at the 1936 Paris Air Show, contrasted sharply with the corpulent fuselage of the nearby M.S.405. When the Potez engine failed to materialise, the airframe was re-stressed to take the larger but considerably more powerful 680-hp HS 12X. The liquid-cooled engine required a bulky radiator, but the Arsenal claim that 500 km/hr ought to be possible immediately attracted the attention of the Air Ministry.[25]

The first flight took place in October 1938 and it was indeed faster than the M.S.406, despite its less powerful engine. Official trials suggested that the internally mounted oil cooler was perhaps taking aerodynamic finesse too far and the engine was constantly overheating. Nevertheless, the maximum speed of 485 km/hr was impressive, better even than the Bf 109 with a similar engine, and there seemed no reason 515 km/hr might not be possible with a larger-diameter airscrew. Basic streamlining had done it rather than exotic configurations. The Arsenal fighter was a remarkable 120 km/hr faster than the similarly powered Dewoitine D.500. Arsenal decided to take the programme one stage further by strengthening the design to take the Hispano-Suiza HS 12Y-31, and it was with some expectation that the Air Ministry awaited the performance of this version.

This was not the only good news for the Air Ministry. While Arsenal set about building what would become the VG-33, it seemed French designers might not have to wait for the HS 12Y-51 engine for more power. Hispano-Suiza had come up with the significantly better Szydlowski-Planiol supercharger, which, with a slight repositioning of the engine-mounted cannon, could be fitted to the standard HS 12Y-31. Also, the French had finally appreciated the significance of the ducted radiator German and British designs were using. Both these improvements could be applied immediately to the M.S.406. The Szydlowski-Planiol supercharger ought to be worth as much as 30 km/hr and the ducted radiator replacing the clumsy retractable system ought to make another 20 km/hr possible. With these improvements applied to the basic M.S.406, the French were well on the way to the 570 km/hr target with a highly manoeuvrable fighter that was already in production. There were growing doubts within the Air Ministry that any of the fighters being developed, including the Dewoitine D.520, were likely to have any advantage over a fully developed M.S.406.[26]

Initial trials with the Dewoitine D.520 did nothing to dispel these doubts. The prototype made its first flight on 2 October, the day after the Arsenal VG-30. For his D.520, Dewoitine resorted to Nieuport's failed wing embedded radiator, but even with the 920 hp HS 12Y-29 engine, could not do better than 480 km/hr, which was slower than the Arsenal VG-30 and M.S.406. He too now turned to the ducted radiator but even with this, the prototype only managed 500 km/hr.[27] The D.520 appeared to be going the same way as the D.513.

As far as Émile Dewoitine was concerned, only more power could save the day and the Merlin was the only engine that could provide it. Switching to the British engine was a drastic step to take. The Merlin was a much heavier engine and the fighter would also lose its engine-mounted cannon, a central feature of the fighter. Wings would need reinforcing if they were to absorb the recoil of cannon. It would be a complete redesign, but it seemed the only option. France was trying to organise licence production, but it would be eighteen months before deliveries could begin. In a rather desperate move, Dewoitine called on the British ambassador in Paris to see if he could get the British to deliver 200 Merlins a month. Britain's refusal to deliver so many cannot have come as a surprise.[28] In truth, Dewoitine was still not getting the most from the engine power available to him. Dewoitine borrowed another idea already being used abroad: exhaust stubs that generated a little more forward thrust. In January 1939, with these, the prototype managed 520 km/hr, becoming the first French fighter to achieve the 1936 speed requirement.[29]

On hearing this news, Caquot, accompanied by the test pilot Détroyat, rushed down to Toulouse to inspect the prototype. Détroyat reported that the fighter was perfectly satisfactory. Indeed, according to Caquot, he considered it to be even more manoeuvrable than the M.S.406. It was a simpler design than the M.S.406 and would be easier to mass produce and now that Dewoitine's Toulouse plant was only building M.S.406-tail units rather than the whole plane, there was plenty of spare production capacity.[30] Caquot wanted to order it immediately, but there were problems. The Air Ministry had used up all the funds for the first stage of Plan V with orders for the M.S.406, the Curtiss H75, the Bloch MB.152, and the Caudron C.714. In any case, there were still many who did not see the Dewoitine D.520 as any great advance over the M.S.406. After all, the Morane-Saulnier fighter could also benefit from the thrust-producing exhaust stubs, ducted radiator and HS 12Y-29 engine, not to mention the Szydlowski-Planiol supercharger. The fixed radiator and Szydlowski-Planiol supercharger ought to push the speed of the M.S.406 up to 540km/hr.[31] Trials with the new exhaust stubs demonstrated these were worth another 37 km/hr. Rather than order a completely new fighter, there was a good case for incorporating these improvements into a proven fighter that was already in production.

Caquot, however, argued that with the same technology, the Dewoitine D.520 ought to be capable of 600 km/hr.[32] This was pure speculation and official trials with the second prototype in March 1939 provided little evidence that he might be right. The fighter still did not have the Szydlowski-Planiol supercharger, but even so, the 527 km/hr achieved scarcely suggested 600 km/hr was possible. Nevertheless, Caquot managed to persuade La Chambre to order 200. The speed with which the first could be delivered was a factor in this decision. Dewoitine was promising the first by September 1939, a mere six months after the order had been placed. This would be before the first engines with the Szydlowski-Planiol supercharger (a combination that became the HS 12Y-45) arrived, so early production models would have to make do with the HS 12Y-31. Trials were ordered with this power plant to see how this would affect performance.[33]

As the order for 200 would actually be over and above the requirements of Plan V and funds for the order did not exist, 200 M.S.406s were made available for export to balance the books. In June 1939, a revised Plan V was introduced, which required a further 810 fighters by the end of 1940, and new contracts included one for 510 more Dewoitine D.520s. In theory, the revised Plan V meant the 200 Morane fighters earmarked for export were no longer surplus to requirements. However, with production of the M.S.406 now running at around 100 per month, La Chambre did not feel he needed any more M.S.406 fighters and the exports were allowed to continue.

It was an extremely relieved La Chambre that confronted the Parliamentary Air Commission in June 1939. The commission still believed it was a mistake to focus on fighter production and was ready to give La Chambre a hard time. Laurent-Eynac led the assault, criticising the lack of bombers and suggesting that fighter production should be cut back so that more could be built. An exuberant La Chambre brushed aside the criticisms. He explained how difficult bombers were to build. The LeO 451 required 60,000 man-hours to build, four M.S.406s or ten Dewoitine D.520s could be built with the same effort. On the question of quality, he agreed that the M.S.406 might not be the most advanced fighter in the world, but it was equally absurd to suggest it was already totally obsolete. Faster fighters were in the pipeline. He pointed out that the improved M.S.450 had flown and was some 75 km/hr faster than its predecessor and this was being considered for production. New Bloch fighters capable of 540 km/hr, he claimed, slightly exaggerating the reported performance, were already rolling off the production lines. The Dewoitine D.520 had also been ordered into production and, once all modifications had been incorporated, this would be capable of 600 km/hr.[34] For the time being, La Chambre had silenced his critics.

Indeed, the news kept getting better. After this meeting, the Loire-Nieuport LN.60, now being developed by the nationalised SNCAO as the CAO.200, and the upgraded Arsenal VG-33 took to the air. Both were still powered by the trusty HS 12Y-31 but both made use of ducted radiators and the new ejector exhaust stubs. The Arsenal VG-33 had lost all vestiges of its lightweight origins and was now heavier than the M.S.406. The CAO.200 was nearly as heavy and with the ultra-low wing areas, arguably both designers were going too far in their quest for speed. Nevertheless, both handled well, and with the CAO.200 managing 550 km/hr and the Arsenal VG-33 560 km/hr, they were impressively fast.[35] Powered by exactly the same motor as the Dewoitine D.510, the two fighters were nearly 40 per cent faster. With the HS 12Y-45, the Arsenal fighter was expected to achieve 590 km/hr. With the HS 12Y-51, the CAO.200 ought to be capable of exceeding the 600 km/hr mark. The June 1939 version of Plan V still required a further 200 fighters to be ordered. The VG-33 had a slight edge in terms of performance. Its wooden structure would also conserve vital raw materials and enable the untapped manpower resources of the carpentry industry to be used. The production version of the Arsenal fighter was to be powered by the HS 12Y-45. At about the same time, it was also decided to abandon the initial HS 12Y-31 version of the D.520 and go straight to the HS 12Y-45 model, even though first deliveries of the engine could not possibly arrive in time for the first D.520 airframes.

As France once more faced the prospect of war, this time over German claims on Polish territory, Vuillemin believed he had good reason to be confident. Little progress had been made with modernising the bomber fleet but he was able to tell Daladier that good progress had been made with reconnaissance squadrons and there had been a transformation in the fighter force. Most fighter units had now completed conversion to modern equipment and would be able to protect army reconnaissance planes and, more significantly for Daladier's piece of mind, guarantee the security of French territory.[36] The French Prime Minister approached the looming crisis a far more confident man.

With hindsight, such confidence seems rather misplaced, but given the state of the fighter force just twelve months before during the Sudetenland crisis, the transformation was nothing short of miraculous. The future also seemed bright. The June 1939 production plan foresaw the delivery of over 600 Dewoitine D.520 and third and fourth series Bloch MB.152 and Bloch MB.155 by 1 May 1940.[37] The first Arsenal VG-33 fighters should also be available by this time and with production of the 1,000-hp HS 12Y-51 due to begin before the end of 1939, it seemed that there was every chance of establishing technical parity with the Germans by the following spring.

The bomber situation was more worrying; the French did not have a single bomber in service that they dare operate by day. However, by the spring of 1940, around 1,000 modern bombers should be in French Air Force hands.[38] If France could delay the decisive confrontation with Germany just a little longer and the production targets could be met, the French would be in a good position to challenge and respond to Luftwaffe attacks on French cities. Whether that was the danger France ought to be worried about was another matter.

10

From Confidence to Panic

On 1 September, German forces invaded Poland and two days later, France honoured her commitment to her eastern ally by declaring war on Germany. The moment for which the French had been planning for the past two decades had finally arrived. For the French nation, the days that followed were anxious times. The air assault, which the experts had proclaimed would herald a new world war, could not be long delayed. Parisians felt particularly vulnerable. Women and children were evacuated. Companies prepared to move their premises outside the capital. Those that remained braced themselves for the carnage the public had been led to believe was inevitable. The emergency services, including special gas squads, stood ready to assist those that remained. The French fighter force prepared to repulse the German bombers. The huge French stockpiles of mustard gas and phosgene bombs were readied for use as French bombers prepared to retaliate as best they could.

The assault, however, never came. Days, then weeks, passed with no sign whatsoever of the Luftwaffe. Even when Poland had been defeated, and the Luftwaffe was in a position to concentrate its might against France, no attempt was made to strike at any target, military or civilian. In Poland, towns had been bombed, but even these appeared to have been legitimate attacks on communication targets rather than deliberate attempts to terrorise the Polish people. The reports reaching France made it very clear that the campaign in Poland did not follow the Douhetian pattern.[1] The Luftwaffe appeared to have focused on supporting the German Army, and no attempt had been made to force victory by air power alone. Poland had been defeated because her army had been overrun, not because the morale of her people had been broken.[2] It seemed that the French Army had been right all along; wars would continue to be decided on the battlefield and not by independent air operations.

The French government was not so sure. It still seemed highly likely that German bombers would eventually launch either terror raids on French cities or attacks on industrial targets. Now that France was at war, it was the latter the government and military feared more. Plans to re-equip the Air Force would be shattered if factories producing the planes were reduced to rubble. Much of French industry was still concentrated in the Paris and Lyon regions and both these areas were well defended; factories elsewhere were less fortunate. On the day war broke out, Vuillemin was ordered to strengthen defences in the rear and the Air Ministry told the fighter factories at Nantes, Toulouse, Châteauroux, and Bourges to organise their own defences with the fighters they were building and ferry pilots.[3]

The reports emerging from Poland, however, were emphasising the tactical use made of air power, not strategic bombing. There was much else to ponder. One striking feature was the intensity of Luftwaffe operations; German pilots were apparently flying up to five sorties a day.[4] French Air Force observers were impressed by the way the Poles had used their own bomber squadrons in low-level air strikes. These had proved to be one of the few effective means the Poles had of slowing down the advancing German panzers. Losses had been heavy to anti-aircraft defences, but some German units had reportedly been held up for twenty-four hours. Armengaud was among the observers and was able to confirm how right he had been about the value of tactical bombing in defence and attack.[5]

These reports affected French planning. Low-level ground-attack, often by the obsolete Henschel Hs 123 biplanes the Luftwaffe had used in Spain, had made more of an impression than the Ju 87 Stuka, so Vuillemin dropped the dive-bomber. He had never been happy with the single-seater Loire-Nieuport LN.411 and those ordered for the Air Force were now handed over to the Navy. The Breguet 698 dive-bomber, and indeed the Breguet 696 light bomber, were also abandoned in order to enable more of the assault version to be built and the six proposed dive-bomber units were replaced by an equal number of assault groups. The decision to abandon the Breguet 696 and the priority given to the reconnaissance version of the Bloch MB.174, rather than the Bloch MB.175 bomber, left the proposed light bomber units relying totally on the Douglas DB-7, so the Martin 167 was switched back to the light bomber role it was designed for.

The Air Ministry was trying to assemble a powerful tactical bomber force. The question was whether the French Army would see the need for it. The Maginot Line ruled out a war of manoeuvre along the Franco-German frontier, but further north the French were planning to advance into Belgium to meet the German Army. In a far more audacious project, if Germany invaded the Netherlands, Gamelin was planning to advance into southern Netherlands to provide a link between the Dutch and Belgium armies. These operations involved French forces operating beyond the artillery support established French lines could provide, and were the sort of situation where close air support had been used in the First World War and the Rif campaign.

The Army, however, was more interested in indirect support. It wanted all Allied bombers to slow down the German advance, to give French forces more time to establish themselves. More intimate support on the battlefield was not needed. The initial mobile phase would only be brief and once the French had established their defensive lines, and the artillery had moved up, it was assumed the front would become static. It was not worth rethinking policy just because of this brief, initial mobile phase. Besides, the fighting in Poland had demonstrated that low-level bombing was very expensive. Also, the Poles had few tanks and little artillery, whereas the French had huge quantities of both. The Poles may have been forced to throw their planes into low-level attacks on tanks but the French would not need to resort to such tactics; French firepower would prevent the sort of breakthroughs achieved in Poland.

Meanwhile, the fighting on the Western Front had taken on an unreal air, with barely a shot being exchanged. The first task of the French reconnaissance aircraft had been to map the German side of the lines and watch out for any signs of offensive action. With only thirty-two of the new Potez 637s available, their resources were hardly adequate. Although considered dangerously slow for such missions, both the Mureaux 117 and Bloch MB.131 had to be used. Even Bloch MB.200 bomber units were used in hair-raising maximum-speed darts across the front line, with crews flying their dated aircraft at continuous full throttle—regardless of the permanent harm this might inflict on the engines. Nevertheless, early operations went more smoothly than anyone had dared hope. The Luftwaffe was almost wholly committed in Poland and aerial opposition was light. During the first four days of hostilities, the French Air Force suffered no losses whatsoever.

Initially at least, the evidence seemed to support Vuillemin's claim that the Curtiss H75 and Morane-Saulnier M.S.406 were good enough to protect the reconnaissance planes. Reports coming in from Poland had reinforced the idea that the much-vaunted Bf 109 lacked the manoeuvrability for fighter-versus-fighter combat. It was even suggested that the slow but agile Polish PZL P.11 was superior to the Messerschmitt. The Poles seemed to think the even less manoeuvrable but powerfully armed Bf 110 was the more formidable foe.[6] Such observations were immediately seized upon by those who still clung to the belief that the low speeds of French fighters need not be a major handicap.

Some early successes over the Western Front were encouraging. The first French victory was gained on 8 September when four Bf 109s engaged a formation of five Curtiss H75s. Initially, the French pilots were taken by surprise, but they soon turned the tables on their assailants, claiming the destruction of two German fighters for no loss to themselves.[7] During the remainder of September, aerial activity remained very light but by claiming twenty confirmed victories for the loss of twelve of their own fighters, the French appeared at the very least to be holding their own. The first French reconnaissance planes (a Potez 637 and a Mureaux 115) were not shot down until the sixth day of hostilities. Over the next couple of days, a further seven reconnaissance and observation planes failed to return.[8] These were hardly the excessive losses predicted before the war, but they were still enough to encourage the French to adopt a more cautious approach.

Using the Bloch MB.200 by day was soon proving too risky. Of three sent out on the 9th, two were shot down and no more Bloch sorties were flown. Indeed, the obvious inadequacies of the bomber fleet, coupled with the failure of any German bomber offensive to materialize, resulted in an instruction on 14 September ordering all bomber units, apart from four Amiot 143 and two Farman F.222 groups, to the rear to await the delivery of more modern equipment. General Têtu, the commander of the recently created Eastern Air Zone (ZOAE: *Zone d'Opérations Aériennes Est*), which controlled all Air Force units along the northern sector of the Maginot Line, could not see the point in transferring bomber units to the rear to wait for equipment that did not exist yet. Instead, he suggested that some of these aircrews should be retrained to reinforce under-strength fighter and reconnaissance squadrons.[9] Têtu was far more worried about the state of these units than the lack of an effective bomber force. A few months later, he would be appointed commander of all Air Force units directly attached to the army along the entire north-eastern front.

Meanwhile those units that remained at the front were instructed to operate with caution. If fighter escorts were not available, reconnaissance squadrons operated at dawn or dusk, so that at least part of the mission would be carried out in poor light. Unescorted missions in broad daylight were only considered if crews could make use of cloud cover. Bomber groups confined their reconnaissance missions to the hours of darkness. The observation squadrons (GAO: *Groupe Aérien d'Observation*) were able to operate without fighter protection, provided they did not stray far from the front line. A limited offensive launched by the French Army on 15 September—a rather half-hearted attempt to take some pressure off the retreating Poles—required the support of these squadrons. Units equipped with obsolete aircraft (the Potez 39, the Breguet 27, and the Potez 25) were instructed to observe enemy positions only while flying over friendly territory and the Mureaux were only allowed to penetrate a few kilometres inside enemy airspace. It was not ideal, but losses in September were kept down to just twenty-two reconnaissance planes during the course of 700 sorties.[10]

During October, there was virtually no fighting on the ground. In the air, French fighters only claimed five confirmed kills, but did not lose a single plane. With no activity on the ground, observation squadrons were virtually grounded while they awaited the arrival of the first Potez 63.11. Reconnaissance or observation missions were only flown if a strong fighter escort was available. It was not unlike 1917. The Air Force once again had a large fleet of reconnaissance planes that were incapable of defending themselves. However, the French were confident that the new Potez 63.11 would prove to be just as effective as the Breguet 14 and Salmson 2 had been in the closing stages of the First World War.

The question was whether France would have enough time to get planes like the Potez 63.11 into service in sufficient numbers. The day war was declared, the Air Ministry set the production target as 742 combat planes per month by March 1940, more than twice the number delivered in August 1939. Caquot felt that even this would not be sufficient. He wanted the Air Force to move to a front line strength of 3,200 planes as quickly as possible. Assuming 50 per cent losses a month, 1,600 new combat planes would have to be delivered each month to maintain this strength. This was actually approved, but it soon became clear it was quite impossible. It was therefore replaced by a less ambitious scheme to raise monthly production to nearly 1,300 planes a month by October 1940.

It was still a very ambitious target and there could be no excuse for holding back. With peacetime expansion plans, there is always an argument for delaying orders and risking a short-term shortage in order to ensure the air force gets more advanced planes. France was now at war; the French were expecting (and indeed the Germans were planning) an autumn offensive on the Western Front. France could not risk a short-term shortage. In peacetime, all production can be used to re-equip units; in wartime, losses have to be replaced as well. Very few aircraft had been lost in September and October, but that would change if a full-scale German offensive was underway. With the American Neutrality Act coming into force, there had to be doubts about future American deliveries despite Roosevelt's assurances. This was not the time to be discarding the tried and tested planes that were already in production. At the time, and indeed in subsequent accounts, there has been a tendency to dismiss the M.S.406 and Potez 63 1934 generation of combat planes. Only planes designed after that could possibly be good enough. However, both the Luftwaffe and RAF would fight the battles of 1939–1940 almost exclusively with planes that evolved around 1934 and had been in production for some time. With full-scale fighting possibly just weeks away, France could not afford to start relying on aircraft that were not even in service yet.

The planes in production were adequate. The Potez 63.11 was arguably the best short-range tactical reconnaissance plane in the world. Even for medium to long-range reconnaissance, nobody had anything better. As a makeshift bomber, the Potez 633 lacked range, but otherwise was broadly equivalent to the British Blenheim and German Do 17. With war approaching, the Air Force had already commandeered the Potez 633 bombers that were supposed to be on their way to Greece and Romania. There was a case for continuing production so that French bomber squadrons would at least have something to help deal with an early German offensive.

Similarly, it was not the time to run down M.S.406 production. The Neutrality Act had halted the delivery of American fighters and the M.S.406 was the only fully tested fighter coming off the production lines in any numbers. Phasing it out was bound to cause a dip in production. There was now an even stronger case for keeping it in production and boosting its performance with a fixed ducted radiator and ejector exhaust stubs. Hispano-Suiza engines were no longer in such short supply. Although its HS 12Y-31 engine was being phased out of production, the December 1939 production programme was predicating a surplus of nearly 500 by May 1940.[11] There was also a strong case for upgrading the M.S.406 with the HS 12Y-45. The M.S.406 was the quickest way of getting this engine into the action. The Szydlowski-Planiol supercharger was the key technology the French needed to get to the front, not more advanced fighter airframes.

La Chambre, however, was totally against any attempt to prolong the life of the Morane-Saulnier fighter. When it was suggested that at least the two-gun wing tested on the M.S.450 could be used, he refused to even consider the idea.[12] No changes should be made that might prevent ending M.S.406 production as quickly as possible. The 550-km/hr Bloch MB.155, 560-km/hr Arsenal VG-33, and 600-km/hr Dewoitine D.520 were the fighters that France needed and Caquot was adamant that phasing out the M.S.406 would only cause a small temporary dip in production in December and January. Monthly output would never drop below the 200 fighters expected in December. Caquot promised that by January 1940, the French aircraft industry would be delivering 100 Bloch and Dewoitine fighters a month, and the first Arsenal VG-33s would be beginning to arrive. By May, French factories would be turning out 500 Bloch MB.155, Arsenal VG-33, and Dewoitine D.520s each month—or at least that was the plan.[13]

The M.S.406 was not being phased out to make way for these new fighters; bombers were to replace the Morane fighter at the Bouguenais and Billancourt plants. With the declaration of war, the number required of all types of warplanes increased dramatically, but the first expansion plan envisaged a greater increase in medium bombers (LeO 451 and Amiot 351/354) than fighters. When the target monthly output was cut from 1,600 to 1,300, planned production of medium bombers increased from 323 a month to 380 while planned single-seater fighter output was reduced from 500 to 400.[14] Long-range bombers had priority over fighters. This was not the direction the Air Force needed to go in.

Soon after the outbreak of war, the Air Ministry placed an order for 400 LeO 451 with the Bouguenais SNCAO plant, with production to begin as soon as they had completed their M.S.406 contract. SNCAC were given an order for 425 Amiot 351/352 bombers, and the Billancourt plant was given the task of building the tail units, once they had completed deliveries of the M.S.406 wings. Even if production went according to plan only twenty-nine LeO 451s and a handful of Amiot tails were expected from these plants by 1 May 1940.[15, 16] This was instead of continuing to turn out 150 M.S.406 fighters a month. In the spring of 1940, France would need fighters, not long-range bombers. It was a serious mistake.

This was not the only production capacity being squandered on the LeO 451. Two brand new factories were also to build the bomber. Eventually, one-sixth of the nationalised industry and nearly 10 per cent of the private sector would be devoted to LeO 451 production.[17, 18] The eventual aim was to have 240 LeO 451 bombers coming off the production lines each month, compared to 150 of the easier to build Amiot 350 series and just 170 of the far more useful Bloch and Breguet assault and light bombers. The Parliamentary Air Commission were getting their way. Douhet still ruled.

At least the Air Force avoided an autumn crisis. Hitler's plans to launch an immediate offensive on the Western Front were frustrated by the weather, and finally ended when a Luftwaffe liaison plane crashed in Belgium with the invasion plans on board. France would have the winter to rearm. On paper, it seemed like there ought to be plenty of time to re-equip the Air Force by the following spring, but it was far tighter than Caquot seemed to realise. Even if there were no teething problems with the new planes, aircrews would need time to get used to their new equipment. By abandoning the old and switching to the new, the French were still taking an enormous risk. It was very optimistic to expect to fight a war in the spring of 1940 with planes that were not in service in September 1939.

Caquot, however, was sure it was possible. Under the revised scaled-back October production plan, 1,300 Bloch MB.152, Dewoitine D.520, and Arsenal VG-33 fighters would be delivered by the following spring, along with over 600 medium bombers (LeO 451 and Amiot 350) and over 400 Breguet and Bloch assault and light bombers.[19] Yet to achieve this, everything had to go without a hitch. At the outbreak of war, the Dewoitine D.520 production programme was already slipping behind schedule, the Arsenal VG-33 had only just been ordered, and even the fully modified Bloch MB.152 had not entered service yet.

Finding the aircrews to fly these planes was even more challenging than building them. It was assumed that losses in personnel would not be as high as material losses. Even so, it was estimated that 40 per cent of front line aircrews would be killed, wounded, or captured each month. To maintain a front line strength of 3,200 planes would require the training of 1,200 pilots each month. It was estimated that the annual turnover of some 15,000 pilots would require thirty-four schools, each training 450 pilots a year. These establishments would in turn require 1,300 instructors and some 5,000 training aircraft. Once the need for adequate reserves was taken into account, aircraft requirements for the training programme were approaching a staggering 10,000 machines. In September 1939, there were only eighteen training schools with just 1,000 planes and 600 instructors. During the whole of 1939, only 500 pilots would emerge from these schools. Considering the predicted 40 per cent personnel losses each month, France would do well just to maintain its current front line strength of 1,600 through the winter of 1939–1940. Only in the spring of 1940, when aircraft production and aircrew training got into its stride, could any increase be contemplated.[20]

However, the enormous anticipated losses at the front did not materialise. In the first few months of war, losses were negligible. Also, the personnel problem was eased by an unexpected source of reinforcement. Following the German occupation of their country, many Czechs had fled to carry on the fight. Between May and August 1939, some 470 Czech airmen, of which half were pilots, arrived in France.[21] The French were rather unsure what to do with them. Initially, they were put in the Foreign Legion but the Czechs were promised that if France should ever find herself at war with Germany, they would get the chance to fight with the French Air Force. The occupation of Poland resulted in an even larger influx of foreign volunteers. When it became clear defeat was inevitable, some 300 assorted aircraft were flown out of Poland to neighbouring countries and many more airmen followed on foot. In October 1939, thousands began arriving on French soil. They included instructors, partially trained airmen from training schools, and a hard core of combat experienced aircrews.[22]

Exiled Polish and Czech leaders soon set about exerting pressure on the Allies to re-form their respective air forces. Two days after the declaration of war, a Czech delegation in Paris informed Daladier that there were sufficient Czechs in France to form a fighter brigade and two bomber groups, with a front line strength of around 150 aircraft, and still have sufficient personnel to form a 100 per cent reserve.[23] In October, Władysław Sikorski, the leader of the exiled Polish contingent, was claiming that there were already 200 Polish pilots in France and soon there would be 650 available for front line duties.[24] If Caquot's figures were to be believed, the aircraft for these foreign volunteers would certainly be available by the following spring. French Air Force strength might be increased very substantially at a stroke.

Caquot's revised plan, however, was soon going off course. Far from increasing, in October, production actually fell and it continued to fall in November. A rather chaotic mobilisation did not help, with workers from aircraft factories called up by mistake. It was November before this was put right. However, increasing M.S.406 production had been largely responsible for the impressive September figure, but this type was now being phased out and the fighters that were supposed to replace it were not arriving in the predicted numbers. Delays with the Dewoitine D.520 were particularly worrying. Problems with the deliveries of various components did not help and, as had always been known, HS 12Y-45 engines could not possibly arrive in time. By the end of July, the first four airframes were waiting for their Olaer undercarriages and Hispano-Suiza engines, but the undercarriages did not arrive until the beginning of September, and the first HS 12Y-45s only arrived at the end of the month; even then, there were only five of the promised thirty.[25] With the Arsenal fighter also lined up to use the engine, it did not seem likely that Hispano-Suiza would be able to meet demand.

The British Merlin was put forward as an alternative. Since Émile Dewoitine had first investigated this possibility in 1938, steps had been taken to set up production in France and Britain had also agreed to export 300 by June 1940. A plan was drawn up in October limiting output of the D.520 with the HS 12Y-45 to just 250. Subsequent machines at the Toulouse plant and those from the new assembly line being set up at Tarbes would be powered by the Merlin. The first Merlin-powered version was supposed to appear in February 1940 and Caquot expected the plane to have the same 600 km/hr top speed as the HS 12Y-45 powered version.[26]

Unfortunately, plans to build the Rolls-Royce Merlin were soon in trouble. Ford Air, a subsidiary of the American Ford car company, was given the contract and the programme relied heavily on American advisers and tools and jigs built in Detroit. However, Henry Ford declared that his company would be neutral in any European conflict and true to his word, when war broke out, American advisors were promptly pulled out of France and the shipment of the required tools and jigs halted. Preparations for the production of the British engine at Ford Air went ahead, but it soon became clear the first Merlins would not be built in time. On 18 November, the Air Ministry abandoned the Merlin-powered D.520 and reverted to the original HS 12Y-45. To free the necessary engines, the Arsenal VG-33 would have to make do with the HS 12Y-31. It was hoped both would be able to switch to the 1,000-hp HS 12Y-51 in July 1940.[27]

Meanwhile, overall output was plummeting. When target monthly production was reduced from 1,600 to 1,300, expectations for December fell from over 700 to just under 400. In fact, little more than 200 were delivered, and there was no sign of an end to the downward trend. The only good news was that Roosevelt kept his promise to find a way round the Neutrality Act. Contracts signed in October called for the delivery of 550 more Curtiss H75s, mostly the more advance 520 km/hr A-4 version. Some 100 of the new Curtiss H81 (P-40), an Allison-powered version of the H75, reported to be capable of 600 km/hr, were also ordered, along with 400 more Martin 167 and Douglas DB-7 light bombers. The French also ordered 6,000 American engines to power variants of French planes (the Lioré et Olivier LeO 458, the Bloch MB.176, the Breguet 695, and the Arsenal VG-32), although none could arrive before the summer of 1940.[28]

American companies had not been deterred by the Neutrality Act and had gone ahead with the construction of the planes already on order. The first 115 Martin 167s had been ordered in February 1939, virtually simultaneously with the plane's first flight and the French had rather optimistically wanted them all delivered by the end of the year.[29] The first production plane flew less than a month behind schedule and remarkably, the first 100 were ready to dispatch by November. By this time, orders had been increased to 345. If anything, the achievement of the Douglas company was even more remarkable. After the crash of the prototype in January 1939, the company set to work on a completely revised second prototype. Despite the problems, the French still wanted 100 by January 1940. The American company completely redesigned their plane and within six months, the second prototype was flying. Simultaneously, a production line was set up and the first example was handed over to the French in October 1939.[30]

Unfortunately, this prodigious American effort was not matched on the French side of the Atlantic. La Chambre had estimated that it would take four weeks to transport these planes across the Atlantic and assemble them.[31] When the Neutrality Act was relaxed on 3 November 1939, the first batch of Martin bombers was already ready to go but a shortage of Allied shipping prevented the first leaving the United States until mid-December, when the first batch of ninety-three Martin and eight Douglas bombers set sail for France. By this time, it had rather belatedly been decided that it was better if the planes were assembled in North Africa: the Atlantic crossing was safer, the winter weather was better for training, and there was no risk of enemy bombing interfering. The first American bombers arrived in North Africa on Christmas Day 1939 and by the beginning of April, 215 Martins and seventy-five Douglas bombers had arrived. Unfortunately, the facilities simply did not exist to assemble the planes and more time was wasted while equipment and personnel were brought over from France. A shortage of machine guns, radios, and bomb racks caused further delays. The first Martin was not officially accepted by the French Air Force until March 1940, seven months after the Americans had handed the first plane over to the French authorities. The first Douglas DB-7 was delivered to the Air Force the following month.[32]

The shortage of ancillary equipment was also plaguing French production. By mid-March 1940, French factories had turned out over 250 LeO 451, which was not far short of Caquot's revised plan. However, as is often the case when output has to increase suddenly, it only takes a shortage of one item of equipment to make these figures meaningless. By the middle of March, the Air

Force had only taken 116 on charge, and even many of these still lacked vital equipment. The Amiot 350 was doing even worse. Deliveries from the SNCAC Amiot production line set up after the declaration of war was not expected to deliver any planes until May 1940, a far less demanding target than those the French Air Ministry had set the American Douglas and Martin companies. Meanwhile Amiot were expected to deliver all 495 ordered from the parent company before the end of April 1940. Amiot thought this a ridiculous target and would only promise to deliver seventy-seven by the end of March. Even this modest target proved beyond Amiot. At the end of March, the Air Force only had twenty-seven, all from the first batch which were unarmed and intended for training only.

The Potez 63 demonstrated what the French aircraft industry was capable of with drive, and a fairly simple plane to build. By the spring of 1940, about 1,000 of the various versions had been delivered. Even this was falling behind schedule and not enough Potez 63.11 had been built to meet the insatiable demands of the reconnaissance and observation squadrons. Breguet managed to deliver fewer than 100 assault bombers by the end of March, little more than half of the output anticipated by the revised November production program, and most of these were powered by the unreliable Hispano-Suiza HS 14AB and could only be used for training. The more reliable Gnome-Rhône 14M was required for the higher priority Potez 63.11. Seventy-eight Breguet 691s came off the production lines before there were enough Gnome-Rhône radials for the Breguet 693.

The training programme was badly affected by the disappointing production figures. There were not enough modern planes needed for the final stages of crew training. No Potez 63.11 could be spared until February 1940, and even then, they were often removed from training centres to keep the front line squadrons happy.[33] There were even fewer modern bombers available. A reasonable number of fighter pilots were still emerging from training schools during the first months of war, but the supply of reconnaissance and bomber pilots virtually ceased.

The large number of trained Polish and Czech airmen should have eased the problem. Vuillemin was certainly very anxious to make best use of these volunteers as quickly as possible. Unfortunately, both the Poles and the Czechs would find their path to front line squadrons beset with problems. The first obstacle was their own insistence that they should be used to form independent Polish and Czech squadrons. This approach had its advantages. Maintaining the traditions and practices of their own air forces boosted morale and the language would also be less of a problem. It was certainly the quickest way of getting them operational.[34]

However, this approach did not appeal to Vuillemin. The French commander was already struggling to coordinate the various chains of command within his own Air Force, not to mention dealing with the various different commands within the Royal Air Force. Separate Polish and Czech air forces, with yet another command structure, was a complication he did not need. In any case, as the Poles and Czechs readily admitted, they did not possess the ground crews to maintain the proposed independent squadrons. It would place less burden on the system as a whole if Poles and Czechs were used to reinforce existing French units.[35]

There were also genuine doubts about the quality of these volunteers. Poland had, after all, been defeated in less than a month and wishful thinking led the French to attribute this to poor training rather than any qualities the German armed forces might possess. Czechs tended to be tarred with the same brush, even though they had not even had the chance to demonstrate their fighting capabilities. The French insisted that foreign aircrews had to be brought up to an acceptable standard and made familiar with French methods and training. Pilots with combat experience against the Luftwaffe were expected to endure a three-month retraining programme before they could join a front line unit.

There was also a political dimension to the problem, which particularly affected the Polish contingent. Most of the Czechs were with the French Foreign Legion and were technically already under French command. There was no recognised Czech government in exile, so it was possible to deal with the Czech airmen as individual volunteers. The Poles, however, had a government in exile led by Władysław Sikorski, which the airmen held allegiance too. Sikorski was not entirely trusted by his allies and the French certainly did not like the idea of a foreign armed force on their soil that might choose not to follow French instructions. Poles had to be under French command.

While the two sides wrangled over the future status of Polish air force units, the aircrews were left biding their time at their Lyon-Bron base. The Czechs were a little more fortunate. A first batch of thirty fighter pilots began training on Curtiss H75s and M.S.406s and these joined front line units in December and January.[36] Yet the French, struggling to implement their own training programme, did not have the resources or facilities to do any more to train Czechs or Poles. However, much Vuillemin might want the Poles and Czechs integrated into the French Air Force, he insisted that the training of French aircrews must have priority.

Meanwhile, the French were finding themselves overwhelmed by the number of Poles arriving. There were so many that in November, the French with difficulty, persuaded the British to take 300 pilots and 2,000 technical personnel off their hands. Denain, brought out of retirement to be the French-Polish liaison officer, was horrified that such a valuable resource was being allowed to leave the country.[37] However, when more Poles arrived the French found themselves persuading the British to take more. Given the treatment they were getting in France, the ones who left considered themselves the

Ader's twin-engine Avion III on display in Paris in 1908.

Caudron G.3 equipped one squadron on the outbreak of war and was the basis for the twin-engined G.4.

Caudron G.4: France's first twin-engined combat plane. (*Raoul Berthelé*)

The Caudron R.4: the plane Barès wanted as the standard multi-purpose combat plane.

Pierre Cot (right) with General Vuillemin (centre).

Air Minister Guy La Chambre (1938–1940).

The high performance of the Martin B-10 forced the French to abandon the BCR concept, and in particular, the drag-evoking nose turret. Ironically, the American bomber achieved its high performance with a nose turret.

The highly streamlined LeO 45 was very advanced but also expensive and difficult to build. (*via Tony Buttler*)

There was a medieval air about the Amiot 140 'flying fortress'.

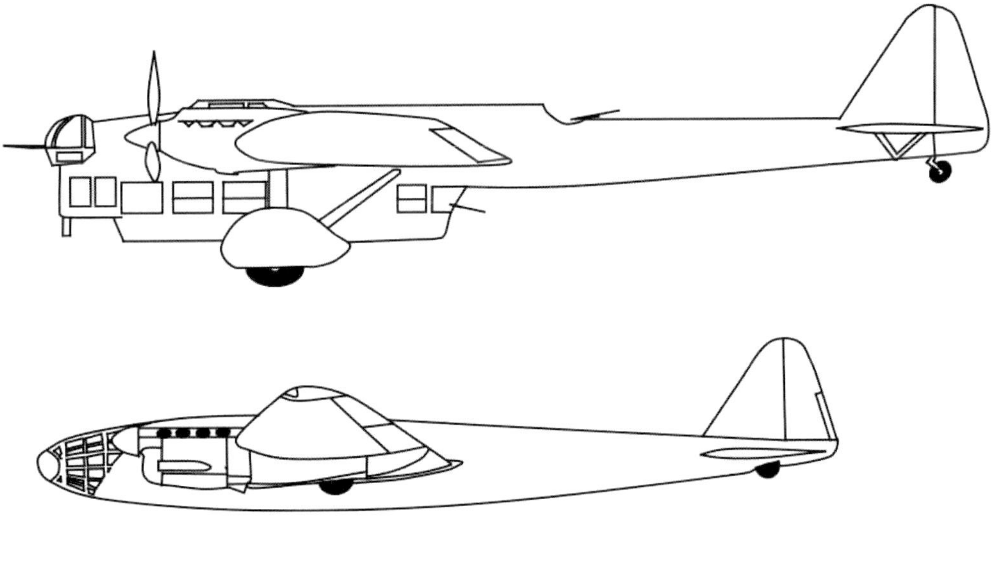

Two planes designed by the same company and powered by the same Hispano-Suiza 12Y-31 engine: (above) the Amiot 142, first flight: January 1935, top speed: 200 mph; (below) the Amiot 370, first flight: July 1937, top speed: 295 mph.

The Breguet 460 with its bulky nose turret. Attempts to tidy up the design led to the Breguet 462 (*below*), but the fundamental bulkiness of the design remained.

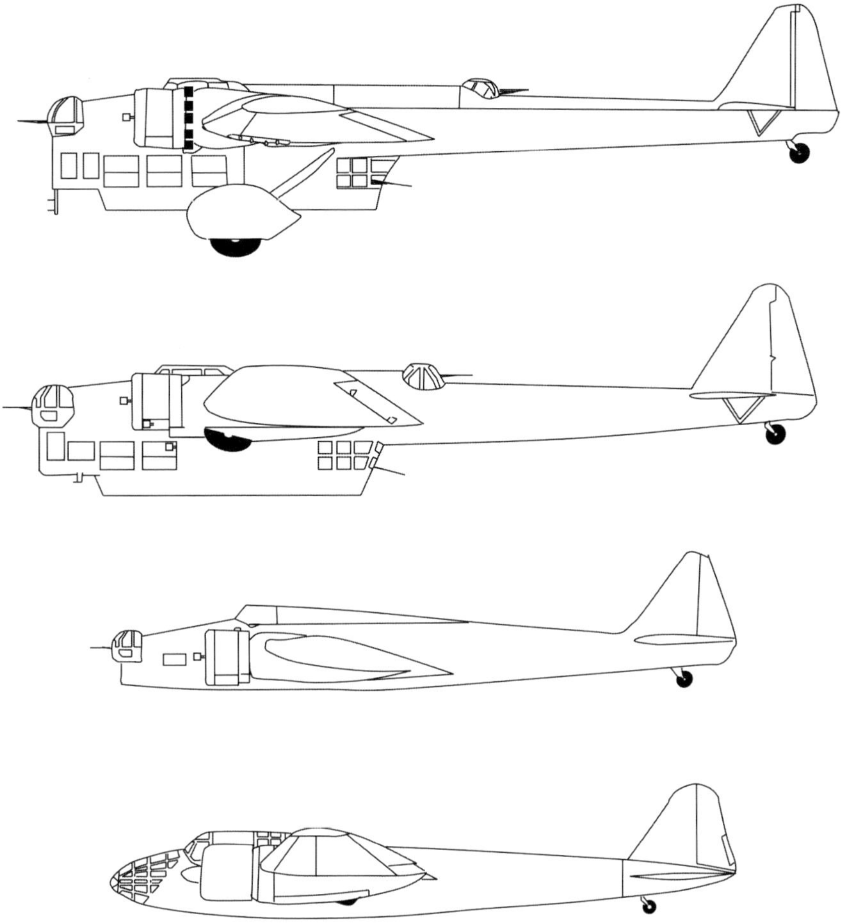

The evolution of the Amiot bombers underlined how important streamlining was becoming: (top to bottom) the Amiot 143 (193 mph); the Amiot 144 (217 mph); the projected Amiot E7 (predicted speed 255 mph); and the Amiot 340 (282 mph). All were powered by the 900-hp Gnome-Rhône Mistral Major, apart from the Amiot 340, which had the 920-hp GR 14N0/1 engine.

The Amiot 340 prototype.

The Dewoitine D.513. The lines of the future D.520 (bottom) are clear but the design was marred by bulky radiator systems.

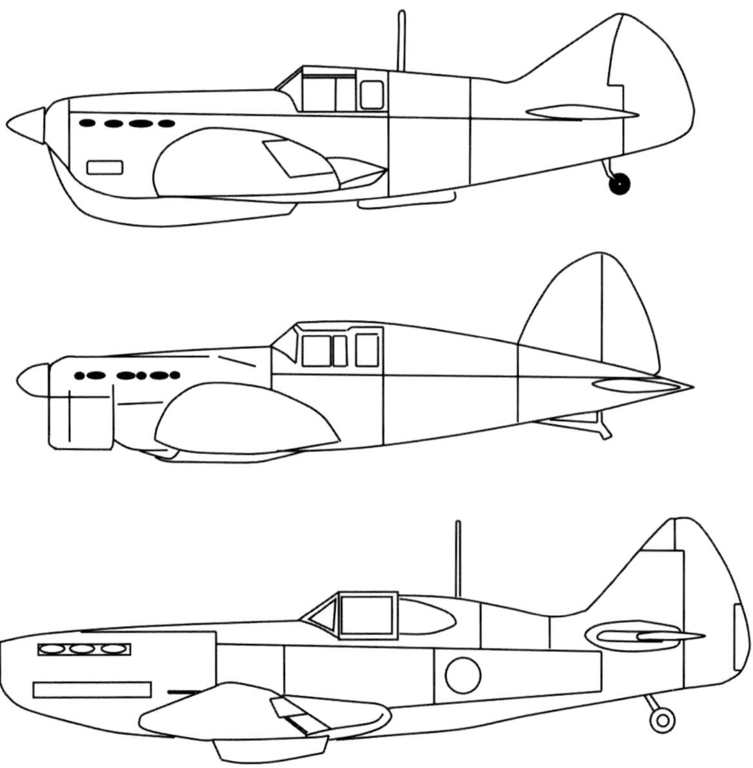

The Caudron C.714 light-weight fighter was actually unsafe to fly, but the Poles still had to use it.

Koolhoven F.K. 58 fighters lined up in the Netherlands ready for delivery to France.

The Potez 630 fighter with a glazed nose became the Potez 63.11 observation plane. Many were fitted with fixed machine guns for defence (here two under each wing). Coincidently, this gave it a ground strafing capability. (*via Ian White*)

The Mureaux 117 was considered obsolete but was no inferior to the German Henschel Hs 126.

The M.S.406 was one of the most agile fighters of its time. (*Tony Buttler*)

The disappointing but rugged and manoeuvrable Bloch MB.152 might have had a successful career as a ground attack fighter (*via Ian White*)

The perceived lack of engine power led to the Air Ministry investigating some radical approaches, including the Nénadovich biplane with the Arsenal-Delanne 10 (*above*) and the Arsenal VB-10 (*below*), with two Hispano-Suiza engines in tandem driving two co-axial propellers. Neither flew until after the surrender. (*via Tony Buttler*)

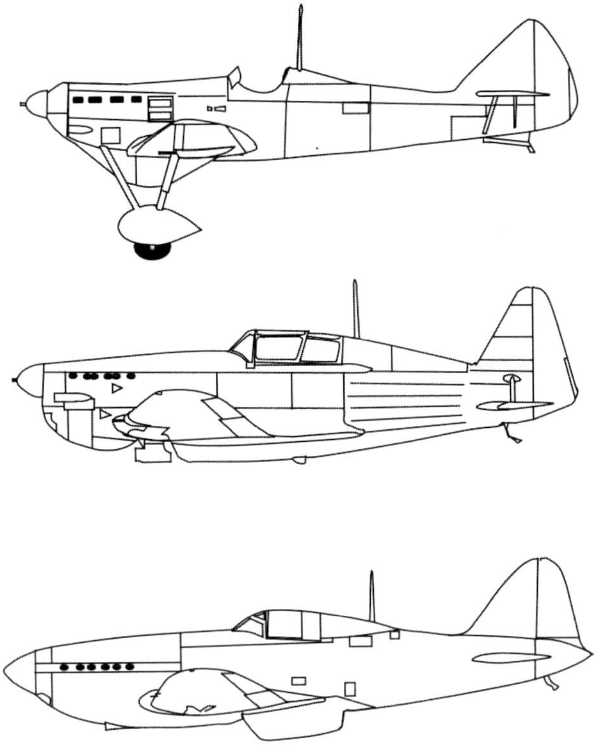

While the usual approach to improving performance is to upgrade the engine, the French effectively kept the engine and changed the airframe. All the above were powered by the 860-hp HS 12Y-31. From top to bottom, the 250-mph Dewoitine D.510, the 303-mph Morane-Saulnier M.S.406, and the 347-mph Arsenal VG-33.

An Arsenal VG-33 captured by the Germans.

One of the surprising features of the campaign was the use made of obsolete planes. Luftwaffe Henschel Hs 123 single-seater ground attack planes and their Bf 109 escorts operated from the same airfield.

The French considered using the Potez 25 as an interim ground attack plane.

Both LeO 257bis (*above*) and Laté 298 (*below*) naval floatplanes were used by day against advancing German columns.

Potez 633s in Greek service. In the late thirties, the Potez 633 was the only modern bomber available to the French.

The Breguet 693 was more advanced than the Potez 633, but arrived too late.

The single-seater LN.401 dive-bomber was designed for naval use and had no rear defence.

The American Curtiss H75 (above) made a valuable contribution, but the excellent Martin 167F (below) arrived too late. (*via Tony Buttler*)

The Bloch MB.174 (*above*), the Dewoitine D.520 and its light weight derivative the D.551 (*below*) were excellent warplanes, but the spring of 1940 was too soon for them to be playing a substantial role.

lucky ones. Those that remained were left kicking their heels in often poorly maintained camps. With little incentive to leave their camps, they were also making little progress with the French language, which was bound to slow down training and integration into the Allied air effort.[38]

The controversy over the constitution of Polish air force units was finally resolved in January when Sikorski and La Chambre reached a compromise whereby the existence of a *Siły Powietrzne* (Polish Air Force), with entirely Polish units, would be permitted. Aircraft would carry the Polish and French insignia, but all units would be under the operational control of the French. Vuillemin, however, still believed that posting Polish personnel to French squadrons was an essential part of their retraining, and ordered that, initially at least, the new Polish units should be broken up and the parts attached to existing French squadrons.

The French agreed to form one reconnaissance and two fighter Polish groups, but even with the departure of 2,300 Poles to Britain there still remained over 6,000 personnel in France, of which several hundred were trained or partially trained pilots. In January, the training of Polish airmen finally got under way with the formation of the Montpellier Group with eighteen fighter pilots.[39] A second batch of seventeen Czech fighter pilots also began retraining, but with several hundred Polish and Czech pilots waiting for something to fly, there was a grave danger that this valuable pool of qualified pilots was going to be wasted.[40]

Meanwhile, the need to strengthen the existing fighter force was being underlined by a sudden shift in the balance of power over the Western Front. French fighters had apparently acquitted themselves well in the opening exchanges of the war. During the first month losses had been light and French pilots had claimed the destruction of no fewer than twenty Bf 109s. There was relatively little aerial activity in October, with the French neither claiming any German fighters nor losing any of their own. The bare statistics for November, seventeen claimed victories for the loss of just six fighters, did not suggest that anything untoward had occurred.[41] Indeed, the month started very well for the French.

On 6 November, nine Curtiss H75s escorting a single Potez 63.11 were surprised by twenty-seven Bf 109s. Once again, the superiority of the Curtiss H75s over their adversaries appeared to be amply demonstrated as the French pilots claimed four confirmed and four probables for the loss of a single H75. This was no exaggeration: four Bf 109s had been forced down on the French side of the front line and a further four crash-landed in German territory. Two German pilots were killed, another seriously wounded, and two more were captured. The engagement shook the Germans and the squadron commander was immediately summoned to Berlin to explain what had gone wrong.[42] Before the end of the month, however, it would be the French who would be desperately trying to find solutions.

For most of November, poor weather restricted operations, but between 21st and 23rd, the weather cleared and several French fighter groups were in action. The results of these combats - nine Bf 109s claimed as destroyed for the loss of four fighters - belied the sense of inferiority French pilots noted in their subsequent reports. All agreed that the Bf 109s encountered outclassed French equipment in every way. The German fighters were faster and could pull away from pursuing French fighters with contemptuous ease. Pilots even reported that the Bf 109 was more manoeuvrable.[43] The Daimler-Benz DB 601-powered Bf 109E was beginning to make its presence felt.

The French had known about the existence of this version of the fighter for some time and indeed believed it had been in production for some time. In fact, various issues delayed production until 1939, but in the first eight months of the year, over 1,000 of these lethal fighters were built. Increased power had pushed speed up to 570 km/hr and, with the exceptionally light airframe, acceleration was spectacular. The early successes achieved by Polish and French fighters against Bf 109s had been rather misleading. The low regard Polish pilots had for the Bf 109 appears to have stemmed from German pilots attempting to dogfight with the agile PZL P.11, rather than using the Bf 109s superior diving and level speeds. There were also still a number of the older Jumo-powered versions in front line service. The successes achieved on 6 November had been against Bf 109Ds. Also, many of the reported successes against the Bf 109 were not victories at all. When pursued, German fighter pilots boosted engine output to a maximum, which tended to send a stream of black smoke out of the exhaust. This was often interpreted by the pursuing Allied fighter pilot as a hit.[44]

The disturbing reports on the superiority of the Bf 109s now coming from the front should not have come as a surprise. The French had captured a fully airworthy example of the German fighter on 24 September when a German pilot landed at a French airfield by mistake. As is their wont, however, the pilots who tested the plane tended to play down the qualities of an unfamiliar design. Those who met it in combat, on the other hand, were left in no doubt about its superiority. The engagements of late November shook the confidence of French fighter pilots. Their commander, General d'Harcourt, demanded the immediate development of a fighter that could defeat the German single-seater. As winter set in and aerial activity declined, the fighter squadrons were granted a welcome respite. However, with a German offensive the following spring a virtual certainty, getting a fighter into service that could match the Bf 109E became the top priority.

Even before d'Harcourt's appeal and indeed the capture of the Bf 109E, steps had been taken to develop just such a fighter. On 11 September, specifications were released requiring a new generation of much faster combat planes in all categories. For single-seater fighters, the aim was simple. The programme required a single-seater fighter that was superior to the Bf 109 in every respect, including horizontal speed. The next generation of fighter had to possess a high rate of climb, be highly manoeuvrable throughout the speed range and have a top speed of 650 km/hr (404 mph). The Air Ministry could no longer be accused of not setting sufficiently demanding requirements. By previous French standards, it was an enormous leap forward. No French prototype had yet achieved the 570 km/hr target set in 1938. If such stiff speed requirements had been set in the early thirties, French fighter development might have taken a different course. The programme was very clear about how designers were supposed to achieve this speed. Perhaps inspired by the reports on the captured Bf 109s, the Air Ministry suggested a return to some of the ideas behind the old 'jockey' lightweight fighter programmes. Weight had to be kept to an absolute minimum. All unnecessary internal equipment had to go and the plane need only carry enough fuel to cruise for two hours.[45]

No matter how much weight was saved or aerodynamic refinement was introduced, it seemed such speeds could only be achieved with the next generation of engine (the 1,200-hp Hispano-Suiza HS 12Z and Gnome-Rhône GR 14R). Bench trials with the HS 12Z were supposed to begin in the autumn of 1939, but the project was running well behind schedule and the first prototypes of the engine were not now expected until well into 1940. Both the Dewoitine D.520 and Arsenal VG-33 airframes were capable of taking full advantage of the engine—the latter actually flew with an early prototype, achieving 624 km/hr—but production was not going to begin until the end of 1940 at the earliest. Gnome et Rhône were doing somewhat better; the first prototypes of their GR 14R radial became available in the autumn of 1939 and it was hoped that production would begin in July 1940. Bloch had initially hoped that it could be used with the MB.150 airframe but the Bloch fighter had been so disappointing, it was felt better to start afresh with a new design. Work began on the much-revised Bloch MB.157, but even in the spring of 1940 the prototype was still nowhere near ready to fly. It seemed that a fighter with a clear advantage over the Bf 109E would remain beyond the capabilities of the French for some time to come. Émile Dewoitine, however, had other ideas. While other designers were putting forward proposals for fighters that would fly faster than 600 km/hr, Dewoitine designed, built, and flew a plane that could go faster than 700 km/hr.

Towards the end of the summer of 1938, Dewoitine had begun work on the D.550 racer. The aircraft was essentially a scaled-down and simpler, lightweight version of the D.520 fighter. Power was to be provided by the new HS 12Y-51, the first prototype examples of which were about to become available. The prototype flew in June 1939 with an HS 12Y-31 motor and, despite its much-reduced wing area, the plane still retained some of the pleasant handling characteristics of the D.520. Dewoitine was soon viewing his racer as a potential successor to the D.520, even though its small airframe would only be able to carry the very minimum of equipment and very little fuel. Then, in September, the Air Ministry released a specification suggesting precisely this approach.[46]

In October, Dewoitine approached the Air Ministry with an audacious proposal to put his new fighter straight into production. Dewoitine claimed the design was so simple that each machine would only require 4,000 man-hours to build, half the number required by the D.520. Dewoitine suggested the creation of two assembly lines for the fighter at the proposed new Tarbes plant, intended for the D.520. The racer could not carry wing guns and armament would have to be restricted to the engine-mounted cannon, but with an immediate decision, the plane could go into production as it was, and the first examples could be delivered by July 1940. With the new HS 12Y-51, which at this point Caquot was still claiming could be in production within a couple of months, Dewoitine promised a staggering top speed of 700 km/hr (435 mph).[47] The anticipated speed seemed to be another example of a rather excitable designer letting his imagination run away with him.

Dewoitine's claim, however, proved to be no exaggeration. On 23 October, the HS 12Y-51-powered version achieved 677 km/hr on its first flight. Eight days later, it managed 695 km/hr. On 22 November, the Dewoitine D.550 became the first French plane to exceed 700 km/hr. Suddenly, Dewoitine's proposal to put the D.550 into production in its existing form seemed like rather a good idea. Caquot dispatched Détroyat to Toulouse to test the plane. He reported that landing speed was on the high side, and would no doubt get higher once military equipment was installed. Visibility from the cockpit was limited and the undercarriage looked decidedly fragile. However, once in the air, the fighter was surprisingly pleasant to fly.[48]

The Air Ministry were sorely tempted to take up Dewoitine's offer and order the D.550 into production as it was. La Chambre and Caquot were certainly keen about using the Tarbes plant to build it. In its existing form, with its limited fuel capacity and need for reasonable airfields to operate from, the fighter might only be useable as a short-range interceptor for the defence of fixed targets in the rear, but with rear defence the major French concern the idea was given some very serious consideration.[49] However, the plane was still more a racer than a combat plane. Indeed, so nervous was Dewoitine about his fragile new creation that he refused to allow the prototype to be transferred to the more primitive official Air Force test centre at Marignane. Caquot still believed the 600-km/hr D.520 would give the French the technical edge over the Bf 109E; even the HS 12Y-31-powered Arsenal VG-33 and the definitive version of the Bloch MB.152 would not be far short. In the end, it was decided that the Air Force would await the delivery of the more fully developed D.551, with increased wing area, six wing-mounted machine guns, higher fuel capacity, a strengthened undercarriage, and a modified cockpit canopy. All these improvements would reduce speed, but it was still expected to exceed the 650 km/hr required by the September programme. In December, ten were ordered, to be delivered between May and July 1940, so that an experimental squadron could be formed.[50] French fighter design was emerging from the doldrums.

Caquot's belief that the D.520 would eventually be capable of 600 km/hr was a matter of faith—the early prototypes had never achieved more than 527 km/hr—but some recent trials seemed to provide some evidence to support the claim. Although it had been decided not to use the HS 12Y-31, trials with the D.520 prototype powered by this engine still went ahead. The Dewoitine fighter apparently took kindly to its new power plant. In September, it achieved 550 km/hr, a higher speed than any previously achieved with the more powerful HS 12Y-29.[51] Climb rate was also improved. Caquot chose not to investigate these puzzling results too closely. Instead he triumphantly announced that his faith in the basic design had been vindicated. With the Szydlowski-Planiol supercharged HS 12Y-45, the D.520 should at least match the speed of the Bf 109E and with the HS 12Y-51 should better it comfortably.

It seemed that d'Harcourt's appeals for a Bf 109E equivalent would soon be met. The first production Dewoitine D.520 had flown in October. The 560-km/hr Arsenal was due in February and by the end of November, the Air Force already had 100 Bloch MB.152s, supposedly capable of 530 km/hr. Over half of the 1,300 fighters expected by the following spring would be the Bloch MB.152 or the 550-km/hr Bloch MB.155. On more than one occasion, the Air Ministry had come close to abandoning the fighter, but their persistence appeared to have paid off. By the following May, 150 would be coming off the production line each month. It was, therefore, no wonder that the news that greeted La Chambre at the weekly meeting of the *Comité de Materiel* on 22 December came as a shattering blow. It emerged that none of the new Bloch fighters being delivered to the Air Force were capable of anything like the performance promised by the manufacturers. Far from attaining 530 km/hr, the planes that the Air Force were testing were only managing 475 km/hr. France was using valuable factory space mass producing a fighter that was slower than the M.S.406, which the Bloch fighter was supposed to replace.[52]

A furious La Chambre immediately ordered a full investigation. It transpired that the figure of 530 km/hr had been passed to the Air Ministry over the phone on 9 May just before that day's *Comité de Materiel* meeting. Only nine days later was the full official report completed and this admitted that the 530 km/hr figure was probably the result of faulty measuring equipment. Unfortunately, the report had somehow been mislaid. La Chambre had certainly never seen it. It also emerged that the highly streamlined engine cowling used during the May trials did not provide adequate cooling and aircraft currently being delivered were equipped with a larger cowling. Furthermore, the plane tested in May was 750 lb lighter than those now being delivered. The first reaction was to cancel the entire Bloch MB.152 production program. Indeed, Caquot immediately ordered that only fighters more than fifty per cent built should be completed and that the remainder should be used for spares.[53] It looked like an ignominious end for the ill-starred Bloch fighter project.

It was a panicky reaction to say the least. At this late stage, France could scarcely afford to abandon a plane that was supposed to equip half the fighter force, however disappointing its performance. Pilots had to have something to fly. But there were plenty of ideas as to how the production space could be better used. Caquot argued that another assembly line should be set up for the Bloch MB.174, a plane which used the same GR 14N-49 engine. He insisted that the loss of fighter output could easily be made up by increasing production of the existing Arsenal and Dewoitine planes. A sceptical La Chambre thought the failure to meet existing targets scarcely justified such high hopes. Vuillemin suggested that the Bloch facilities be used to start up another Dewoitine line immediately and did not rule out the possibility of using it to produce the Dewoitine D.550. The November confrontations with the Bf 109E and d'Harcourt's appeal for something superior to the German fighter had breathed new life into the Dewoitine D.550 debate. The latest reports claimed that the D.550 prototype was not only extremely fast but also more manoeuvrable than the M.S.406, particularly in turning performance, a somewhat dubious claim given the plane's high wing loading.[54]

Dewoitine was still pushing hard for production of the D.550 to begin at the Tarbes plant and he was letting it be known among his political friends that only Air Ministry obstinacy was preventing deliveries of this highly promising fighter by May 1940.[55] However, following the Bloch MB.152 fiasco, there was little appetite for taking a chance with a fighter simply based on company claims and one flight by a Ministry test pilot. Production of the plane's HS 12Y-51 engine was also running behind schedule. Switching the Bloch production plant to the D.520 was considered, and the rapidly increasing numbers of Hispano-Suiza engines being built might make this possible, but it would mean dependence on Hispano-Suiza engines and the destruction or damage of Hispano-Suiza production plants might cripple the fighter arm. There were advantages to having at least one fighter powered by another engine.[56]

On 15 January 1940, details emerged of yet another modified version of the Bloch fighter. Apparently, alterations made by the manufacturers had enabled the plane to achieve 517 km/hr (321 mph). This was still below what the Air Ministry had been promised, but it was a slight improvement on the M.S.406. La Chambre was even less impressed when he discovered the plane tested was unarmed. However, the Bloch MB.155 version was supposed to be slightly faster and the modifications required by both versions were not major and could be applied quickly. With a German offensive probably only months away, La Chambre felt obliged to reinstate the fighter in the production program, though at a considerably reduced rate.[57] It was a disaster all round. Two months' output had been lost as the production lines started up again and the Bloch MB.152 was clearly not the answer to the Bf 109E.

Everything now depended on the Arsenal VG-33 and the D.520. Some 500 of these were still expected by the end of April. In December, an experimental flight equipped with the first D.520 was set up with personnel from GC I/3. To speed things up, the first production models were rushed to this unit early in January without armament or various other non-essential equipment. During the first months of 1940 production of the Dewoitine D.520 finally got into its stride. Then, La Chambre was hit by another bombshell. Far from being capable of the 600 km/hr Caquot was predicting or the 570 km/hr its designers were promising, the fighters that the Air Force was getting were struggling to exceed 500 km/hr.[58] There was bemusement that the plane was far slower than the version using the less powerful HS 12Y-31. Engineers and designers set to work on the second production machine, but even after numerous modifications, they could only squeeze 535 km/hr out of the plane. The experimental flight also discovered numerous defects that had been overlooked in the haste to get the fighter into production. By the end of February, seventy-four had left the SNCAM production line, but only thirty-one had been officially taken on strength by the Air Force and none of these were considered fully operational. In fact, at this point, although production at the Toulouse plant continued, the Air Force stopped accepting any more machines until all the problems had been sorted out.[59]

Meanwhile, the Arsenal VG-33 production schedule was also slipping behind. There was a major shortage of raw materials, especially the spruce required by the wooden fighter. First deliveries were not now expected until April. Far from re-equipping the majority of fighter units by the spring, La Chambre was reduced to hoping that he would have two or three groups equipped with the Arsenal or Dewoitine fighters in time for the expected German spring offensive. Rather optimistically, he hoped these would be enough to establish local air superiority.[60]

With the performance of both the Bloch MB.152 and Dewoitine D.520 lower than expected and production behind schedule, the decision not to update the M.S.406 and continue production was beginning to look like a serious error. It was too late to put it back into production, but perhaps not too late to improve its performance. All M.S.406 were to get a more efficient constant-speed Ratier airscrew, which greatly improved acceleration and climb. It was too late to install the Szydlowski-Planiol supercharger but in February, it was decided to modify 500 M.S.406 with the two-gun wing, fixed radiator, and ejector exhausts, the updated version becoming the M.S.410.[61] Priority would go to recently built M.S.406 with the newest engines. The conversion would require 400 man-hours per machine and would take about three weeks. It was hoped to build up to a daily output of eight M.S.410s, with fifty being completed by 15 May. There was no time to test all the modifications on a single plane so final performance was a matter of conjecture, but the fixed radiator was supposed to be worth up to an extra 20 km/hr, and the new exhaust system up to 37 km/hr. These improvements were not necessarily achieved at the same altitude so could not simply be added to the existing top speed, and given recent testing errors, they could perhaps not be entirely trusted, but there was no doubt that the M.S.410s would be superior to the M.S.406. The French also hoped that more advanced versions of the Curtiss H75, the 511 km/hr H75 A-3, and 520 m/hr H75 A-4, would soon be arriving but none of these gave La Chambre the 570 km/hr fighter to match the Bf 109E. Finding something that could achieve the magic 570 km/hr became a priority bordering on obsession.

Breguet seemed to have the solution. They had been developing an upgraded Breguet 690 with two of the more powerful but much larger and heavier GR 14N-49 engines replacing its lightweight low-powered GR 14M *Mars*. The result, the Breguet 697, had flown in October 1939 and achieved an impressive 560 km/hr. At the time, this did not provoke too much interest, especially as there were reports that the plane was far from easy to fly and the engines tended to overheat.[62] However, in the aftermath of the Bloch affair, La Chambre persuaded himself that the twin-engined Breguet was the instant solution to the problems facing the French Air Force. The plane did not seem so dissimilar to the Bf 110, which had so impressed the Poles and which French pilots were still waiting with some trepidation to take on for the first time. The GR 14N-49-powered Breguet might be the French answer.

The Air Minister asked Détroyat to test the Breguet plane, and when he reported that it was actually capable of 570 km/h, the issue was settled for La Chambre. This was what his demoralised pilots must have. As the Breguet 693 was already in production as an assault bomber, the fighter version could become available almost immediately. La Chambre insisted that part of the Breguet 693 production facilities be switched to the fighter version. Mindful of the way previous designs seemed to suffer a dramatic reduction in performance when they went into production, La Chambre ordered that no changes whatsoever should be made to the plane. The production model must be identical in every respect to the version flown by Détroyat.[63]

The decision brought a storm of protest. Breguet were well aware that in its existing form, the Br 697 was scarcely safe to fly. It was not possible simply to replace the smaller Gnome-Rhône *Mars* with the larger GR 14N-49 and expect a satisfactory plane. The basic Breguet 690 airframe was not strong enough; the plane would tear itself apart in any violent manoeuvre. Breguet were planning on having a strengthened prototype ready by July with production possibly starting in November. Others objected to the plane on purely tactical grounds. It was no good ordering any plane just because it was capable of the same speed as the Bf 109E. It was not at all clear how the Air Force would use the twin-engined fighter and its production would reduce the number of assault bombers available. The ever optimistic Caquot dismissed the technical objections. It was simply necessary to add a few extra rivets and these would be incorporated into the Breguet 700 production version. La Chambre remained adamant that it was essential to get something into service that could match the speed of the German fighters. All objections were brushed aside. Breguet were told that from April, twenty-eight Breguet airframes per month would be equipped with Gnome-Rhône GR 14N-49 motors and deployed as fighters. Armament would be two cannon and six machine guns.[64]

With the French fighter force looking like it might struggle, frantic efforts were made during the winter of 1939–40 to give French reconnaissance planes and bombers a better chance of fighting off the Messerschmitts by adding armour and guns.[65] To counterattacks from below, Breguet assault planes and Potez and Bloch reconnaissance planes were fitted with ventral machine guns on wobble mounts. They could not be aimed but the weapons were loosely hinged so that the vibration of their firing caused bullets to be sprayed in all directions. These might have boosted the morale of French crews, and enemy pilots might have found it disconcerting but it is difficult to see how such random defensive fire could be effective. Dorsal weapons and fixed forward-firing were also increased in number, although it was difficult to see how the latter could help much defensively. After modification, some Potez reconnaissance planes were carrying as many as ten machine guns. Coincidently, these weapons did give these planes a ground strafing capability.

Any ideas that the LeO 451 and Amiot 350 would be too fast to be intercepted or even fast enough to force enemy fighters to attack from the rear had now evaporated. The dorsal cannon could not fire sideways and even against attacks from the rear, it was not proving a great success. The drums only had a limited firing time and had to be constantly replaced. With the Amiot 350, changing the drum proved virtually impossible and the dorsal cannon had to be abandoned completely. Alternative arrangements with machine guns covering more angles were being hurriedly tested.[66] Only the 530 km/hr Bloch MB.174 had the speed to make interception difficult, but the three-seater did not have the same priority as the larger four-seater bombers. The Air Force did not get its first Bloch MB.174 until December 1939 and only fifty were on order. When these were built, production switched to the Bloch MB.175 light bomber version and this inevitably halted deliveries temporarily

– France could not afford to lose a couple of months' worth of production just to enable the plane to carry larger bombs. Even worse, only sixty-five of the Bloch MB.175 would be built as its GR 14N-49 engines were needed by the LeO 451 and Amiot 351/354. The priority long-range bombers were getting over short-range tactical bombers meant the Bloch reconnaissance bomber would have to make do with the American Pratt and Whitney engines, which would reduce top speed to just 470 km/hr.[67] France was effectively planning to abandon the only bomber-reconnaissance plane it had with the performance to survive without escort in Messerschmitt-infested skies.

The vulnerability of the Potez 63.11 was forcing the French to rethink their approach to reconnaissance. An observer had always been considered a vital member of the reconnaissance plane's crew, but there was no point in having a specialist observer with an excellent view if the plane was not going to make it back. Single-seater fighters were generally faster and more capable of looking after themselves. For photo-reconnaissance, an observer was not essential and even for more general visual reconnaissance, it was better to bring back some information than not to return at all. There were suggestions that M.S.406s discarded by units re-equipping with more modern fighters could be distributed among reconnaissance squadrons.[68] Three Dewoitine D.520s were to be fitted with cameras for photo-reconnaissance trials, and an extra four Dewoitine D.551 prototypes were ordered for similar duties. This would prove to be the right way to go, but it meant even more fighters would be needed.

Quite what the future equipment of the observation squadrons would be was a conundrum. The September 1939 development programme still wanted a twin-engined, three-seater, with a top speed of 600 km/hr (375 mph) that could land in a field. It was simply impossible. The Dewoitine D.720 was supposed to be the next specialist observation plane, but this was not even as fast as the Potez 63.11. In September 1939, it was dropped, but nobody had any idea what would replace the Potez 63.11. The observation squadrons were the heart of the French Air Force; they made up one quarter of front line strength. As far as the Army was concerned, these, and the reconnaissance squadrons, were why the French Air Force existed. Suddenly, there were major doubts about how any of these squadrons would be able to operate at all, if fighters were not around to protect them.

Fighters were the key. As the First World War had demonstrated, it was impossible to have too many. This was especially true if there were doubts about the quality of available fighters. Ideally, the French needed numerical superiority to offset their technical inferiority. Unfortunately, although fighters still had priority, ever since Plan V had been introduced, the bomber lobby had been chipping away at this priority. Each successive adjustment had seen the proportion of fighters drop and the number of long-range bombers increase.

All that changed in February 1940 with Plan Vbis. Fighter production was to be restored to the level originally proposed in March 1938 (500 fighters a month) and medium bomber production would be slashed. Planned fighter strength was doubled to 1,500 fighters, which was to be achieved by the end of 1940 if possible. Large numbers of Curtiss P-46, Bell P-39, and Lockheed P-38 single-seaters were ordered from the United States.[69] As a proportion of total strength, the fighter arm was to rise from forty to fifty per cent, which was approximately the proportion which had existed at the end of the First World War. Arguably, this was still not enough as, in 1918, the French fighter force had not been expected to provide comprehensive cover for targets in the rear. Compared to the November production scheme, the new plan was to double monthly output of the Dewoitine D.520 and triple Arsenal output. The Bloch MB.152 would be replaced by the Bloch MB.155, but this type would be phased out completely before the end of the year.[70] The single-seater fighter force of the future would be built around the Arsenal, Dewoitine D.520, eventually the D.551, and American fighters. Although the Dewoitine D.551 prototype had not yet flown, a new production line was expected to be delivering 100 a month by 1941.[71]

The medium bomber force would be cut by more than half while the assault force was to be nearly doubled. Both Amiot 350 and LeO 451 production would be cut but it was the latter that would be reduced the most. The LeO 451 was a difficult plane to fly and with the possibility that the medium bombers would have to operate by night, the less demanding Amiot 351/354 was looking ever more attractive. From the autumn of 1940, some LeO 451 squadrons would begin converting to the Amiot 350. New versions would include the Amiot 353 and 356, with the Merlins that the Dewoitine D.520 had been going to use. The Amiot 352 with Hispano-Suiza HS 12Y engines would begin rolling off the production lines in October 1940. The plan was to use the HS 12Y-51, but initially it would use up the surplus HS 12Y-31 engines.[72] The bomber was finally going into production with the engine that had been available since Amiot first drew up his high-speed E7 bomber proposal in 1933.

It was a much better-balanced air force that was emerging, but it was very late in the day. As spring and the inevitable German offensive approached, the French Air Force seemed little better prepared than it had been at the outbreak of war. By the end of February, fewer than 200 of the 1936 generation of combat planes, the only modern planes according to La Chambre and Caquot, had been taken on strength by the Air Force; many of these still lacked vital parts and could not be issued to squadrons. For the French, time was running out.

11

Desperate Measures

The first months of 1940 had been extremely stressful for La Chambre and the strain was beginning to show. His almost irrational determination to get the Breguet 700 into production suggested he was coming to the end of his tether. The Air Minister and Caquot were both becoming the target of growing criticism. In January 1940, Caquot was forced to resign. In February, La Chambre was once again forced to account for the current state of the Air Force before an increasingly hostile Parliamentary Air Commission. The year before, La Chambre had been able to dismiss their criticisms. However, the 600 km/hr fighters he had promised had not materialised and in January, the number of planes taken on charge by the Air Force fell below 200. Incredibly, this was the lowest since the outbreak of war.

The Air Commission had no intention of letting La Chambre off the hook. He was reminded once again that the fighters he had ordered in such large numbers were all at least 80 km/hr slower than the Bf 109E. The new Dewoitine and Arsenal designs would not arrive before July and even these were inferior to German fighters. He was also reminded that France had virtually no modern bombers, a deficiency the members of the Air Commission believed was particularly worrying. La Chambre defended himself as best he could. When he had taken over at the Air Ministry, the M.S.406 had been the only modern fighter available and he had had no choice but to order it, nor was he responsible for the failure to develop a satisfactory bomber.[1] However, there were few who would support him now.

On 19 March 1940, La Chambre was forced to step down and his place was taken by Laurent-Eynac. The wheel had turned full circle. The appointment of the founding father of an independent Air Ministry represented a victory for those who still yearned for a long-range bomber fleet that would force potential enemies to cower. Laurent-Eynac had not substantially altered his outlook. He still believed the bomber was all important. With more time, Laurent-Eynac might have re-orientated Air Force expansion to reflect his beliefs but he kept La Chambre's Plan Vbis, approved as Plan VI, with its emphasis on fighter and assault bomber production. The only change he made was to drop the contentious Breguet 700 fighter, and concentrate on the production of the Breguet 693 assault version.

Ironically, the month that saw the departure of La Chambre also saw the first real signs of an increase in aircraft production. The first of the latest modified version of the Bloch MB.152 left the factories and were immediately rushed to units making do with the early versions. By the end of April, around seventy had reached the seven Bloch fighter groups, but units were still having to use substandard Bloch MB.152s and even Bloch MB.151s. By the end of March, 139 Dewoitine D.520 fighters had been built, but apart from a few test models, none were considered fully operational. There were so many faults, a second production line had to be set up to modify the planes already built. There were still hopes that with further tinkering, the plane might yet achieve the promised 570 km/hr, but there was no time for any more changes. The German spring offensive could not be far off. The fighter would be used as it was with a top speed of 535 km/hr (332 mph). Towards the middle of March, work began on bringing a first batch of twenty-two Dewoitine D.520s up to full operational standard and the first modified machines reached GC I/3 on 17 April. This group handed its non-operational Dewoitine fighters to GCs II/3, III/3, and I/7 so that these groups could get some training going. By 10 May, around 250 Dewoitine D.520 fighters had been built but fewer than fifty were ready for combat; only GC I/3, with thirty-four D.520s, was close to becoming operational.[2] The first production Arsenal VG-33 flew on 21 April. These too suffered from being put into production too hastily and plans to form an experimental squadron in May had to be postponed.

The squadrons were also getting their first Bloch MB.174s. The first three were delivered to GR (*Groupe de Reconnaissance*) II/33 on 19 March and the first batch of fifty Bloch MB.174s had been completed by the end of that month. All three strategic reconnaissance groups had some examples of the plane by the end of April, but then deliveries ceased as the production line was readied for the bomber Bloch MB.175 version. The first of these would not arrive until May.

Substantial numbers of bombers were now leaving French factories. By March, the second Breguet 693 and LeO 451 production lines were up and running and the second Amiot 350 assembly line was due to come into operation the following month. By the end of April, over 650 LeO, Amiot, and Breguet bombers had been built and production was running at around 150 a month and increasing.[3] With the 300 Martin and Douglas bombers that had been transported across the Atlantic, this was more than enough to re-equip the entire bomber fleet and provide a substantial reserve. However, the shortage of key items made these figures meaningless. Fewer than two-thirds of the LeO 451 bombers built had actually been accepted by the Air Force and more than a third of these were still awaiting vital parts. At the beginning of May, only two bomber groups were operational on the LeO bomber. Only one third of the Breguet 693s built had been officially accepted by the Air Force. Two assault groups (*Groupe de Bombardement d'Assaut*: GBA I/54 and GBA II/54 of *Groupement* 18) were ready for operations, but at the beginning of May, even these units lacked bomb release gear. The Amiot 351/354s delivered were all from the first batch, which were only supposed to be used for training and were not even fitted with bomb sights.

Fewer than a third of the Douglas bombers that had been shipped across the Atlantic had been assembled and no units were yet operational on the type. A slightly higher proportion of the Martin bombers were flying, but again, many lacked essential equipment. The first two operational Martin units flew from North Africa to France at the beginning of May, although to do this, the bomb racks had to be replaced with fuel tanks. Until the bomb racks caught up with these units, they too remained non-operational. Astonishingly, although some 1,000 bombers had been built or arrived from the United States, instead of having a force of 400 day bombers ready to strike the invading German Army, the French Air Force had just two bomber groups with twenty-six LeO 451s ready for action.

It was not just the very latest planes France was short of. It was only quite late in the day that it was realised just how chronically short the French Air Force was of all types of war planes, old and new. When war broke out, Vuillemin had managed to get all exports halted, but not everyone thought it was necessary. Caquot was insisting that France would soon have more planes than it knew what to do with.[4] Weygand, now commanding French forces in Syria, had ambitious plans for using the Balkans as a springboard for operations against Germany. There were even bizarre plans to bomb Soviet oil fields in the Caucasus.[5] Wishful thinking persuaded many that the war on the Western Front would stay phoney and the real fighting would take place in somebody else's country, and so Weygand got the reinforcements he wanted. By the spring of 1940, his air units were remarkably well equipped. While some observation squadrons on the Western Front were still having to make do with Potez 25, Potez 39, and Breguet 27s, Weygand's reconnaissance squadrons were equipped entirely with the Potez 63.11. In February, GC I/7 (with twenty-six M.S.406s) was sent to Syria and Weygand had even acquired a group of priceless Martin 167 bombers. More modern planes were earmarked for friendly air forces in the region. Vuillemin found himself committed to the delivery of thirty M.S.406 fighters to Turkey and in December, it was agreed that fifty M.S.406s should be sold to Yugoslavia and Greece.[6] When the Soviet Union invaded Finland, France immediately promised the delivery of 175 war planes, including 150 fighters.

Vuillemin desperately sought to put a stop to this drain on his resources. Fighters like the M.S.406 were still required by front line units and even when they had been replaced by more modern equipment, they would still be needed for training. Instead of supplying Morane-Saulnier fighters, Vuillemin suggested that nations promised French help should make do with the Caudron C.714, Bloch MB.151, or Koolhoven F.K.58, none of which he wanted. The Caudron C.714 had been declared dangerous to fly and many of the early series unsatisfactory Bloch MB.151 fighters had been stored away. Seventeen complete Koolhoven F.K.58s were flown to France before the declaration of war and more unassembled fighters had been shipped to France, but such was Caquot's overconfidence, nobody had bothered to assemble any more. If friendly powers had to have French fighters, it should be these, not M.S.406s, Vuillemin insisted.[7]

It was only early in 1940 that the French suddenly realised how exaggerated Caquot's claims had been and how desperate the situation really was. Only seventy fighters were delivered to the Air Force in January, the first-time monthly production had fallen below 100 since the previous April. Deliveries would drop even further in February. Vuillemin finally got his way and no more M.S.406 would be exported once the Turkish and initial Finnish batch had been delivered. The remainder of the Finnish order would be made up of Caudron C.714 and Koolhoven F.K.58s. The Greeks and Yugoslavs would have to make do with the Dutch fighter or the Bloch MB.151. In fact, the growing equipment crisis in France was so grave, even deliveries of these were halted. Just six Caudron C.714s went to Finland and nine Bloch MB.151s to Greece.

It seems strange that aircraft were being exported when many Polish and Czech pilots still found themselves without any sort of aircraft to fly. By the spring of 1940, there were 950 Polish pilots, 148 student pilots, and 763 aircrew undergoing training. It was planned to form four fighter, two reconnaissance, and one bomber group, but only GC I/145, with thirty-three pilots and around twenty M.S.406s, was close to being declared fully operational.[8] Eighteen pilots of the Montpellier squadron had been sent to various French units to gain combat experience. The training of a 3rd Polish fighter group, with a handful of Caudron C.714 and M.S.406 fighters, was considered to be sufficiently advanced to enable this formation to be declared semi-operational and capable of assisting in the defence of the Lyon district if required.[9] Among the Czechs, there were 195 fighter, thirty-three bomber, and 119 reconnaissance pilots with twenty pilots in training.[10] A second batch of eighteen pilots had joined fighter squadrons at the front, bringing the total to sixty-nine Poles and Czechs with French units, but it seems that more than 300 more fully trained Polish and Czech fighter pilots remained available, along with nearly 200 fully trained reconnaissance and bomber pilots.

Many of these had not flown any sort of French plane since they had arrived in the country.

There was very little for the foreign volunteers to fly. Even M.S.406s were in short supply. Around 1,000 had been built and some 400 were still in service at the front, with around another 150 in training schools. This should have left enough for an ample reserve.[11] However, the decision to upgrade 300 to M.S.410 standard cut into the number available. In March, another problem came to light. For some time, Morane fighter pilots had been complaining about the gradual deterioration of the performance of the fighter. Pilots claimed that after a while most machines found it difficult to manage 450 km/hr. Some claimed the top speed of some Moranes had dropped as low as 420 km/hr (260 mph). The problem was the engine. All fighter types are stretched to their limits in combat situations, but in the case of the M.S.406, these problems were made worse by the extra strain on the engine caused by the inefficient retractable radiator and the original two-pitch propeller. By the spring of 1940, most M.S.406s had the variable pitch airscrews, but by this time many of the M.S.406 engines were in need of a major overhaul. A plan was drawn up to inspect all engines that had clocked up more than 100 hours in the air.[12]

D'Harcourt was horrified. He argued that he could not afford to have the number of M.S.406 fighters available reduced any further. The alternative, however, was that French pilots should be sent into action with aircraft that were not only technically inferior but were also powered by worn out engines. It is not clear what was finally decided but on 10 May, for one reason or another, nearly 250 M.S.406s were either undergoing repair, modification, or were for some reason unserviceable. Once combat losses, exports, the needs of training schools, and planes sent to overseas units were taken into account, there were just eleven left as a reserve. Vuillemin had managed to limit the export of the M.S.406, but France now needed the 200 that he had been unable to prevent leaving the country. With each passing month, the decision not to keep the M.S.406 in production was looking like an ever more serious mistake.

Controversy would later surround the value of the 1,700 combat planes (800 fighter, 800 reconnaissance 100 bombers) stored away in the rear. One general would later claim that his attempts in January 1940 to make use of some 150 unarmed 'modern' Bloch fighters stored at Tours had been blocked by the Air Force.[13] With hindsight, it might appear that the French could have made a greater effort to distribute these and other fighters among the Polish and Czech pilots. At a time when some British pilots were still flying Gladiators and Belgian and Dutch pilots were forced to fly fighters of similar or even lower performance, it could be argued that the 200 Bloch fighters sitting in stores could have made a contribution. Even obsolete aircraft like the Potez 25, of which there were at least 600 stored away in France, would have enabled the Czech and Polish bomber and reconnaissance pilots to train.[14,15] If the French had been aware how close they were to total defeat, there might have been more urgency about using some of these substandard resources, but nobody was anticipating what was about to happen. Arguably, the French were right to focus on maximising the number of modern planes available, rather than waste manpower mobilising obsolete equipment. However, there was also a reluctance to accept that apparently obsolete planes could still be useful. The Air Ministry and Air Force were convinced that only the very latest 1936 generation of planes could possibly be of any value. The 1934 generation had already been dismissed as inadequate; anything older or less capable was not even considered. Unfortunately, wars have to be fought with what is available, not with what commanders would like to be available. As the May–June campaign would demonstrate, obsolete aircraft can be surprisingly effective if used wisely.

With winter turning to spring, and the inevitable German offensive approaching, the French fighter force found itself relying on virtually the same equipment it had possessed at the outbreak of war. However, the fighting at the front still did not suggest these fighters would be overrun. In the first six months of war, only twenty-one French fighters had been lost in combat. This hardly seemed to substantiate the grim picture painted by front line pilots after the encounters of the previous November. Perhaps d'Harcourt had been overreacting when he had claimed all French fighters were inferior to German equipment. Mock combats with the captured Bf 109E suggested the D.520 was only slightly inferior and, a little optimistically, that the superior manoeuvrability of the Bloch MB.152 would enable the fighter to hold its own. A complacent report on the eve of the invasion claimed that the poor manoeuvrability of the Bf 109 and British fighters demonstrated that you could not increase the performance of a fighter simply by reducing wing area and increasing power.[16]

Certainly, in the hands of experienced pilots, the Curtiss H75 and M.S.406 were tricky opponents. The manoeuvrability of these two fighters might enable French pilots to hold their own until better material became available. Both lacked the necessary speed to dictate terms to the enemy but in a close escort role, they were capable of at least occupying the attentions of German fighters heading for the vulnerable French bomber and reconnaissance planes. The desperately disappointing Bloch MB.152 offered few advantages over the Morane and H75, although it was rugged and was powerfully armed. The French claim that it was more manoeuvrable than the Bf 109E was only true at low altitudes. Above 3,000 metres, the performance of the plane dropped off alarmingly. To make matters worse, the late arrival of the definitive version of the Bloch MB.152 meant that Bloch pilots had no opportunity to learn how to get the best out of their fighter in actual combat. This was particularly unfortunate as many of the Bloch squadrons were manned by the most recently trained, least experienced pilots. With its two cannon, the Bloch fighter was capable of inflicting heavy casualties, if it could evade the Bf 109 escorts. Perhaps with this in mind, most Bloch squadrons were in the rear, defending civilian and industrial targets beyond the range of the Bf 109.

The Dewoitine D.520 was the only plane that could take on the Bf 109E on reasonably equal terms. At low and medium altitudes, even this plane was outclassed by the German Bf 109E, but at higher altitudes, thanks to its excellent Szydlowski-Planiol supercharger, the gap in performance closed and above 7,000 metres, the Dewoitine fighter was actually faster in horizontal flight and climb.[17] The French had an excellent high-altitude air superiority fighter, capable of providing lesser French fighters with the necessary protection, but it was only just reaching the squadrons, and pilots would have no time to find out how to get the best out of their new mount.

Rear defence was still uppermost in French minds and in the future campaign, much would depend on how quickly resources were switched from the rear to the front. The scattered rear regional defence squadrons were formed into four new fighter groups, which were still mainly deployed in the rear, but these more substantial units could be more easily moved elsewhere. These brought the number of groups available in France to twenty-five. Of these, seven were defending the Lower Seine, Paris, Lyon, and Marseilles. The British constantly complained about the poor early warning and tracking systems that directed these and RAF fighter squadrons. Helpfully, they were providing the French with radar sets, although they knew these did not work well over land; even Dowding's Fighter Command used the eyes and ears of the Royal Observer Corps for inland tracking. Radar was of limited value for rear defence and could play no part in the forthcoming tactical air battles. Germany led the world in radar, but it was their panzers and Stukas that were going to be decisive. British complaints about the French air defence system were not helpful as they merely intensified French fears about how vulnerable their cities and factories were.

With seven fighter groups covering the rear, eight more attached permanently to various armies, and another four re-equipping, only six groups were available as a central reserve to reinforce the rear or any particular sector of the front. Vuillemin was gradually working his way towards a more centrally controlled fighter force. Much to the annoyance of the Army, the six groups they controlled would be last to move from their peacetime strength of twenty-six planes to their official wartime strength of thirty-four.[18] Also, none of the new units being formed would be under Army command. By the end of 1940, the proportion of fighter strength directly attached to armies would be reduced from one quarter to one tenth.

In April, the fighter groups were organised into *groupements*. *Groupement* 21 covered the Paris and Lower Seine; *Groupement* 22, the northern end of the

Maginot Line; *Groupement* 23, the Ardennes-Belgium front; *Groupement* 24 the southern end of the Maginot Line; and *Groupement* 25 would protect the advance into the Netherlands. The idea was that fighter groups could be quickly switched to the *groupement* where they were needed. It looked flexible, and the needs of the Army seemed well catered for, but the Army had good reason to be nervous. While Vuillemin made much of the need for a centralised flexible force that could be focused over the front or in the rear, it was the nightmare of devastated French cities that still haunted the Air Force commander.

With the vast majority of the day bomber force still waiting for something to fly, other ways of striking an invading German Army were already being considered. Têtu wanted the obsolete Amiot 143 bombers used by day if there was a rupture of the front line; on 14 April, Vuillemin formally instructed General d'Astier, the commander of the Northern Air Zone (ZOAN: *Zone d'Opérations Aériennes du Nord*), to use the obsolete night bombers in this way if necessary.[19] Using these slow, ungainly multi-seaters seemed an unnecessarily desperate measure; there were far better alternatives.

Fighters were one option. Operational instructions for fighter groups made it clear that they too might be needed for ground-attack in an emergency. Trials took place with the Bloch MB.151, Dewoitine D.510, and Potez 63 in the ground-attack role.[20] The Curtiss H75 was being viewed as a potential specialised low-level ground-attack plane or dive-bomber, once these aircraft were no longer required by fighter units. Trials in 1939 involved H75s carrying five 10-kg anti-personnel bombs under each wing and releasing them in 45-degree dives.[21]

The Hispano-Suiza cannon French fighters carried gave them a very useful ground-attack capability. Trials held in January 1940 demonstrated that this weapon could penetrate 15 mm of armour with ease and up to 30 mm if the shells struck at the right angle. In practice, this meant that both the Panzer I and II, which made up half the German tank force, were vulnerable. More luck would be needed to knock out the more heavily armoured Panzer III and IV.[22]

Of all the fighters available to the French, perhaps the most suitable for the ground-attack role was the Bloch MB.151/152. At low levels, it was fast and manoeuvrable and its rugged airframe and air-cooled engine increased the chances of surviving ground fire. The plane was also armed with two Hispano-Suiza cannon. Even the Bloch MB.151 could carry the cannon; the trainer version was only armed with machine guns to conserve weapons. Interestingly, when the plane had been relaunched in 1938, the Bloch company, perhaps realising the design might never make it as a fighter in its own right, advertised their product as an '*avion d'assaut*'.[23]

There was no shortage of the substandard versions of this plane in stores, nor was there a shortage of trained Polish and Czech pilots who would have welcomed the opportunity to attack an invading German Army. It was a lot less desperate than using clumsy Amiot bombers. Given the opportunity, the Bloch might have joined the ranks of those fighters, which, having proved disappointing in their original role, went on to make a name for themselves as fighter-bombers. The trials that were being organised demonstrated that the Air Force was moving in the direction of using fighters for ground-attack. If the Army had shown more interest in tactical bomber support, there might have been more urgency about developing the idea.

Using reconnaissance and observation planes was another alternative. Although the Army had always opposed equipping these units with planes capable of operating as bombers, all French reconnaissance aircraft were designed to carry light bombs, and using them in an emergency as ground-attack planes was policy. In March 1940, the strategic reconnaissance group GR I/33 was involved in trials with the 3rd Light Mechanised Division, to see how effective Potez 637 would be knocking out enemy batteries that were holding up the advance of the tanks.[24] Finally, the French Navy could also help out. It had four dive-bomber squadrons, two with the French Liore-Nieuport LN.401/411 and two the American Chance Vought V-156-F, and three of these were already earmarked to support the French advance into southern Netherlands.

Meanwhile, the opposing air forces continued to test each other out in sporadic fighting over the front. March 1940 brought better flying weather and aerial activity on both sides increased sharply. Even so, the 1,700 sorties flown by French fighters could hardly be described as intensive use of the available resources. Luftwaffe fighter squadrons were now much more in evidence, with sweeps being flown well inside French territory. This month saw the long-awaited appearance of the Bf 110. In their first engagements with the twin-engined German destroyer, French pilots were as impressed as the Poles by the speed and firepower of this machine. It seemed the problems were mounting. French pilots were having little success intercepting high-flying German reconnaissance planes. Even when contact was made, pilots discovered the defensive fire of the German planes was very effective and the planes themselves robust. Following the destruction of two German reconnaissance planes on 2 March, the French fighter force could not manage a single confirmed 'kill' during the remainder of the month.[25]

However, there still appeared to be little evidence that the French fighter force was being overwhelmed. Even a disastrous encounter on the last day of the month seemed to be largely bad luck. Twenty Bf 109s surprised eleven Moranes from GC III/7, shooting down three and seriously damaging another four. An enquiry discovered there were mitigating circumstances. As was standard practice, six of the Moranes had been flying at 6,000 metres, providing protection for two lower formations. Unfortunately, the leader of the higher patrol had a problem with his oxygen mask and was forced to dive to 4,000 metres. The rest of the formation, not realising what the problem was, followed suit, losing their altitude advantage in the process. At this moment, the German fighters pounced on the disorganised French formation. All the aircraft shot down were in fact from the higher patrol.[26] It was felt that not too much should be read into what seemed like a rather freakish sequence of events. Even so, Morane losses were mounting. In the first few days of April, six more were lost before poor weather brought some respite to the French pilots.

These were still hardly excessive, but even this scale of loss was beginning to expose problems that would become more severe when the fighting intensified. Strangely, given that there were so many unemployed Polish and Czech pilots in France, there was an acute shortage of ferry pilots. Those that were available were used to deliver twin-engined planes, leaving fighter groups to make their own arrangements. In the context of the Phoney War, with aerial activity relatively low, this did not seem an unreasonable burden. The lack of urgency the Phoney War engendered tended to make the replacement procedure even more inefficient. Depots in the rear tended to work on a peacetime basis. Just weeks before the German offensive, d'Harcourt was complaining that even when planes were available in stores and fighter units sent their own pilots to collect them, it sometimes took up to a week for the replacements to arrive.[27] The whole French administrative system was slowing down to the pace of the Phoney War. The tactical air/land battle that was about to unfold would be fought at a much faster pace and the French were not ready for it.

It was not just the speed at which replacement fighters could be delivered that was worrying d'Harcourt. Even more worrying was the shortage of available fighters. Instead of the substantial reserves all French expansion plans since 1938 had called for, on 10 May, the entire French fighter reserve consisted of just thirty-one single-seater machines. There were just eleven M.S.406s and the last few were trickling off the production line. Virtually all the Curtiss H75s delivered were with the squadrons and training schools. On 10 May 1940, there were only five available as reserves and the first examples of the third batch of H75 A-3s were only just beginning to arrive. There were large numbers of substandard Bloch fighters but there were still not enough of the fully modified version to equip front line units. On 10 May, there were just fifteen in the rear ready to be sent to front line squadrons.[28] The reserves were wafer thin.

The month that preceded the German offensive turned out to be a reasonably successful one for the French. Fourteen planes were lost, of which ten were fighters, but a total of eighteen Luftwaffe aircraft were claimed. These included one of the new high-speed Junkers 88 intercepted by an MB.152 of GC III/9, the first victory achieved by the Bloch fighter.[29] The D.520 was on the way. On 7 May, GC I/3 received the last of its full complement of thirty-four machines. The day before, the first group of GC II/3 pilots had been dispatched to Toulouse to pick up this unit's first fully operational fighters. By this time, machines with all the required modifications already incorporated were rolling off the main Toulouse assembly line and with the improvised line modifying early production models, around fifteen a week were reaching the Air Force. The first Arsenal VG-33 and Bloch MB.155 fighters were being readied for delivery while deliveries of the first Hispano-Suiza HS 12Y-51 engines were now only weeks away. The first 150 sets of modified wings for the M.S.410 existed. One machine had been converted and work had started on another twenty.[30] Better fighters would be arriving very soon. The French just had to hang on.

Even before the battle started, the French were paying the price for their weakness in the air. During April, the number of German reconnaissance sorties steadily increased, a sure sign that a major offensive could not now be far away. Vuillemin, however, found himself having to prohibit any French reconnaissance missions, if cloud cover or fighter protection was not available.[31] During April, the French only dared fly under 200 reconnaissance missions along the entire front, compared to nearly 700 in the first month of war.[32] Whereas the German High Command had a very clear picture of where the Allied forces were, the French only had a sketchy idea of German dispositions and intentions.

There were few clashes between French and German forces in the first days of May. On 9 May, the number of German reconnaissance flights increased dramatically with most Allied airfields in the battle zone being visited. The French fighter force seemed particularly powerless to intervene. Only one French fighter squadron managed to make contact with the enemy, five M.S.406s from GC III/7 intercepting a Do 17 near Dijon. The German plane was damaged, but was still able to pull away from its pursuers and flee across the frontier.[33] The engagement did not augur well for the forthcoming campaign.

12

Dutch Misadventure

On 10 May, the Germans launched their long-awaited offensive. The Luftwaffe had available over 1,000 medium bombers, 400 Stuka dive bombers and Hs 123 assault planes, 300 observation planes, and 300 reconnaissance planes, with over 1,000 single-seater fighters and 350 twin-engined fighters to protect them. As German troops crossed the Dutch and Belgian frontiers, 500 medium bombers struck targets deep in the rear while the Stukas and Hs 123s supported the Army's drive through Dutch and Belgian frontier defences.

The Dutch immediately began withdrawing to the more easily defendable Fortress Holland and the Belgians prepared to hold the Germans on the line running along the Albert Canal line and the River Meuse. The French Navy started transporting infantry to Flushing and the 100 tanks and associated motorised infantry and artillery of the 1st Light Mechanised Division raced through Belgian to link up with them. British and French forces started advancing towards the Dyle and Meuse with two French light mechanised divisions bolstering the Allied line in the 'Gembloux gap' between these two rivers. In the Netherlands, the Ockenburg, Ypenburg, and Valkenburg airfields outside The Hague were occupied by German airborne troops. Further south, more paratroopers captured the bridges at Moerdijk, Dordrecht, and Rotterdam, with the aim of giving the 9th Panzer Division a clear run on The Hague. The remaining nine armoured divisions pushed westwards towards Gembloux, Dinant, Monthermé, and Sedan, with the heaviest blow falling in the south.

While the Stukas supported the drives towards Gembloux and Rotterdam, the principal objectives of the German medium bomber force on this first day were Allied airfields and lines of communication. Some of the targets were to the west of Paris, but aerial defences in the Paris region were avoided. To the south, Luftwaffe bombers penetrated as far as Lyon. Many of the targets were beyond the range of the Bf 109 and some beyond the range of the Bf 110. By penetrating so far inside French air space, the Germans were taking a

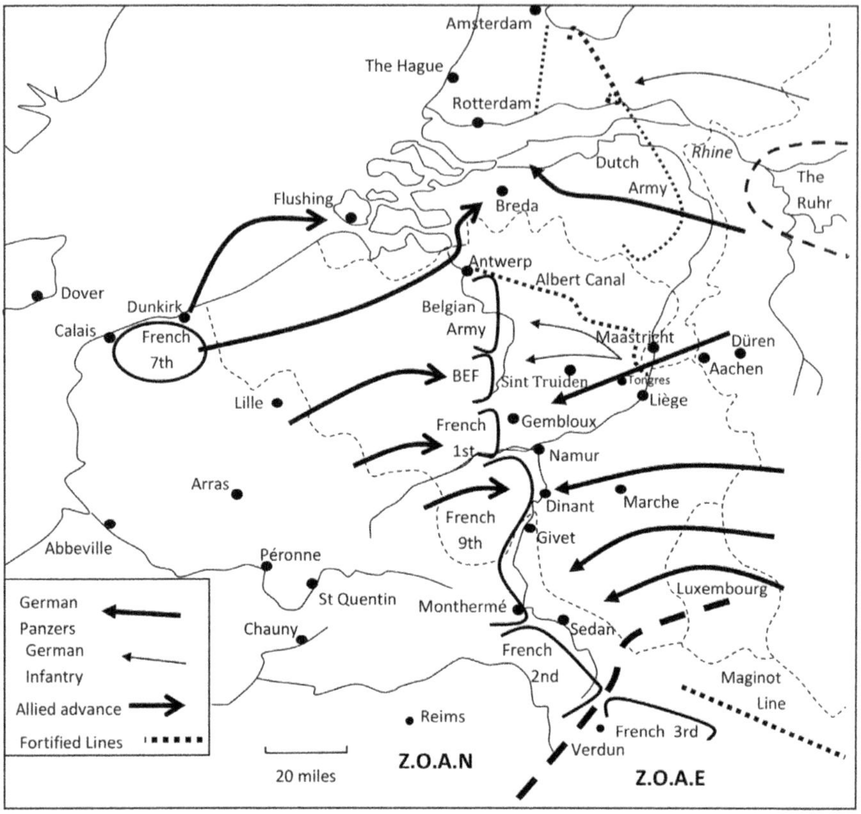

German offensive, 10 May 1940.

chance. Unlike the lone reconnaissance planes, the bombers would be carrying bombs and flying much slower in formation. Without escorts, they would be vulnerable. Even bombers operating within fighter range often had to do without an escort. The lumbering Ju 52 troop transports the Germans were using in the Netherlands were in far greater need of protection. The Panzers making their way through the Ardennes also needed protecting, as did the bridges and airfields the Germans had captured; not even the Luftwaffe had enough fighters to cover everything.

The sheer range of targets the Luftwaffe attacked enabled Allies to bring into play a high proportion of their rather scattered fighter units. The decision not to bomb targets in Britain or the Paris area did eliminate from the fray half the fighters available to the Allies. Even so, the areas the Germans were operating in were covered by some 700 British, French, Dutch, and Belgian fighters. Dutch resistance was fierce. Even Fokker T.V bombers took off to take on the waves of German bombers and transports. The Dutch squadrons had very little warning. One squadron of Fokker G.1s was caught on the ground and virtually wiped out, while many other fighters were caught climbing, but twenty-one German planes were claimed during the course of fifty defensive sorties for the loss of twelve. It was a very creditable performance in difficult circumstances. Pilots returned to find their home bases badly damaged or captured but despite the problems, Dutch pilots were soon flying their second sortie of the morning.[1]

Meanwhile, the German transport planes were running into problems. Anti-aircraft fire, fighters, and obstacles strewn across likely landing grounds destroyed large numbers. The Dutch immediately ordered any plane capable of offensive action to attack the occupied airfields. From 7 a.m., some forty bombing and ground strafing sorties were flown by bombers, fighters, and reconnaissance planes against the surrounded German airborne troops. The planes used included 150-mph Fokker C.V biplanes, broadly similar to the French Potez 25 in performance and age. During the course of the first day, the Dutch Air Force had flown around 150 sorties, including approximately 100 by fighters. By the end of the day, Dutch claims had risen to twenty-seven.[2] These claims do not appear to be exaggerated. KG 4 alone lost fourteen bombers over the Netherlands during the course of the day. In extremely difficult circumstances, obsolete planes used aggressively had performed well. By the evening, Dutch forces had routed the German paratroopers that had landed around The Hague, but failed to dislodge those hanging on to the bridges leading to Rotterdam. The spirited resistance put up by the poorly armed Dutch forces seemed to justify Gamelin's decision to send troops into the south of the country. In the early hours of the 11th, reconnaissance elements of Giraud's 7th Army pushed into the Breda area, just ten miles from the German held bridge at Moerdijk.

Further south the airborne troops had captured key positions on the main Belgian defensive line along the Albert Canal. The bridge over the Canal at Canne, immediately north of Eben-Emael, was successfully demolished before the German forces could take it, but those at Veldwezelt and Vroenhoven were captured intact and the troops landed on Eben Emael by glider had soon neutralised the fort's artillery. The German panzers heading west were briefly held up by the Dutch demolition of the bridges over the Maas in Maastricht but the 3rd and 4th Panzer Divisions were soon across the river and the Albert Canal and heading for Gembloux.

Meanwhile, the first large-scale clashes between the Allied and German air forces were taking place in the skies over France. The six French-based RAF fighter squadrons used flew around 200 sorties, losing fifteen machines but claimed forty-two enemy planes. Many French airfields were bombed but by and large the fighter squadrons emerged unscathed. The most serious loss occurred at Cambrai-Niergnies where thirteen M.S.406s of GC III/2 were either destroyed or seriously damaged. If adequate reserves had existed, these would have been easily replaced, but these losses alone were more than the entire existing reserve. The surviving planes managed to fly forty-four sorties during the course of the day, claiming three German planes.[3] At Lyon-Bron, home to GC I/145 and GC III/9, the commander of GC III/9, gamely flying an old Dewoitine D.501, led four of his pilots against the bombers attacking his airfield. They failed to bring down any of the raiders, but the commander was showing a willingness to use whatever was available, which was going to become all the more necessary in the weeks ahead.[4]

The Curtiss H75s of GC I/5 claimed nine bombers over their base, despite the presence of a Bf 110 escort, and the M.S.406s of GC III/1 claimed another nine in defence of their airfield, demonstrating both these fighters were capable of making inroads into the German bomber formations.[5, 6] Elsewhere, however, the results were less encouraging. Pilots from GC III/3 claimed that after making an initial pass at a German bomber formation, their Moranes lacked the speed to manoeuvre into a position to repeat the attack.[7] GC III/7 started the day with twenty-one serviceable M.S.406s but by the end of the day, this number had been reduced to just five, and the unit had not been able to claim a single German plane.[8]

GC I/5 may have coped with the Bf 110 escorts but the similarly equipped GC II/4 struggled in their first encounter with the twin-engined German fighter. Like so many meeting the plane for the first time, the pilots of this group were impressed by the fighter's speed and firepower, and blamed their lack of success (just one plane claimed) on the Messerschmitt escort. So demoralised were the pilots, they insisted that the twin-engined Bf 110 was more manoeuvrable than their Curtiss fighter.[9]

Other French fighter squadrons were failing to make any contact with the enemy. The German decision to avoid the Paris area meant that the Bloch MB.152 groups stationed there could play almost no part in the fighting. Four bombers did fly over the base of GC I/1, but the group received no warning and the patrol on standby was unable to get into the air in time to intercept.[10] A patrol from GC II/l did encounter two He 111s and claimed the destruction of one of them, but GCs II/10 and III/10, both in the Le Havre region, did not encounter a single plane during the entire day.[11, 12] Another Bloch unit, GC II/8, was providing air cover for the Allied naval expedition heading for the Netherlands, but the Luftwaffe made no attempt to interfere with this operation.

As soon as it was clear the German attack was coming in the north, some effort was made to focus fighter effort there, but these moves were dogged by a lack of urgency. GC III/3, part of the Paris defence force, sent forward one of its Morane squadrons to provide more protection for the Allied forces heading for Walcheren. However, despite the intense Luftwaffe activity over northern France, the group only flew six sorties during the day, one patrol over its airfield, and another over Dunkirk. Elsewhere, the transfer of a group seemed to virtually eliminate it from the day's fighting. Both GC I/4 and II/6 were transferred to *Groupement* 25, supporting the advance into the Netherlands, but neither began full scale operations until the following day. Even those groups not involved in transfers were underused. After its initial successful encounter with the enemy, GC III/1 received no further orders until the afternoon. GC II/5 had to wait until 5.50 p.m. before getting any orders at all.[13] Many of these instructions were still arriving as written orders. The French were finding it difficult to adjust from the pedestrian pace of the Phoney War. It was all in sharp contrast to the way in which Dutch squadrons, evicted from their own bases by German paratroopers, were almost immediately flying sorties from auxiliary airfields. For the Dutch, 10 May had been a desperate fight for survival. For the French, it was just the first day in what was expected to be a long drawn out struggle.

Of the twenty-five fighter groups available to the French, five stationed in the south played no part in the fighting and the seven defending the Paris and Lower Seine region or assigned the defence of Allied shipping heading for Walcheren were only involved on the periphery. Some groups flew as many as fifty sorties, but overall the sortie rate was low with the 418 serviceable fighters flying 360 sorties, a lower rate than RAF and Dutch fighter squadrons. Altogether, French fighter units were credited with thirty-eight confirmed victories and seven probables.[14] In combat, twelve fighters were lost or seriously damaged. Four pilots were killed, five wounded, and another five baled out unharmed and were able to return to their squadrons. Aircraft lost on the ground pushed fighter losses up to forty-two for the day, which was heavy, but would not have caused any great alarm had adequate reserves been available. However, the reserves did not exist and the losses caused huge alarm. Vuillemin issued urgent instructions to all rear bases to make the maximum number of M.S.406, Curtiss H75, D.520, and the latest version of the Bloch MB.152 available for the front. The situation was grave, he emphasised. The Germans had substantial reserves and unless urgent steps were taken to create adequate French reserves, the French fighter force would be destroyed in a fortnight.[15] It seemed a little late. Urgent measures had been required for some time; Vuillemin could not afford to be fussy about which version of the Bloch MB.152 was sent to the front. Squadrons were already using early versions on operations, although, it would seem not the Bloch MB.151s many squadrons still had.

During the course of the day, German medium bombers carried out about 150 raids on various targets in the Netherlands, Belgium, and France, around half which were against airfields. In Belgium and the Netherlands, some sixty combat planes were destroyed on the ground. The French naval dive-bomber squadron, AB 3, lost all twelve Chance Vought 156-Fs. M.S.406 bases seemed to attract German bombers, with twenty-two destroyed or badly damaged, but elsewhere, losses were light. In all, around fifty French aircraft were destroyed.[16] The attacks carried out on various communication targets in eastern and central France did not cause serious damage, but they served to remind the French of the dangers of risking troop movements by day. The French either limited movement to the short May nights or rerouted them through tortuously long detours far in the rear. More delay was caused by the fear of what might happen than any actual physical damage caused. The Luftwaffe had no intention of interfering with the advance of the BEF to the Dyle, but further south, a raid on the Hirson railhead did cause considerable damage and reduced the flow of materials to the 9th Army advancing towards the Meuse.

Allied bombers were supposed to strike as soon as it was clear an offensive was underway. Even before reconnaissance planes had identified the main line of advance, the plan was for bombers to hit predetermined targets on the German side of the frontier.[17] As soon as reconnaissance had identified more specific targets, effort would focus on these. Barratt's AASF was to concentrate on targets in Luxembourg while French bombers and RAF No. 2 Group would deal with any advance through central Belgium. Both Barratt and d'Astier were reluctant to carry out this plan, Barratt because of the losses he feared his squadrons would suffer and d'Astier because he only had two LeO 451 bomber groups, and was reluctant to commit them too soon. By 7.30 a.m., the first news of appropriate targets was beginning to filter through to d'Astier and Barratt's joint headquarters at Chauny. A reconnaissance plane of the 3rd Army had spotted German columns advancing through the southern Ardennes and the fierce fighter opposition encountered by the plane suggested this was no minor diversionary attack. It was probably with some relief that d'Astier received instructions at 8 a.m. to restrict operations in neutral Belgium and the Netherlands to fighter and reconnaissance missions, even though Dutch bombers were already in action. Three hours later, the instruction was reversed and during the course of the afternoon, Barratt tentatively dispatched thirty-two Battles to attack various targets in Luxembourg. D'Astier later complained about the indecision higher up the chain of command, but even with the go ahead, he decided not to commit his LeO 451 squadrons.[18]

The low-level Battle missions were a disaster. Fifteen were lost, which was not encouraging for d'Astier's Breguet 693s. The first French bomber sorties were not flown until the night of the 10/11th. The four Amiot 143 groups could only muster twenty-nine serviceable machines on the morning of the tenth and some of these were either destroyed or damaged on the ground. When night fell, just twelve set off for German airfields.[19] Given that some 1,000 Luftwaffe sorties by day had resulted in the destruction of little more than 100 Allied planes, it was hardly surprising that the French effort by night should have no effect whatsoever on the Luftwaffe.

The Amiot groups also flew some nocturnal reconnaissance missions. Some pilots returning from these reported German columns advancing through the Ardennes with headlights blazing. Clearly, the Germans were quite happy to sacrifice surprise for speed. Having no bombs on board, the French planes could only strafe the German columns. These were clearly more easily identifiable targets than enemy airfields. Even scattered attacks on these columns might have at least forced the Germans to stop driving with headlights on.[20]

Little more than a dozen sorties in twenty-four hours from a force that should have been capable of putting over 400 planes into the air is a statistic, which graphically highlights the tragedy that had overtaken the French bomber force. If the Germans had adopted a different strategy, the weakness of the French force might not have been so cruelly exposed. However, the Germans had deliberately opted for a high-risk strategy that involved pushing the vast majority of their motorised and armoured divisions through the limited Ardennes road network. It would be three days before the first major line of French resistance was even reached and during this time the armoured forces would be vulnerable to air attack. Much to their surprise and relief, the Germans were able to advance virtually unhindered.

German commanders were equally surprised by the almost total lack of Allied reconnaissance flights behind their lines. With so many French groups dealing with the German raids on targets well inside French territory, the only fighters available to escort reconnaissance missions were those attached to armies, which was some justification for the Army's insistence on retaining control of fighter units. However, these units were struggling to defend their own bases, and there were simply not enough fighters on any sector of the front to cover reconnaissance missions as well. In the end, the French only risked eight long-range reconnaissance missions along all fronts.[21] Only one plane failed to return, but German fighters forced others to beat a hasty, premature retreat before they had got far. As a result, reconnaissance missions in the Ardennes only reported columns in the south of Luxembourg, which led to the impression the main German drive in Luxembourg was south of the capital rather than to the north. This in turn led to the few Battle bombing sorties that were flown being too far south.

Both sides could view the first day's fighting with satisfaction and concern. The German landings around The Hague had been defeated and a staggering 200 Ju 52 transports had been lost. The Luftwaffe had also lost 120 combat planes. Nearly 100 bombers had failed to return or were so badly damaged they had to be written off. Many more returned with less severe damage but with dead and wounded crew members. Even at the height of the Battle of Britain, Luftwaffe losses would not be this heavy. If it had been an air-only offensive, like the Battle of Britain, it would have been a victory for the defending fighters. However, it was not a purely air offensive. Panzers were advancing on Rotterdam, Gembloux, Monthermé, Dinant, and Sedan and in the skies above them, the Allies were already losing the tactical air battle.

From the 11th, German bombers operated in larger formations with escorts against targets closer to the front, but the longer-range efforts of the first day had left their mark on the French. Most of the targets had been communications, but industrial targets, some as far south as St Etienne, had also been bombed. These were almost certainly either attacked by mistake or by crews who could not find their primary target, but it took very little to revive French fears of a possibly crippling air offensive against the French industrial heartland and its civilian population. Panzer divisions were bearing down on the French defences, but the first French reaction was to stiffen air defences in the rear.

The instruction to commanders of the various Air Regions to put on alert any fighter groups in the rear converting to more modern material was sensible enough. However, GC III/6, which was operating over the southern sector of the Maginot Line along with the 8th Army's own GC II/7, was available to move north to the active front, but instead, it was told to reinforce the fighters defending Lyon.[22] The half-forgotten decision of the previous September to form rear defence flights was suddenly put into effect. On 11 May, an order was issued requiring flights to be established at the four aircraft plants mentioned in the original September 1939 instruction and these were to be reinforced by Polish and Czech pilots. Over the next few days, orders would be issued for the creation of further ELDs (*Escadrille Légère de Défense*) at Romorantin, Chartres, Étampes, Tours, Avord, Montpellier, Bordeaux, and Orléans, all to be manned by foreign pilots. These flights were supposed to consist of six pilots and three planes each, the pilot/plane ratio underlining how short the French were of any sort of fighter. They used whatever fighters happened to be available. Those defending the Bloch and Curtiss H75 plants used the fighters they were assembling; others were to get the Morane-Saulnier M.S.406 and Bloch MB.151. Dewoitine D.520s were too precious, so the flight defending the Toulouse plant used Dewoitine D.501s. The new units were created with remarkable speed, evidence that would suggest that more could have been done sooner to make use of the pool of foreign pilots in France. A first victory was claimed on the 12th by a ferry pilot from the Châteaudun flight.[23, 24, 25]

Eventually, some twenty-five of these flights would be formed, each with between three and nine fighters. At their peak, these units probably mustered 100 planes. Most of the towns protected were to the west of Paris and Lyon, where German bombers rarely penetrated and contacts with the enemy were even rarer. Following the success achieved on the 12th, there was probably only one further victory in May. While it was reasonable to organise test pilots and instructors already based in the rear in this way, the 100 Poles and Czechs that found their way into these flights would have been far better employed where they were needed: over the front.

So too would the fighter groups defending the rear. One squadron from the five groups defending Paris and the lower Seine had been sent forward to support the drive into the Netherlands, but the rest stayed in place. The only other reinforcement for the northern front was GC II/4 transferred from ZOAE (covering the Maginot Line). On the morning of the 11th, the fighter groups defending Rouen, Paris, Lyon, and Marseilles together with the four fighter groups attached to the 3rd, 4th, 5th, and 8th Armies, to the south of the German offensive, made up more than half the available French fighter strength. Seven and a half groups (fifteen squadrons) were available to the four French armies on the 125-mile long active front from the southern Netherlands to Luxembourg. It was not enough to protect the troops at the front, communications to the rear, and provide escorts for reconnaissance planes and bombers.

Initially, French attention on the 11th was focused on Giraud's 7th Army and its attempt to link up with the Dutch. Gamelin was determined it should be allocated the resources necessary for it to succeed and the 7th Army possessed some of the best equipped motorised divisions in the French Army, including the 1st Light Mechanised Division (DLM), one of the Army's six priceless armoured divisions. In the air too, it was well-supported, with its standard reconnaissance group, three observation squadrons, and fighter cover provided by *Groupement* 25. On the morning of the 10th, it possessed GC III/1 (the 7th Army's own fighter group), and the naval cooperation group GC II/8, but was soon reinforced by GC I/4 and one squadron from GC III/3, transferred from the Paris region. French naval squadrons were also supporting the operation. These included two fighter squadrons equipped with the Potez 631 and three dive-bomber squadrons (two LN 401/411 and one Chance Voight 156-F). There were also three Laté 298 reconnaissance bomber floatplanes squadrons and the French could also count on the two Hurricane and two Blenheim squadrons Fighter Command had promised for the operation. Altogether, the force had nearly 200 fighters and 100 bomber reconnaissance planes. Bloch MB.152 and Morane units moved forward to bases in northern Belgium to cover the operation but the longer-range Curtiss H75s and naval Potez 631s had the range to operate from bases in France.

Despite Dutch counterattacks, on the 11th, German airborne troops were still holding the three bridges leading to Rotterdam. By midday, advance units of the 9th Panzer Division had made contact with reconnaissance elements of Giraud's 7th Army in the vicinity of Tilburg, just east of Breda. At this stage, the main body of the German forces was still 25 miles from the Moerdijk bridges. The situation was extremely fluid with both sides exposed, but equally both were in an excellent position to seriously embarrass the other. However, the Luftwaffe was already giving the German Army the edge. While no effort was made to use the naval bombers to slow down the German advance, the Luftwaffe launched a series of heavy raids on the troops disembarking at Flushing, inflicting heavy casualties. The shaken French commander decided his troops were in no position to carry out their instructions to advance eastwards. The fear of Luftwaffe attacks also persuaded the commander of the 1st Light Mechanised Division to

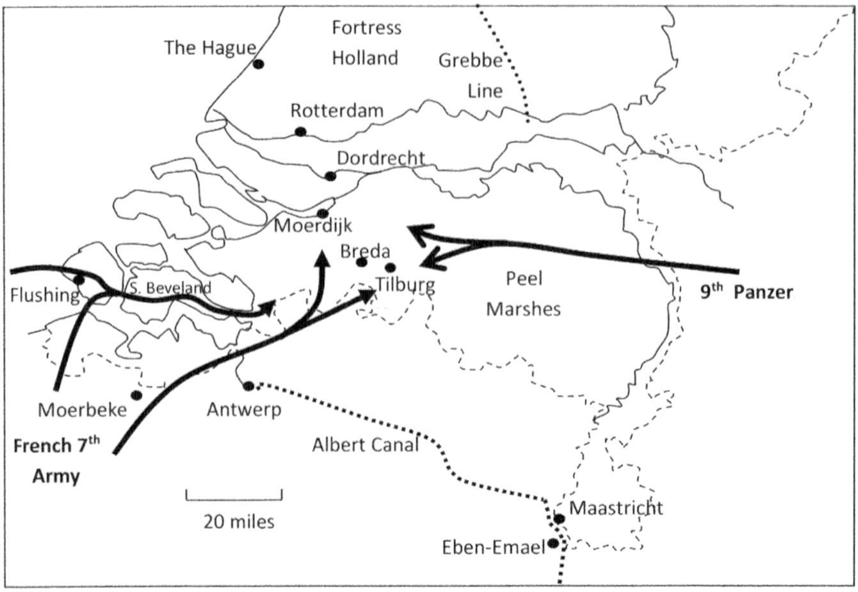

Operations in southern Netherlands.

detrain his tanks south of Antwerp so they did not make such an easy target for German bombers. Then, it was decided not to risk them in southern Netherlands at all, which left the French force short of any real punch.

Despite the bombing throughout the morning of the 11th, no use was made of GC I/4, which was moved the day before specifically to support the Dutch operation. In the afternoon, one of the two French battalions making for Breda suffered a particularly vicious air assault. Casualties were heavy and the unit was held up for two hours. In response, at 3.50 p.m., the French finally ordered GC I/4 to the area. This was the unit's first major mission of the campaign. An hour later, twenty-six Curtiss H75s were patrolling the skies over Breda. A formation of bombers was spotted, but the French fighters were set upon by the Bf 109 escort and a fierce dogfight ensued. The French claimed five victories but two French pilots were killed, three wounded, and most of the planes that made it back to base were damaged. The following morning, the group could only muster six serviceable machines and further operations were cancelled until a reasonable number of planes could be repaired. It was the evening of the 13th before the group was back in action.[26] A single engagement with the enemy had effectively eliminated the fighter group for forty-eight hours. During the Phoney War, the group might have two days to recover, but not during a fast-developing enemy ground offensive. The group claimed a couple of bombers on the 13th but these would be the last victories for several days.

Operating from Moerbeke in northern Belgium, CC III/1 claimed a couple of German planes on the 11th. However, the number of unserviceable M.S.406s was rising rapidly and the situation was not helped by having to move to a second airfield in northern Belgium on the evening of the 12th. The number of sorties flown by the group steadily dwindled and after the successes of the 11th, no further victories were recorded by this unit while based in Belgium. On the 13th, the surviving planes were ordered back to France. In four days of operations, personnel losses were just four pilots wounded, but aircraft losses meant the unit had ceased to have any fighting value. The squadron detached from GC III/3 did have more success. This unit claimed five confirmed victories over Breda on the 13th for the loss of just a single M.S.406. Four of these claims were for Bf 109s. In fact, only two Messerschmitts were shot down, but on this occasion at least the M.S.406s had not been overwhelmed. However, the French fighters had failed to break through to the bombers.

Meanwhile, Giraud was doing his best to help the Dutch, but under constant attack and without the tanks of the 1st DLM, there was not much he could do. A couple of half-hearted attempts were made to dislodge the German forces holding the Moerdijk bridges but the French lacked the firepower and these efforts were easily repulsed. In the First World War, air support for such assaults had been improvised overnight. Giraud may not have had a First World War Air Division at his disposal but he did have dive-bomber squadrons he could have called on, but they remained unused. The commanders of the 7th Army did not appear to make much use of their short-range observation planes either. In a fluid situation where anticipating the enemy was essential, French commanders might have been expected to risk the occasional Potez 63.11 sortie, but in the first three days of the operation, neither GAO 501 nor GAO 516 flew a single operational mission.[27] Further north, the Dutch were using their far more limited resources much more aggressively. In three days, the four Dutch Fokker C.V squadrons had flown sixty-five reconnaissance and ground-attack sorties, losing five planes.[28, 29] Giraud did not seem to want to use his planes for reconnaissance, never mind the sort of low-level attack missions the ancient Dutch Fokkers were flying. A bolder use of the available French ground and air forces might have recaptured the Moerdijk bridge before the 9th Panzer could relieve the lightly armed airborne troops holding it. There were no excuses for this failure to act decisively. This was an operation the French had been planning for some time; they were scarcely victims of unexpected circumstances. Unfortunately for the Dutch, French Army commanders had forgotten how useful air power could be in such situations and using the available bombers did not seem to occur to anyone.

While the French hesitated, the Germans pushed on. The French forces in the Breda area were soon beginning to look rather exposed and on the 13th General Billotte, who had been given the task of coordinating all French,

British and Belgian forces on the northern front, ordered Giraud to pull his forces out of the Netherlands. Soon after midday on the 13th, the 9th Panzer Division linked up with the German paratroopers still holding the Moerdijk bridges and the German tanks then pushed rapidly northwards, reaching the southern end of the Willems bridge, on the outskirts of Rotterdam, by nightfall.

The next day, the airborne troops and panzers planned to storm the city. Unlike the French attempts to recapture the Moerdijk bridges, the Germans were willing to use air power to substitute for artillery. The attack was called off when it seemed the Dutch were willing to surrender, but half of the bomber force did not get the message. The bombing was fierce and accurate. Warehouses full of inflammable materials were soon ablaze and the flames spread like wildfire through the surrounding timber buildings. Initially, the death toll was put at 30,000 people. The actual death toll was a tragic 900, but the initial exaggeration was generally accepted at the time. The message seemed clear enough: leave your cities devoid of fighter protection at your peril. The French, and indeed the British, took note and both cast even more anxious glances at their vulnerable cities.

While the citizens of Rotterdam counted the cost, French forces further south were in serious trouble. Already on the 13th, French units in the Breda area were in danger of being cut off by the German drive on Tilburg and Antwerp. On the morning of the 13th, a French reconnaissance plane had spotted German tanks already south-west of Breda. Rather bizarrely, Battles from the AASF, based 150 miles to the south, were called in to cover the retreat while the naval dive-bombers assigned to the operation remained unused. By the 15th, German forces were threatening to break through the French defences and capture Flushing before the evacuation could be completed. Only at this point did the French begin to use their dive-bombers. Between the 15th and 18th, the three squadrons flew forty sorties against the German forces closing in on Walcheren. Naval Potez 631 and the H75s of GC I/4 provided escorts and only one bomber was lost.[30]

Earlier in the campaign, when only the advance guards of the two armies were in contact and small groups of German paratroopers were clinging on to the bridges they had captured, the small number of bombers available to the French might have had more impact. Now, they were far too few to make much impression on the gathering German might and were completely overshadowed by the efforts of the Luftwaffe. On the 16th, a powerful German assault on the ground, preceded by a fierce Luftwaffe aerial bombardment, forced the French to retreat to Walcheren. The final defensive line was breached on the afternoon of the 17th and before the end of the day, Flushing itself was in German hands. The next day, GAO 516, one of the three observation squadrons that was supposed to support the French forces, flew its first operational mission, which rather summed up the complete failure to make use of the air resources available.

With the Breda operation, the French had chosen a strategy which made air superiority and close air support even more crucial. To succeed, it needed the sort of mobile firepower the Air Division had provided in the First World War and Jauneaud and Armengaud had wanted developed in the interwar years. Instead of the boldness and decisiveness required, from the very beginning, the operation was dogged by caution. Naval dive-bomber squadrons were only introduced when the tide of battle was turning against the French. The French fighters were deployed too late and lacked the numbers to challenge German air superiority. The available reconnaissance planes were scarcely used at all. The German commanders, on the other hand, received full support from the Luftwaffe from the outset.

The Dutch adventure was an embarrassing setback rather than a catastrophe. Unfortunately for the French, the mechanised land and air forces involved in the effort were now desperately needed elsewhere. Further south, a far more serious threat was developing. Nine panzer divisions were bearing down on the defensive line the French were establishing along the Meuse, with the aim of rupturing the Allied line between Gembloux in the north and Sedan in the south.

In southern Belgium, two German panzer divisions were pouring across the pontoon bridges over the Maas and the captured Veldwezelt and Vroenhoven bridges over the Albert Canal. The French 1st Army was racing towards them in an effort to establish a line between the Dyle and the Meuse. By the evening of the 11th, German forces were fewer than thirty miles from Gembloux and the German columns streaming westwards and the bridges over the Maas and Albert Canal they were using were priority targets. News that the Albert Canal bridges had not been blown by the defenders only reached d'Astier on the morning of the 11th. Destroying them would be a major setback for the German plans. The bridges ran 60 feet above the canal below and crossing it any other way would be difficult. However, as the RAF had discovered over the Somme in August 1918, bridges are not easy targets to destroy; even near misses tend to have little effect. The temporary pontoons over the Maas would also require a high level of precision, but would at least be more vulnerable to near misses. It was precisely to destroy targets like bridges that that for years French Air Force commanders had been demanding more manoeuvrable low-level and dive-bombers. Medium bombers like the LeO 451 could not do it from their normal operating altitudes and were too vulnerable at lower altitudes. The Breguet 693 provided the low-level precision but could only carry 50-kg bombs, which were no more powerful than those the British had used in their attempts on the Somme bridges in the First World War.

The bridges were all quite close to the German frontier and only a few minutes flying time from German fighter bases, another parallel with the attacks on the Somme bridges in August 1918. On the 11th, the Belgians and British flew around thirty bombing sorties against the Albert Canal bridges and the roads leading westwards. At the end of the day, the French carried out their first daylight bombing mission of the campaign, attempting to destroy the bridges over the Albert Canal. Twelve LeO 451s were drawn from GB I/12 and II/12 and escort was provided by eighteen M.S.406s of GCs II/6 and III/3. The protection was certainly needed. The French fighters ran into powerful formations of Bf 110s and Bf 109s. A fierce dogfight ensued with the French fighters claiming five of the enemy. Three Moranes were lost, but the French escort had achieved its task and the bombers reached the target. However, the fighters could do nothing about the flak. The bombers attacked at an altitude of 800 metres to ensure maximum accuracy, but it was neither low enough to be accurate nor high enough to avoid the worst of the flak. All the French bombers were hit, one bomber already damaged by flak was shot down by a Bf 109 and two more badly damaged machines crashed attempting to land. Only one of the planes involved in the raid would be available for operations the following morning.[31, 32] On the 11th, Georges, the commander of French armies in the field, ordered the night bombers to switch their efforts to routes running through Düren and Aachen towards Maastricht. Amiots on reconnaissance missions also now carried bombs to attack targets of opportunity, but the surviving Amiots managed even fewer sorties than on the 10th.

On the evening of the 11th, Georges ordered that the priority for the following day should, once again, be routes leading westwards from Maastricht. French reconnaissance planes were reporting German forces moving through the Ardennes around Marche and along routes west of Luxembourg, clearly heading for Givet.[33] Georges was well aware of this, but the 1st Army had to be given time to establish itself to the east of Gembloux. The threat in the Ardennes had to wait until the situation had been stabilised further north. On the 12th, British squadrons flew around sixty sorties on the Maastricht-Tongres road and twenty-nine of the unescorted bombers were lost. At 6.30 p.m., twelve LeO 451s bombed convoys on the Maastricht–Sint Truiden road. Once again, a close fighter escort was provided and all the bombers returned. The escorts were proving their worth.

The bomb release gear *Groupement* 18 needed for its Breguet 693s was rushed to these units on the night of the 10th–11th, and for the next day, the *groupement* was ordered to dispatch six three-aircraft patrols to seek out enemy columns west of Maastricht. The Breguets flew to the airfield at Maubeuge-Élesmes to pick up their eighteen-strong Morane escort, provided by GC III/3, and set off for their objectives at tree-top altitude. On paper, both planes had approximately the same speed, but the worn out Moranes struggled to keep up with the brand new Breguets; the assault bombers had soon left their escort behind. As it turned out, German fighters did not turn out to be the danger.

There was no shortage of targets for the Breguets and they delivered their attacks from the lowest possible altitude with precision. The cannon and light bombs caused havoc among the German columns, but the Germans were quick to turn every available weapon on the low-flying bombers and the results for the French were catastrophic. Only one of the seven Breguets from GBA II/54 was shot down by the flak but of the eleven Breguets from GBA I/54, no fewer than seven were shot down in the target area, one badly damaged plane crash-landed on the way back, and another was so badly damaged it was a write off.[34]

With heavy losses also being suffered by the British, Gamelin's pre-war prediction that the Air Force would 'not play the part in the next war some military commentators foresee' but would 'burn itself out in a flash', now had a prophetic ring about it, although it seemed only for Allied planes.[35] The Army had always insisted that low-flying ground-attack would be too dangerous, and on the evidence of this mission, they were right. However, there were extenuating circumstances. Low-level missions are always hazardous, even for experienced crews, but the dangers were even greater for inexperienced crews flying their first missions in a plane making its operational debut. It takes time and experience to get the best out of any equipment. The dangers of low-level attack did not mean that tactical air support was impossible, as the Luftwaffe was demonstrating. Nevertheless, new tactics were needed and the French responded quickly. Future Breguet missions would try shallow dive-bombing from around 1,000 metres, and this would prove far less hazardous.

In two days, the Allies had flown around 150 sorties against Maastricht and the routes leading westwards. None of the bridges in the area were destroyed, but the Germans reported that the bombing had caused considerable delays.[36] Allied bomber squadrons had paid a heavy price, but their efforts had not been entirely in vain. The delays imposed on the German advance at least helped to compensate for the delays inflicted on the French 2nd and 3rd Light Mechanised Divisions by the Stukas of the Luftwaffe's VIII Air Corps as they raced towards Gembloux. When caught unescorted, the Ju 87 was as vulnerable as any Allied bomber, and on occasions, the Allied fighters were getting through to the Stukas and inflicting heavy losses. On the 12th, the Luftwaffe had to release fighters protecting the Maastricht bridges to provide more substantial escorts. If the Luftwaffe, with its 1,200 fighters, was finding it difficult to meet all its commitments, it was hardly surprising the French fighter force was struggling.

However, it was not just a case of the numbers of fighters available; the intensity with which the available fighters were used was also a factor. On the 11th, the French fighter force increased its effort to around 400 sorties from the 387 serviceable machines that were available at the beginning of the day, but the next day, it slumped to just 263 sorties from 345 serviceable planes. Even their best effort on the 11th was low by Luftwaffe standards. During the course of the 12th, JG 27, with only eighty-five serviceable fighters at the beginning of the day, flew 340 sorties.[37] This was much higher than the entire French fighter force. JG 27 pilots sometimes had only a forty-five-minute break between missions and some flew five sorties that day. There was not the same degree of urgency about using French fighter squadrons as the use of the Bloch MB.152 squadrons in the Paris region demonstrated. These were used over the front for the first time on the 12th but this just involved GC I/1 sending one of its squadrons forward for the day, flying one patrol east of Gembloux, and then returning to Paris in the evening. The lack of intensity was a more significant factor than the lack of numbers.

The 11th and 12th were bad days for both the British and French fighter forces. The Bloch mission mentioned above was typical. Six of GC I/1's Blochs flew at medium altitude, while twelve M.S.406s flying at a higher altitude attempted to provide some protection against the marauding German fighters. However, the M.S.406s were unable to prevent German fighters swooping on one flight of three Blochs, destroying one and damaging the other two before disappearing.[38] All along the front it was a similar story. Allied fighter pilots were being caught out by the German hit and run tactics. The French lost thirty-six fighters in combat on the 11th and 12th with another eight destroyed on the ground. On the morning of the 13th, the number of serviceable machines had dropped to just 314. Allied pilots were also claiming fewer enemy planes and most of these tended to be the escorting fighters. German fighter losses actually increased slightly on the second and third days of the campaign, showing the struggle with Allied fighters was not so one-sided, but total daily Luftwaffe losses fell to around fifty combat planes on the 11th and 12th. These were still heavy losses that were unsustainable over a prolonged period of time, but perfectly acceptable if it helped bring a quick victory in the land battle below.[39]

On the 12th, French tanks clashed with the advance elements of the 4th Panzer Division. A fierce tank battle, lasting two days, followed. The French force suffered heavily, but the German advance was halted. The Allied bombing was scarcely decisive, but it had made a contribution. Unfortunately for the Allies, an even greater threat was developing further south.

13

Disaster on the Meuse

While the battle for Gembloux raged, French reconnaissance units continued to monitor the build-up German forces in the Ardennes. Substantial quantities of armour and units with bridging equipment were reported heading for Dinant, Givet and especially Boullion.[1] By the afternoon of the 12th, Georges and Têtu, the commander of the fighter, reconnaissance, and observation units attached directly to armies, were sufficiently concerned to order bomber units to switch their efforts from the Maastricht–Gembloux axis to the front of the 2nd Army. Billotte countermanded the instruction, ordering two-thirds of Allied bomber effort to be applied to the front of the 1st Army at Gembloux and only the remainder in the Ardennes.[2] Even one-third of a full-strength French bomber fleet could have inflicted serious delays and losses on the German units winding their way through the Ardennes. As it was, the argument over who should benefit most from Allied bomber support was largely academic. Barratt had decided to rest his bombers and d'Astier only had four already badly battered groups.

During the first three days, the cavalry units the French had pushed east of the Meuse were already suffering at the hands of German bombers. Whenever these weak French screening forces threatened to slow down the German advance, Wehrmacht commanders called in the Stukas to disperse the opposition. The 2nd and 9th Armies had their own fighter groups (GC I/5 and GC II/2) but the rest of *Groupement* 23 was focusing its efforts over the 1st Army around Gembloux. To the south, the 3rd Army's GC II/5 was supposed to provide some protection for the southern flank of the two armies on the Meuse. The group had two successful days on the 11th and 12th claiming seven certain and one probable bomber victories for the loss of one Curtiss H75, but was operating too far south to be of any use to the French forces in the Ardennes. The M.S.406 equipped GC III/7 in ZOAE was supposed to be available to d'Astier but only appears to have flown any sorties well to the south-west of the Ardennes. On the morning of the 12th, the Curtiss H75s of GC I/5 broke up a Stuka attack on French cavalry near Bouillon, claiming eleven, but probably only shooting down three and damaging two more. Nevertheless, it was a rare success in the battle zone; for the most part, Luftwaffe assaults from the air went unhindered.[3] By the evening of the 12th, the battered French cavalry had pulled back to the west bank of the Meuse.

The Germans had reached the Meuse three days quicker than the French had anticipated but the situation still did not appear in any way alarming. All the bridges over the Meuse had been destroyed and as a precaution, two armoured divisions (the 2nd and 3rd DCR) were ordered to take up positions behind the 9th and 2nd Armies. The 1st DCR, deployed around Charleroi in case of a German breakthrough at Gembloux, was also well placed to intervene against any German success in the Dinant region. The French estimated it would take the Germans another four days to move up the artillery any serious attempt to cross the river would require.

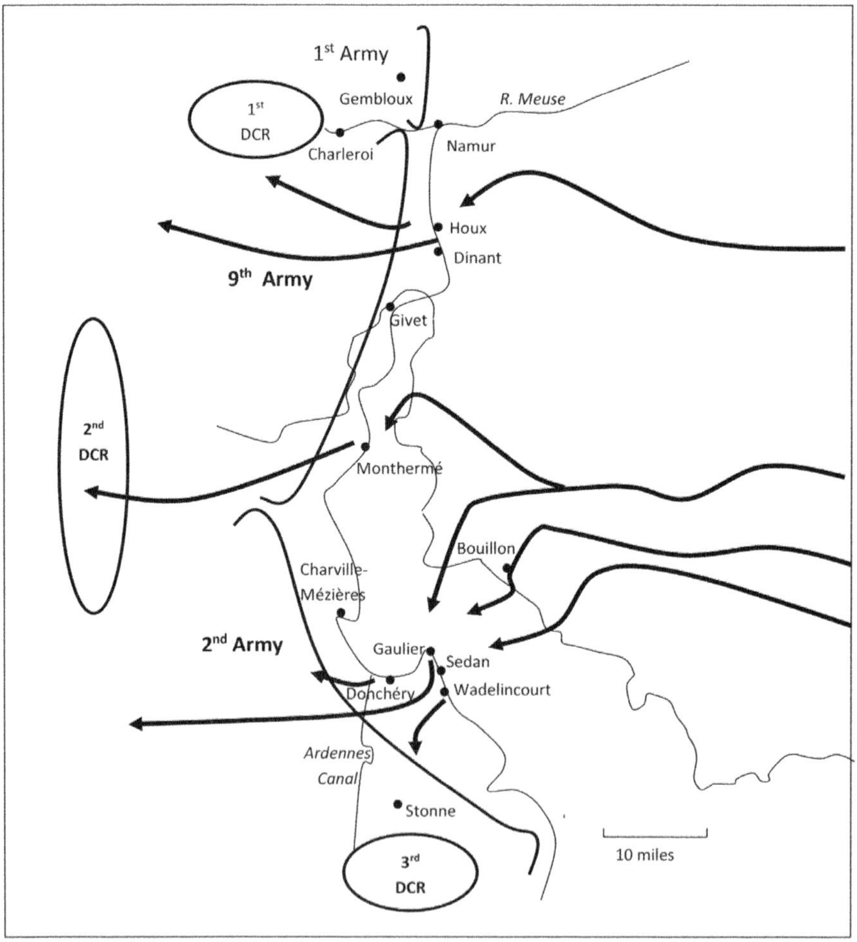

The German advance, 10–15 May.

The Germans, however, had no intention of waiting for more artillery to arrive. Richthofen's VIII Corps was switched from the Gembloux front to the Meuse and Luftflotte 2 stopped bombing targets in the rear and prepared to support German infantry attempting to cross the river. To escort the bombers and protect the forces on the ground, the Germans gathered together an impressive force drawn from five fighter wings. To ease the escort problem, Luftwaffe commanders wanted to deliver a few heavy attacks, but German Army commanders insisted on a continuous assault to ensure the defenders kept their heads down.[4] With the Luftwaffe escorts stretched, the Allied fighters, operating from airfields much closer to the front, would be well-placed to disrupt the German bombardment and inflict heavy losses, if the French could get enough fighters in the right area.

Early on the 13th, reports from a reconnaissance mission flown the previous night persuaded Billotte to agree with George's and Têtu's assessment that the main danger now was in the Ardennes and ordered the Air Force to make a greater effort in the Sedan region. D'Astier, however, had little to play with; most of his fighters were either tied to armies or already committed to the operation in the Netherlands.[5] The Bloch MB.152 equipped GC I/8 moved to ZOAN on the 12th, GC III/7 was also available, and the Dewoitine 520s of GC I/3 would join *Groupement* 23 during the course of the 13th. The decision had also been taken to transfer the Bloch equipped GCs II/10 and III/10 from the Paris region to *Groupement* 23, but these would not arrive until the 14th.

Although the main Luftwaffe effort on the 13th would come at Sedan, the Luftwaffe was also active further north, on the 9th Army front. During the night of 12th–13th, a reconnaissance patrol from Rommel's 7th Panzer Division discovered an undefended weir at Houx just north of Dinant and established a small bridgehead on the west bank of the Meuse. At dawn, another small party of German infantry, using the cover provided by early morning mists, managed to expand the bridgehead by crossing the river further south. By midday, the pocket was about 3 miles wide and 2 miles deep. The French were aware of the danger developing and General Corap, commander of the 9th Army, ordered units to the north and south to eliminate the bridgehead.

Billotte informed d'Astier that these counterattacks did not need any bomber support. It probably did not even occur to Corap to ask for any. According to d'Astier, it did occur to the 9th Army's air commander, but his request for attacks on targets on the east bank of the Meuse in the Houx area were not considered precise enough.[6] It also occurred to the pilot of a French reconnaissance plane. Having spotted the German forces on the west bank at Houx, he headed for the base of No. 12 Squadron, which was on standby with its Battles for any targets of opportunity that might emerge. Barratt, however, did not feel he could risk more losses and permission to attack Rommel's forces was denied. What did not occur to any Frenchmen was to use planes from the five GAO squadrons attached to the 9th Army. Disorganised forward troops were precisely the sort of target even obsolete planes can attack with some chance of success. Like the other thirty-three GAO squadrons attached to other armies, these planes were just sitting on airfields and occasionally getting destroyed by German bombing raids. By the evening of the 12th, the GAO had lost twenty-two planes on the ground, but it seems they had hardly flown any sorties of any description. Just one plane had been lost flying a mission.[7]

Meanwhile, the Luftwaffe was operating all out and the constant bombing was causing endless problems for the French. To the north of Rommel's bridgehead, the 5th Motorised attempted to organise a counterattack, but it took a reserve battalion nine hours to move 10 miles. When the attack was eventually launched at around 2 p.m., more bombing immediately broke it up.[8] A more substantial counterattack with tanks supported by infantry was planned for the evening, but again enemy bombing slowed down the units trying to move into position.[9]

The only fighter group immediately available was the 9th Army's own GC II/2 with the M.S.406. This unit had flown a dawn patrol of six planes over Givet, south of Dinant, but apart from a few sorties in defence of their own airfield, the only mission the group was called upon to perform during the remainder of the morning was the escort of a reconnaissance plane. In the afternoon, seven M.S.406s from this group took off to escort another reconnaissance plane. At this point, Corap decided something had to be done about the constant bombing. At 4.45 p.m., a straightforward instruction was passed to GC II/2. The group was to halt the bombing of 9th Army positions with all available means. All eleven available fighters were immediately scrambled and those already in the air on the escort mission were diverted to the front line. The Moranes took on a formation of Dorniers and damaged a couple, but three French fighters were shot down by the escorting Bf 110s. The group had done its best, but eighteen fighters could make little impression. By the end of the day, the group had just seven serviceable fighters.[10, 11]

By late afternoon, Billotte seems to have changed his mind about bomber support. The 2nd Army had not had to move from its Phoney War positions, and its artillery was in place, but the 9th Army had moved forward into Belgium and its artillery was still moving up. At 4.20 p.m. he told d'Astier that artillery was controlling the situation at Sedan and his bombers should be used to support the forces at Dinant. In the evening, six LeO 451s attacked the pontoon bridges already under construction around Dinant and troop columns in the area. Some twenty-seven Bloch MB.152s from GC I/l and GC I/8 provided direct escort for the bombers and a further eighteen Dewoitine D.520s of the newly arrived GC I/3 flew two patrols—one at high, one at low altitude—as indirect support. The Bloch close escort did not encounter any

German fighters, but the Dewoitines claimed four enemy planes without loss, three of which were Henschel observation planes.[12] As necessary as escorts were, it was a lot of fighters to protect six bombers and the Army might legitimately argue that under their control they might have been used earlier and more usefully to reinforce the efforts of their own fighter group. Whether even this would have been enough to protect the French units that were trying to counterattack is open to question. With so few fighters, there were no easy solutions.

Most of the counterattacks on the Dinant bridgehead planned for the 13th had to put off until the following morning, mainly because of the delays caused by bombing. One attack from the south was launched, but the infantry had not arrived so the tanks set off on their own. For a while, they caused considerable panic among Rommel's forces, but without the infantry to consolidate the gains, the effort was wasted. By the end of the day, the construction of pontoon bridges that would carry the German tanks across the Meuse was well underway.

Even the limited German air support on the 9th Army front had played a significant part in the day's operations, but the Luftwaffe's main effort on the 13th would come further south at Sedan. From 11 a.m., medium and dive-bombers maintained a continuous attack on artillery positions, reserves and strong points along the river edge. Confusion reigned as telephone lines were cut and movement disrupted. As the day wore on, the artillery of the 55th Division holding the sector gradually became less effective as the gunners were cut off from their forward observers. The continuous attacks were also sapping the morale of the French troops holding the front line. At 3 p.m., the commander of the 55th Division, General Lafontaine, appealed for fighter protection and got the backing of his Corps commander, General Grandsard, but no fighters arrived to beat off the attacks.[13] At around 4 p.m., just as Billotte was deciding the real danger was further north at Dinant, the aerial assault reached a climax and German forces in rubber dinghies made their way across the river, almost unnoticed by the defenders taking cover from the aerial bombardment.

Where were the French fighters? *Groupement* 23 had GC I/8 and one squadron from GC I/l available to reinforce the 2nd and 9th Army's own fighter groups (GC I/5 and GC II/2). The 3rd Army's GC II/5, was supposed to provide some support on the 2nd Army's southern flank and the Moranes of GC III/7 were available to D'Astier. The Dewoitine D.520s of GC I/3 would arrive during the course of the day. However, not even these meagre resources were committed with any vigour. GC III/7 flew a patrol well north of Namur in support of the 1st Army. At 9.35 a.m. the squadron from GC I/1 flew a patrol over Namur then remained on standby for the rest of the day, but was not called upon until the LeO 451 escort mission in the evening.[14] GC I/8 was also not called upon until the escort mission. The 2nd Army's own fighter group GC I/5, flew three operations before 10 a.m., but after that, confined itself to sorties in defence of its own airfield and an attempt around 6.p.m. to hunt down a non-existent balloon. GC II/5 flew a patrol at 5 a.m. but apart from an abortive attempt to intercept a reported German spotter plane, flew no more sorties until 5 p.m. and even this last operation was probably not in the critical area. It certainly did not encounter any enemy planes.[15] At 4.20 p.m., just as the aerial assault on the Sedan front reached its climax and German troops began crossing the Meuse, Billotte instructed d'Astier to use the Blochs of GC I/8, GC I/1, and the newly arrived D.520s of GC I/3 to escort the LeO 451 Dinant mission.

Despite the difficulty the 2nd Army was in and the appeals of Lafontaine and Grandsard, it would appear that no fighter sorties were flown over the Sedan sector of the front after 10 a.m. This failure to make use of the fighters that were available appears to have been the result of a serious miscalculation by the 2nd Army's commander General Huntziger. Although fully aware of the dangers of aerial bombardment, he saw the assault as a necessary experience for his troops. After nine months of 'phoney war', they had at last received their baptism of fire and would emerge far tougher soldiers for the experience. It would seem the French commander was also anxious not to over commit his fighter group and risk unnecessarily high losses at, what he thought, was still a very early stage of the battle.[16] Huntziger was resting the fighter force on what would turn out to be the most critical day of the campaign.

On the 13th, the French fighter force only flew 260 sorties. Nearly one quarter of these were over southern Netherlands. *Groupement* 23 flew about 160, but many of these were escort missions or were flown over the 1st Army in Belgium. Most of the rest were flown over the 9th Army. At least on this front, there was some urgency about attempting to halt the bombing. Over Sedan, no attempt was made to stem the aerial bombardment. Even if, by some miracle, the entire French fighter force had been re-equipped with the Dewoitine D.520, on the 13th, over Sedan, it would have made no difference; no fighters were called for.

The consequences would be catastrophic. As evening approached, the French line at Sedan was still holding. Then, in the space of a couple of hours, the morale of the 55th Division suddenly collapsed. A rumour that German tanks had penetrated well behind the front line spread like wildfire through the ranks of the troops manning the artillery in the rear. Men abandoned their guns and fled. The German assault troops immediately noticed the slackening in French fire, as did the French infantry holding the front line. As soon as they realised they were no longer getting artillery support, they too abandoned their positions and joined the disorderly retreat. In no time, the 55th Infantry Division had virtually ceased to exist. The German bridgehead rapidly expanded to fill the vacuum.

Grandsard immediately attempted to restore the situation. Even before the Germans had started crossing the Meuse, he had instructed two tank battalions and two infantry regiments forward from the reserves. With nearly 100 tanks, it was a force that was perfectly capable of dispersing the German infantry on the west bank and re-occupying the territory vacated by the 55th Division. At 7 p.m., the mixed force of infantry and tanks was ordered to pass through the retreating 55th Division and drive the Germans back over the Meuse, but once again, just the threat of German bombing was enough to influence events. In order to avoid destruction from the air, the commander of the counterattacking force decided to wait for darkness before moving forward. Another opportunity to strike an early blow at the German bridgeheads had been lost. It was another victory for the Luftwaffe.

The battle along the Meuse was approaching a critical phase far sooner than the French High Command had believed possible. At Dinant and Sedan, German engineers had begun building the pontoon bridges that would carry the tanks across to the west bank. The counterattacks rescheduled for the 14th would have considerably less chance of succeeding if the German panzers were well-established on the west bank. The battle hinged on the bridges. Billotte appealed to d'Astier to deploy all available bombers against the crossing points, especially those at Sedan. There was no time to lose. He did not even want to wait until the next morning; he wanted the bombing to start that night.[17]

It was a significant moment in the campaign. Up until this point, the French knew that they faced a difficult task, but no one believed France was in imminent danger of losing the war. Suddenly, it became very clear to all from Georges at the front to the Prime Minister Reynaud in Paris that catastrophe was looming. The French could no longer treat the battle as the opening moves in what would be a long, drawn-out campaign. Immediate and bold action was required.

The French knew exactly where their bombers were needed. Unlike their British allies, they were not distracted by distant and irrelevant strategic targets. The focus was clear but they had hardly any bombers. The planes the squadrons in the rear were waiting for might be superior to the Luftwaffe bombers that had just smashed the French 9th Army, but they were no use if they were not available.

D'Astier did not think it was possible to do much about the crossing points that night; even in daylight, he believed that they would be difficult targets. D'Astier might have been right. Even so, given the gravity of the situation, it was perhaps worth trying. Instead, twenty-four Amiots set off to bomb and strafe German columns on the congested roads leading into Sedan, which was the next best target. For operations the next day, the severity of the crisis forced the French to implement the emergency plan to use the Amiot 143 groups, even though they would have already flown the night before. Using this large, ungainly plane in daylight was a desperate step to take and d'Astier was not happy about it.[18] Whatever the crisis, he did not believe the risks were worth it. Arguably, a less desperate step might have been to use some of the available reconnaissance planes in the ground-attack role, but while to the Dutch, this had seemed the obvious step to take in their struggle, no French commander even suggested it.

D'Astier was also expected to put the maximum number of fighters over the crumbling Meuse front. The instructions were clear: protection was to be total and continuous. There could be no excuse for holding anything back now. The French fighter force had suffered some heavy losses but was still a substantial force. There was no shortage of pilots. By the evening of the 13th, some forty French pilots had been killed, wounded or were missing. However, with the return of those on leave and the arrival of some reinforcements, including the first of what would become a flood of Czechs and Poles, there were around forty more pilots with the fighter groups on the north-eastern front on the morning of the 14th than there had been on the 10th.[19]

The problem was whether there were fighters for them to fly. The loss of forty-two fighters on the first day of the offensive, more than the entire reserve, had shaken Vuillemin. On the 11th, he had just eleven M.S.406s and four Curtiss H75s available. At this rate, he warned the government, the French fighter force would be eliminated in a fortnight.[20] By the evening of the 13th, forty-four replacement fighters had reached the squadrons but losses had risen to 116 planes destroyed or so badly damaged they had to be written off. Hardest hit were the M.S.406 groups. These had received just twenty-five machines to replace the eighty-two they had lost. The number of pilots available had increased to 467 since the 10th, but the number of serviceable fighters had dropped from 419 to 323.[21, 22]

Even the 300 odd fighters available on the morning of the 14th was a substantial force, if it could be focused where it was required. The disaster that had overcome the French on the 13th was focusing minds. The Potez 631 night-fighter squadrons defending Paris were to be used by day, to free more single-seater squadrons for use over the front.[23] There was more urgency about using the groups defending the Paris-Le Havre region. On the 13th, two Bloch groups defending Paris had been ordered to work with *Groupement* 23 from the 14th. Now the two Bloch groups based at Rouen and Le Havre were also ordered to operate over the front, this time the instruction taking effect immediately. However, even these moves were still somewhat half-hearted. Each day, each Bloch group would still only be sending forward one of its two squadrons, with the squadron returning to its home base in the evening. Vuillemin could not leave the Paris region undefended. Groups defending Lyon and Marseilles also stayed in place. On the 14th, the 5th Army's GC

II/4 was ordered to join *Groupement* 23. For the first time, a fighter group was being detached from the Army it was assigned to, but it was still only a half measure; two other groups (GC II/7 and GC I/2) remained attached to their respective armies in the Maginot Line, and too far from the critical front to help. The French were still only employing a little over half of their available fighters over the active front and, with commitments over southern Netherlands and Belgium, not all of these could be deployed over the crucial sector along the Meuse. On this most critical of days, little more than a third of the operational fighter groups were available to operate over Sedan.

During the night of the 13th–14th, German forces extended their Sedan bridgehead to a depth of ten and a width of five miles and German engineers began working on pontoon bridges at Donchery, Wadelincourt, and Gaulier. It was up to the Air Force to make sure they did not complete their work. It was ironic that given their rather dismissive interwar opinion of the value of short-range tactical bombers, the French Army was now relying totally on the success of the day's bombing missions to prevent the Germans getting substantial forces across the Meuse.

The prospects for the proposed assault on the Sedan crossing points were better than they had been at Maastricht. If the attacks on the Albert Canal bridges paralleled the ill-starred RAF attempts to destroy the Somme bridges in August 1918, the bombing of the Sedan crossing points was more like the successful French attempts to disrupt the German advance over the Marne in July 1918. The action was taking place further away from German airfields, so it was more difficult for the Luftwaffe to provide continuous fighter cover, and the pontoon bridges themselves were far easier to destroy than permanent bridges. If the Allies could strike quickly before the Germans could organise their anti-aircraft defences, there was every chance the flow of German reinforcements over the Meuse could be severely reduced, just as it had been over the Marne in 1918.

At 5.15 in the morning of the 14th, d'Astier was told that a local counter-attack was being organised to stabilise the situation in the Sedan area and that a more substantial counterattack would follow to eliminate the bridgehead.[24] The former was a reference to the assault by the two tank battalions put off the evening before and now rescheduled for dawn of the 14th. The latter referred to Flavigny's XXI Corps, with the 3rd DCR, a motorised division and a cavalry brigade, which was assembling south of Sedan, with instructions to strike north towards Wadelincourt. Billotte expected both operations to receive full air support. D'Astier complained that he was not given any details of when or where these counterattacks were to take place, but as far as the bombing operation was concerned, Billotte had made clear what he wanted. The crossing points were the target and he wanted them attacked as soon as possible.

That should have meant at first light, but D'Astier did not want to attack so soon. There was the very legitimate fear that the early morning mists that often shrouded the Meuse valley would conceal the target, although equally they might also conceal the approach of the bombers. He was also anxious to give his battered squadrons as much time as possible to make the highest number of planes serviceable.[25] This was doubly unfortunate for not only would it enable the Germans to start moving their panzer divisions across unhindered but it would also give them time to extract the anti-aircraft units from the congested approach roads and deploy them around the crossing points.

Barratt had ruled out using his Battles at all, but a couple of early morning raids were delivered on the Sedan crossing points with just the loss of one plane forced to crash land at its base. The pilots spotted powerful German formations just south of Sedan and Barratt passed this information on to d'Astier who ordered the available Breguet 693s to bomb these columns.[26] Eight Breguet 693s set off with a thirty-strong fighter escort. Following their disastrous operational debut on the 12th, the Breguets bombed from around 800 metres, with less precision but considerably greater safety. In fact, as with the Battles, little flak was encountered and all the French planes made it back to their base. All the indications were that a more vigorous response at this time, when the German defences were still not organised, might have brought the Allies greater reward at less cost than would be endured latter in the day.

As the Breguets attacked, the tanks of the German 1st Panzer Division were already beginning to cross the Meuse over the only completed bridge at Gaulier. The arrival of the German armoured division on the west bank transformed the prospects for the French counterattacks. The first was supposed to be launched at dawn, but the two tank regiments were held up in equal measure by German bombing and the routed retreating 55th Division. The attack finally got underway at 7 a.m. with just one infantry and one tank regiment. The French tanks had little difficulty in pushing back the German infantry and, initially at least, made good progress. At 8 a.m., however, the inevitably confrontation with the German Panzers occurred and by 9 a.m., the French were in retreat. The failure to destroy the one bridge available was proving decisive. By 8.30 a.m., the 2nd Panzer Division was making its way over to the west bank. The situation was getting more critical by the hour and Barratt now agreed to throw his Battles into an all-out assault. The French would attack first at around midday. The AASF would follow. Both sets of bombers would rearm and attack again. An evening attack by No. 2 Group Blenheims and a second mission by the Breguet 693s would conclude the day's operations. In this way, the Allies hoped to squeeze about 250 sorties out of their meagre resources.

D'Astier's first wave comprised just nineteen Amiot 143s and eight LeO 451s. Bloch MB.152s from GC I/8 and nine Dewoitine D.520s from GC I/3 provided the indirect escort. Twelve M.S.406s from GC III/7 provided the vulnerable Amiot 143s with close escort but the LeO 451s had to do without this luxury. Six of the Amiots missed the rendezvous with their escort and turned back to base. This most critical assault, therefore, eventually consisted of just twenty-one bombers. The Germans had by this time set up their anti-aircraft defences around the bridges and the French bombers were greeted by intense flak and large numbers of German fighters. The French escort fought valiantly to defend their vulnerable charges. Only one Amiot was the victim of fighters, and this only after it had been damaged by flak, but four more were destroyed by German ground fire.[27] The large unmanoeuvrable Amiot was too inviting a target. One of the LeO 451s was also lost. It was even worse for the AASF Battles and Blenheims. Seventy-one set off but forty failed to return. So many of the returning French and British bombers were damaged the second round of attacks had to be called off.

At dusk, No. 2 Group flew another twenty-eight sorties losing seven planes, but the evening attack by Breguet 693s had to be postponed until the following day because there were no fighters available to escort them.[28] It would seem that none of the pontoon bridges were destroyed, but the bombing did cause delays. German commanders complained that all three panzer divisions had been forced to endure constant air attack, the bridge at Donchery had not been completed because of the bombing and there were demands for better fighter protection.[29, 30] The French bombers were hitting the right targets, but there were simply not enough of them and they could not maintain the pressure. At least for the fighter force, there were reasonably modern planes available; for most of the bomber force, there was nothing.

As well as escorting bombers and reconnaissance planes, *Groupement* 23 was also supposed to ensure there was no repeat of the previous day's demoralising German bombing. There was now much more urgency about French fighter operations. Telephoned instructions replaced written orders. The Curtiss H75s of GC II/4, brought up from the south, flew their first mission within half an hour of landing at their new base.[31] However, the number of sorties flown was still relatively low, given the scale of the crisis. It would appear that *Groupement* 23 managed around 200 sorties over the Meuse. About sixty of these were used to escort the bombing raids in the Sedan area and some of the remainder escorted reconnaissance planes or were patrols in defence of their own airfields.

Those that did operate over Sedan were ordered to avoid enemy fighters wherever possible and concentrate on the bombers, but this was easier said than done. It turned out to be the worst day for the French fighter force so far. The Bloch units moved forward from the rear suffered particularly heavily. Blochs from GCs I/1 and II/1 shot down two Stukas and damaged two more in a morning patrol over Sedan for the loss of a Bloch. Another patrol from GC I/1 over Dinant was less successful, with Bf 110s forcing two Blochs to crash land, although both pilots were safe. Four more GC II/1 Bloch fighters were lost in the afternoon escorting a Potez 63.11 over Dinant. In the evening, twenty-seven Bloch MB.152s from GC III/10, GC II/10 and GC I/1 were ordered to provide fighter cover for the 1st Armoured Division in the Charleroi area. The fighters formed three patrols at low, medium, and high altitude. The lower flight from GC III/10 was surprised by German fighters and lost six. The flight from GC II/10 2,000 metres above them suffered almost as severely; three were destroyed and the rest so badly damaged that on their return to base, all were found to be in need of major repairs. The problems of the Bloch groups were compounded by the low endurance of the fighter. Many of those that survived clashes with the Luftwaffe were forced to put down at the nearest available airfield and the Bloch groups soon found they had stranded unserviceable machines scattered all over the place. At the end of the day, GC II/1 had just one serviceable machine and four pilots were missing, although three of these would eventually make their way back to the group. All the aircraft from GC II/10 were badly damaged and of the twelve sent forward by GC III/10, seven had been destroyed or badly damaged. Only GC I/1 emerged relatively intact from the day's operations.[32, 33]

Nineteen Bloch MB.152s had been lost in a single day. The fighter was struggling against the Messerschmitts, and was not getting into positions where it could use its powerful cannon armament against bombers. At least the fighter's ruggedness was getting their pilots back to friendly bases; only three Bloch pilots had been killed. If the French had possessed a fighter capable of shielding the Bloch from the German Messerschmitts, there might have been more opportunities to exploit the plane's strengths. The Hispano-Suiza HS 12Y-45 provided the performance to tackle the Messerschmitts, but the only fighter with the engine was the Dewoitine D.520. GC I/3 claimed ten confirmed victories on its first full day of operations, but there were too few of them. The French would have been better off using the 500 available HS 12Y-45 engines in the tried and tested M.S.406 airframe.

On the 14th, the French fighter force lost ten pilots, with a further eleven wounded. These were the heaviest personnel losses suffered so far; however, the French fighter force did claim its highest number of confirmed victories this day, forty-six from 340 sorties flown, which was broadly in line with the RAF striking rate of thirty victories from around 200 sorties. Yet even on this day of maximum French effort, the British were, proportionally, getting more sorties out of their fighter force.

The Allied effort in the Sedan area did not go unnoticed. German commanders reported intense fighter activity, which severely affected the activities of the short-range reconnaissance squadrons. However, if the primary aim of the Allied fighter force was to protect the troops on the ground, the effort was largely misdirected. On the 14th, German bombers were focusing their efforts on the Dinant sector. Those squadrons operating over Sedan found themselves for the most part grappling with the fighter squadrons the Germans had detailed to protect the bridges. The German fighters did not have it all their own way, the loss of twenty-one fighters in a single day was their heaviest so far.[34] However, with the French losing thirty-three and British more than twenty, even this narrow tactical battle was going the Luftwaffe's way.

The sacrifices of the Allied bomber and fighter crews would have been worthwhile if the French Army had been able to take advantage of the temporary respite gained. Flavigny's XXI Corps to the south was a powerful force with around 200 modern tanks. On the morning of the 14th, Georges ordered this force to strike northwards into the flank of the German bridgehead. The assault was supposed to get underway at 11 a.m. Guderian, commanding the panzers, had been warned by German reconnaissance planes of powerful French armoured units to his south, but decided to swing the 1st and 2nd Panzer Divisions westwards over the Ardennes Canal, leaving 10th Panzer to cover the southern flank. However, this unit had been delayed, in part by Allied bombing. If the French had launched their assault as planned, the armoured force would find itself moving into the vacuum vacated by Guderian's tanks. There was an opportunity to turn the tables on the Germans, just as the French had done on the Marne in 1914.

Unlike the Marne in 1914, however, French reconnaissance did not pick up the direction the German forces were taking. Huntziger's army reconnaissance group, GR II/22, was in the throes of moving base to avoid the advancing panzers. One sortie was flown around 5 p.m. in the Sedan area, but this does not seem to have picked up anything significant. Flavigny's Corps was supposed to have two observation squadrons but one was in the south of France re-equipping and the other, if it flew, does not appear to have provided any useful information. French long-range reconnaissance had been able to identify the general direction of the German thrust through the Ardennes, but only 100 sorties had been flown by the entire reconnaissance force in the first five days and this level of activity was not enough to detect more detailed developments.[35] Both Flavigny and Huntziger feared that the German breakthrough at Sedan was aimed at outflanking the Maginot Line and that Guderian would swing south, not west. The priority was therefore to halt any advance southwards. Flavigny called off the assault and distributed the armoured units defensively along a wide front. The opportunity was missed. The mistake underlined how right the Army had been about the importance of an effective reconnaissance force.

While Guderian's panzers, without substantial air support, were pushing the French forces well behind the Meuse at Sedan, the 9th Army further north were experiencing the full weight of the Luftwaffe. During the night of the 13th–14th, the first German tanks crossed the Meuse and gradually, under constant air attack, the French were pushed back. By the end of the day, they were still holding the line but were close to collapse. Reinforcements were continuously harried by the Luftwaffe, with some units scattered before they could even reach the front. Further south at Monthermé, the French front held until an evening assault, with powerful Luftwaffe support, finally broke through. The French rallied and a new defensive line established, but German engineers were soon throwing more bridges across the Meuse, enabling the panzers to cross to the west bank.

There was on the 14th within the 9th Army, both at the front and in the rear, a general resentment at the way they had been abandoned by the Air Force. The Moranes of the 9th Army's own GC II/2 were powerless to intervene. On the 14th, it managed just sixteen sorties, and nine of these were in defence of its own airfield. *Groupement* 23 provided the odd reconnaissance plane with an escort, but was for the most part engaged further south over Sedan. It did not have enough fighters to make its presence felt over Sedan and Dinant.

By the evening of the 14th, German fighter losses had risen to seventy-three, British losses were sixty-five and the French 140. French squadrons had only received fifty-one fighters as replacements and to make matters worse, ground crews were overwhelmed by the number of planes returning damaged.[36] This was true for all squadrons and the scale of the problem took the French by surprise. A report on the 14th, and another on the 24th, emphasised that front line squadrons needed far more specialist ground staff and equipment to effect repairs, but nothing could be done about this overnight.[37] It would not have mattered so much if there had been plentiful reserves to replace damaged machines but reserves were almost non-existent. A combination of insufficient reserves and inadequate repair facilities was crippling squadrons. By the morning of the 15th, the number of serviceable fighters available to d'Harcourt's squadrons had dropped below 300.

Even 300 fighters were still a considerable force if it had been possible to focus them; however, with the French forces battling fiercely around Gembloux and pulling out of the Netherlands could scarcely be abandoned, and with Rotterdam very much in the news, rear defence could not be neglected either. D'Astier had nothing like the necessary resources to cover all these commitments. For the 15th, Georges and Billotte again instructed d'Astier to give priority to the Sedan region. In the early hours of the 15th, however, Corap, aware that his battered divisions were close to collapse, felt he had to order a general retreat to the frontier positions his units had held before their advance into Belgium. He phoned d'Astier and pleaded for maximum fighter protection at dawn to cover the manoeuvre. D'Astier, ignoring Georges's orders, promised to do his best.[38]

The Bloch groups around Paris were once more each asked to send one squadron forward to operate over the front. Once again, this might be considered a less than total response, although in truth the squadrons that had been operating the previous day were scarcely capable of contributing much. GCs II/10 and III/10 were supposed to operate together in the rear to the east of Soissons between midday and 6 p.m., covering the movement of reserves up to the front. The nine planes from GC III/10 somehow got sent to Le Havre by mistake and the group did not catch up with its sister unit until late afternoon. Bf 110 escorts prevented either unit from any success against the bombers that were encountered.[39] The two squadrons from GCs I/1 and II/1 attempted to make their presence felt over the front in mid-afternoon to the south-west of Dinant and a couple of bombers were claimed. For the most part, however, the German fighter escorts continued to pose an almost insurmountable barrier. The Blochs of GC I/8 joined forces with what was left of the 9th Army's GC II/2, but the latter's contribution amounted to a handful of Moranes patrolling the home base.[40] GC I/8 operated over the front between Charleville-Mézières and Monthermé. The lower patrol spotted bombers but then became involved in a fierce dogfight with Bf 109s and Bf 110s. On this occasion, the Blochs acquitted themselves well, claiming four of the German fighters without loss, but once again the German escort had done its job. The French pilots could only claim one of the bombers.[41]

The H75s of GC II/4 found themselves in the same predicament. The unit was ordered to use all available fighters to patrol the Dinant sector of the front. Unfortunately, on the morning of the 15th, this amounted to just seven planes. These set off at 11 a.m. but, over Reims, long before they reached their assigned zone, they spotted a formation of nine bombers with half a dozen Bf 109 escorts. In a rapidly descending dogfight the French were able to claim three Messerschmitts without loss to themselves. A couple of H75s managed to get through to the bombers, claiming two. All the French fighters made it back to base, although again many were seriously damaged.

The M.S.406s continued to find life difficult. GC III/7 was instructed to break up German bombing attacks in the Verdun region, well to the south of Sedan. To give themselves a sufficient speed advantage, the Morane pilots felt they had to be patrolling well above any bombers, but before they could even reach a reasonable altitude, they were caught up in a dogfight with Bf 110s. At midday, another patrol from the same group was ordered to break up German bombing raids in the Namur-Charleroi region, north-west of Dinant. The bombers were sighted but so was a large Bf 110 escort. In the circumstances, the squadron commander decided it was pointless even to attempt to reach the bombers and turned his squadron away. As they returned, they were surprised by Bf 109s; five Moranes were shot down and only four of the French fighters made it back to base.[42] The squadron lost two pilots killed that day and two wounded.

On the 15th, another twenty-seven fighters were lost. Once again, the most successful fighters were the Dewoitine D.520s of GC I/3. These claimed four

German bombers and two fighters, but the unit lost nine fighters during the course of the day, five of them trying to escort a Potez 63.11. Escort was becoming the main task for the fighter force. In mid-afternoon, no fewer than twenty-seven Bloch MB.152s escorted sixteen British Blenheims attacking German columns between Monthermé and Charleville-Mézières. A few hours later, nine Breguets and six LeO 451s attacking targets in the same region benefited from a fighter escort drawn from four different fighter groups. This was a high proportion of fighter effort. During the course of the day, the entire French fighter force managed just 254 sorties.

For the German fighter force, the 15th had been another hard day with twenty-five lost, but they were blocking the path to the bombers. Only twenty-two bomber and reconnaissance planes were lost and Allied air resistance was getting noticeably weaker. It seemed the Luftwaffe had air superiority. The consequences were all too apparent to French Army commanders. All movement was hampered by the continuous German bombing and French reconnaissance was becoming ever patchier. Often, French commanders did not know the whereabouts of their own troops, never mind those of the enemy. The French Army was not short of reconnaissance planes, but it was short of fighters to protect them. About one fifth of those sent out on missions failed to return and many more returned damaged.

Instead of sending a reconnaissance plane with a squadron of fighters for protection, it seemed to make more sense just to send a fighter to do the job. On the 15th, Corap began doing just that, using the M.S.406 of his Army's GC II/2; for the remainder of the campaign, this would become an increasingly important task for fighter squadrons.[43] Using fighters for reconnaissance was being considered before the German offensive; the reality of war was turning a possibility into a necessity.

There was no fighter protection for the GAO observation squadrons and Vuillemin's pre-offensive edict seemed to rule out any sorties if there was no cloud cover. The five GAO of the 9th Army had hardly flown a mission. Just one plane had been lost in combat, but losses on the ground were constantly eating into their strength.[44] There was a danger they would waste away without being used for anything. To get anything from the force they had to be used wisely. On the morning of the 13th, a Potez 63.11 of GAO 502 was asked to survey enemy movements along a fifteen-mile stretch of the front from Dinant to Namur to a depth of twenty-five miles. In a mission lasting nearly two hours, the plane meandered around in enemy air space, covering over 100 miles. This plane made it back, but it is not surprising others did not.[45] As the Dutch Fokkers had demonstrated, short-range missions with limited objectives, even hit and run ground-attack missions, were perfectly possible with even the most obsolete planes. What French observation planes could not afford to do was roam around behind enemy lines for hours at a time.

The domination of the skies by the Luftwaffe, the continuous bombing attacks and the lack of clear information on exactly what was happening ensured that the 15th would be a black day for the French Army. Corap's decision to pull back to the French frontier proved to be a disaster. With inadequate transport, the manoeuvre would have been tricky in the best of circumstances. German bombing made a difficult operation virtually impossible and the retreat soon became a rout with Panzer units overtaking the surviving elements of Corap's army. By the evening of the 15th, the 9th Army had virtually ceased to exist.

The last hope of restoring the French line lay with the two heavy armoured divisions (DCR) the French had positioned behind the 9th Army. Both were preparing to counterattack the German bridgehead and with 160 modern, well-armed and armoured tanks each, they might prove to be a very unpleasant surprise for the advancing German panzers. Unfortunately, the two armoured divisions had no idea what was happening ahead of them. On the 15th, both units were still attempting to gather their forces following their transfer to the combat zone. It did not help that the 1st DCR's observation squadron was still in the south of France re-equipping. The division was refuelling near Charleroi when German tanks burst past the retreating 9th Army. Far from surprising the German panzers, the French were taken aback by the sudden appearance of enemy tanks. With many of its own tanks immobilised through lack of fuel, the division could do nothing as Rommel's 7th Panzer raced past and it was at a severe disadvantage in the fierce, but one-sided, tank battle that followed with the 5th Panzer. By the end of the day, the 1st Armoured Division had virtually ceased to exist. The 2nd Armoured Division had been sent north, then south, and was strung out over a large tract of territory. The advancing Panzers sliced right through the French division without ever being aware of encountering a major French formation. How much use was made of the Armoured Division's observation squadron (GAO 546) to clarify the situation is not clear, but its planes had certainly not been shot out of the skies by the Luftwaffe. It was the evening of the 15th before the unit suffered its first casualty: a Potez 63.11 forced down south of Charleroi.[46]

With the 3rd DCR engaged in a defensive battle against 10th Panzer Division around Stonne, the three French heavy armoured divisions had been neutralised. The breakthrough was complete. The French line had been ruptured on a 45-mile front from Dinant to Sedan. No sizeable units remained in the path of a German drive to Paris, or, if the Germans so chose, the English Channel.

14

Missed Opportunities

The morning of the 16th found the political and military leaders of France in a mood of deep despair. Reports the previous night suggested that German tanks were already approaching Laon, just 80 miles from the capital. No one could doubt the seriousness of the situation. The impossible had happened. The French armies along a major sector of the front had disintegrated and German tanks were racing into the French rear almost unopposed. Total defeat was staring the French in the face. In 1914, the French had faced a similar crisis, but a valiant counterattack into the flank of the advancing German Army had saved the day. Again, in 1918, the Germans had broken through British lines along a 40-mile stretch of the front, only to be first slowed by aerial attack and finally halted by the timely arrival of French reinforcements. Could the Allies save the day once again?

The situation was far more difficult in 1940. The panzers were moving much faster than the infantry in the First World War and German bombing provided support for the advance and threatened the movement of reinforcements in the rear. Yet the German war machine was not quite as invincible as it might appear. The troops that would have to hold the flanks were not as mobile or as well-equipped as the panzer and motorised divisions spearheading the breakthrough and the gap between the two was a constant concern to the German High Command. A well-timed Allied counterattack might slice straight through the German salient and leave the advancing panzers stranded. The Allies might yet be capable of grasping victory from the jaws of defeat.

The German supply routes were also vulnerable to attack from the air. Much of the German transport was still horse drawn, little different from what had proved to be so vulnerable in 1918. Junkers Ju 52 transports were available, but even a full-strength fleet could only carry a fraction of what an advancing army required. As it was, half the fleet had been lost in the Netherlands. By day, they would also be very vulnerable to any resurgence in Allied fighter effort. The Germans were all too aware that long, supply columns and forward airstrips made extremely inviting targets. The Luftwaffe was also beginning to feel the strain. In the first six days, over 350 combat planes had been written off (about 10 per cent of their original force) and the high sortie rates were taking their toll on man and machine. On the 15th, Guderian was already complaining that 'vigorous, extensive' reconnaissance was impossible.[1] The front line was also passing beyond the effective range of planes like the Bf 109 and Stuka. The Germans had become adept at moving their squadrons forward to keep up with the advance on land, but there was a limit to the number that could be moved forward and kept supplied. From the 15th, French fighter pilots noticed bomber escorts were not as strong as they had been.[2]

As the panzers raced westwards, the Allies desperately tried to form a defensive line north and south of the 'panzer corridor' and create the offensive forces to counterattack. The British garrisoned the town of Arras and the 7th Army, with its largely unused mechanised division, was hastily recalled from northern Belgium to bolster the 1st Army. A British armoured brigade had just arrived in France, and this was ordered to the Arras region. To the south, divisions in the process of being formed, including de Gaulle's 4th DCR armoured division, were rushed north.

These forces, however, would need more effective support and protection than the French Air Force had been able to provide thus far. There could be no sudden increase in the quality of the force. The latest A-3 version of the Curtiss H75 only offered only a small increase in speed at the expense of some of the fighter's excellent handling characteristics. The Dewoitine D.520 was undoubtedly the best fighter available. Output was rising rapidly and GCs II/3 and II/7 were hurriedly re-equipping but GC I/3, the only group using the fighter, was already suffering heavy losses and it was difficult to replace these and equip new units. Bloch production was also getting back into its stride and GCs II/9 and III/9 were re-equipping with this fighter, but daily losses at the front far exceeded output. Even deliveries of the Curtiss H75 were struggling to keep up with losses. It was difficult to see how existing units could be maintained, let alone new units re-equipped.

Any French fightback would have to rely on what already existed. Unfortunately, this did not amount to much. There were not even enough M.S.406s. So desperate was the shortage of fighters of any description, rear establishments were told to make serviceable and arm the previously unwanted Bloch MB.151s, Caudron C.714s, and Koolhoven F.K.58s languishing in various depots. Schools were told to prepare for combat any fighters they had. On the 12th, GC I/145 was told that it would no longer be getting the Bloch MB.152.[3, 4] Indeed, it would not even be keeping its M.S.406s. These were needed by units at the front. The Poles would have to make do with the Caudron C.714. The ECDs being established would have to use the Koolhoven F.K.58 and Bloch MB.151. Perhaps the most drastic step was the decision to abandon plans to convert 300 M.S.406s to M.S.410 standard. By 15 May, only one had been completed, about twenty were at various stages of the modification process, and work was about to begin on another seventeen. All these machines were immediately handed back to the Air Force. Some had a few of the proposed modifications, but machines on which work had only just begun were hastily returned to their original state.[5]

These measures helped produce a temporary increase in the flow of replacements. In the first six days of the fighting, only sixty-three fighters had arrived to replace the 176 fighters lost. On the 16th, however, no fewer than forty-three arrived—a substantial increase—but even this was nowhere near sufficient. Nor could it be maintained; on the next two days, only four more followed.[6] Pilots did not pose the same problem; there were already far more pilots at the front than planes and the French were also starting to make more use of the large numbers of Poles and Czechs. On the 17th, sixteen Polish and no fewer than thirty-three Czech fighter pilots were ordered to join various fighter groups.[7] GC II/1 found that the six Poles sent to them did not speak any French, so they formed their own patrol and operated independently.[8] It was not ideal, but it was the sort of flexible use of resources that the crisis demanded. It was perhaps time to stop sending any of these foreign volunteers to distant parts of France to form ELD defence flights. Planes like the Bloch MB.151 might not be ideal, but it was no slower than the Dutch Air Force Fokker D.XXIs. France could not afford to be choosy about the fighters it used. The substandard Bloch fighters would not be capable of defeating the Bf 109, but as escorts, they might give reconnaissance planes a better chance of getting through, or indeed they could just be used for reconnaissance.

About six modern bombers were leaving French factories every day and more were arriving from the United States; there was now more urgency about getting these, and the hundreds awaiting vital equipment, up to operational standard. However, as with the fighter groups, units converting in the rear and those already operating at the front were competing for these machines. Although only four bomber groups had been used operationally in the first days of the German offensive, their losses exceeded output.

The Breguet 691s of GBA II/35, with their unreliable engines, were only supposed to be used for training, but times were desperate and these, along with any aircrews considered sufficiently trained, were used to make good the losses suffered by *Groupement* 18. *Groupement* 19 (GBAs I/51 and II/51) joined *Groupement* 18 on 20 May, bringing with it the Potez 633 they had been using for training and these too would be used on operations. There were enough LeO 451s among the converting groups to make one group (GB I/31) operational and this joined *Groupement* 6's GB I/12 and GB I/12. The units handing over these bombers were told to make their way to the front and use their obsolete Bloch MB.210s by night. The few Amiot 351/354s that had trickled through to the bomber groups were all from the initial batch intended solely for training and did not even have bombsights, but even these were to be used by night in the hope that by flying low, they would be able to hit something. Far from phasing out the old Amiot 143 and Bloch MB.210, units in the rear were told to haul planes out of stores and make as many as possible serviceable.

Light bomber units re-equipping with American planes in North Africa were ordered to cross the Mediterranean with any planes they had. Two more Martin 167 groups arrived on the 15th but like the two units already in France, they could not be used until their bomb racks caught up with them. The five Douglas DB-7 groups just about had enough planes between them to make two groups operational and GBs I/19 and II/19 arrived on the 18th, flying their first missions a few days later.[9]

On the evening of the 15th, Vuillemin and Têtu instructed d'Astier to make an all-out effort against the advancing German forces. Nothing was to be held back. Fighters were to be thrown into the ground-attack role and the old Amiot 143s were once more to be sent out by day. As soon as the evacuation from Walcheren was complete, D'Astier would also get the naval dive-bomber units being used in the Netherlands. D'Astier was told to use the twin-engined Potez 631 fighter for ground strafing and Vuillemin ordered that Curtiss H75s should be equipped with racks for 10-kg anti-personnel bombs.[10, 11, 12] It seemed that the French were rising to challenge as their forefathers had done in 1918.

On the 16th, reconnaissance planes landing at GB I/12's base provided immediate targets on which to start this all-out offensive. German forces were heading for Montcornet and GB I/12's base. The LeO 451s headed off for a more secure airfield, but first took a detour to bomb the enemy columns heading their way. The other LeO 451 units, GB II/12 and the recently arrived GB I/31, joined in the attack and by the end of the day, the three groups had flown twenty-nine sorties, losing four planes. Two more were lost when a badly damaged plane collided with a parked plane while trying to land. These were heavy losses, made worse by the need to abandon unserviceable planes as the three groups retreated to more secure bases.[13, 14]

The Breguet groups were also in action. Having flown two missions on the 14th and 15th without suffering any losses, the commander of the Breguet wing felt sufficiently confident to allow a return to the hedge hopping tactics of the 12th. Eight Breguets set off in pairs to attack targets around Montcornet, but three more were lost to flak. For the remainder of the campaign, the assault groups would use their planes in low-level shallow dive-bombing attacks.[15, 16]

The only way of maintaining any sort of offensive was to use aircraft outside the specialist bomber units. French commanders would have to start improvising, as they had done in 1918. Then, fighters and reconnaissance planes had joined the bombers. Similar boldness was required in 1940. Vuillemin was leading the way by suggesting the Potez 631 and Curtiss H75 fighters be thrown against the advancing German columns. Têtu's decision to risk the Amiot 143s again suggested a willingness to use everything. Yet Têtu had under his command the thirty-two GAO units along the north-eastern front with some 300 planes and these had a secondary bombing capability. However, once again, using this largely unused resource was not even considered. Indeed, far from throwing the unused GAO along the Maginot Line against the German columns, on the 16th, Têtu ordered all the GAO belonging to the 1st, 7th, and 9th Armies to hand over any Potez 63 they had to reconnaissance squadrons and make their way to the rear with their remaining equipment and await instructions.

Fighters were another option. Cannon-armed fighters could surely be more effective than the SPADS of 1918. Eighteen ground strafing sorties were flown by Potez 631 fighters on the 17th, and the six planes lost seemed ample proof such missions were not worth it. However, the next day five Bloch MB.152s of GC I/8 returning from a patrol, repeatedly strafed German columns they came across near Hirson, without suffering any losses.[17] The rugged Bloch seemed a far more suitable plane for the role than the lightweight Potez 631. The Bloch ELD defence flights in the rear might have been able to contribute far more to the cause if they had been used as ground-attack fighters.

The attempt to equip the H75s with bomb racks ended in fiasco. D'Astier recounts how 'one evening in May', presumably soon after Vuillemin's order of the 14th, the depot at Nanterre was phoned to get hold of the necessary bomb racks, only to find the office was closed and the staff had gone home.[18] It was easy to use this as just another example of how rear services still seemed to be working on a peacetime basis, but, just as significantly, nobody seems to have rung again the following morning when they were open for business. There was no real conviction about French efforts to use fighters for ground-attack.

The problem was not office hours in the rear, it was a lack of flexible thinking. Enormous risks were taken with obsolete Amiots 143s, unsafe Breguet Br 691s and trainer Potez 633s because they were bombers, but Têtu did not see the reconnaissance Mureaux 117, Potez 637 and 63.11 under his command as bombers. Similarly, using fighters for ground-attack was not how they were supposed to be used. After the campaign, d'Astier would make much of the fact that right up to the very end, his Air Force had been used in a controlled, correct way, but this was not a time for orthodoxy; boldness and risk-taking were required.[19] Commanders were not using the available resources as flexibly as they had in 1918.

D'Astier was no more enthusiastic about committing the Amiot 143 by day than Têtu was about using his observation planes as bombers. However desperate the situation might be, d'Astier insisted that the available forces had to be used in a rational manner and pointless sacrifice avoided. He refused to carry out Vuillemin's verbal instruction to use the Amiot 143 by day unless he received written orders. These never arrived and the Amiots were not used. Nor was D'Astier happy about using fighters for ground-attack. D'Astier would not preside over a reckless all-out attack on the advancing Germans with whatever was available. Vuillemin lacked the courage to order it; Gamelin and Georges, unlike Foch and Pétain in similar circumstances in 1918, did not see its value. D'Astier's logical and compassionate stand might have saved the lives of many French aircrews, but the price of defeat and occupation by the Germans would prove to be far higher.[20]

Even if all resources available to the French had been used, they could not have matched the widespread delays imposed on the German advance in March 1918. In 1918, Allied fighters were controlling the skies. However, they might be able to achieve something similar over a limited sector of the front. Focusing the available limited fighter and bomber resources was crucial, and the obvious focus were the counter-attacks Georges was planning. The first of these took place on the 17th. General Giraud, who had taken over what remained of the 9th Army, was to strike south towards Montcornet while de Gaulle was to strike north towards the same area with the 4th Armoured Division. There was no realistic chance of the proposed counterattack sealing off the German breakthrough; the front was already shattered as far north as Dinant. Nevertheless, the town of Montcornet was well-chosen. The lines of communication of three panzer divisions ran through it and its recapture by the French would be a serious blow to the southern wing of the German advance.

The true state of the forces available to Giraud was unknown to Georges, but he was realistic enough to assume that de Gaulle's as yet uncommitted armoured division posed the more substantial threat to the German advance and d'Astier was instructed to concentrate air support here. As far as Georges was concerned, this meant fighter cover. The French commander still did not appreciate the role the bomber might play in such an attack. Têtu, it would appear, did see the potential value. In a covering note, he explained that the circumstances were particularly unusual and that this particular counterattack was so important it would also have to have maximum bomber support.[21] Têtu clearly believed a lengthy explanation was required to justify his change of heart on the tactical bomber support issue. All available French bomber units, apart from the Farman F.222 heavy bombers, would participate.

Unfortunately, this did not amount to much. After the losses of the previous day, the two Breguet groups had just four serviceable planes and were unable to fly any missions and *Groupement* 6 only had a dozen LeO 451s. These and the Potez 631s d'Astier had been told to use for ground strafing were all that

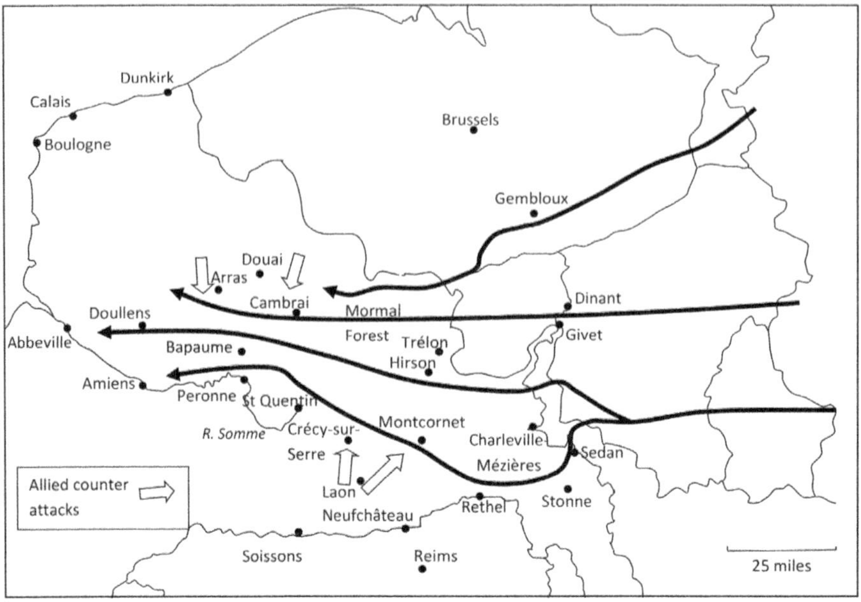

German advance, 16–20 May.

was available. The arrangements for using this tiny force were extremely vague; targets were to be worked out with 'the appropriate authorities'. In fact, they would simply be given instructions about which area to operate in, or more accurately, where the French tanks would be and thus the areas to avoid. There were no formal arrangements for Giraud or de Gaulle to call up direct air support if they should require it, and neither would have known what to do with it if they had been able to, but at least the French bombers would be operating in the right areas. The night before the attack, the Amiot 143s bombed German columns north-east of Montcornet, but these enfeebled units could only manage fourteen sorties. At dawn, de Gaulle's 100-odd tanks set off, completely unaware that the air cover he had been promised had been withdrawn at the last moment. D'Astier had decided the fighters were needed elsewhere.

While de Gaulle struck northwards, Giraud was discovering that many of the units that he was supposed to use to strike south no longer existed. There appeared to be only scattered forces covering the area west of Monthermé and in places German panzers were advancing unopposed. With all thought of even attempting to drive south gone, Giraud set about trying to establish some sort of defensive line. At 6 a.m., he appealed to d'Astier for the maximum possible air support in the Anor area on the Franco-Belgian frontier, well north of Montcornet.[22] Here, the 1st North African Division had already repulsed several assaults, but had suffered heavy casualties and were being constantly bombed.

D'Astier's own night reconnaissance also suggested the Germans were making most progress in this region and he ordered all air units to operate there instead of around Montcornet. This included eighteen ground-strafing Potez 631 fighters and twelve LeO 451 bombers. No escort was provided for the LeO 451 formation and four out of twelve failed to return, two shot down by Bf 109s and two by flak.[23] These were the most serious losses yet suffered by *Groupement* 6. The lack of escort, we shall see, was no oversight on d'Astier's part.

With all sectors of the front demanding fighter protection, d'Astier's dilemma is clear, but whether to support Giraud's defensive efforts in the north or de Gaulle's counterattack in the south, was not his decision to make. Initially the lack of fighter cover did not prove to be a disadvantage for de Gaulle. Although only three of his battalions were in position in time, his force, with some 100 tanks, was reasonably formidable and the attack seemed to be going well. De Gaulle's battalions advanced 15 miles to the outskirts of Montcornet, unspotted by German reconnaissance aircraft and scattering the light German screening forces defending the town. The Germans hastily threw together an improvised defensive line with any light flak and self-propelled artillery that happened to be in the vicinity and this was enough to block the advance. With no artillery to overcome these defences or infantry to hold the ground gained, de Gaulle felt he had to withdraw.

It seemed to confirm pre-war thinking that the tank could not sustain an advance against any sort of organised resistance without artillery support. In fact, the situation de Gaulle found himself in outside Montcornet was precisely one in which a German tank commander would have been able to call in air support. As Giraud had demonstrated that very day, it was not impossible to get fairly speedy intervention. De Gaulle did not perhaps have Giraud's access to d'Astier, but more significantly, using air support as a substitute for artillery simply never occurred to de Gaulle. As if to bring home to de Gaulle the options that were available to commanders, as he pulled back, his tanks were harried by German Ju 87s called up by the forces defending Montcornet.[24]

Meanwhile, d'Astier was questioning the sense of using the available fighters for escort. On the 15th, eight LeO 451s had been escorted by fighters drawn from four fighter groups. On the 16th, twenty-four Bloch fighters had escorted a single raid by LeO 451s. Escort missions seemed to be absorbing a disproportionate fraction of fighter effort at a time when ground forces were desperately appealing for protection. At around midday on the 17th, d'Astier requested Vuillemin's permission to abandon escort missions, even if this meant reducing the number of day bombing sorties flown or restricting the force entirely to night attacks. Instead, all fighter units should concentrate on intercepting German bomber formations.[25]

It seemed a reasonable enough suggestion. The problem with the policy was that German escorts had been making it impossible for the fighters to get through to the bombers and there had to be doubts that this was a battle the French fighters could win. Nevertheless, d'Astier felt that it was his duty to try and re-establish some sort of French fighter presence over the front; that was what his fighters were for. With Georges and Gamelin appealing for better protection for their troops, Vuillemin felt he had little choice but to agree but insisted that if the situation warranted it, daylight bombing missions would have to be flown without fighter cover. After their single ground-attack mission, the Potez 631s were redirected to defend the stations in the rear where French reinforcements were arriving and further bombing missions for the day were cancelled.

Defending the French Army did indeed seem more important than defending a few bombers. The ideal solution, however, was to get the fighters in the rear to the front so that both escort and protection missions could be attempted. The change in policy ended any hope of Vuillemin's all-out air offensive against the advancing German columns gaining any momentum. On the night of 17th–18th, French bombers did their best to maintain some pressure on the enemy by bombing routes heading westwards from Monthermé. Even the huge four-engined Farman 222 heavy bombers were involved, flying low-level attacks on enemy columns moving from Charleville-Mézières towards Hirson. In all, though, the six night bomber units could only manage around twenty sorties.[26] Just eight day-bombing sorties were flown on the 18th—four Breguet 693s and four Breguet 691s attempting to relieve the pressure on French troops falling back on the Forêt de Mormal. With RAF night bombers focusing on the Ruhr and British day bombers unable to operate, Vuillemin's all-out assault was fast fizzling out.

The forces on the ground were in desperate need of the cover D'Astier was hoping to provide and there were some encouraging signs that it might be possible. Since the 15th, French pilots had been reporting that German escorts were noticeably less common and less strong.[27] Whether the French fighter force would be in a position to take advantage was another matter, especially following the catastrophic events of the 15th. GC II/6 was wiped out, losing virtually all of its M.S.406s in a bombing raid and was withdrawn to re-equip with Bloch MB.152s. GCs II/2 and III/2 had to abandon seventeen unserviceable Moranes as they retreated to new airfields. Following the loss of nine D.520s in combat on the 15th, GC I/3 had another two destroyed on the ground, with seven others damaged, during another German raid on the 16th. All the damaged fighters had to be abandoned as this group too was forced to retreat. When the unit reached its new base on the 17th, its strength had been reduced to just eighteen planes, of which only six were serviceable. In all, seventy-nine fighters were lost on the 16th and on the 17th, only three arrived to replace them.[28] Ten GC I/3 pilots were dispatched to the Toulouse factory to pick up replacement D.520s but it would be the 20th before the first of these was actually handed over.[29]

The pilot situation was far more encouraging; some of the Poles now reaching the front were battle-hardened veterans who had already notched up victories in Poland. The Poles and Czech were especially welcomed by groups like the hard-hit GC II/2. On the evening of the 17th, three French and nine Czech pilots, with their training school M.S.406s, reached the group. Unfortunately, the planes they brought with them were particularly worn out.[30]

In the rear, frantic efforts were being made to equip more fighter units. GC II/9 moved to the airfield at the SNCASO plant at Châteauroux to take delivery of Bloch fighters as they came off the assembly line. The pilots, most of whom were fresh out of training school, were hurriedly introduced to their new Bloch fighters and the group's first squadron was declared operational on the 18th and the second the next day. Between the 10th and the 20th, thirty-six D.520s were delivered to GC II/3 and the unit declared operational. The Polish GC I/145 moved to Villacoublay on the 17th and collected a first batch of fourteen Caudrons the following day. However, any chance of the group becoming operational disappeared when, a couple of days later, a Pole lost his life flying the fighter. Polish engineers declared the Caudron unsafe to fly and the plane was grounded.[31] With the evacuation of southern Netherlands complete, the fighter units that had been supporting the 7th Army were now available. On the 17th, GC I/6 moved up from the south to replace the shattered GC II/6, but the front needed more than just replacements. With the crisis at the front so acute, there were still far too many fighters being held back to cover the rear.

For the 18th, day fighter groups from *Groupement* 23 were ordered to provide permanent air cover west and south-west of the Forêt de Mormal while others covered rail links in the Paris area and reinforcements arriving south of the Aisne. The first day of this new strategy did have at least one major success; the Curtiss H75 fighters of GC I/5, transferred from ZOAE for the day to provide cover for reinforcements arriving in the Soissons region, joined forces with the Curtiss fighters of GC II/4 and Moranes of GC II/2 to shoot five He 111s with three more Heinkels returning damaged; at least two of the escorting Messerschmitts were also lost. Most claims for that day were bomber or reconnaissance planes. The twenty-five enemy aircraft claimed was scarcely a decisive victory, but the fighters were getting through to the bombers. Pilots described how enemy planes dropped their bombs haphazardly and fled as soon as they were attacked.[32] Just the presence of fighters will always make bombing less effective. D'Astier could claim his policy had brought some reward, but with so few fighters available, they could only have any serious influence on events if they focused effort where it might make a significant difference.

De Gaulle's second counterattack on the 19th provided the perfect focus. This time, he would be striking towards Crécy-sur-Serre. The attack was never intended as more than a raid, an attempt to remind Guderian that he dare not push too far to the west. Like his previous counterattack, the assault was to receive some indirect air support, with bombers hitting targets to the east of his proposed line of advance, but again, there was no question of de Gaulle being able to call up air support if his forces should get bogged down. As well as bomber support, D'Astier was instructed to provide fighter protection.

D'Astier, however, seemed to be running the air war as he saw fit rather than the instructions he was receiving from the Army. On the 18th–19th, the night bombing offensive was reinforced by two groups flying a mixture of Bloch MB.210 and Amiot 351/354s. With more crews than planes, bomber groups began using the same plane twice with different crews. Even so, the force managed only thirty-four sorties. However, all these missions were in the Hirson region in support of the French forces falling back on the Forêt de Mormal rather than the area where de Gaulle was attacking.[33]

The day bomber support was to come from *Groupement* 6 and AASF Battles, but the LeO 451 element never materialised. The French bombers were about to set off to attack German tanks reported north-west of Rethel, some way from de Gaulle's counterattack, when their airfield was heavily bombed and most of the wing's aircraft destroyed. The fighter cover for de Gaulle's operation also never materialised. D'Astier claimed that he had been misinformed about the time of the attack and had his fighters operating in the Forêt de Mormal region.[34]

This time the lack of fighter cover was felt. German reconnaissance planes had spotted the French build up and almost immediately de Gaulle's force came under attack. The aerial assault was intense and losses heavy, particularly among the supporting infantry. Nevertheless, by 9 a.m., the French had reached the River Serre, but again, a hastily assembled defensive line prevented any further advance. Without greater artillery support and under intense Luftwaffe bombardment, once again, de Gaulle could see no way forward and withdrew.

Late in the afternoon, d'Astier finally got to hear of the difficulties de Gaulle was in. At 5 p.m., eight hours after de Gaulle's advance had ground to a halt, GCs III/1 and II/2 were ordered to put all available fighters over the region between Laon and Crécy-sur-Serre. Unfortunately, these two units had already been badly battered in a dogfight with Bf 109s in the Forêt de Mormal region. Two patrols from GC III/1 at low altitude were covered by three higher patrols from GC II/2, but Bf 109s prevented the Moranes from getting through to the bombers pounding de Gaulle's force.[35]

Meanwhile, further north, d'Astier was using the naval dive-bombers that might have helped de Gaulle continue his advance, to shore up the defences around the Forêt de Mormal. At 6 p.m., twenty LN 401/411s from AB 2 and AB 4 attacked German panzer units in the village of Berlaimont in the Forêt de Mormal. After completing several missions in the Netherlands without suffering serious casualties, the units were confident, perhaps over-confident. The two squadrons were supposed to be escorted by naval Potez 631s but they missed their escort and pushed on to their target anyway. This could have proven fatal for the defenceless single-seater Liore-Nieuport dive-bombers, but on this occasion, fighters were not the problem. The flak that greeted the unit over the target proved to be far more devastating than anything encountered over the Netherlands. The two squadrons spotted the armoured formations. To ensure maximum accuracy, they released their bombs at a very low altitude, but this made them very vulnerable as they pulled out of their dives.[36] Eight were shot down by flak and a ninth had been damaged by flak was shot down by Bf 109s; to complete a disastrous day, a tenth was shot down by French anti-aircraft fire.[37] It was a reminder of how vulnerable the dive-bomber could be if anti-aircraft gunners are prepared to stand their ground.

By the 20th, the battered units of the 1st Army had been pushed north and west of the Forêt de Mormal but a reasonably secure line was being established along the Escaut Canal and the River Sensée to the British garrisoned Arras on the River Scarpe. It would be from this area that any attempt by the northern armies to link up with those in the south would come. The units cut off in the north were far better equipped than the forces scraped together to defend the Somme to the south, so the main attack would have to come from the surrounded forces. It was, perhaps, not the time to strip the northern armies of their remaining air units. However, the RAF had begun evacuating back to Britain on the 19th and the remaining French fighter units flew south on the 20th.

On the 18th, 19th, and 20th, the French fighter force flew around 300 sorties daily with its 250 serviceable fighters, which was an improvement on previous days, but still hardly the degree of intensity the crisis merited. There was some evidence that d'Astier's decision to concentrate French fighters against German bombers had paid dividends. French fighters were able on occasion to take advantage of the less numerous German escorts to disrupt some attacks. Even the Potez 631s gained some successes defending railway stations in the rear. Even so, between the 17th and 20th, the French claimed fewer than eighty confirmed victories, about the same number as the smaller British fighter force. German bomber losses only increased significantly on the 19th and this was largely the result of some fierce clashes with British Hurricanes in the Lille-Arras region. It was here, over the front line, that the critical battle was being fought and the French fighters needed to be, but even units moved north were often based well to the rear. The Bloch equipped GC II/9 arrived from the south on the 18th but was based to the west of Paris and saw little action. Despite the reinforcements arriving, by the 20th, the number of serviceable fighters had dropped to around 200. There were too few fighters and they were far too scattered.

On the evening of the 20th, elements of the 2nd Panzer Division reached the Channel coast north of Abbeville, cutting off forty-five French, British and Belgian divisions in the north. The Germans had achieved the complete breakthrough that had eluded them in March 1918. This time, Allied efforts never gained the momentum of the 1918 counter air offensive. Daylight attacks on the advancing enemy rarely rose above 100 sorties a day; this was never going to be sufficient to be decisive. In 1918, the intervention of the Allied air forces had bought the time the ground forces had needed to contain the German advance. In 1940, the mobility of the panzers and the power of the Luftwaffe, but also the less focused and flexible Allied use of the available air resources, ensured history did not repeat itself.

The German arrival on the Channel coast placed the Allied armies in an extremely serious but not hopeless situation. The Wehrmacht's own position was far from secure. The cordon of troops protecting the southern flank was being stretched thinner every day. Little more than 25 miles separated the British stronghold at Arras and French forces south of the Somme. On the 19th, Gamelin was replaced by the bustling, confident (some would say cocky) Weygand. Spirits in Paris rose. The new French commander hoped to create the forces required by the breakout attempt by shortening Allied defensive lines in Belgium. Freed British divisions would join the forces in the Arras-Douai region, drive south to Cambrai and Bapaume, and link up with French forces driving northwards from Amiens. Weygand hoped rather optimistically that the required redistribution of forces could be achieved as early as the 23rd.

The Air Force would have an important role to play, not just by providing reconnaissance and fighter cover, but bomber support too. The night before the counter-attack, German airfields were to be raided and on the day of the attack, each bomber crew would be expected to fly up to three sorties, with maximum effort coinciding with the launching of the attack. Day bombing meant fighter escorts would be required again. The number of fighters was decreasing and the number of tasks was increasing. Which targets the bombers would hit remained vague and effectiveness would depend on how many bombers the Allies could put into the air. Churchill promised Weygand the full support of the RAF. Vuillemin would do his best.

On the 20th, after ten days of operations, *Groupement* 6 was withdrawn south to rest and re-equip. To replace it, GBAs I/54 and II/54 became available with a makeshift force of eleven Potez 633s, ten Breguet 691s, and six Breguet 693s. Four Martin 167s and two Douglas DB-7 groups would fly their first missions over the next few days. GBs I/11 and II/11 pooled their available LeO 451s to dispatch the equivalent of one group to the front on the 25th. GB I/23, having handed its LeO 451s over to *Groupement* 6, moved up to support the night bombing offensive with eighteen Bloch MB.210s. Even when all these reinforcements had arrived, the French could, at best, put fifty bombers into the air by day and a similar number by night.

Other elements of the Air Force were no better off. The reconnaissance groups could only muster forty-eight serviceable planes on the morning of the 21st. The fighter force was reinforced on the 20th by the arrival of the M.S.406-equipped GC III/6 from the southern sector of the Maginot Line and more significantly by thirty-three brand new D.520s of GC II/3. On the same day, the ten pilots of GC I/3 received the first eight replacement D.520s, but waited for the delivery of the final two on the 23rd before making their way back to their unit on the 24th.[38] There was a strange mixture of frenzy and casualness about the French reaction to the crisis. While GC I/3 waited for the pilots to return, the group was virtually grounded.

The collapse of the French armies in the north enabled Vuillemin to achieve the centralisation of the fighter forces that the Air Force had always wanted. The 7th Army in the Netherlands had been disbanded, the 9th had ceased to exist, and the fighter group belonging to the 1st Army was no longer able to operate from within this army's ranks. From the 18th, all fighter units in the north were under the full operational control of either *Groupement* 21, responsible for the defence of the rear, or *Groupement* 23, which was operating over the front. In the east, along the Maginot Line, the same centralisation was enforced with GC I/5, GC II/5, and GC I/2 of the 2nd, 3rd, and 4th Armies respectively now operating as a single force, and the new armies being formed to cover the Somme and Aisne would not get their own fighter group. This ended the system that the Army had fought so hard to retain. Reconnaissance units too were to be organised at a higher level. The remnants of the army reconnaissance groups in the north were now under the direct orders of d'Astier, although reconnaissance units in ZOAE remained attached to their armies.

The situation on the ground was extremely fluid. To the south and west of Arras, German panzer units were advancing unchecked. The port of Boulogne was already threatened. As the panzers swung north, they would be cutting straight into the rear of the Arras garrison. West of Arras, there was not even the pretence of an Allied defensive position. The French response in the air was as scattered as their forces were on the ground. On the 20th, the three remaining serviceable LN.401s joined a dozen Chance Vought V-156-Fs in an attempt to slow down German forces by destroying a bridge just east of St Quentin. British Hurricanes were supposed to provide the escort but the RAF was in the throes of evacuating France and the escort did not materialise. The Chance Voughts were caught by a formation of Bf 109s and five were shot down. The LN 401s managed to avoid the German fighters but lost one of their number to flak.[39] Vuillemin was right about the vulnerability of the dive-bomber, but the German Stukas were demonstrating how effective they could be if they were protected. Fourteen *Groupement* 6 LeO 451s, either in small formations or singly, and without fighter escort, attacked various German columns in the St Quentin and Péronne regions, the last missions flown by this unit before it withdrew south. Again, losses were heavy, with four failing to return, all the victims of German fighters.[40] The lesson was clear: bombers had to have escorts. Breguets and Potez 633s flew thirteen sorties much further north in the Arras area. Scattered over such a wide area, such a low number of sorties could not have much impact.

By night, the French Bloch MB.210, Amiot 143, Amiot 351/354, and four-engined Farman F.222 heavy bombers were making the maximum possible effort in the brief summer nights. Efforts to make operational as many aircraft as possible were bearing fruit. On the 20th, *Groupement* 9 received no less than fourteen Amiot 143s, nineteen Bloch MB.210s, and four Amiot 354s.[41] The following night, the French were able to fly fifty-nine sorties from the available thirty-seven planes.[42] It was impossible to do more with the limited numbers available. The effectiveness of these night attacks varied considerably, but for pilots willing to fly low enough, there were enemy columns, often with headlights blazing, to strafe and bomb. Some planes were flying so low, they were returning with damage from their own exploding bombs.

There were successes. The Germans reported that bombing had caused considerable damage on forward airfields in the Guise region, which Ju 52s were using to fly in supplies for advanced Luftwaffe units and the Wehrmacht panzers. As a result of these raids, the number of sorties the Luftwaffe could fly from forward airstrips had to be limited.[43] Poor weather and ageing equipment made it difficult to keep up the pressure. Night operations were also beginning to prove as hazardous as daylight missions; on the night of 25th–26th, two Bloch MB.210s crashed attempting to take off in bad weather.

As a preliminary to Weygand's planned push south, British and French forces in the Arras region planned to strike southwards on the 21st in the hope of slowing down Rommel's panzers sweeping round to the north of Arras. A simultaneous French attack towards Cambrai had to be postponed until the following day because the forces were not in position in time. The French had promised air support for the largely British drive from Arras, but d'Astier ordered French fighters to make their major effort further east, north of Cambrai, where he apparently still believed the French attack was going ahead. Despite the intervention of Stukas, the British counterattack made some progress but like French efforts from the south, it ground to a halt as soon as any serious resistance was encountered. The Breguet assault planes and Potez light bombers of *Groupements* 18 and 19 were operating much further south, engaging Germans columns that were already establishing bridgeheads across the Somme. These were worthy targets but the little air support that was available would have been better used where the Allies were trying to take the initiative.

The next day, the French armoured units struck south-eastwards towards Cambrai. Again, it was not an attempt to link up with the southern French armies, but the capture of Cambrai would cut the lines of communication of both the 5th and 7th Panzer Divisions. D'Astier still appeared to be in the dark about the attack. On the evening of the 21st, he was told that the operation was to take place the following day, but was apparently not told the time nor the precise axis of attack. However, the Army had made it clear what they wanted: bombers were to operate to the east of the proposed advance and the 1st Army wanted fighter cover north of Cambrai.[44]

No particular orders appear to have been passed to the night bomber squadrons to support the counterattack, although the communication targets French bombers continued to bomb south-west of Cambrai were vaguely appropriate. For day operations, the Martin and Douglas bombers had finally become available but d'Astier still only had a total of around thirty day bombers. On the morning of the 22nd, one flight of three Potez 633s and two flights of Breguets set off to bomb columns on roads leading to Cambrai from the south, and eighteen Martin 167 and Douglas DB-7s attempted to hit columns approaching Cambrai from the south-east.[45] In the circumstances, that was about as close as the bomber support could be. Even this was a wasted effort; fog prevented most of the Martin bombers from finding their targets.[46] Some effort was made by the French to reconnoitre the area. Four reconnaissance missions were flown on the 22nd. Two failed to return, but the two that did make it back reported German concentrations to the west of Arras. D'Astier sent six Breguets to attack these, but the targets were too distant to be an immediate threat to the counterattack towards Cambrai.[47, 48] D'Astier liked to think as Air Force commander, he was in the best position to decide where to use his forces but as is often the case, targets chosen by air force commanders tend not be where ground forces most need support.[49]

French fighters seemed particularly ineffective. Although a total of 244 sorties were flown, until a late afternoon mission by the D.520s of GC II/3, no French fighters were lost but the only claim was a reconnaissance Do 17 shot down by the H75s of GC I/4 near St Quentin.[50, 51] The poor weather was no doubt a factor, but it did not seem to stop the Luftwaffe. The French tanks advancing on Cambrai were soon spotted by a German He 46 observation biplane. The obsolete 250 km/hr (150 mph) reconnaissance plane dropped a message on Cambrai airfield, now occupied by II/LG 2, a ground-attack unit equipped with equally antiquated 340 km/hr (210 mph) ground-attack Henschel 123 biplanes. These were immediately scrambled along with their own personal Bf 109E escort. The Henschel biplanes bombed the advancing French columns and the Bf 109 fighters strafed with their cannon, causing heavy losses, especially among the lorry-mounted infantry.[52] It was another example of what could be achieved by prompt action with obsolete aircraft used purposefully and modern planes used flexibly. The French tanks were eventually brought to a halt by an improvised defensive line on the outskirts of Cambrai. All afternoon, the attack remained bogged down and was becoming the object of increasingly violent dive-bombing attacks. No French fighters appeared to have arrived until late afternoon when the Dewoitines of GC II/3 managed to break up one Ju 87 attack, claiming eight dive-bombers and a couple of Henschel Hs 126 observation planes.

The failure of the British and French counterattacks left the Allied forces in the Arras area in a precarious position. With their lines of communication now secure, the Panzers were able to continue their swing round to the north-west of Arras. By the 22nd, many of the units earmarked for Weygand's counter offensive were being drawn into defensive battles. Somewhat controversially, the British had already decided to retreat north in order to evacuate from any Channel ports still held, effectively ending any hope of striking south.

By the 23rd, the battle for the Channel ports had already reached a critical stage. Boulogne and Calais were already surrounded and the Germans were advancing on Dunkirk. In desperation, the French Navy threw all their bombers into the struggle. On the 23rd, thirty daylight ground-attack sorties were flown by Chance Vought 156-F dive-bombers and Laté 298 floatplane bombers on targets in and around the Boulogne. Four of the floatplanes were brought down by flak and fighters. Again, the French seemed willing to use any plane, even floatplanes, in the ground-attack role, however unsuitable, provided it was a bomber. By the evening, only isolated groups of Allied troops were managing to hold on and a couple of days later, these surrendered. Calais also soon fell, leaving Dunkirk as the only port the Allies could use. This was held and a remarkable evacuation organised, which enabled most of the surrounded troops to escape. While the British Navy was plucking one third of a million Allied troops from the Dunkirk beaches, the French were preparing for the battle that would decide whether their country stayed in the fight.

15

Lessons Learned Too Late

To some, the task now facing France seemed hopeless. The Dutch and Belgian Armies had been defeated, only one British division remained in the front line, and one third of the French Army had been lost. On 10 May, the Allies had outnumbered the Germans. Now, the French stood virtually alone and outnumbered in every respect. There seemed to be good reason for French pessimism.

The short-term prospects of the French may have been bleak, but if the Army could hold on, all was not necessarily lost. Fresh divisions were already arriving from North Africa and the French divisions plucked from the Dunkirk beaches were heading back to France. Better planes were on the way and production was rising rapidly. The delivery of nearly 200 modern fighters was expected in June and by August, it was hoped that monthly output would have risen to 400, which was far more than the German aircraft industry was turning out.[1] Even more significant was the improved quality of these fighters. On 12 May, the HS 12Y-51-powered Dewoitine D.523 achieved 562 km/hr and two days later, a similarly powered Arsenal VG-35 managed 590 km/hr. French fighters would finally have the speed to intercept German bombers with ease and the ability to take on German fighters on equal terms. The delivery of the first 200 HS 12Y-51 motors was expected in June and deliveries of the D.523 were due to begin in July. Production of bombers was also rising fast. French factories were expected to build over 200 in June and with deliveries from the United States also increasing, very soon, some 500 would be becoming available each month.[2] However, all of this would mean nothing if France could not stem the German tide; to do this, everything available would have to be thrown into the struggle.

The brief lull in the fighting on the Somme and Aisne fronts as the Germans concentrated their efforts on the Allied forces surrounded at Dunkirk gave the French a brief opportunity to reflect. Valuable lessons had been learned and Georges was anxious to apply them. He was particularly struck by the speed with which German commanders could get air support; he estimated bombers could be over a target within fifteen minutes of the request being made. He claimed this feat was only possible because the German Army and Air Force were under a single commander.[3] This was not quite the case, but they were part of the Wehrmacht, which acted as one. Georges's comment was clearly a swipe at the whole concept of an independent *Armée de l'Air*. In truth, however, it had been this independent Air Force that had argued for tactical close air support and the Army that had been reluctant to incorporate the idea into its thinking.

Georges now accepted the enormous impact the direct intervention of bombers on the battlefield could have. Quite correctly, however, he observed that although the psychological impact had been great, the actual physical harm done was often limited. Fighter units had to be called in quicker; in terms no French general would have trouble understanding, he explained how rapid fighter intervention against bomber attack was just like a counter-artillery barrage. He was, however, careful not to lay all the blame for the collapse of French Army formations on the Air Force. He recognized that the Army had simply not done enough to prepare the troops for the shock of aerial bombardment. The reaction of French soldiers had been far too passive and this had bred a feeling of helplessness. He urged all commanders to instil in their troops the need to turn all weapons on the attacking aircraft. He pointed out that French aircraft were often returning from missions riddled with small arms fire. French troops had to be trained to take a more active part in their own defence. This would reduce the accuracy of German bombing, lower the morale of German aircrews, increase Luftwaffe losses, and, most importantly of all, lift French morale.[4]

The role of the GAO observation groups also came under close scrutiny. As Têtu now freely admitted, these units had played virtually no part in the fighting. Seven months before, the commander of the observation forces had suggested that the crews of the grounded bomber groups in the rear should be retrained as reconnaissance pilots. Now, he was proposing removing all observation squadrons from army corps, creating fewer larger units under his direct control and using surplus crews to reinforce bomber and fighter units.[5]

In the last three weeks of May 1940, the French made more progress towards a more modern air force than they had managed in the previous decade. The Army now appreciated that the bomber was a battlefield weapon, and the need for more fighters had been hammered home. It was now accepted that a disproportionate amount of effort had been put into observation squadrons at the expense of other branches of the Air Force. The Army was still suspicious of Air Force intentions, and with the way d'Astier had been running air operations, they had good reason, but there was agreement about the need for more centralised control of the Air Force at a higher level of command.

While all this was now plain to the French High Command, it would be some time before these new ideas filtered through to commanders in the field and time was something the French did not have. On 29 May, the outlines of a German offensive across the Somme and Aisne were already being drawn up. The German Army had so far suffered surprisingly light losses, but advances of several hundred miles inevitably imposed considerable wear and tear on equipment. Hitler, however, was determined not to give the French any time to recover and there would only be the briefest of rests before the attack was renewed. The next offensive would be launched on 5 June. The stakes were high. If it failed, the Germans would be forced to give their units time to rest and refit. This in turn might give the French time to complete the re-equipment of their Air Force, rearm the French troops that had escaped at Dunkirk, and put into practise the lessons they had learned. On the other hand, an immediate German success on the Somme and Aisne might lead to the disintegration of the French Army and the defeat of the nation. The French felt if they could just hold the next offensive for a week, the situation would begin to look very different.[6]

Once any attempt at linking up with the forces in the northern pocket had been definitively abandoned, Weygand turned his attentions to strengthening the defensive lines along the Aisne and Somme. The French Air Force was required to protect French reinforcements disembarking at railheads in the rear, disrupt the German build-up on the Somme and Aisne, and support French efforts to eliminate the bridgeheads at Abbeville, Amiens, and Péronne. From the 26th, the Luftwaffe was concentrating on Dunkirk and enemy air activity over the southern front was light. On the last three days of the month, the same bad weather that helped the Dunkirk evacuation succeed also brought French aircrews a welcome respite.

The French used this time to refit their squadrons as best they could. The M.S.406 was to be replaced as quickly as possible. After losing all its M.S.406s on the 16th, GC II/6 moved to the Châteauroux Bloch MB.152 plant; between 23 May and 1 June, the group took delivery of thirty-four as they came off the production line. The pilots flew patrols in defence of the factory as they got used to their new mounts and demonstrated they were fully operational by claiming four He 111 bombers that attacked the factory on 5 June. Other groups converted even more rapidly. On 29 May, GC III/2 handed over its surviving M.S.406 to other groups, and between 31 May and 5 June, the group took delivery of thirty recently arrived Curtiss H75 A-3. The unit flew its first operation with the plane on 6 June. This was not nearly enough time to become fully familiar with a new plane, but it was the sort of urgency that France would need to have any chance of surviving. GC II/7 received thirty-five D.520s between 20 and 29 May and flew its first mission with the fighter on 1 June. GC III/3 got its first D.520 on 25 May and flew its first mission with the plane on 5 June.[7]

With the reduced aerial activity, replacement Bloch MB.152 and Curtiss H75s reaching squadrons for once exceeded combat losses and there was time to repair damaged machines. Even so, most H75 and Bloch groups had fewer fighters than on 10 May. Dewoitine groups at the front were particularly short of equipment as nearly all new output was being used to convert M.S.406 units. At least the few remaining M.S.406 groups had no problems with reserves; the remaining units were turning away machines being offered to them by groups converting to new types.[8] By the beginning of June, the number of fighters available had risen to 356. French losses among fighter pilots amounted to 160 killed, wounded, or captured, but these had been largely made good. A total of 175 pilots arrived from training schools in May. In the first days of June, another fifty fighter pilots arrived and another 100 were expected to become available in a matter of days. These were supplemented by some instructors hastily called back to front line duties to see France through the crisis.

Bomber units were also benefiting from increased production. There were still no fully operational Amiot 351/354s, which meant the bomber could still only be used by night at low level. *Groupement* 6 returned to the front on the 28th after a week's rest and refit. At the beginning of June, there were six LeO 451, four Breguet 693, four Martin 167, and two Douglas DB-7 groups available for day operations, with a paper strength of around 200 bombers, although only a half, at most, were serviceable at any one time. Another eight groups were available for night operations.

The GAO and reconnaissance units had lost around sixty Potez 63.11 reconnaissance planes in combat since the beginning of the campaign, but around 100 more had been destroyed on the ground or abandoned. Eighty replacements helped restore Potez strength to around 130, of which eighty-five were serviceable, an improvement on the forty-eight that had been available on 21 May.[9] Those GAO still at the front contributed another 120, of which around seventy were serviceable. However, there was a reluctance to risk any of them if fighters were not available for escort duties. The Bloch MB.174 could operate without an escort, and Vuillemin ordered a special effort to be made to ensure as many as possible were made available to front line units but switching production from the Bloch MB.174 to the Bloch MB.175 meant deliveries of new machines had virtually ceased. On 5 June, there were only nine serviceable Bloch reconnaissance planes along the entire front.[10] Interestingly, older planes like the Mureaux reconnaissance machines were not even listed. France was not in a position to be so cautious about which planes it used.

The shortage of modern planes was chronic but there was no shortage of aircrews. French naval squadrons had been heavily involved in the fighting, and they now expected a proportion of the modern planes that were coming off the production lines. On 31 May, the first ten Dewoitine D.520s were handed over to re-equip one of their four fighter squadrons. The Navy also got its first LeO 451s and Martin 167s. Large numbers of Belgian aircrews were now joining the Poles and Czechs in the rear. The aircrews of the 1st, 7th, and 9th Army observation squadrons sent to the rear were also still waiting for something to fly.

More Poles and Czechs were finding their way to front line squadrons. On 28 May, eighteen Polish fighter pilots were posted to front line squadrons.[11] On 3 June, another thirty-three Poles followed.[12] There was now far less resistance to the idea of units manned entirely by foreign personnel. On 24 May, the first Polish bomber unit was finally formed and was expected to become operational with the LeO 451 in mid-June. Other Poles were to begin training on Martin 167s.[13] On 1 June, the morale of the Czech contingent was given a boost by the signing of an agreement finally allowing an independent Czech Air Force within the framework of the French Air Force, along the lines of the agreement already made with the Poles. Two Belgian squadrons began converting to the LeO 451, but the aircrews from eleven more were waiting for something to fly. On 4 June, another 100 Polish fighter and fifty bomber pilots completed their training.[14] At a time when units were being converted to new types and thrown back into action within days, it was not too late to make use of these pilots, if planes could be found for them to fly.

The French still held out hope that even at this late stage, the United States might save the day. Since 23 May, the French, apparently armed with a detailed list of planes held in American stores, had been preparing a request for more American help. By the time it was made, it had become a frantic appeal for anything, however obsolete, the Americans could send. Aware of the many American planes the French already had, but through lack of vital equipment could not be used, Reynaud made it clear that they had to arrive fully armed and ready for use. Astonishingly, within a couple of weeks, the Americans had gathered together ninety-three obsolete Northrop A-17A attack bombers and fifty Curtiss SBC biplane dive-bombers and the first batch left for France on 16 June.[15]

Did the French have to wait for the Americans to go through their reserves and ship what they could find across the Atlantic? Should the French Air Force have looked more closely at their own stored obsolete equipment? The French Army was already hauling obsolete mothballed 75-mm guns out of stores and dispatching them to the front to be used as anti-tank guns over open sights. Soon after the Germans launched their attack, Vuillemin had ordered storage units to make available as many fighters and bombers as possible. Bloch MB.151s and Koolhoven F.K.58s had been hastily made serviceable and used to equip rear defence flights, but nothing older than these relatively new fighters was considered. The plea for bombers saw much effort put into preparing old Amiot 143 and Bloch MB.210s for combat. Indeed, so many were arriving at the Avord air base, they did not know what to do with them and told the units to stop sending them. These ungainly, difficult to fly bombers were better than nothing, but perhaps it would have been better to focus effort on cannon-armed Dewoitine D.501and D.510 single-seater fighters for ground strafing, or Mureaux reconnaissance planes for bombing. Perhaps it was even time to see if the old Potez 25s could be used like the Dutch used their Fokker C.Vs. It seems, however, that to the very end, the French default preference was large multi-seaters.

On the ground, Weygand had few options. With the Luftwaffe controlling the skies, the last thing the French wanted was a war of manoeuvre. Even a limited retreat from the position they now held might prove catastrophic. Weygand opted for a static defence in depth, with towns and villages turned into strong points and their garrisons instructed to hold on, even if bypassed by German forces. By holding key communication centres, the French hoped that the panzer spearheads would be starved of supplies and that the German offensive would eventually fizzle out. In the circumstances, it was the strategy which offered the French the best chance of success.

Weygand's policy was not entirely defensive. If the French could recapture bridgeheads the Germans had established at Abbeville, Amiens, and Péronne, it would boost French morale and make the German task more difficult. With the Germans fully occupied around Dunkirk, there would be no better time. There was now a new-found determination to integrate bomber support with operations on the ground. Georges wanted these counterattacks supported by 'rigorous bomber action' and Weygand demanded the maximum bomber effort against the panzers forces assembling in the bridgeheads.[16] Vuillemin, Weygand, Georges, and Têtu all now agreed on the need for bomber support on the battlefield.

On the 26th, the four Breguet 693 groups and two fighter groups—GC III/2 and GC III/3—were made available to General Frère's 7th Army to support attempts to eliminate the German bridgeheads at Amiens and Abbeville, where de Gaulle's 4th Armoured Division was in action. This Assault Brigade and its accompanying fighter groups were, in effect, now being used in much the same way as the Air Division of the First World War. To speed up the response time, flights of fully armed Breguets, with their engines ticking over, were kept on alert at forward airstrips ready to intervene immediately an appropriate target was identified, a practice a previous generation of Breguet tactical bomber units had used in the Rif campaign.[17] Poor weather limited the opportunities of the brigade, but about forty sorties were flown against various targets in and around Abbeville and Amiens in the last four days of May. Four Breguets and Potezs were lost, all the victims of fighters.

The last day of the month proved to be a particularly unfortunate one for the entire bomber force. Nine out of twenty-one LeO 451s were lost, as were four out of twelve Douglas DB-7 bombers and two out of eighteen Martin 167s, again all the victims of fighters.[18] Weygand wanted the German bridgeheads pounded with everything the Air Force had and demanded that these attacks should continue but Vuillemin feared that his force would be exhausted before the Germans even launched their offensive. In the end, a compromise was worked out whereby the light and assault bombers continued to provide the Army with support by day, while the LeO 451 groups would operate by night until the Germans attacked, although following the heavy losses of the 31st, no missions would be flown until the night of 4–5 June.[19]

Meanwhile, the counterattacks on the German bridgeheads across the Somme were continuing. General Altmayer's 10th Army had now taken over the Abbeville sector of the Somme front. On 3 June, the Assault Brigade with forty-three Breguets and forty fighters, was put at his disposition, for a further assault on the Abbeville bridgehead planned for 4 June. The army commander was also told that a further fifty bombers and 100 fighters were available for more general support. 'What am I to do with all this aviation? I've already got more than sufficient artillery,' he is reputed to have replied.[20] Altmayer made no attempt to call upon the resources put at his disposal either before or during his counterattack. Altmayer can hardly be blamed. The Army had always insisted bombers did not have an important role to play on the battlefield. At the top of the Army command structure, Weygand and Georges may have come to appreciate that ideas had to change but it was expecting a lot of Altmayer to enthusiastically embrace this use of air power overnight. Although the French counterattacks reduced the size of the German bridgeheads, none were eliminated, so strategically, the attacks were failures.

While the French troops along the Somme and Aisne awaited the German offensive, in the rear, a threat of a different kind was causing far more concern. On the first two days of June, the Luftwaffe launched a series of powerful raids against targets in the Rhône valley, including industrial targets around Lyon and the port of Marseilles, where reinforcements were arriving from North Africa. It was a timely reminder to the French that they dare not reduce their aerial defences in the rear. Even more disturbing was the mounting evidence that the Germans were planning a major air assault on the French capital. For Parisians, this was a much greater threat than the panzers just sixty miles away. For Vuillemin too, the danger was still in the rear. On 29 May, he made it very clear to d'Astier that the defence of Paris had to have priority over support for the armies at the front.[21]

The danger to Paris was far more acute than it had been a few weeks before. The Germans were not quite as near to Paris as they had been in 1918, but the speed of modern bombers meant that the capital was little more than fifteen minutes flying time from the front. Before 10 May, the Bf 109E had not been capable of reaching the Paris area; now, it could escort German bombers all the way with ease. With the world still stunned by the destruction of Rotterdam, the French believed they had good reason to be worried. For French civilians and government, the moment of truth was at hand.

French intelligence was correct. 'Operation Paula' was never intended as a pure terror raid—the targets were military rather than civilian—but the Germans hoped an attack on Paris would shake French morale. Targets included communication centres, airfields, and factories. Targeting factories scarcely suggested that the German High Command were entirely convinced they would soon be in their hands. About 500 German bombers, escorted by an equal number of fighters, would take part in the raid.

For some time, both *Groupements* 21 and 23 had been on standby for the expected Luftwaffe attack. *Groupement* 22 in the east had also been told that it should try and intercept German formations as they headed back towards Germany. The Potez 631 squadrons would try and follow the bombers and report their positions. Ground controllers, using the Eiffel tower radio mast, would transmit instructions to the fighter squadrons. The Dewoitine D.520 groups would tackle the German escorts, while other fighters would concentrate on the bombers. With only fifty serviceable Dewoitine D.520s, it was a daunting task.

Soon after midday on 3 June, the raids began on targets in and around Paris as well as airfields well beyond Paris. The Potez 631s did what they could but the scrambling fighter squadrons were always going to be desperately short of time and their task was complicated by the Germans jamming the instructions from the ground controller. GCs III/1 and II/1 both had to take off amid falling bombs. GCs I/1 and II/9 were both caught by enemy fighters as they climbed towards the bombers and eight of their Bloch fighters were shot down. The Moranes of GC III/7 once more found they lacked the speed to catch the German bombers, and were then set upon by German escorts. By good fortune, the arrival of the Dewoitines of GC I/3 enabled them to escape. GCs I/5, I/6, and I/8 spotted bomber formations but found it difficult to break through the German escorts. To the west of Paris, three Polish pilots from GC I/145, flying their unsafe Caudron C.714s, entered the fray claiming three Bf 109s, but they too failed to get through to the bombers. Four pilots from the Belgian Air Force unit GC II/2, still flying their Fiat CR.42 biplanes, gamely attempted to stop Do 17s attacking their airfield at Chartres, and contributed to five of the attacking Dorniers returning badly damaged. Seventeen French fighters were lost, thirteen pilots were killed, and eight were seriously wounded. They claimed seventeen certain victories, although the Luftwaffe lost just seven fighters and only four bombers. In the air, it was another emphatic victory for the German fighter force.[22, 23]

However, the raid itself achieved little. Only five aircraft were destroyed and four damaged at the thirteen airfields bombed. About 250 Frenchmen lost their lives in the attack.[24, 25] While heavy, these casualties were not on the cataclysmic scale predicted by so many experts before the war. There was no panic or public disorder in the streets of Paris and no extra pressure on the government to seek an end to the war. The threat that had dominated and distorted French thinking for two decades had finally materialised, and while it was by no means an empty threat, it was far more manageable than the prophets of doom had predicted. In the overall scheme of things, the much-feared bomber threat turned out to be irrelevant. The fate of France would be decided on the Somme and Aisne battlefields, not in the skies above her cities; on those battlefields, the Army would need the cheaper light bombers that could have been built instead of large expensive planes that the long-range deterrent bomber force required.

This was still not so easy to see at the time. It was not easy to switch mindset in a matter of days. The Paris raid and others in the rear ensured the French still kept back strong fighter forces. The principal task of four Bloch groups and GC I/145 remained the defence of the capital and Lower Seine. At Lyon, there was a semi-operational Polish group created from pilots awaiting transfer to front line squadrons, which offered some protection for the area, but it was still felt necessary to keep GC III/9 there. GC II/7, one of the few Dewoitine D.520 groups, and GC II/2 were based well to the south of the Aisne line, covering the Dijon and Tours regions. GC III/6, converting to the Dewoitine D.520, provided some protection for Marseilles, but it was still felt necessary to have GC III/1 there too. More than twenty light defence flights were also covering targets in the rear.

There were good reasons for covering the rear. Reinforcements arriving from North Africa via Marseilles were very worthy candidates for protection and the desperate shortage of planes made it difficult to leave aircraft factories undefended. Nevertheless, it was not in the rear that the fate of France would be decided. If the front line held for a week and every French factory in the rear had been destroyed, France would still be in the war. If the line did not hold, it did not matter how many factories were building aircraft. Indeed, if the Luftwaffe could be persuaded to bomb French factories rather than the French Army, France's chances of survival would be considerably improved. It was a mistake the German High Command was unlikely to make. Guarding against this potential threat, however, was also a mistake. The French could not understand why, at such a critical stage, the British were holding back 600 fighters in the UK to meet an attack that had not so far materialised. France had more reason to fear bombing attacks—her cities and towns were being bombed—but they were just as guilty of holding fighters back. To survive, the French had to take chances, and one chance was to leave the rear exposed and focus all air effort on holding the front line. French fighter units were not well placed to do this. Once the German offensive was underway, the French would have to get as many fighters over the front as quickly as possible, if they were to have any chance of halting the Wehrmacht juggernaut.

As far as retaliation was concerned, the French were not quite as helpless as they had been in 1918. All medium and heavy French bombers had been designed with Berlin in mind as the principal target. Ironically, now that retaliation was required, they were far too valuable tactically to squander on a long-range bombing offensive. The two Farman F.222 groups were ordered to bomb Munich and seven sorties were flown on the night of the 3rd–4th.[26] The following night, seven LeO 451s joined four Farmans for a second attack on Munich.[27] Retaliation against the German capital itself was left in the hands of the Navy. Its sole Farman F.223.4 long-range reconnaissance bomber had the remarkable ability to carry 2,000 kg of bombs along the Channel, North Sea, and Baltic coasts and then south to Berlin. The Germans were taken completely by surprise, both by the raid itself and the direction from which it came. There were no blackout precautions and the French crew found their target with little difficulty.[28]

The raid was only a gesture, but this was all that was required. The next day, the French press were able to lift the morale of the nation with a slightly exaggerated account of how a formation of naval bombers had struck the German capital and neutral embassies were certainly able to confirm an attack had taken place. After all the effort that had gone into the creation of a bomber force capable of attacking the German capital, a single long-range bomber, and a naval one at that, was all that was needed to satisfy French honour.

Meanwhile, the Germans were preparing to launch the offensive that would decide the fate of France. French reconnaissance planes did a fairly good job of identifying where the Germans were concentrating for the attack. It seems only around a dozen sorties a day were flown, and with fighters on standby to meet the expected attack on Paris, most of these missions were unescorted, but only four reconnaissance planes lost in the first four days of June. The densest concentrations of tanks were identified in the Péronne region with smaller groupings spotted around Amiens.[29, 30] With these threatening Paris directly, there was little doubt in French minds that this was where the greatest danger lay.

The German plan did not involve any great tactical or strategic novelty. The ten available German panzer divisions were divided equally between the five proposed lines of advance. On 5 June, three of these would strike westwards from Abbeville, Amiens, and Péronne. The French would be forced to commit their reserves to counter these thrusts. Then, after three days, the Germans would use their remaining two armoured corps to strike south across the Aisne from the Rethel region.

The German attack again involved intensive use of level and dive-bombers over the French front line, but this time, there was no repeat of the panic on the Meuse. The French troops now knew what to expect and tenaciously resisted the German advance. All the available light and assault bombers were thrown against the advancing panzers. The sixty-eight Breguets, Martins, and Douglas bombers focused their efforts on the roads leading west from the

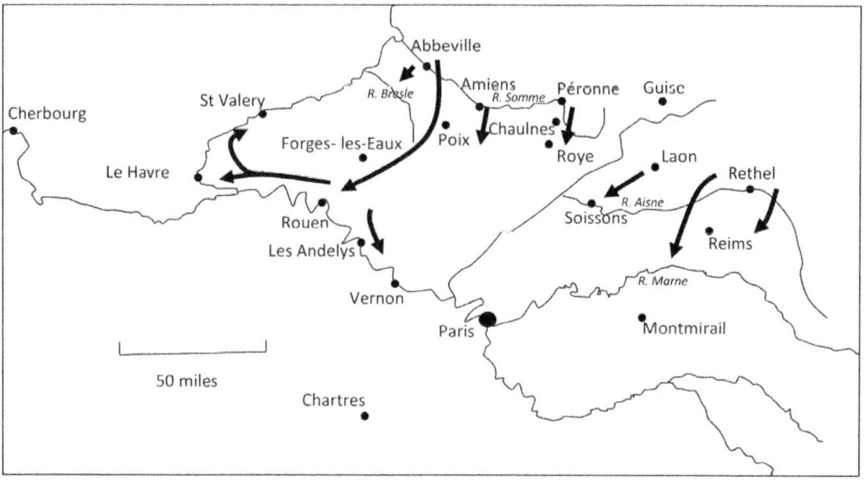

German offensive, June 1940.

Péronne bridgehead southwards to Chaulnes, but when fighter escorts were not available, the results were disastrous. An escorted early morning strike by ten Breguets suffered no losses but a second strike at 9 a.m. was savaged by Bf 109s, with nine out of the twelve Breguets shot down. A formidable force of D.520s, Bloch MB.152s, and H75s was assembled to cover more Breguet attacks in the afternoon and evening. The fighters did their job, and no more Breguets were lost. Twelve ground-strafing Moranes joined these attacks, losing two to ground fire, but it was still a tactic Vuillemin was very reluctant to use.[31, 32]

As soon as it became clear the northern front was bearing the brunt of the new offensive, four fighter groups (GCs II/2, II/5, II/7, and II/6) were ordered to support the fighters on the Somme front. GCs II/2, II/5, and II/7 were heavily involved in the afternoon escort missions, the Moranes of GC II/2 joining in the strafing attacks. GC II/6 at the Châteauroux Bloch factory did not get involved over the front until the next day. The Bloch groups defending Paris were operating over the front but both GC II/10 and III/10 were held back to cover the Lower Seine. This was now much closer to the fighting than it had been on 10 May, but it was not where the fate of France was being decided. GC II/10 was in action, shooting down three Heinkels in an early morning raid on Rouen and a couple of Ju 88s in an evening raid, but GC III/10 did not encounter a single German plane throughout the course of the day. It was not sensible to have a fighter group idle while an unescorted Breguet attack was being decimated by Messerschmitts.

During the 5th, French fighters flew 487 sorties, the highest number on any day of the campaign to date. Even so, it was still far from an all-out effort. Two pilots from GC II/10 flew five sorties during the day, which was the level of intensity the crisis required, but along the entire front, an average of only one sortie was flown for each serviceable plane. It was the most successful day for the French, with pilots claiming fifty-two confirmed victories. In fact, the Luftwaffe lost forty planes, of which twenty-two were bombers. However, nearly all the bombers had been lost in the rear, especially in the fierce clashes with Bloch MB.152s and RAF Hurricanes over Rouen. Over the front, where French troops were under constant attack, French fighters did not have the same success. Curtiss H75s claimed a couple of Henschel Hs 126 observation planes and the Moranes of GC I/6 shot down two Hs 123 ground-attack planes, but that was about it. The Luftwaffe lost just a single Stuka during the course of the day, and this was a victim of anti-aircraft fire.[33] The French fighter force was not succeeding where it was needed. It was low over the battlefield the fighters could make a difference, not deep in the rear over Rouen.

At the end of the day, the French front south of Amiens was still fairly secure. Many of the strong points had been surrounded but these were still holding out. One of the final missions flown by the Air Force was the dropping of supplies to encircled French units to the south-west of Péronne. Further north, the situation was more worrying. South of Abbeville, Rommel had advanced 6 miles against weakening opposition. This was now where air support was urgently needed, but neither Weygand nor Altmayer were aware of how serious the situation was becoming. It seems very few missions were flown by reconnaissance groups, apparently because there were no fighters to escort them.[34] Only two planes from reconnaissance groups were actually lost, and perhaps more should have been risked. The reconnaissance was most needed on the Abbeville sector, not so far from the unused Bloch group defending Rouen. Escorting reconnaissance planes would have been another more useful way of using the Bloch group.

On the 6th, the number of fighter sorties flown fell by nearly a half. Why is not entirely clear, the number of serviceable planes available was about the same as the previous day. French bombers continued to focus on the Chaulnes and Roye area. The lack of fighter cover proved disastrous for the LeO 451 groups. Ten of the twenty-four dispatched failed to return, all the victims of Bf 109s. The escorted Martin 167s, Breguets, and Douglas DB-7s were doing much better, flying around ninety sorties and losing five. The lack of fighter cover did not help but it was also clear to d'Astier that the LeO 451 was simply not a suitable bomber for tactical air support; the American Douglas and Martin bombers were 'infinitely more suitable'.[35] D'Astier felt that he had no choice but to use the LeO bombers by night, or at least late evening when the gathering gloom provided some cover.

The French fighter force lost sixteen fighters on the 6th, the Luftwaffe fourteen. In the struggle between the two fighter arms, the French might seem to be holding their own. In the context of a long-term battle for aerial superiority, fought independently of ground operations, these losses would not have been cause for too much concern. However, in the context of the battle being fought on the ground, this superficial parity was irrelevant. The German fighter force was enabling the Luftwaffe to operate with freedom. Luftwaffe bomber and reconnaissance losses were negligible. Not one of the Stukas pounding the French was lost. French fighters were not enabling their own Air Force to operate with freedom. German domination of the skies was increasingly apparent to the troops on the ground. A French counterattack by an under-strength 1st Armoured Division towards Chaulnes brought some relief to the defenders, but air cover was totally lacking and Stukas inflicted heavy losses on the tanks.[36]

Even more serious was that French reconnaissance was not picking up the danger further north. By the end of the day, Rommel had reached Poix and was poised to outflank both the Franco-British force holding the River Bresle to the north and the 7th Army still containing the German attempts to break out of the Amiens and Péronne bridgeheads. How many reconnaissance sorties were flown is not clear, but it was not German defences creating an insurmountable obstacle; only one French reconnaissance plane was lost along the entire front. Despite the fierce struggle taking place just sixty miles to the east, the two Bloch units on the Lower Seine remained idle.

On the 7th, most of the 100-odd bombing sorties were again flown in the region around Roye. Although it was becoming clear there was a problem further north, the only French Air Force bomber operation in the area was a raid by half a dozen Martin 167s on German columns north of Poix. By the end of the day, the Anglo-French forces north of the German advance faced encirclement on the coast and the forces further south on the Somme were also having to fall back to protect their flank.

On the 7th, the number of fighter sorties increased to around 300 as the French finally committed the two Bloch groups covering the Lower Seine, but again, Luftwaffe losses were extremely light; only five bombers failed to return. Six French pilots were killed and two wounded, but again, the fighters had failed to break through to the bombers. Ominously, the number of available French fighters dropped dramatically to around 300 as squadrons were forced to abandon bases in the path of the German advance.

By the 8th, the full magnitude of the disaster in the north had become clear to Weygand and d'Astier. Nine Breguet and twenty-one Martin bombers attacked columns heading for Rouen. For the first time, fighters were ordered to join in the attack on a large scale, with forty M.S.406s from GCs I/6, II/2, and III/7 ground strafing enemy columns around Forges-les-Eaux. It was perhaps a day too late. In the late evening, twenty LeO 451s bombed columns south of Péronne, where the line was just about holding. However, French reconnaissance was detecting concentrations of tanks further south along the Aisne, and an attack there seemed imminent. Twenty Breguets and twelve Douglas DB-7s and Martin 167s had to be used to disrupt concentrations around Soissons. Some 100 sorties spread along a 100-mile front was not enough to make a significant difference.[37, 38]

The 8th saw the most intensive use yet of the available fighters with 430 sorties flown from the 300-odd serviceable machines. However, the effect on the Luftwaffe bomber force was minimal. As an interceptor force, the French fighter groups were not having any effect on the course of the battle. In a ground-attack role, they might still make a difference. The floodgates were creaking and it was surely time to throw everything, fighters, reconnaissance planes, anything that could attack the advancing enemy. However, this was not d'Astier's way of operating. Later, he would make much of the fact that at the end of the battle, his Air Force, unlike the Army, was still a coherent fighting force, but this was not much consolation for a nation humiliated by such a rapid defeat. Nor was it an observation that was likely to be well-received by an Army under constant Stuka attack.[39]

The situation was now disintegrating fast. By the morning of the 9th, the Germans had reached the Seine and Rouen had fallen. In the south, the French had already been pushed back well beyond Soissons. The only good news was that all the bridges over the Seine had been blown and the first task of the German forces on the east bank was to complete the defeat of the Allied forces pinned to the Channel coast. However, on the 9th, the Germans opened the second phase of their offensive along the Aisne. As on the Somme, the French forces resisted fiercely, despite the pounding they were taking from the Luftwaffe. French fighter groups were rushed to the new front. The number on the Aisne front rose to eleven, leaving six on the Somme and four along the Maginot Line. Some 280 sorties were flown but efforts to disrupt the German bombing continued to bring little reward. The Caudron C.714s of the Polish GC I/145 attempted to intercept a formation of Do 17s near Rouen but the Bf 109 escort shot down three Caudrons and another five were forced down with varying degrees of damage. No Dorniers were lost. There were French victories. West of Paris, the D.520s of GC I/3 shot down six Bf 109s for the loss of just one fighter, but along the entire front, the Luftwaffe lost only six bombers.[40] Only in the close escort role were French fighters contributing, but by this time, there were few bombers to escort. The efforts of the previous four days had broken the back of the bomber force. On the 9th, only twenty-seven sorties were flown.[41]

On the 10th, the desperate situation forced the LeO 451s to return to day operations. The French had scraped together 150 tanks for a counterattack south of Rethel, but just eight LeO 451s and nine Douglas bombers could be mustered to support it. These bombed targets 5–10 miles ahead of the advancing French tanks. It was the best that could be organised in the circumstances, but such limited resources would have been more useful against the inevitable improvised anti-tank screen that once again halted the French advance. As was the case in the very first days of the campaign, when the French were trying to recapture the Moerdijk bridge in the Netherlands, this was where a small number of bombers might make a difference.

The Breguet bombers in the Rif campaign might have been able to deliver, but such close coordination could not be recreated overnight.

The remaining twenty-odd bomber sorties flown that day concentrated on the German forces already advancing well to the south-west of Reims, and the bridgeheads the Germans were already establishing across the Seine. Six ground strafing Bloch MB.152s of GC I/8 took part in the attacks on the latter, the first time the Bloch had been used for ground-attack since 18 May.[42] Again, no Blochs were lost, but this second experiment was not repeated. German fighters were constantly strafing French airfields and any other targets they came across, but this was not how d'Astier wanted to use his fighters.

By the end of the 10th, the position seemed hopeless. The Aisne line had been punctured and the forces did not exist for a serious attempt to hold the Seine. On the 11th, Paris was declared an open city and the following day, Weygand ordered his battered armies to pull back to the River Loire. The Air Force tried to buy the Army some time. Eighteen Breguets bombed bridges the Germans were constructing over the Seine at Les Andelys and Vernon while twenty-one LeO 451s attacked columns around Rethel. On the 12th, thirty-one Martin 167s bombed columns already advancing beyond Reims. On the 13th, an all-out effort was made by fifty bombers to slow down German forces sweeping past Montmirail and overtaking the retreating French forces. Even Amiot 354s, still without bombsights, were used in low-level evening attacks, but only aircraft from regular bomber groups were being used in these desperate efforts to slow down the German advance.

Most now believed the only serious military option was to evacuate as much equipment and as many men as possible to North Africa and continue the war from there. Even this became problematic when, on 10 June, Mussolini decided that the time had come for his country to take advantage of France's predicament. Fortunately for the French, the Italian entry into the war was more a political gesture than a military threat and the weak French forces remaining in the south were able to hold the half-hearted Italian attempts to advance along French Mediterranean coast.

The Panzers did not cross the Seine until the 16th, but east of Paris, eight Panzer divisions were streaming south. The rapid retreat forced squadrons to abandon equipment and unserviceable planes. By the 13th, the French only had around 150 serviceable fighters. The only protection French troops now received was from the weather, which fortunately was severely hampering the operations of both sides. By the 16th, the Germans had already reached Dijon, effectively cutting off the line of retreat of units belatedly pulling out of the Maginot Line.

The mighty French Army was doomed, but the Air Force had the mobility to flee and fight another day. Although battered and bruised, the force still had enormous potential. Losses in aircrews had been no heavier than those suffered by the RAF, and the survivors were now battle-hardened veterans of enormous value to the Allied cause. They might yet play a crucial part in North Africa and even in the battle that would surely follow in Britain.

French confidence was already being restored by the first clashes with the Italian Air Force. French pilots soon discovered that the technical superiority of planes like the D.520 over the Italian Fiat CR.42 was as great as the German Bf 109E over the M.S.406. With production facilities in France lost, the French Air Force would have to rely entirely on American imports, but these were already arriving in some numbers and the evacuation of existing stocks of planes should enable units to remain operational on French types for a while.

On the 16th, a full-scale evacuation of the French Air Force began. Groups equipped with planes like the M.S.406 and MB.152 that lacked the range to cross the Mediterranean, would continue to cover the remnants of the French Army. The five Breguet 693 groups along with three LeO 451 units and two Amiot 143 groups, also stayed, together with four reconnaissance and twenty observation squadrons.[43] Other units made their way to North Africa with whatever equipment they possessed or could lay their hands on. Many brand new machines were picked up direct from factories and flown straight to North Africa without so much as a test flight. On occasions, pilots were actually flying that particular type for the first time. Ferry pilots, instructors, and partially trained students all managed to fly valuable combat planes out of the country. Even General d'Harcourt flew a D.520 out. By the end of June, some 700 modern aircraft had been flown across the Mediterranean.[44, 45] With 300 modern planes already in North Africa, there was more than enough to keep the fourteen fighter, twenty-two bomber, and nine reconnaissance groups based there operational for a while. Doubtless far more equipment and personnel could have been evacuated, yet this was not to be. On the 22nd, the French government accepted peace terms offered by the Germans and two days later, a treaty was signed with Italy. Fighting officially ended on all fronts at 12.25 a.m. on the morning of the 25th.

Until the very end, those Air Force units that remained in France continued to oppose the German advance. At Cherbourg, French naval units, including ponderous LeO 257 floatplanes operating by day, flew against the panzers advancing on the port, but could not prevent its fall on the 19th. In the south, when weather permitted, the Breguets and LeO 451s continued to fly against German and Italian targets. On the 23rd and 24th, in one last defiant gesture, all fighter units were ordered to ground strafe German columns advancing down the Rhône valley. Three weeks earlier, such a bold move might have been more than a mere gesture. The last French victory was a Henschel 126 shot down by a pilot of GC I/2 on 24 June and the last French Air Force casualty was suffered just hours before the Armistice came into effect when S/Lt Raphenne of GC I/6 was shot down and killed while strafing German panzers just north of Valence.[46]

Conclusion

From 10 May until 11 June, the British and French air forces lost around 1,850 aircraft in combat, of which some 950 were French. Luftwaffe losses were around 1,100. These figures suggest a clear victory for the Luftwaffe, but even they give no idea of the scale of the defeat suffered by the Allied air forces. Such heavy losses, indeed even heavier losses, would have been perfectly acceptable if they had enabled the Allied armies to avoid such a total and catastrophic rout.

Most French problems stemmed from the way long-range bombing dominated French thinking at all levels, political and military. The threat the bomber posed to French cities was overestimated and what it might achieve on the battlefield underestimated. Paranoia over the long-range bomber had emerged long before the outbreak of the First World War. In 1914–1918, the needs of the front prevented this from dominating military thinking, but in peacetime, the theory and the fear were able to flourish. French politicians assumed bombing could bring swift and total defeat and ruin to their country.

The idea that bombers alone would decide future wars was a far more radical notion than the *blitzkrieg* that would eventually defeat France. The German strategy was just a restatement of the importance of mobility, with the internal combustion engine replacing the horse. Douhetism envisaged an entirely new form of warfare in which armies would be irrelevant. It is perhaps no coincidence that these theories took root most strongly in the democracies (France, Britain, and the United States) where public anxiety over aerial bombardment could find an effective political voice. In the totalitarian states (Germany, USSR, Italy, and Japan), where public opinion had less influence, more pragmatic military uses of air power prevailed.

The French are often accused of trying to fight the Second World War with the weapons and ideas of the First World War. This is true for some aspects of policy, but as far as the air war is concerned, in 1940, France needed the sort of Air Force it had in 1918. The Great War had underlined the value of aerial reconnaissance and the need for the strongest possible fighter force to enable the reconnaissance fleet to operate. The Air Division had demonstrated how effective air power could be as a flexible defensive and offensive weapon. In 1940, the French did not have enough fighters, they had no equivalent of the Air Division and were completely taken by surprise when the Luftwaffe turned their very similar VIII Air Corps on the French Army. Instead of building on the close air support tactics developed in the First World War, the French focused on developing a long-range deterrent bomber force. How fast, how far, and how many tons bombers could carry became the yardstick for measuring French air strength. Ironically, once the country was at war, it was the Ju 87, the slowest German bomber with the least range and lowest bomb load, that proved so decisive.

The French Army never believed the long-range bomber could be decisive; they had no doubts that wars would still be won or lost on the battlefield. Unfortunately, the zeal with which the Douhet-style conflict was promoted induced a scepticism within the Army about all forms of bombing, strategic and tactical. Battlefield bombing in direct support of ground forces proved to be far more effective than the generals imagined, and, more importantly, meant armies did not have to wait for artillery. The French found themselves facing a German Army that could advance far more rapidly than they believed possible. This was at least as significant as the actual damage bombing inflicted.

Yet developing a long-range bomber force was not a mistake. It might not decide the outcome of a war, but it did have huge influence in peacetime. Politicians needed the security a powerful bomber fleet provided. Bargaining positions were determined by how many bombers you had. Foreign policy was shaped by the bomber. The value of a powerful bomber fleet was amply demonstrated during the Rhineland and Sudetenland crises. Hitler got his way without firing a bullet. At the time, it did not occur to the Air Force or the politicians that the long-range bomber was not a decisive war winning weapon, that its value was political and psychological rather than military. Without fully understanding what was happening, it was difficult to see that a balance was required between what the politicians needed in peacetime and the military needed for fighting a war. Attempts to match the German bomber fleet led to far too much effort being devoted to strategic bombers at the expense of shorter-range tactical bombers. It was the latter that France would need when it came to war. They also happened to be much easier to build. The LeO 451 was not only the least effective and suffered the highest loss rate of any French bomber, but it also required far more resources to build.

The lack of trust between Army and Air Force was another major problem. Even in the tactical domain, the Army felt that in the First World War, the Air Force had tended to disregard Army needs and go its own way. The Air Force focus on independent strategic air warfare in the interwar years increased the mistrust. The more independent the Air Force became, the less the Army trusted it. The Army had good reason not to trust their sister service. Even in the May–June campaign, d'Astier tended to run air operations as he thought best, rather than as the Army wanted.

As far as the Army was concerned, centralised control meant Air Force control, and the only way the generals felt they could be sure of getting the air support they needed was to attach squadrons permanently to army units, even though this made it even more difficult to focus air effort where it was needed. Ironically, as the Army did not think tactical bombing was so important, control of the bomber force was centralised, and it could be switched to where it was required. Fighter squadrons, however, were attached to armies, which stretched available resources along the length of the front. Fears that French cities and industry would be wiped out by German bombing meant fighters also had to defend these targets. In the end, French fighter resources were stretched in two directions: along the front and deep into the French rear. Even if the French fighter force had matched the Luftwaffe in terms of quality in 1940, it would have still been at a disadvantage numerically because of the way it was dispersed.

The inability to secure local air superiority meant that the large fleet of reconnaissance planes the French had assembled, and into which so many resources had been poured, could not function. The French were quite right to emphasise the importance of reconnaissance, but a smaller reconnaissance fleet with a larger fighter force to protect it, would have enabled the French to gather more information.

On the technical side, the French fascination with large multi-seater, multi-purpose planes proved particularly unfortunate. France missed out completely on the Blenheim and Dornier Do 17 generation of bomber design and as a result, the French bomber force had nothing suitable to fly by day when war broke out. Even in the 1940 campaign, the products of the *multiplace de combat* era flew nearly as many sorties as the French bombers that were supposed to replace them. Perhaps more significantly, the low speeds expected of the turret laden bombers, meant required fighter speeds were too low, and although the BCR multi-purpose plane was abandoned in 1934, French fighter design never quite caught up with what was being achieved elsewhere.

France started rearming much later than Germany, but it was not fatally late. The mistake was the planes the French decided to build. The RAF and Luftwaffe fought the air battles of 1940 largely with planes conceived in the early thirties or upgrades of these designs. For France, this was the Amiot 340, M.S.406, Potez 63, and Mureaux 113 generation. France, however, decided these were not good enough and placed all their trust in the next generation. This was not necessary. The makeshift Potez 633 was a reasonable equivalent to bombers like the Dornier 17. The Mureaux 117 was no more obsolete than the Henschel Hs 126 the Luftwaffe used successfully. An upgraded M.S.406 could not have matched the Bf 109, but it might have been good enough. These were the only planes that France could have built in sufficient numbers in time for the 1940 campaign.

In peacetime, there was a case for waiting for the very latest designs, but once war broke out, continuing to rely on the 1936 generation became a fatal mistake. The Dewoitine D.520 and Bloch MB.174 were excellent planes that would have played an increasingly important role from mid-1940 onwards. The Martin 167 and Douglas DB-7 did go on to have very successful careers with the RAF. They were all capable of making some contribution in the spring of 1940, but it was too soon to be relying on them. New planes invariably have teething problems and aircrews need time to become familiar with them. In the end, the Dewoitine D.520 was no more successful than the Curtiss H75, because the H75 pilots had learned how to get the best out of their fighters. Fighter production plummeted when the M.S.406 was phased out. The Potez 633 was easy to build and could have been built in large numbers. In the end, France fell between two stools: it did not have enough combat planes of either the old or the new generation.

Even with the resources that were available in 1940, the French could have done better. No battle is lost before a shot is fired. On the ground, there were opportunities for the French to rescue the situation even after the breakthrough at Sedan. Once it was obvious how serious the situation was, there was plenty of urgency, but little flair or improvisation. During the 1918 crises, doctrine had been ditched and instinct took over. Fighters and reconnaissance planes, as well as bombers, were thrown into the ground-attack role, regardless of doctrine. In 1940, everything was done by the book. Tremendous risks were taken by committing large ungainly multi-seaters and floatplane bombers to daylight operations. Frantic efforts were made to make obsolete long-range bombers available for operations, but there was no thought about how smaller, more manoeuvrable fighters or reconnaissance planes might be used for ground-attack. A striking feature of the campaign was how obsolete biplanes like the Henschel Hs 123 and Fokker C.V could be used for ground-attack, provided they were not expected to attack targets far beyond the front line. The way French aircraft were used was determined by what they were designed to do rather than what they might be capable of doing. The French had far more useable planes than they imagined but the lure of the ultra-modern that had led them to reject the 1934 generation of combat planes also blinded the French to how even older equipment might make a contribution.

The strange contrast between frenzy and inaction was another striking feature of the French reaction to the crisis. Rear defence flights were formed and squadrons converted to new equipment in days, but elsewhere, trained foreign and French aircrews were left kicking their heels with nothing to fly. Army and Air Force commanders called for maximum effort, but at the height of the battle, some units remained unused and with those that did operate, sortie rates throughout the campaign were low by comparison with other Allied and enemy air forces. D'Astier placed too much emphasis on using his squadrons in a controlled, measured way, but in some ways, it was too measured. He insisted that available planes had to be used correctly, when the crisis facing the French demanded a more radical approach. The way any combat planes are used has to depend on the situation and how what is available can make a contribution rather than peacetime practice, doctrine and theories about how planes ought to be used.

Much is often made of various quotes which seem to prove that French Army generals did not understand the importance of air power. Although they underestimated the value of close air support, they never doubted the need for a powerful air force. The Army's fierce fight to retain control of the Air Force is proof of that. Many of the quotes were provoked by frustration at the constant talk of bombers deciding wars on their own. The expressions '*lutte aérienne*' or '*bataille aérienne*', were standard ways of describing the Douhetian aerial struggle. Those who use these quotes tend to confuse these references to battles fought by opposing bomber fleets, with the battle for air superiority fought by rival fighter forces. It was the former the Army opposed, not the latter. On hearing the dreaded Douhetian '*bataille aérienne*' mentioned yet again at a lecture in the summer of 1939, a frustrated Gamelin famously interrupted to point out that 'There is no such thing as the "aerial battle", there is only the battle on land.'[1] This did not mean he saw no need for fighters to secure the skies above the battlefield. He was just objecting to the idea that bombing cities wins wars. He was right. The Second World War was decided on the battlefield by all arms working together, not by air forces fighting their own independent bombing war.

The French Air Force failed in 1940, not so much because it was stuck in the past, but because it had been seduced by radical and unproven theories on the way air power would develop in the future. In the process, it forgot how it had used air power successfully in the First World War. France was not alone. For most of the interwar years even the German military did not believe bombers were a battlefield weapon. Initially, the fighter force had a low priority in the new Luftwaffe. Both Germany and France began revising their ideas about the same time. Crucially, the Germans had the experience in Spain and Poland to speed up the process. Even so, in 1940, the gap was not as wide as it might appear. As Liddell Hart put it, the German Army was successful not because 'it was overwhelming in strength or thoroughly modern in form, but because it was a few vital degrees more advanced than its opponents'.[2] With their superior tanks and growing appreciation of tactical air support, the French were arguably more than a just few degrees ahead of their British ally. In June 1940, French Army and Air Force commanders were a lot closer to understanding what was required to defeat the German Wehrmacht than their British counterparts. The loss of this expertise was as big a blow to the Allied cause as the lost manpower resources and industrial capacity. If France had managed to hang on, the war would have been won a lot sooner.

APPENDIX I

French Re-equipment/ Expansion Plans

<table>
<tr><th></th><th>Actual, 1918</th><th>Ideal Air Force, 1924</th><th>Planned 186 Sqn, 1924</th><th>Plan I (metropole), 1933</th><th>Denain's 1935 Plan</th></tr>
<tr><td>Single-seater day fighter</td><td>1,182 + 285 rear defence</td><td>1,050</td><td>580</td><td>180</td><td rowspan="3">320</td></tr>
<tr><td>Night fighter</td><td></td><td>375</td><td>120</td><td></td></tr>
<tr><td>Two-seater fighter single-engined</td><td>18</td><td></td><td></td><td>70</td></tr>
<tr><td>Twin-engined multi-seater-fighter</td><td>90</td><td></td><td></td><td>80 (BCR)</td><td>80</td></tr>
<tr><td>Reconnaissance</td><td>205</td><td rowspan="2">1,400</td><td rowspan="2">540</td><td>240 (BCR)</td><td>30</td></tr>
<tr><td>Observation</td><td>1,340</td><td></td><td>114</td></tr>
<tr><td>Single-engined reconnaissance bomber</td><td></td><td></td><td></td><td></td><td>115</td></tr>
<tr><td>Dive bomber</td><td></td><td></td><td></td><td></td><td>20</td></tr>
<tr><td>Assault bomber</td><td></td><td rowspan="4">1,200</td><td></td><td></td><td>20</td></tr>
<tr><td>Light bomber</td><td></td><td rowspan="3">180</td><td></td><td></td></tr>
<tr><td>Single-engined medium day bomber</td><td>225</td><td></td><td></td></tr>
<tr><td>Twin-engined medium bomber</td><td></td><td>120 (BCR)</td><td>289</td></tr>
<tr><td>Heavy bomber night</td><td>245</td><td>1,200</td><td>440</td><td>120</td><td>15</td></tr>
<tr><td>Very heavy</td><td></td><td></td><td></td><td>16</td><td></td></tr>
<tr><td>Hydro-bomber</td><td></td><td></td><td></td><td></td><td>17</td></tr>
<tr><td>Total</td><td>3,590</td><td>5,225</td><td>1,860</td><td>826</td><td>1,020</td></tr>
</table>

Plan II (metropole), 1936	Plan V, March 1938	Plan V reinforced, March 1939	Plan VI, March 1940	Theoretical, May 1940	Actual, 10 May 1940
252	960	900	1500	714	724
	38	90	90	60	58
72	85	225	180	16	17
108	168	252	168	169	156
342	468	450	720	418	380
	108	72			
	72	72	288	65	0
	276	276	216	117	0
420	264	396	240	182	26
24	24	24		26	78
24	12	12			
1,242	2,475	2,769	3.402	1,767	1,439

APPENDIX II

Aircraft Performance

Unless otherwise stated, mg refers to 0.303-calibre machine guns.

Fighters				
	Prototype first flight	Engine	Speed (mph) at altitude (ft)	Range (miles)/ endurance (hours)
Morane-Saulnier N	01/06/1914	80 hp le Rhône 9C	96/10,000	1.75 hours
Nieuport 11	1915	80 hp Gnome	97/0	2.5 hours
Fokker E-1	1915	80 hp Oberursel	82	1.5 hours
Nieuport 17	1916	110 hp Le Rhône 9J	107/6,500	2 hours
SPAD S.VII	1916	150 hp Hispano-Suiza 8Aa	120/6,500	2.25 hours
Morane-Saulnier MoS. 27	1917	150-hp Gnome 9N	135/9,800	1.75 hours
SPAD S.XIII	04/04/1917	200-hp Hispano-Suiza 8b	130/6,500	2 hours
Nieuport 29	1918	300-hp Hispano-Suiza 8 Fb	147/0	2.5 hours
Nieuport-Delage 42	1924	500-hp Hispano-Suiza 12Ha	154/16,400	400 miles
Morane-Saulnier M.S.225	1932	440 hp Gnome-Rhône 9K	203/16,400	435 miles
Dewoitine D.500	18/06/1932	690-hp Hispano-Suiza 12X	223/13,120	534 miles
Dewoitine D.510	14/08/1934	860-hp Hispano-Suiza 12Y31	244/13,120	373 miles
Curtiss H75 A-2	1935	1,050-hp Pratt & Whitney R-1830-S1C3-	303/10,000	677 miles

Climb to (ft/min-sec)	Ceiling (ft)	Empty weight (lb)	Loaded weight (lb)	Wing area (sq ft)	Armament
10,000/12	13,000	633	976	118	1 mg
9,800/18	15,000	759	1,210	140	1 mg
6,500/20	10,000	788	1,239	172	1 mg
10,000/9	17,400	825	1,233	160	1/2 mg
9.800/11-30	18,000	1,100	1,550	192	1 mg
9,800/7-25	27,000	926	1,428	144	1 mg
9,800/8-75	22,300	1,225	1,815	215	2 mg
9,800/7-35	25, 300	1,874	2,433	283	2 mg
16,400/14-34	26,200	3,040	4,000	332	4 mg
16,400/10-07	31, 170	2,544	3,485	185	2 mg
13,120/5-11	36,100	2,837	3,770	178	2/4 mg
13,120/5-30	34,450	3,298	4,253	178	2 mg and 1 × 20-mm cannon
15,000/4-54	33,000	4,620	5,996	236	4/6 mg

Messerschmitt Bf 109B	29/05/1935	680-hp Jumo 210D	289/13,120	430 miles
Morane-Saulnier M.S.406	08/08/1935	860-hp Hispano-Suiza 12Y31	302/16,000	497 miles
Potez 631	01/04/1936	2 × 660-hp Gnome-Rhône 14M	277/13,120	2.5 hours
Messerschmitt Bf 110C	12/05/1936	2 × 1,100-hp Daimler-Benz 601A	349/22,965	565 miles
Bloch MB-151	01/10/1937	920-hp Gnome-Rhône 14N35	301/13,120	398 miles
Messerschmitt Bf 109E	Summer 1938	1,100-hp Daimler Benz DB 601A	354/12,300	412 miles
Dewoitine D520	02/10/1938	910 hp Hispano-Suiza 12Y45	329/19,685	777 miles
Bloch MB.152	01/12/1938	1,080-hp Gnome-Rhône 14N49	320/13,120	373 miles
Arsenal VG- 33	Spring 1939	860-hp Hispano-Suiza 12Y31	347/17,060	745 miles
Dewoitine D.551 (predicted)	23/06/1939	1,100-hp Hispan-Suiza 12Y51	411/19,700	

Bombers			
	Prototype first flight	Engine	Speed (mph) at altitude (ft)
Voisin III	1914	130-hp Salmson (canton-Unne) 9M	76/0
Breguet-Michelin 4	1914	200-hp Renault 8G	83/0
Farman F.60	01/1919	2 × 260-hp Salmson CM9	100/0
Liore et Olivier LeO 20	1927	2 × 480-hp Gnome-Rhône 9A	119/9,800
Farman F.222	26/05/1932	4 x 950-hp Gnome- Rhône 14N	199/13,120
Amiot 143	August 1934	2 × 900-hp Gnome-Rhône 14K	188/13,120

19,685/ 9-48	26,900	3,318	4,740	174	2 mg
16,400/ 6-0	30,800	4,189	5,364	172	2 mg 1 × 20-mm cannon
13,120/9	29,500	6,526	9,921	352	2 × 20-mm cannon 4 mg fixed 2 mg moveable
18,000/ 8-30	32,000	11,466	14,884	413	2 × 20-mm cannon 4 mg mixed 1 mg moveable
16,400/7	32,800	4,374	5,706	161	4 mg
16,500/ 6-12	36,000	4,421	5,523	174	2 mg 2 × 20-mm cannon
13,120/ 4-0	36,090	4,608	6,129	172	4 mg 1 × 20-mm cannon
16,400/6	32,800	4,453	5,908	161	2 mg and 2 × 20-mm cannon
	36.090	4,519	5,856	151	4 mg and 1 × 20-mm cannon
19,700/5-08	38,200		4,740	118	1 × 20-mm cannon and 6 mg

Range (miles)/ endurance (hours)	Ceiling (ft)	Empty weight (lb)	Loaded weight (lb)	Wing area (sq ft)	Bomb load (lb)/ armament
300 miles	11,485	2,094	2,976	534	460 1–2 mg
248 miles		2,557	3,384	581	600 1–2 mg
800 miles	15,400	6,283	11,450	1,735	3,477 3 mg
620 miles	18,000	5,840	11,850	1,138	2,200 4 mg
1,240 miles	26.250	23,122	41,226	2,002	9,260 3 mg
750 miles	25,000	13,526	21,970	1,034	4,000 5 mg

Bloch MB.200	26/06/1933	2 × 900-hp Gnome-Rhône 14K	181/13,120
Potez 540	14/11/1933	2 × 690-hp Hispano-Suiza 12X	196/13,120
Dornier Do 17 Z-2	1934	2 × 940-hp Bramo Fafnir 323 P	255/13,120
Bloch MB.210	23/11/1934	2 × 1,030-hp Gnome-Rhône 14N20/21	201/13,120
Lioré et Olivier LeO 451	16/01/1937	2 × 1,060-hp Gnome-Rhône 14N48/49	292/16,400
Bristol Blenheim IV	24/9/1937	2 × 920-hp Mercury XV	266
Amiot 354	06/12/1937	2 × 1,060-hp Gnome-Rhône 14N48/49	298/13,120

Tactical reconnaissance/ground-attack			
	Prototype first flight	Engine	Speed (mph) at altitude (ft)
Breguet 14	21/11/1916	300-hp Renault 12 Fey	121/0
Breguet 19	01/03/1922	550-hp Renault 12Kc	149/0
Fokker C.V	01/05/1924	650-hp Rolls-Royce Kestrel	155
Potez 25	1925	450-hp Lorraine 12Ed	137/0
Mureaux 115	1931	860-hp Hispano-Suiza 12Y-31	210
Junkers Ju 87 B-2	1935	1,200-hp Jumo D	237/13,120
Henschel Hs 123	08/05/1935	870-hp BMW 132Dc	212/3,940
Henschel Hs 126	1936	830-hp BMW Bramo Fafnir 323 A-1	221/9,840
Chance-Vought 156F	04/01/1936	825-hp Pratt & Whitney Twin Wasp Junior	251
Westland Lysander	16/06/1936	890-hp Mercury XII	229/10,000

620 miles	26,400	8,570	15,730	721	2,645 6 mg
790 miles	34, 500	8,444	12,844	819	1,102 6 mg
720 miles	22,965	11,484	18,931	592	2,205 6 mg
1,210 miles	32,000	12,540	21,120	829	4,410 6 mg
1,530 miles	22,000	16,437	24,350	732	4,470 1 × 20 mm cannon, 2 mg
1,460 miles	22,000	8,700	13,400	469	1,000 4 mg
1,553 miles	32,810	10,417	24,912	721	2,200 1 × 20 mm cannon 2 mg

Range (miles)	Ceiling (ft)	Empty weight (lb)	Loaded weight (lb)	Wing area (sq ft)	Bomb load (lb)/ armament
300	14,000	2,280	3,480	550	500 2–3 mg
500	25,600	3,273	5,093	538	3–4 mg
500	21,330	4,233		423	440 3 mg (two fixed) 2 fixed
410	23,000	2,641	5,512	506	440 3 mg
620	32,800	3,874	6,360	375	440 1 × 20 mm cannon 4 mg (2 fixed)
370	26,000	6,051	9,336	343	1,102 3 × mg (2 fixed)
534	29,525	3,316	4,888	267	440 2 x mg (fixed)
360	27,000	4,480	7,209	340	330 2 mg (one fixed)
630	27,500	4,713	6,379		1,000 2 mg (1 fixed)
600	26,000	4,065	5,920	260	500 3 mg

Bloch MB.131	16/08/1936	2 × 910-hp Gnome-Rhône 14N10	217/13,120	
Potez 633	1937	2 × 660-hp Gnome Rhone 14M	273/13,780	
Loire-Nieuport LN401	1938	690-hp Hispano-Suiza 12X	236/13,100	
Bloch MB.174	15/02/1938	2 × 1,060-hp Gnome-Rhône 14N48/49	329/17.060	
Breguet 693	23/03/1938	2 × 660-hp Gnome-Rhône 14M	304/16,000	
Douglas DB-7	26/10/1938	2 × 1,050-hp Pratt & Whitney R-1830-SC3G	305	
Potez 63.11	31/12/1938	2 × 660-hp Gnome-Rhône 14M	264/18,050	
Martin 167	14/03/1939	2 × 1,050-hp Pratt & Whitney R-1830-SC3G	294/13,000	

Naval planes				
	Prototype first flight	Engine	Speed (mph) at altitude(ft)	
Lioré et Olivier H-257bis	07/07/1932	2 × 870-hp Gnome-Rhône 14K	118/0	
Latécoère 298	08/05/1936	860-hp Hispano-Suiza 12Y31	180/6,560	
Loire-Nieuport LN 411	01/06/1938	670-hp Hispano-Suiza HS12X	236/13,120	

800	23,800	10,340	17,438	581	500 3 mg
810	26,250	6,393	9,436	352	880 2 mg
746	31,168	4,945	6,250	266	496 1 × 20 mm cannon 2 mg (fixed)
800	36,100	12,346	15,784	409	880 7 mg
790	27,900	6,403	10,614	313	880 3 × mg (1 fixed) 1 × 20 mm cannon
462	31,650	11,400	15,150	465	1,000 6 mg (four fixed)
932	27,900	6,911	9,987	352	440 3-10 mg
1,870	27,200	11,000	17,890	452	1,800 6 mg (four fixed)

Range (miles)	Ceiling (ft)	Empty weight (lb)	Loaded weight (lb)	Wing area (sq ft)	Bomb load (lb)/ armament
745	26,000	12,370	22,530	1,440	1,900 3 mg
500	21,325	6,750	10,140	340	1,100 3 mg
746	31,168	4,945	6,250	266	500 1 × 20 mm cannon 2 mg

APPENDIX III

French Aircraft Deliveries 1936–1940

1936	Jan.	Feb.	Mar.	Apr.	May	Jun.	Jul.	Aug.	Sept.	Oct.	Nov.	Dec.	To
Dewoitine D.500/501	38	23	10	17	3	1	0	11	9	9	9	2	13
Dewoitine D.510										9	2	14	2
Bloch MB.200	12	2	1	14	13	5	6						5
Bloch MB.210				2				1		5	7	10	2
Amiot 143				15	10	14	14	11	4	4			7
Potez 540	5	15	18	11	15	16	5	5	8	9	11	3	12
Mureaux 113/117	18	13	16	3							7	12	6
Loire 46						1				8	5	8	2
Farman F.221						2	1		2	2	1	1	9
LeO 257bis					4	4	4		5	3			2
Total	73	53	45	62	45	43	30	28	28	49	42	50	54

1937	Jan.	Feb.	Mar.	Apr.	May	Jun.	Jul.	Aug.	Sept.	Oct.	Nov.	Dec.	Tot
Dewoitine D.510					3	2	2		12	7	3		2
Dewoitine D.371		5	5	7	1								1
Bloch MB.210	9	7	10	8	15	11	11	6	10	9	14	14	12
Amiot 143											4	5	9
Potez 540	11	7	8	-	2	5	8	4	5	8	4	4	6
Mureaux 117	10												1
Loire 46	-	8	7	5	11	5	2						3
Farman F.221/2	1	-	-	2	3	2	2	-	1	1	-	4	1
Spad 510			1	2	12	8	17	16	3	1			6
Total	31	27	31	24	47	33	42	26	31	26	25	27	37

938	Jan.	Feb.	Mar.	Apr.	May	Jun.	Jul.	Aug.	Sept.	Oct.	Nov.	Dec.	Total
.S.406				2	1	2	4	-	3	4	7	4	27
.510	2	9	11	6	3	3							34
otez 30/631					4	-	5	2	14	16	16	16	73
loch B.210	18	6	12	5	9	12	10	6	7	7	2	3	97
miot 143	6	5	5	-	3								19
arman .222	2	4	3	4	5	1	1						20
loch B.131					1	5	3	-	2	14	15	15	55
otez 540	4	1	1										6
ureaux 117	-	-	18	2	13	14	7	4	9	1	1	1	70
otal	32	25	50	19	39	37	30	12	35	42	41	39	401

939	Jan.	Feb.	Mar.	Apr.	May	Jun.	Jul.	Aug.	Sept.	Oct.	Nov.	Dec.	Total
.S.406	25	20	34	60	95	101	63	147	132	103	83	69	932
loch MB.151/ B.152			2	5	5	3	50	58	91	85	66	50	415
otez 63	25	27	48	38	58	50	20	14	52	76	68	65	541*
loch MB.210	2	2	1	1									6
arman F.222						2	1	2					5
loch MB.131	21	22	22	9	6	2	2						84
ureaux 117					2	3	4	9					18
urtiss H75		16	30	36	17	5	34	38	24				200
reguet 691						3		7	6	7	12	13	48
eO 451							3	8	6	12	18	19	66
miot 350												6	6
loch MB.174												1	1
otal	73	87	137	149	183	169	177	283	311	283	247	223	2322

*Includes eighty-four Potez 630, 206 Potex 631, thirty-six Potex 633, and sixty-one Potez 637.

1940	Jan.	Feb.	Mar.	Apr.	May	Total to 31/5/40	Jun. **	Comments
M.S.406	41	42	26	7	9	1,084	4	
Bloch MB.150 series	5	1	71	72	55	619 (incl. MB.151)	72	140 Bl.151, 200 Bl.15 2 (GR 14N25), 88 Bl.152 (GR 14N49 but substandard 200 Bl.152 (GR 14N49 bon de guerre), 9 Bl.155
Curtiss H75				6	51	257	50	
Caudron C.714	1	8	28	15	1	53	3	
Dewoitine D.520	12	27	12	31	146	228	196	
Arsenal VG-33					3	3	6	
Potez 63	69	63	130	96	85	1,057	42	85 P. 630, 208, P.631, 37 P.633, 61 P.637, 723 P.63.11
Martin 167F		11	33	69	53	166	27	223 arrived in North Africa
Douglas DB-7		2	7	16	21	46	29	100 arrived in North Africa
Bloch MB.174 /175	14	16	2	10	9	53	15	
Breguet 690/693	9	6	23	29	58	173	54	
LeO 451	22	20	47	64	111	330	65	507 built
Amiot 350	5	9	7	11	19	57	10	
Koolhoven F.K.58**	12	0	1	1		14		
Total	190	205	387	427	621	4,140	573	Plus eight Farman 223.4 in May 1940.

** aircraft accepted by air force storage units (including those repaired).

Endnotes

SHD means files from the Service Historique de la Défense in Vincennes, NA from the National Archives, Kew. When the Service Historique de l'Armée de l'Air (SHAA) became part of the tri-service Service Historique de la Défense (SHD), some of the file numbers were changed; as this book goes to print, the SHD have been unable to find any record of how the new file numbers relate to the old. This mainly affects 'B' series files. Where I could not locate the original file, I have used the old SHAA number.

Introduction

1 Speidel, *The German Air Force in France and the Low Countries*, pp. 74, 224.
2 Chadeau, *L'Industrie Aeronautique en France 1900-1950* (1987), p. 435.

Chapter 1

1 SHD *G/696/1*, *L'Aviation Militaire Française* (unpublished), *Vol. 1*, p. 13, Vol. 2 Annex 12.
2 Ader C., *L'Aviation Militaire*, (1909) pp. xxxiv, 24, 118).
3 G/696/1, *op. cit.*, Vol. 1, p. 52.
4 *Ibid.*, Vol. 1, pp. 53, 58.
5 *Ibid.*, Vol. 1, pp. 64–65.
6 *Ibid.*, Vol. 1, pp. 93–96.
7 SHD G/762, Patin, *L'organisation de l'aviation militaire française de 1909 à 1918.*
8 *G/696/1, op. cit., Vol. 2, Annexes 27 November 1912 report.*
9 Martel, *French Straegic and Tactical Bombardent Forces of World War 1*, (2007), pp. 3–4.
10 G/696/1, *op. cit.*, Vol. 2, Chapter 3 (27 November 1912).
11 Patin, *op. cit.*
12 *G/696/1, op. cit., Vol. 2 Annexes (16 April 1913).*
13 Etévé, *La Victoire des Cocardes* (1970), p. 148.
14 Patin, *op. cit.*, (16 December 1914).
15 Martel, *op. cit.*, p. 22.
16 *Ibid.*, pp. 22, 33.
17 *Ibid.*, pp. 49–52.
18 *Ibid.*, p. 66.
19 *Ibid.*, pp. 61–65.
20 NA, Air1/204/4/67 (August 1915).
21 Martel, *op. cit.*, pp. 97–98.
22 Jones, *The Origins of Strategic Bombing* (1973), p. 108.
23 Martel, *op. cit.*, pp. 109–115.

24 Etévé, *op. cit.*, pp. 217–218.
25 SHD Barès File (2 January 1916).
26 Etévé, *op. cit.*, pp. 156–159.
27 *Ibid.*, pp. 193–194.
28 Icare, *L'Aéronautique Militaire Française 1914–1918*, Vol. 1, p. 54.
29 NA, AIR1/1303/204/11/169, (15 May 1916).
30 Voisin, *La Doctrine de L'Aviation Française de Combat* (1932), pp. 1–4.
31 *Ibid.*, p. 12.
32 NA, AIR6/3 (24 October 1916).
33 Icare, *L'Aéronautique Militaire Française 1914–1918* Vol. 2, p. 13.
34 *Etévé, op. cit.*, pp 203–204, 223–224.
35 *Ibid.*, pp. 223–224.
36 Voisin, *op. cit.*, p. 36–38.
37 Franks, Guest, Bailey, *Bloody April...Black September* (1995), p. 111.
38 *Icare*, L'Aéronautique Militaire Française 1914-1918 Vol. 2, pp. 22–23.

Chapter 2

1 Martel, *French Straegic and Tactical Bombardent Forces of World War 1*, (2007), pp. 259–260.
2 *Ibid.*, p. 263.
3 Voisin, *La Doctrine de L'Aviation Française de Combat* (1932), p. 73.
4 Jones, *The Origins of Strategic Bombing* (1973), p. 108.
5 Morrow, *The Great War in the Air* (1993), p. 200.
6 SHAA *Historique sommaire du developpement de l'aviation de combat française novembre 1914-novembre 1918, Annexe 1.*
7 Voisin, *op. cit.*, p. 84.
8 *Icare, L'Aéronautique Militaire Française 1914–1918* Vol. 2, p. 29.
9 SHAA, 2A12.
10 Bruce, *Warplanes of the First World War Volume 5*, (1972), pp. 114–117.
11 *Ibid.*, p. 118.
12 Chadeau, *L'Industrie Aeronautique en France 1900-1950* (1987), p. 435.
13 Martel, *op. cit.*, pp. 289.
14 NA AIR1/881/204/5/596.
15 Martel, *op. cit.*, pp. 330–332.
16 *Ibid.*, p. 335.
17 Voisin, *op. cit.*, p. 98.
18 *Ibid.*, p. 98.
19 Martel, *op. cit.*, pp. 351–352.
20 *Ibid.*, pp 354–355.
21 *Ibid.*, p. 356.
22 *Revue Forces Aerienne* (1929).
23 SHD 1A89/1 (1921–1924).
24 *Ibid.*
25 Martel, *op. cit.*, pp 366-369.
26 SHD 1A89/1 (1921–1924).
27 Voisin, *op. cit.*, p. 159.
28 Larson, *The British Army and the Theory of Armoured Warfare*, (1984), pp. 90–91.
29 Voisin, *op. cit.*, p. 72.
30 Etévé, *La Victoire des Cocardes* (1970), p. 267.
31 SHD *Discussion des Conferences sur l'emploi du bombardment et de la chasse au centre d'Etudes aeronautique e Versailles* and associated Ménard notes (1920).
32 Bruce, *Warplanes of the First World War, Vol. 4*, (1972), pp. 70–72.
33 Franks, Guest, Bailey, *Bloody April ... Black September* (1995), p. 170.
34 Etévé, *op. cit.*, p. 287.
35 Danel, Cuny, *L'Aviation de Chasse Française 1918–1940* (1974), p. 15.
36 Bruce, *op. cit., Vol. 4*, (1972), p. 103.

37 Etévé, *op. cit.*, pp. 289–290.
38 Danel, Cuny, *L'Aviation de Française de Bombardment et de Renseignement 1918–1940* (1978), p. 26.
39 SHD 1A25/3.
40 NA AIR6/3 (24 October 1916).
41 *Icare, L'Aéronautique Militaire Française* 1914–1918, Vol. 2, p. 39.
42 *Les Ailes*, (8 December 1932).
43 Martel, *op. cit.*, pp. 243–248.
44 AIR 1/2266 (20 September 1917).
45 Martel, *op. cit.*, p. 308.
46 Huber, *La Population de la France pendant la guerre* (1931) pp. 312–313.

Chapter 3

1 *La Revue de Paris*, (July 1926) pp. 724–725.
2 NA FO371/8248 (29 December 1921).
3 FO371/9390 Air Attaché annual report (January 1923).
4 SHD 7N3456 (June 1922).
5 Danel, Cuny, *L'Aviation de Française de Bombardment et de Renseignement 1918–1940* (1978), pp. 37–38.
6 NA FO371/8248 (29 December 1921).
7 SHD 1B3, Hergault note to Weygand, annex 1 (19 May 1932).
8 Chadeau, *L'Industrie Aeronautique en France 1900-1950* (1987), p. 435.
9 Horne, *To Lose a Battle* (1969), pp. 51–52.
10 Messenger, *The Art of Blitzkrieg* (1976), p. 54.
11 Jauneaud, *J'Accuse Le Maréchal Pétain* (1977), p. 22.
12 SHD *Discussion des Conferences sur l'emploi du bombardment et de la chasse au centre d'Etudes aeronautique e Versailles* and associated Ménard notes (1920).
13 *Revue Militaire Française, Considerations sur notre aviation militaire* (Dec 1923).
14 NA FO371/8248, Air *attaché* report (29 December 1921).
15 SHD 1A89/1 (1921–1924).
16 SHD 7N3464 (25 March 1922).
17 Danel, Cuny, (1978), *op. cit.*, p. 50.
18 SHD 7N3464 (21 June 1926).
19 SHD Report by General Ragueneau for CSDN (30 November 1923).
20 Etévé, *La Victoire des Cocardes* (1970), pp. 296-297.
21 *Ibid.*, p. 296.
22 Foxworth, T., *The Speed Seekers* (1989), pp. 134–138.
23 Danel, Cuny, *L'Aviation de Chasse Française 1918–1940* (1974), pp. 26–27.
24 SHD 7N3456, (21 November 1919).
25 *Ibid.*, (February 1923).
26 SHD 1A89/1 (1921–1924), section II.
27 Etévé, *op. cit.*, p. 297.
28 SHD 7N3456.
29 Danel, Cuny, (1974), *op. cit.*, pp. 26–27.
30 Armengaud, *Revue Militaire Française* (April 1928) pp. 152–153.
31 *Ibid.*, pp. 159, 168.
32 NA FO371/11917, (10 April 1926).
33 Armengaud, *op. cit.*, (March-May 1928).
34 *Ibid.*, (April, May 1928).
35 Danel, Cuny, (1974), *op. cit.*, p. 52.
36 NA FO371/11917, (13 February 1926).
37 Armengaud, *op. cit.*, (May 1928), p.163.
38 Messenger, *op. cit.*, p. 89.

Chapter 4

1 SHD CSDN (3, December 1923, January 1929).
2 NA AIR9/20 (16 July 1926).
3 *Ibid.*, (June, December 1922).
4 SHD 7N3464 (February 1923).
5 SHD 1A89/1 (1921–1924).
6 SHD 7N2345 (13 February 1924).
7 SHD 7N3456, Note for CSDN (11 September 1925).
8 SHD 1B3, Pujo notes (March 1933).
9 NA FO371/8248.
10 SHAA 2B188 (14 January, 15 February and various undated notes 1929).
11 Castex, Laspalles, *José Barès* (1994), pp. 135–163.
12 SHD CSDN (15, 26 February 1929, 1 July 1930).
13 *Ibid.*, (15, 26 February 1929).
14 *Ibid.*, (13 April 1929).
15 *Ibid.*, SHD CSDN (8 January, 30 July 1931).
16 SHAA, 2B188, undated note referring to previous Weygand July 1931 note.
17 Douhet, *The Command of the Air* (1942).
18 *Ibid.*, p. 101.
19 *Ibid.*
20 *Ibid.*
21 SHD 1B3 Pujo notes (March 1933).
22 SHD Armengaud to Hergault and Weygand (1 October 1932).
23 SHD 1B3, (19 May 1932).
24 *Ibid.*, (2 May 1932).
25 *Ibid.*, (3 June 1932).
26 *Ibid.*
27 *Ibid.*
28 SHD personal study by Armengaud for Hergault and Weygand (1 October 1932).
29 SHD Cot to War Ministry (27 February, 1 March 1933).
30 SHD *Conception d'emploi et organisation des forces aeriennes* (27 February 1933).
31 SHD Armengaud note (1 October 1932).
32 SHD 1B3, (27 February 1933).
33 SHD Haut Comité Militaire (27 March 1933).
34 *Revue d'Histoire de la Deuxieme Guerre Mondiale*, (January 1969) p. 17.
35 SHD 1B3 (19 March 1933).
36 Danel, Cuny, *L'Aviation de Française de Bombardment et de Renseignement 1918-1940* (1978), pp. 93, 99.
37 SHD 2B111 (formerly SHAA 2B104) (1933).
38 SHD 1B1 (19 September 1934).
39 SHD 1B4 (formerly SHAA 1B1) (30 October 1934).
40 SHAA 3B8 (late 1934–early 1935).
41 SHD 1B4 (30 October 1934).
42 *Ibid.*
43 *Ibid.*, (30 October, 5, 17 November 1934).
44 SHAA 2B131 (undated 1935).
45 SHD 1B1 (30 October 1934).
46 *Les Ailes* (3 January 1935).
47 SHD 2B111 (22 August 1935).
48 *Les Ailes* (3 January 1935).
49 SHD 2B111 (22 August 1935).
50 SHD 1B4 (1 August 1935).
51 SHAA 1B2 (9 December 1935).
52 *Ibid.*, (1 August 1935).
53 SHD 2B111 (10 April 1936).
54 SHAA 1B2 (December 1935–January 1936).

55 *Ibid.*, (August, December 1935, 7 January 1936).
56 SHD 1B4, (10 March 1936).
57 SHD 2B163 (formerly SHAA 2B131) (15 June 1936).
58 SHAA 1B2 (7 January 1936).
59 SHD 1B4 (1 August 1935).
60 SHAA 1B2 (14 January 1936).
61 *Ibid.*, (1 August 1935).
62 *Ibid.*, (14 January 1936).

Chapter 5

1 SHAA 2B131, (29 March, 5 April 1929).
2 Kosin, *The German Fighter Since 1915* (1988), p. 92.
3 SHAA 2B131 (5 April 1929).
4 Danel, Cuny, *L'Aviation de Chasse Française 1918–1940* (1974), *op. cit.*, p. 57.
5 *Ibid.*, pp. 48, 52, 65.
6 *Les Ailes*, (10 October 1930).
7 Danel, Cuny, (1974), *op. cit.*, pp. 75, 79.
8 Danel, Cuny, *Les Avions Dewoitine* (1982), p. 84.
9 Danel, Cuny, (1974), *op. cit.*, pp. 75–86.
10 Danel, Cuny, (1982), *op. cit.*, p. 90.
11 *Ibid.*, 103-104.
12 *Revue de l'Armée de l'Air*, (January 1935).
13 Danel, Cuny, *LeO 45*, *Amiot 350* (1985), p. 245.
14 SHAA 3B8 (late 1935–early 1936).
15 *Les Ailes* (26 December 1935, 23 April 1936).
16 Kosin, *op. cit.*, p. 117.
17 SHD Report to CSDN (27 November 1929).
18 SHD 1B3 (2 May 1932).
19 *Ibid.*, (27 January 1933).
20 SHAA 1B2 (undated 1935).
21 SHD 2B120 (1935–1936).
22 SHAA 2B113 (28 March 1936).
23 SHD 1B4 (19 September 1934).
24 SHAA 1B2 (undated probably February/March 1935).
25 SHD 1B4 (1 August 1935).

Chapter 6

1 Danel, Cuny, *L'Aviation de Française de Bombardment et de Renseignement 1918-1940* (1978), pp. 95, 103.
2 *Revue d'Histoire de la Deuxieme Guerre Mondiale* (January 1969), pp. 92–93.
3 Frankenstein, *Le prix de Réarmement française 1935-1939*, (1982), pp. 58–59.
4 SHD 1B4 (April 1935).
5 Danel, Cuny, (1978), *op. cit.*, p. 93.
6 *Ibid.*, p. 108.
7 Frankenstein (1982), *op. cit.*, pp. 60–61.
8 SHD 1B4 (undated, late 1934).
9 *Ibid.*
10 Shirer, *The Collapse of the Third Republic* (1970), pp. 248, 253–255.
11 Irving, *The Rise and Fall of the Luftwaffe* (1976,) p. 46.
12 SHD 2B110 (formerly SHAA 2B103) (23 April, 18 August 1936).
13 Danel, Cuny, (1978), *op. cit.*, pp. 148-153.
14 *Ibid.*, p. 153.
15 *Revue d'Histoire de la Deuxieme Guerre Mondiale*, (January 1969) p. 23.
16 SHD 2B163 (15 June, 18 September, 11 October 1936).
17 *Revue d'Histoire de la Deuxieme Guerre Mondiale*, (January 1969) p. 24.

18 SHAA, 1B2 (1 December 1936).
19 Danel, Cuny, *L'Aviation de Chasse Française 1918–1940* (1974), p. 124.
20 SHD 2B78 (formerly SHAA 2B75) (16 January 1937).
21 SHD 2B111 (27 January 1937).
22 *Ibid.*, (15, 31 May, 9, 13 October 1937).
23 *Ibid.*, (January 1939, 26 February 1940).
24 SHAA 2B103 (20 March 1939).
25 SHD 2B78 (March 1937).
26 SHD 2B163 (8 May 1937).
27 Jauneaud, *J'Accuse Le Maréchal Pétain* (1977), Annex 2, pp. 207–210.
28 SHAA 2B1, (25 September 1937).
29 SHAA 2B132 (November 1938).
30 Danel, Cuny, (1978), *op. cit.*, p. 143.
31 Messenger, *The Art of Blitzkrieg* (1976), p. 114.
32 Gunsburg, *Divided and Conquered* (1979) pp. 43–44.
33 SHD 7N3456 (7 May 1937).
34 SHAA 2B75 (22 October 1937).
35 *Ibid.*
36 *Ibid.*
37 *Ibid.*
38 *Ibid.*, (31 May 1937).

Chapter 7

1 SHAA 2B131 (15 June 1936).
2 SHD 2B163 (18 September 1936).
3 Danel, Cuny, *LeO 45*, *Amiot 350* (1985), p. 42.
4 *Ibid.*, p. 45.
5 *Ibid.*, pp. 244–248.
6 *Ibid.*, pp. 306–309.
7 Danel, Cuny, (1978), *op. cit.*, pp. 119, 129.
8 SHD 2B63 (former SHAA 2B60) (7 July 1937)
9 SHAA 3B8 (Late 1935/early 1936).
10 Danel, Cuny, *Le Dewoitine D.520* (1980), p. 22.
11 *Flight* (25 March, 16 July 1936).
12 *Aeroplane* (22 April, 12 May, 16 June 1937).
13 SHAA 1B2 (December 1937).
14 Danel, Cuny, *L'Aviation de Chasse Française 1918–1940* (1974), pp. 115, 129.
15 NA FO371/20693 (8, 10 February 1937).
16 SHAA 2B131 (18 February 1937).
17 SHD 2B163 (18 February 1937).
18 Green, *The Ausburg Eagle* (1980), pp. 24–26.
19 Danel, Cuny, *L'Aviation de Française de Bombardment et de Renseignement 1918-1940* (1978), pp. 141, 145.
20 Frankenstein, *Le prix de Réarmement française 1935-1939*, (1982), Table 12.
21 SHAA, 2B1 (25 September, 13 November 1937).
22 NA AIR FO371/20694 (29 June 1937).
23 *Ibid.*, (24 September 1937).
24 *Ibid.*, (1 October 1937).
25 *Ibid.*, (27 November, 3, 7, 8, 11, December 1937).
26 *Ibid.*, (13 December 1937).
27 Danel, Cuny, (1974), *op. cit.*, p. 134.
28 SHAA 2B132 (December 1937).
29 SHD 1B3, CPDN (8 December 1937).
30 SHD 1B3, CPDN (8 December 1937).
31 Danel, Cuny, (1985) *op. cit.*, p. 255.

Chapter 8

1 Danel, Cuny, *L'Aviation de Chasse Française 1918–1940* (1974), p. 134.
2 Danel, Cuny, *L'Aviation de Française de Bombardment et de Renseignement 1918-1940* (1978), pp. 199–200.
3 Danel, Cuny, (1974), *op. cit.*, p. 136.
4 SHD 1B5 (11 March 1938).
5 SHD 2B124.
6 SHD 3D493 (June 1939).
7 McVicker Haight *American Aid to France 1938-1940* (1970), pp. 6–8.
8 *Ibid.*, p. 9.
9 *Ibid.*, pp. 9–12.
10 SHD 1B6 (April 1938).
11 *Ibid.*, (8 July 1938).
12 SHAA 3B8 (April 1935).
13 SHD 1B6 (13, 25 May 1938).
14 *Ibid.*, (31 March 1938).
15 *Ibid.*, (25 May 1938).
16 Danel, Cuny, (1974), *op. cit.*, p. 139.
17 *Ibid.*, pp. 138, 143.
18 SHD 1B6 (20 May 1938).
19 Danel, Cuny, (1985) *LeO 45, Amiot 350* (1985), p. 47.
20 SHD 1B6 (1 April 1938).
21 Danel, Cuny, (1985) *op. cit.*, pp. 254–255.
22 SHD 1B6 (28 April 1938).
23 *Ibid.*, (31 March, 1, 28 April 1938).
24 SHD 6N325 (February 1938).
25 SHD 1B6 (15 April 1938).
26 Danel, Cuny, (1985) *op. cit.*, pp. 255, 258.
27 SHD 1B6 (20 May 1938).
28 *Ibid.*, (8 April, 6 May 1938).
29 SHD 1B5 (June 1938).
30 Bonte, *L'Histoire des Essais en Vol* (1974), p. 141.

Chapter 9

1 Irving, *The Rise and Fall of the Luftwaffe* (1976,), p. 63.
2 Facon, *L'Armée de l'Air dans le Tourmente* (2005), p. 27.
3 Shirer, *The Collapse of the Third Republic* (1970), p. 357.
4 Facon, *op. cit.*, (2005), p. 28.
5 Danel, Cuny, *L'Aviation de Chasse Française 1918–1940* (1974), p. 150.
6 SHD 1B6 (April, September 1938).
7 Danel, Cuny, (1974), *op. cit.*, p. 144.
8 *Ibid.*, p. 139.
9 SHD 1B6 (22 December 1939).
10 Danel, Cuny, *L'Aviation de Française de Bombardment et de Renseignement 1918-1940* (1978), pp. 203–204.
11 *Ibid.*, pp. 203–204.
12 McVicker Haight *American Aid to France 1938-1940* (1970), pp. 92–97.
13 Danel, Cuny, (1978), *op. cit.*, p. 199.
14 SHD 1B6 (9 November 1938).
15 *Ibid.*, (January 1939).
16 Bonte, *L'Histoire des Essais en Vol* (1974), p. 220.
17 SHD 2B60 (April 1938).
18 SHAA 2B132 (15 October 1938).
19 SHD 1B6 (25 September 1938).
20 *Ibid.*, (6 October 1938).

21 SHD 3D493 (June 1939).
22 SHD 1B6 (9 May 1939).
23 *Ibid.*, (30 June, 22 July 1938).
24 *Ibid.*, (12 August, 21 October 1938, 16 May, 5 July, 19 September 1939).
25 *Ibid.*, (12 August 1938).
26 *Ibid.*, (9 September, 21 October 1938).
27 Danel, Cuny, *Le Dewoitine D.520* (1980), p. 32.
28 NA FO371/21597 (21 December 1938).
29 Danel, Cuny, (1980), *op. cit.*, p. 34.
30 *Ibid.*, p. 44.
31 SHD 1B6 (21 October 1938).
32 *Ibid.*, (12 August, 21 October 1938).
33 Danel, Cuny, (1980), *op. cit.*, p. 45.
34 SHD 3D493 (1 June 1939).
35 SHD 1B6 (9 August 1939).
36 Danel, Cuny, (1978), *op. cit.*, pp. 217–218.
37 Danel, Cuny, (1974), *op. cit.*, p. 149.
38 Danel, Cuny, (1978), *op. cit.*, pp. 203–204.

Chapter 10

1 SHD 7N3020.
2 SHD 1D32 (19 September, 4, 21 November 1939)
3 SHD 2B7 (September 1939).
4 SHD 7N3020.
5 SHD 1D32 (September-November 1939).
6 SHD 1D32 (19 September 1939).
7 Shores, *Fledgling Eagles* (1991), pp. 54–55.
8 Ehrengardt *et al.*, *Les Aiglons* (1983), p. 48.
9 SHD 1D2 (19 November 1939).
10 Ehrengardt, *et al. op. cit.*, pp. 48, 132.
11 SHD Engine production schedule (1 December 1939).
12 SHD 1B6 (26 October 1939).
13 Danel, Cuny, *L'Aviation de Chasse Française 1918–1940* (1974), p. 185.
14 Danel, Cuny, *L'Aviation de Française de Bombardment et de Renseignement 1918-1940* (1978), pp. 203–204, 230–234.
15 *Ibid.*, pp. 234–235.
16 Danel, Cuny, *LeO 45*, *Amiot 350* (1985), p. 265.
17 *Ibid.*, pp. 48–49.
18 Chadeau, *L'Industrie Aeronautique en France 1900-1950* (1987), pp. 493–494.
19 Danel, Cuny, (1978), *op. cit.*, p. 234.
20 SHD 2B124.
21 Smoldas, *Ceskoslovensti letci v boji proti fasismu* (1987), p. 79.
22 Cynk, *History of the Polish Air Force 1918-1968* (1972), pp. 156–157.
23 SHD 2B108 (5 September 1939).
24 SHD 7N3020 (October 1939).
25 Danel, Cuny, *Le Dewoitine D.520* (1980), p. 56.
26 SHD 1B6 (7, 26 October 1939).
27 Danel, Cuny, (1980), *op. cit.*, p. 62.
28 Danel, Cuny, (1978), *op. cit.*, pp. 232–234.
29 *Ibid.*, pp. 199, 203.
30 Gann, *The Douglas A-20* (1967), pp. 4–5.
31 SHD 3D493 (June 1939).
32 McVicker Haight *American Aid to France 1938-1940* (1970), pp. 239–244.
33 SHD 1D1 (18 March 1940).
34 SHD 2B108 (September 1939).
35 *Ibid.*

36 Smoldas, *op. cit.*, pp. 154–163.
37 SHD 7N3020 (11 October 1939).
38 Cynk, *op. cit.*, p. 156.
39 *Ibid.*, p. 157–158.
40 Smoldas, *op. cit.*, pp. 154–163.
41 Ehrengardt, *et al. op. cit.*, p. 138.
42 Shores, *op. cit.*, pp. 102–103.
43 SHD D'Harcourt note to Vuillemin (12 December 1939).
44 Shores, *op. cit.*, pp 54–55.
45 SHD 2B163 (formerly SHAA 2B131) (11 September 1939).
46 Danel, Cuny, (1980), *op. cit.*, p 180.
47 SHD 1B6 (7 November 1939).
48 Danel, Cuny, (1980), *op. cit.*, p 180.
49 SHD 1B6, (10, 23, 25 November 1939).
50 Danel, Cuny, (1980), *op. cit.*, p. 186.
51 *Ibid.*, p. 38.
52 SHD 1B4 (22 December 1939).
53 *Ibid.*, (10 January 1940).
54 *Ibid.*, (22 December 1939, 10 January 1940).
55 *Ibid.*, (14 December 1939).
56 *Ibid.*, (10 January 1940).
57 *Ibid.*, (15 January 1940).
58 Danel, Cuny, (1974), *op. cit.*, p. 176.
59 Danel, Cuny, (1980), *op. cit.*, p. 68.
60 SHD 1B4 (12 January 1940).
61 Danel, Cuny, (1974), *op. cit.*, p. 169.
62 SHD 1B4 (26 October, 21 November 1939).
63 SHD 1B4 (10 January 1940).
64 SHAA 2B133 (9 January 1940), SHD 1B6 (26 January 1940).
65 SHD 1D3 (1 December 1940).
66 Danel, Cuny, (1985) *op. cit.*, p. 279.
67 Green, *War Planes of the Second World War Vol. 7* (1967), p. 117.
68 SHD 1D3 (1 December 1939).
69 Danel, Cuny, (1974), *op. cit.*, pp. 171–172.
70 Danel, Cuny, (1974), *op. cit.*, p. 174.
71 Danel, Cuny, (1980), *op. cit.*, p. 189.
72 Danel, Cuny, (1985) *op. cit.*, pp. 266–268.

Chapter 11

1 SHD 3D493 (9 February 1940).
2 Danel, Cuny, *Le Dewoitine D.520* (1980), pp. 72–84.
3 Danel, Cuny, *L'Aviation de Française de Bombardment et de Renseignement 1918-1940* (1978), pp. 252, 261.
4 SHD 1D36 (20 December 1939).
5 Shirer (1970), *The Collapse of the Third Republic* (1970), pp. 521–523.
6 SHD 1D36, (20 December 1939).
7 *Ibid.*, (20 December 1939).
8 SHD 2B108 (6 April 1940).
9 Cynk, *History of the Polish Air Force 1918-1968* (1972), p. 159.
10 Smoldas, *Ceskoslovensti letci v boji proti fasismu* (1987), p. 91.
11 Danel, Cuny, *L'Aviation de Chasse Française 1918–1940* (1974), p. 182.
12 SHD 1D1 (23 March 1940).
13 Horne, *To Lose a Battle* (1969), p. 354.
14 Danel, Cuny, (1974), *op. cit.*, pp. 181-182.
15 Danel, Cuny, (1978), *op. cit.*, pp. 251-254.
16 SHD 2B63 (February, 8 May 1940).

17 Danel, Cuny, (1980), *op. cit.*, pp. 255-256.
18 SHD 1D1 (9 April 1940).
19 SHD 1D2 (12, 14 April 1940).
20 SHD 2B111 (19, 29 June 17, July, 4 November 1939), 1D3, (1 December 1939).
21 *Ibid.*, (November 1939).
22 *Ibid.*, (26 February 1940).
23 *Les Ailes* (31 March 1938).
24 SHD 1D3 (28 March 1940).
25 Ehrengardt, *et al. Les Aiglons* (1983), p. 138.
26 Shores, *Fledgling Eagles* (1991), p. 185.
27 SHD 1D1 (9 April 1940).
28 Danel, Cuny, (1974), *op. cit.*, p. 182.
29 Ehrengardt, *et al. op. cit.*, pp. 132, 138.
30 *La Fanatique de l'Aviation* (March 1978).
31 *Icare No 59, 1939–1940 La Bataille de France Vol. IV*, p. 84.
32 Ehrengardt, *et al.*, *op. cit.*, p. 132.
33 *Ibid.*, p. 131.

Chapter 12

1 *Icare, No. 79, 1939-1940 La Bataille de France Vol. IX*, p. 38.
2 *Ibid.*, p. 46.
3 SHD GC III/2 campaign record.
4 SHD GC III/9 campaign record.
5 SHD GC I/5 campaign record.
6 SHD GC III/1 campaign record.
7 SHD GC III/3 campaign record.
8 SHD GC III/7 campaign record.
9 SHD GC II/4 campaign record.
10 SHD GC I/1 campaign record.
11 SHD GC II/10, campaign record.
12 SHD GC III/10 campaign record.
13 SHD GC II/5 campaign record.
14 SHD Compilation of GC campaign records.
15 SHD 1D51 (11 May 1940).
16 Cornwell, *The Battle of France Then and Now*, (2007), pp. 188–189.
17 NA AIR35/22 (21 February 1940).
18 D'Astier de la Vigerie, *Le Ciel N'Etait Pas Vide* (1952), pp. 87–88.
19 Paquier, *L'Aviation de bombardement française en 1939-1940* (1948), p. 232.
20 *Icare No. 57, 1939-1940 La Bataille de France Vol. IIII*, p. 88.
21 Paquier, *L'Aviation de renseignment française en 1939–1940* (1947), pp. 89–90.
22 SHD GC III/6 campaign record.
23 SHD 3D497 (May 1940).
24 Cornwell, op. cit., p. 253.
25 SHD 2B7 (11–14 May 1940).
26 SHD GC I/4 campaign record.
27 *Icare No. 59, 1939–1940 La Bataille de France Vol. IV*, p. 141
28 *Icare No. 79, 1939–1940 La Bataille de France Vol. IX*, p. 46..
29 Cornwell, *op. cit.*, pp. 193, 236, 250.
30 *Icare No. 61, 1939-1940 La Bataille de France Vol. VI*, p. 59.
31 Danel, Cuny, *LeO 45, Amiot 350* (1985), p. 101.
32 Cornwell, *op. cit.*, pp. 234–235.
33 Paquier (1947) *op. cit.*, pp. 89–90.
34 Cornwell, *op. cit.*, pp. 247–248.
35 Shirer, *The Collapse of the Third Republic* (1970), p. 586.
36 Ellis, *The War in France and Flanders 1939–1940* (1954), p. 54.
37 Bekker, The Luftwaffe War Diaries (1966), pp. 166–167.

38 SHD GC I/1 campaign record.
39 IWM Luftwaffe daily returns of aircraft losses.

Chapter 13

1 Paquier, *L'Aviation de renseignment française en 1939–1940* (1947), p. 91.
2 D'Astier de la Vigerie, *Le Ciel N'Etait Pas Vide* (1952), pp. 96–97.
3 SHD GC I/5 campaign record.
4 Bekker, *op. cit.*, p. 118.
5 D'Astier de la Vigerie, *op. cit.*, p. 104.
6 *Ibid.*, p. 105.
7 SHD 1D45.
8 Chapman, *Why France Collapsed* (1968), pp. 110–111.
9 Horne, *To Lose a Battle* (1969), p. 318.
10 SHD GC II/2 campaign record.
11 Cornwell, *The Battle of France Then and Now*, (2007), pp. 259, 265.
12 Danel, Cuny, *LeO 45, Amiot 350* (1985), p. 101.
13 Shirer (1970), *The Collapse of the Third Republic* (1970), p. 625.
14 SHD GC I/1 campaign record.
15 SHD GC campaign records.
16 Shirer, *op. cit.*, p. 625.
17 D'Astier de la Vigerie, *op. cit.*, p. 107.
18 *Ibid.*, pp. 111–114.
19 SHD 1D51.
20 *Ibid.*, (11 May 1940).
21 SHD 1D45.
22 SHD 1D51.
23 SHD 1D2 (13 May 1940).
24 D'Astier de la Vigerie, *op. cit.*, pp. 109–110.
25 *Ibid.*, p. 107.
26 *Ibid.*, p. 110.
27 Cornwell, *op. cit.*, pp. 273–274.
28 D'Astier de la Vigerie, *op. cit.*, p. 111.
29 Ellis, *op. cit.*, p. 54.
30 Horne, *op. cit.*, p. 379.
31 SHD GC II/4 campaign record.
32 SHD GCs I/1, II/1, II/10. III/10 campaign records.
33 Cornwell, *op. cit.*, pp. 274–275.
34 IWM Luftwaffe daily returns of aircraft losses.
35 Paquier, *L'Aviation de renseignment française en 1939–1940* (1947), p. 95.
36 SHD 1D51.
37 SHD 1D3 (24 May 1940).
38 D'Astier de la Vigerie, *op. cit.*, p. 127.
39 SHD GC III/10 campaign record.
40 SHD GC II/2 campaign record.
41 SHD GC I/8 campaign record.
42 SHD GC III/7 campaign record.
43 SHD GC II/6 campaign record.
44 Cornwell, *op. cit.*
45 *Icare No. 59, 1939–1940 La Bataille de France Vol. IV*, pp. 127–129.
46 Cornwell, *op. cit.*, p. 284.

Chapter 14

1 Ellis, *op. cit.*, p. 56.
2 SHD 1D6 (22 May 1940).
3 SHD 1D1 (12 May 1940).

4 SHD 1D6 (12 May 1940).
5 *La Fanatique de l'Aviation* (March 1978).
6 SHD 1D51.
7 SHD 1D6 (17 May 1940).
8 SHD GC II/1 campaign record.
9 Cornwell, *The Battle of France Then and Now*, (2007), p. 346.
10 SHD 1D1 (14 May 1940).
11 SHD 1D2 (16 May 1940).
12 D'Astier de la Vigerie, *Le Ciel N'Etait Pas Vide* (1952), p. 136.
13 Danel, Cuny, *LeO 45*, *Amiot 350* (1985), pp. 102–103.
14 Cornwell, *op. cit.*, p. 396.
15 D'Astier de la Vigerie, *op. cit.*, p. 140.
16 *Icare, No. 80 1939–1940, La Bataille de France Vol. X*, p. 25.
17 SHD 3D497.
18 D'Astier de la Vigerie, *op. cit.*, p. 141.
19 *Ibid.*, pp 143–144.
20 *Ibid.*, pp 142–144.
21 SHD 1D2 (16 May 1940).
22 D'Astier de la Vigerie, *op. cit.*, p. 150.
23 Danel, Cuny, (1985) *op. cit.*, p. 104.
24 Horne, *To Lose a Battle* (1969), pp. 479–482.
25 D'Astier de la Vigerie, *op. cit.*, p. 155.
26 Paquier, (1948) *op. cit.*, p. 234.
27 SHD 1D6 (22 May 1940).
28 SHD 1D51.
29 Danel, Cuny, *Le Dewoitine D.520* (1980), *op. cit.*, p. 90.
30 SHD GC II/2 campaign record.
31 Danel, Cuny, *L'Aviation de Chasse Française 1918–1940* (1974), p. 189.
32 SHD 1D6 (22 May 1940).
33 Paquier (1948) *op. cit.*, p. 234.
34 SHD GC II/2, III/1 campaign records.
35 SHD GC II/2, III/1 campaign records.
36 *Icare* No. 61, 1939-1940 La Bataille de France Vol. VI, p. 105.
37 Cornwell, *op. cit.*, p. 324.
38 Danel, Cuny, (1980), *op. cit.*, pp. 84, 90.
39 Cornwell, *op. cit.*, p. 333.
40 Danel, Cuny, (1985) *op. cit.*, p. 105.
41 *Icare* No. 57, 1939–1940 La Bataille de France Vol. III, p. 64.
42 Paquier, (1948) *op. cit.*, pp. 234–237.
43 Speidel, *op. cit.*, Vol. 2 p. 192.
44 D'Astier de la Vigerie, *op. cit.*, pp. 187–188.
45 Cornwell, *op. cit.*, p. 346.
46 Paquier, (1948) *op. cit.*, pp. 212–213.
47 *Icare* No. 80 1939-1940 La Bataille de France Vol. X, Table 6.
48 D'Astier de la Vigerie, *op. cit.*, pp. 189–190.
49 *Ibid.*, p. 155.
50 SHD 2D24.
51 Cornwell, *op. cit.*, p. 347.
52 Bekker, *op. cit.*, p. 121.

Chapter 15

1 Danel, Cuny, *L'Aviation de Chasse Française 1918–1940* (1974), p. 185.
2 Danel, Cuny, *L'Aviation de Française de Bombardment et de Renseignement 1918-1940* (1978), p. 261.
3 SHD 1D35 (27 May 1940).
4 *Ibid.*, (27, 31 May 1940, 3 June).

5 SHD 1D2 (3 June 1940).
6 NA AIR35/343 (7 June 1940).
7 Danel, Cuny, (1974), *op. cit.*, pp. 187–189.
8 SHD 1D2 (2 June 1940).
9 SHD 1D51.
10 SHD 1D1 (3 June 1940).
11 SHD 1D6 (28 May1940).
12 *Ibid.*, (3 June 1940).
13 SHD 1D1 (29 May 1940).
14 SHD 1D6 (1 June 1940).
15 McVicker Haight, *American Aid to France 1938-1940* (1970), pp. 251–255.
16 D'Astier de la Vigerie, *Le Ciel N'Etait Pas Vide* (1952), pp. 222–223.
17 *Icare* N. 80, 1939–1940 La Bataille de France Vol. X, p. 30.
18 Cornwell, *The Battle of France Then and Now*, (2007), pp. 400–401.
19 SHD 1D2 (31 May 1940).
20 D'Astier de la Vigerie, *op. cit.*, p. 238.
21 SHD 1D2 (29 May 1940).
22 *Icare* No. 54, 1939–1940 La Bataille de France Vol. I, pp. 60–61, 125–127.
23 Cornwell, op. cit., pp. 416–418.
24 *Icare* No. 54, 1939–1940 La Bataille de France Vol. I, pp. 60–61, 125–127.
25 Cornwell, *op. cit.*, p. 418.
26 1D2 (3 June 1940).
27 Paquier, *L'Aviation de bombardement française en 1939-1940* (1948), pp. 240–241.
28 *Icare No. 61, 1939-1940 La Bataille de France Vol. VI*, pp. 97–99.
29 Cornwell, *op. cit.*, pp. 403–421.
30 Paquier, *L'Aviation de renseignment française en 1939–1940* (1947), p. 115.
31 *The Battle of France Then and Now*, (2007), p. 424–425.
32 Danel, Cuny, *Le Dewoitine D.520* (1980), p. 96.
33 Cornwell, *op. cit.*, pp. 427–429.
34 Paquier (1947) *op. cit.*, p. 117.
35 Paquier (1948) *op. cit.*, pp. 209–210.
36 Chapman, *op. cit.*, p. 244.
37 Paquier (1948) *op. cit.*, pp. 222–223.
38 *Icare* No 54 1939-1940 La Bataille de France Vol. I, p. 63.
39 D'Astier de la Vigerie, *op. cit.*, p. 10.
40 Cornwell, *op. cit.*, pp. 452-453.
41 Paquier (1948) *op. cit.*, pp. 222-223.
42 SHD 3D497.
43 Danel, Cuny, (1978), *op. cit.*, p. 265.
44 Danel, Cuny, (1980), *op. cit.*, pp. 84-88;
45 Danel, Cuny, (1978), *op. cit.*, p. 269.
46 *Icare* No. 54, 1939–1940 La Bataille de France Vol. I, p. 64.

Conclusion

1 Shirer, *The Collapse of the Third Republic* (1970), p. 586.
2 Liddell Hart, *History of the Second World War* (1970), p. 22.

Bibliography

Books

Ader, C., *L'Aviation Militaire*, (Paris: Berger-Levrault, 1908)
Bailey, F. and Cony, C., *The French Air Service War Chronology 1914-1918* (London: Grub Street, 2001)
Bekker, C., The Luftwaffe War Diaries (London: Macdonald, 1966)
Bonte, L., *L'Histoire des Essais en Vol* (Paris: Larivière, 1974)
Bruce, J., *Warplanes of the First World War Volume 4*, (London: Macdonald, 1972)
Bruce, J., *Warplanes of the First World War Volume 5*, (London: Macdonald, 1972)
Cain, A., *The Forgotten Air Force* (Washington: Smithsonian Institute, 2002)
Castex, J., Laspalles, L., *José Barès* (Paris: NEL, 1994)
Chadeau, E., *L'Industrie Aeronautique en France 1900-1950* (Paris: Fayard, 1987)
Chapman, G., *Why France Collapsed* (London: Cassell, 1968)
Cornwell, P., *The Battle of France Then and Now*, (Old Harlow: Battle of Britain International, 2007)
Cynk, J., *History of the Polish Air Force 1918-1968* (Reading: Osprey, 1972)
Danel, R. and Cuny, J., *L'Aviation de Chasse Française 1918-1940* (Paris: Larivière, 1974)
Danel, R. and Cuny, J., *L'Aviation de Française de Bombardment et de Renseignement 1918-1940* (Paris: Larivière, 1978)
Danel, R. and Cuny, J., *Le Dewoitine D.520* (Paris: Larivière, 1980)
Danel, R. and Cuny, J., *LeO 45, Amiot 350* (Paris: Larivière, 1985)
Danel, R. and Cuny, J., *Les Avions Dewoitine* (Paris: Larivière, 1982)
Danel, R., *Émile Dewoitine* (Paris: Larivière, 1985)
D'Astier de la Vigerie *Le Ciel N'Etait Pas Vide* (Paris: Julliard, 1952)
Douhet, G., *The Command of the Air*, (New York: Coward-McCann, 1942)
Ehrengardt, C., Shores, C., Weisse, H., and Foreman, J., *Les Aiglons* (Paris: Lavauzelle, 1983)
Ellis, L., *The War in France and Flanders 1939–1940* (London: HMSO, 1954)
Etévé, A., *La Victoire des Cocardes* (Paris: Robert Laffont, 1970)
Facon, P., *L'Armée de l'Air dans le Tourmente* (Paris: Economica, 2005)
Foxworth, T., *The Speed Seekers* (Sparkford: Haynes, 1989)
Frankenstein, R., *Le prix de Réarmement Francaise 1935–1939*, (Paris: Publications de la Sorbonne, 1982)
Franks, N., Guest, R., and Bailey, F., *Bloody April ... Black September* (London: Grubb St, 1995)

Frieser, K., *The Blitzkrieg Legend* (Maryland: Naval Institute Press, 2005)
Gann, H., *The Douglas A-20* (Leatherhead: Profile Publications, 1967)
Green, W., *The Ausburg Eagle* (London: Jane's, 1980)
Green, W., *War Planes of the Second World War Volumes 1, 6, 7, and 8* (London: Macdonald, 1961-1967)
Gunsburg, J., *Divided and Conquered* (London: Greenwood Press, 1979)
Hébrard, J., *Vingt-Cinq Années d'Aviation Militaire* (Paris: Albin Michel, 1946)
Henshaw, T., *The Sky Their Battlefield* (London: Grub Street, 1995)
Horne, A., *To Lose a Battle* (Harmondsworth, Penguin, 1982)
Huber, M., *La Population de la France pendant la guerre* (Paris: 1931)
Irving, D., *The Rise and Fall of the Luftwaffe* (London: Futura Publications, 1976)
Jauneaud, J., *J'Accuse Le Maréchal Pétain* (Paris: Pygmalion, 1977)
Jauneaud, M., *L'aviation militaire et la guerre aérienne* (Paris: Ernest Flammarion, 1923)
Jones, N., *The Origins of Strategic Bombing* (London: William Kimber, 1973)
Kosin, R., *The German Fighter Since 1915* (London: Putnam, 1988)
Larson, R. *The British Army and the Theory of Armoured Warfare* (London: University Associated Press, 1984)
Liddell Hart, B., *History of the Second World War* (London: Cassell, 1970)
Liron, J., *Les Avions Farman* (Paris: Lariviére, 1984)
Martel, R., *French Strategic and Tactical Bombardent Forces of World War 1*, (Plymouth: The Scarecrow Press, 2007)
McVicker Haight, J., *American Aid to France 1938-1940* (New York: Athenum, 1970)
Messenger, C. *The Art of Blitzkrieg* (London: Ian Allan, 1976)
Morrow, J., *The Great War in the Air* (Shrewsbury: Airlife Publishing, 1993)
Niessel, A. *La maîtrise de l'air* (Paris: Perrin & Cie, 1928)
Offenberg, J., *Lonely Warrior* (St Albans: Granada Publishing, 1974)
Paquier, P., *L'Aviation de bombardement française en 1939-1940* (Paris: Berger-Levrault, 1948)
Paquier, P., *L'Aviation de renseignment française en 1939-1940* (Paris: Berger-Levrault, 1947)
Patin, *L'organisation de l'aviation militaire française de 1909 à 1918*, (Vincennes: SHAA, 1973).
Pitt, B., *1918 : The Last Act* (Barnsley: Pen and Sword, 2003)
Shirer, W. *The Collapse of the Third Republic* (London: Cox and Wyman, 1970)
Shores, C., *Fledgling Eagles* (London: Grub Street, 1991)
Smoldas Z., *Ceskoslovensti letci v boji proti fasismu* (Prague: Nase Vojsko, 1987)
Speidel, W., *The German Air Force in France and the Low Countries* (unpublished)
Voisin, A., *La Doctrine de L'Aviation Française de Combat* (Paris: Berger-Lvrault, 1932)
Young, R., *In Command of France* (London: Harvard University Press, 1978)

Periodicals

Aeroplane (22 April, 12 May, 16 June 1937).
Flight (25 March, 16 July 1936).
Icare, La Bataille de France, Nos 54, 57, 59, 61, 79, and 80.
Icare, L'Aéronautique Militaire Francaise 1914–1918 Nos 85 and 88.
La Fanatique de l'Aviation (March 1978).
Revue de l'Armée de l'Air, (January 1935).
Revue d'Histoire de la Deuxieme Guerre Mondiale, (January 1969)
Revue Forces Aerienne (1929)
Revue Militaire Française (December 1923; March, April, and May 1928)

Index